Chennault's Forgotten Warriors

Carroll V. Glines

CHENNAULT'S FORGOTTEN WARRIORS

THE SAGA OF THE 308TH BOMB GROUP IN CHINA

CARROLL V. GLINES

Schiffer Military/Aviation History
Atglen, PA

*To all those living and dead who served
with the 308th Bomb Group in China during World War II.*

Book Design by Robert Biondi.

Printed in the United States of America.
ISBN: 0-88740-809-5

We are interested in hearing from authors with book ideas on related topics.

Published by Schiffer Publishing Ltd.
77 Lower Valley Road
Atglen, PA 19310
Please write for a free catalog.
This book may be purchased from the publisher.
Please include $2.95 postage.
Try your bookstore first.

CONTENTS

FOREWORD

The story of Major General Claire L. Chennault's Flying Tigers has been told so many times that, like the famous Lafayette Escadrille of World War I, it is now part of American aviation folklore. However, the feats of the P-40 fighters of the Flying Tigers are only one part of the story of the air war in the China-Burma-India theater during World War II. A most important contribution made by Chennault's B-24 Liberator heavy bombers of the 308th Bombardment Group has been overlooked and unreported until now.

The 308th's wide-ranging activities through nearly three years of bitter air warfare are virtually unknown, despite the fact that it performed some of the most accurate bombing of the U.S. Army Air Forces, and used the first American "smart bomb" called the Azon. The 308th also sustained the highest casualty rate in the USAAF, for its missions were long and hard, often conducted at very low level and at night through the very heart of Japanese-occupied territory and over their controlled sea lanes.

A study of the records of World War II reveals that every bomber crew had stories to tell that were as interesting as those of any fighter pilot. Colonel C. V. Glines has woven these fascinating personal narratives into a wider story of the air war in China.

Chennault's Forgotten Warriors combines political intrigue, military valor and personal hardships to a degree not found elsewhere. From its inception, the 308th was the object of intense personal interest to three Allied leaders: President Franklin D. Roosevelt, Prime Minister Winston Churchill, and Generalissimo Chiang Kai-shek, who made it the focus of their attention. As a result of their agreement, the 308th was to be the only heavy bomb group assigned to Chennault's small fighting force that eventually became the 14th Air Force.

Thus the 308th was in the political limelight from the moment of its birth, and continued to be as it conducted some of the most dangerous and effective bombing in the history of aerial warfare. And yet, when the war ended, the three-year saga of the 308th and its companion units was unheralded and overshadowed in the literature of the war by the P-40s of Chennault's American Volunteer Group and the China Air Task Force.

The 308th flew nearly 600 combat missions under conditions that would have been deemed impossible in Europe. At the end of a 12,000-mile supply line, every ounce of gasoline, every bomb, every spark plug, had to be dragged over the hazardous, high altitude route across the mountains, along what became known as "the Aluminum Trail" for the plane wreckage scattered along the way. There were few radio or navigational aids, and the weather was usually bad. Midway through the war, crews viewed combat missions as less stressful than the haul over the Hump. It took about four trips hauling supplies to be ready for one bombing mission.

The 308th went into action almost immediately after its arrival in the theater in the spring of 1943. As Chennault's only heavy bomb group, it covered the widest geographical area of any bombing group in the world. Their B-24s had been designed for high-level precision bombing and that's how the crews had been trained, but the 308th quickly created new tactics for the war against Japan's merchant marine and navy. The enemy recognized the threat of the 308th's presence and reacted strongly to it by reinforcing their air forces and making frequent raids on their airfields. Chennault's fighters responded with the usual superb defensive tactics he had imparted to the original Flying Tigers. Meanwhile, he sent the 308th's B-24 Liberators beyond the Japanese lines to hammer their air fields, storage depots, docks and ships.

The story of the 308th is told in the following pages in the context of the times, so that the reader is aware of the military and political events which dictated its formation and then influenced its operation. At long last, a void in the literature of World War II has been filled.

Walter J. Boyne
Former Director
National Air & Space Museum

ACKNOWLEDGMENTS

This story of the 308th Bombardment Group is the end result of one man's desire to honor the aircrew members and the ground personnel who served in China with him during World War II and those who followed after he completed his CBI tour. He is Colonel Howard H. Morgan, a pilot with the 375th Squadron, who arrived with the original contingent of the 308th and flew 79 combat missions and 410 combat hours during his tour of duty there.

It took many months of letter writing, telephoning and sending questionnaires to over 600 former 308th members, plus visits to Air Force archives for him to gather the official reports, reminiscences, letters and diaries which provide the background for this study of a unique World War II air unit. Without his dedication to the task, persistence in running down facts, and ability to persuade former members of the 308th to tell their stories and submit photos, this book could never have been written. When reading the official orders, folded letters, and moving personal narratives that were loaned, now yellowed and brittle after being tucked away in footlockers and storage chests for half a century, one quickly discovers that the men of the 308th were not different from those in other bomb units. Its pilots, navigators, bombardiers and enlisted crew members were bright young men right out of combat training schools, most in their early twenties. The ground personnel, many too young to have ever had a job in civilian life, kept the planes and armament in fighting shape despite never-ending supply shortages. Yet the record of the 308th comprises one of the brightest elements in the history of the China-Burma-India theater during World War II, the theater which was the most demanding and least publicized of all the World War II combat areas.

An enthusiastic supporter of this project was Ming Chen Hsu, one of five presidentially-appointed commissioners serving with the Federal Maritime Commission in Washington, D.C. Born in Beijing, China, she fled to Kunming with her family to escape the Japanese. Fluent in English by virtue of attendance at the Shanghai American School, she was a teenager when she met many of the members of the 308th's Squadrons. She came to the United States in 1944, became a citizen and rose to the vice presidency of RCA Corporation before being appointed by President Bush and confirmed by the Senate to her position as commissioner. Her knowledge of the conditions under which the 308th had to fly and fight were essential to this writer in gaining background about the wartime conditions in China which she had witnessed. Her continuing support during the preparation of the manuscript was invaluable.

Besides the many former 308th members who submitted stories and photographs about their service in China, others sent maps, propaganda leaflets and copies of "blood chits" which were used to persuade the Chinese to assist downed airmen. Families of deceased members also sent materials. Special appreciation is extended to Sandra E. Beebe, daughter of the late highly respected Brigadier General Eugene H. Beebe, who furnished photographs and other materials concerning his service as an aide to General Henry H. "Hap" Arnold and as the commander of the 308th.

Especially helpful was Milt Miller, editor of the *Jing Bao Journal,* the official publication of the Flying Tigers of the Fourteenth Air Force Association. Miller was a member of the 375th Squadron and keeps the spirit and memories of the surviving Flying Tigers alive through the lively, 50-page bimonthly magazine he publishes. He graciously supplied answers to questions as well as a number of back issues from which many of the stories submitted by participants were excerpted with his and their permission.

Gratitude is also extended to the anonymous archivists of the Center for Air Force History and the National Archives for their assistance in locating material pertaining to the 308th.

Last, but far from least, thanks are due to those who returned the questionnaires sent out by Howard Morgan to 600 former 308th members. Unfortunately, because of lack of space, not all of the stories could be used but the willingness to respond is sincerely appreciated.

Carroll V. Glines
Dallas, Texas

Chapter 1

PRELUDE TO WAR FOR THE 308TH

I t can be said that the history of the 308th Bombardment Group in China had its beginning before World War II when Japanese militarists decided to embark on a war of conquest in the mid-1930s. A nation without great natural resources but a burgeoning industrial capacity, Japan relied on imports of raw materials to produce goods to satisfy a hunger for international trade and acceptance as a power on the world stage. Its nearest neighbors, China and Korea, were the first targets for domination.

The decade of the 1930s, often referred to by aviation historians as the Golden Age of Flight, was also known in the world of American military aviation as the Age of Anxiety. While the United States was suffering from the economic chaos it called the Great Depression, other nations besides Japan were also shaping their national economies to prepare for war and were developing strong air forces.

In Italy, dictator Benito Mussolini, who wasn't being taken seriously, built hundreds of planes and declared war on defenseless Ethiopia. In Germany, Adolph Hitler, another dictator, was threatening to build an overwhelming air force. Recognizing the threat, Great Britain established a four-year expansion plan for the Royal Air Force in 1934. British Intelligence later reported an increase in German aerial capability and Britain changed her plan to match.

When still another dictator made a bid for control of Spain, the German proponents of fascism supported him with air weapons and personnel. Proponents of an opposing ideology – communism – supported his antagonists in kind. In the major nations of the world, with the notable exception of the United States, the airplane was considered a major weapon around which their war machines were built.

In those days, it was the policy of the United States to arm for defense only. Yet Billy Mitchell and his followers who believed in the potential of air power knew, as any high school football coach knows, "the best defense is a good offense." The mounting signs of conflict could not be seen by the man in the street, nor his elected representatives. President Franklin D. Roosevelt, former Assistant Secretary of the Navy, was a romanticist when it came to ships and the sea. There would be no expansion of the Army Air Corps unless he willed it.

Mitchell was firm in his belief that the president felt that war in the Far East would be impracticable and that an attack upon the United States by the Japanese was inconceivable. In a meeting with friends shortly before he died in 1936, Mitchell prophesied:

> "The Japanese will not politely declare war. They are treacherous and will stop at nothing. Hawaii, for instance, is vulnerable from the sky. It is wide open to Japan. Yet we bring our Navy in at Pearl Harbor and lock it up every Saturday night so that sailors can spend their week's pay to please the merchants and politicians who have arranged that routine because they think it's good for business. And Hawaii is swarming with Japanese spies. As I've said before, that's where the blow will be struck - on a fine, quiet Sunday morning."[1]

The blow was struck on a "fine, quiet Sunday morning" – December 7, 1941. The next day, President Roosevelt went to Capitol Hill and addressed a joint session of Congress:

> "Yesterday, December 7, 1941 - a date which will live in infamy - the United States of America was suddenly and deliberately attacked by naval and air forces of the Empire of Japan.
> "...Yesterday the Japanese Government launched an attack against Malaya.
> "Last night Japanese forces attacked Hong Kong.
> "Last night Japanese forces attacked Guam.
> "Last night Japanese forces attacked the Philippine Islands.
> "Last night the Japanese attacked Wake Island.
> "And this morning the Japanese attacked Midway Island.
> "...I ask that the Congress declare that since the unprovoked and

dastardly attack by Japan on Sunday, December 7, 1941, a state of war has existed between the United States and the Japanese Empire."

The six months following Pearl Harbor were the darkest this nation has ever experienced. Four days after the United States declared war on Japan, Germany and Italy declared war on the United States. On December 11, the United States reciprocated. Within a week, some 35 nations had chosen sides.

The United States, facing an enemy in both directions which it could not fight with equal vigor, had to choose a major theater of war. Unknown but to a few, the issue had already been decided. The previous spring an agreement with the British had been made which specified that in the event of war, "the High Command of the United States and the United Kingdom, will collaborate continuously in the formulation and execution of strategic policies and plans." It was further agreed that "the Atlantic and European area is to be considered the decisive theater."

Despite the Pearl Harbor disaster, the strategy thus determined that the war in the Pacific or in Asia would not receive priority in the master plan. This fact, plus the factors of distance, climate and lack of even the barest facilities spelled almost total defeat for American forces in the Pacific during the first six months of hostilities. The only bright spot in the dismal war news was the April 18, 1942, surprise raid against five Japanese cities, including Tokyo, the capital, by Lt. Col. James H. "Jimmy" Doolittle and sixteen North American B-25 medium bombers. The damage inflicted was not great but the tremendous boost in morale it gave to America and her allies was incalculable. And the tremendous psychological blow to the Japanese was worth the risk. Air, sea and ground forces were ordered back from the war zones to defend the home islands and the Japanese militarists were forced to restructure their plan of conquest.

To prevent further attacks, the Japanese decided to launch an attack against Midway Island and occupy it to keep the Americans at bay and force the American Navy into a decisive naval battle. Landings were made on Attu and Kiska in the Aleutian Islands to further distract the Americans from any more such raids.

The ensuing Battle of Midway was decisive all right – in favor of American air power. The planes from three American carriers destroyed four Japanese carriers while losing only one of their own. The Japanese, with a fleet which also included six powerful battleships, limped home in defeat. It was the beginning of the end for Japanese power in the eastern half of the Pacific but it was not the end of their desire for conquering vast land areas in their half of the globe.

With the major nations of the world engaged in a life-or-death struggle, there was a clear need for "Combined Operations" – close cooperation and coordination of land, sea and air power – which was essential if the Allies were to overcome the coalition of armed might arrayed against them. It was the only way to combat deadly, ingenious enemies.

To carry out the U.S. Army Air Forces' portion of the team effort, sixteen "numbered" air forces were formed. The 1st, 2nd, 3rd and 4th were the domestic air forces that contributed so heavily to training and defense of the Continental United States. The 5th, 6th, 7th, 8th, 9th, 10th, 11th, 12th, 13th, 14th, 15th, and 20th Air Forces were the overseas combat forces. But there were many differences in the modus operandi of each Air Force because of the mission assigned, types of planes on hand, number of personnel, geographical location, climate, and the nature of the enemy threat against them in their respective areas.

While each numbered air force fought its battles in its own way, it fell to the lot of the 10th and 14th Air Forces in India and China respectively to have to wait until men, planes and materiel could span the 12,000 miles of the longest military logistical supply lines the world had ever experienced. The history of the first of these two air forces – the 10th – began when Major General Lewis H. Brereton, veteran of the last-stand Allied action in the Philippines and Java, arrived in Ceylon, on February 25, 1942. He had one Douglas LB-30 light bomber, five war-weary Boeing B-17s, $250,000 wrapped in a blanket, and orders to take command of the 10th Air Force.

The 10th Air Force had been activated at Patterson Field, Ohio, on February 12, 1942, before Brereton arrived at Ceylon. But it was a paper organization, and the units that were to make up the 10th eventually gathered in India only after some lengthy wanderings. Air operations against the Japanese in this theater were officially inaugurated on April 25, 1942, by an attack of Boeing B-17Es on warships at Port Blair, capital of the Andaman Islands. The attack was directed by General Brereton himself. It was the first time that an Air Force general had ever led a raid in person.

By the fall of 1942, the 10th Air Force consisted of subunits in India and China - the India Air Task Force under Brigadier General Caleb V. Haynes, and the China Air Task Force (CATF) under Brigadier General Claire L. Chennault. It was these two units and their descendants, separated by miles of the world's worst terrain, that eventually broke the back of Japan's land campaign. But the end result was not accomplished without great difficulty for both organizations.

It was a time of great danger and confusion in the Far East. The Japanese were pushing through Southeast Asia toward the sprawling subcontinent of India, where they could deliver a severe blow to the Allied cause in the Orient. The Burma Road, China's only land link to India, was being cut off. Before Pearl Harbor, the Nationalist Chinese, led by Generalissimo Chiang Kai-shek, had made numerous appeals to President Roosevelt for dollars and planes under a lend-lease agreement to fight the ever-encroaching enemy forces. Chiang's brother-in-law, T.V. Soong, was his chief representative in Washington.

When the Soviets and Japanese made a neutrality pact, the situation became alarming, although Roosevelt had no intention of changing the basic strategy of defeating Germany first. With Soong's urgings, plans were quickly made to send Chiang some money and supplies; however, only a trickle of the supplies was able to get through.

Before this, however, in mid-April 1941, President Roosevelt had signed an executive order, which he did not publicize, authorizing American military airmen to resign from their respective services for the specific purpose of forming a volunteer civilian group in China called the American Volunteer Group (AVG).

Thus, the thread of the China Air Task Force and its successor, the Fourteenth Air Force, actually goes back to the summer of 1941. Five months before the Japanese attack on Pearl Harbor, a small group of Army Air Corps, Navy, and Marine pilots were given flight checks in the States and arrived in China to become privately engaged in the war with Japan. They had agreed to give up their commissions and fly for the nation that since 1937 had been fighting a giant Japanese war machine intent on complete domination of the Far East. The AVG, more popularly known as the Flying Tigers, was formed and trained to fight for China under the leadership of Claire Lee Chennault, a U.S. Army Air Corps captain who had been retired for physical disability. Although the United States did not experience war until that "date that shall live in infamy," he was one American who had already been at war with the Japanese for more than four years.

The primary mission of the AVG was the defense of the Burma Road, China's last remaining ground avenue of logistical support from the outside world. It meant trying to conduct effective fighter and bomber operations along a 5,000-mile front which extended from Chungking and Chengtu in the north, to Indo-China in the south, from the Tibetan plateau and the Salween River in Burma in the west, to the China Sea and the Island of Formosa in the east.

Chennault's task, stated in military terms, was six-fold: (1) defend his command's own lifeline over the Himalayas; (2) ferret out and destroy Japanese aircraft and troop concentrations; (3) destroy enemy military and naval installations in China; (4) smash and disrupt Japanese shipping along the China coast and on the numerous inland waterways of China; (5) destroy enemy supplies and military installations in Indo-China, Thailand, Burma and Formosa; and (6) encourage Chinese resistance and provide all possible aerial support to their ground forces.

Chennault was given a new directive by Generalissimo Chiang Kai-shek. After the capture of Rangoon by the Japanese on March 4, 1942 and their rapid advance to the Salween River in China, the Generalissimo directed him to move the AVG, less one squadron to be left at Kunming, to Chungking, which had been the "most bombed" city in the world during 1941. The defense of Chungking then became the AVG's primary mission and Chennault was given complete freedom to deploy his forces as he desired but "to permit no bomb to fall in the city of Chungking during the summer of 1942."

The move was no secret to the Japanese and since they knew the AVG was guarding Chungking and Kunming, both cities became prime targets for their air attacks. Chennault decided to defend Chungking by taking the offensive in east and south China.

Moving in small formations, Chennault moved his two squadrons of P-40 fighters to previously prepared fields at Hengyang, Lingling and Kweilin. The Japanese attacked promptly and the AVG countered by attacking Japanese-occupied fields at Hankow, Wuchang and Canton. Any planes requiring minor repairs and engine changes were flown back to Chungking so that there were always two or three planes plus two "squadrons" of bamboo-and-fabric P-40 dummies there.

At the highest levels of the American government, T.V. Soong, China's Minister for Foreign Affairs and the personal representative of Generalissimo Chiang Kai-shek to the American government, met with President

Roosevelt and Harry Hopkins, the president's closest advisor, in May 1942. Soong had been assured that there would be sufficient air transport from India to China to be the lifeline for the supply of the thousands of Chinese troops. A minimum of five thousand tons of supplies per month of key military supplies had been promised. Soong doubted that it could be done, especially with the twin-engine aircraft that General Henry H. "Hap" Arnold, chief of the newly-named Army Air Forces, had said would be available. Soong had hoped that four-engine transport aircraft with their greater load-carrying and high altitude capability that were coming into the inventory would be provided. In a May 19, 1942 letter to Arnold, Soong expressed his concerns:

> "China does not care whether the planes used are one-engine, two-engine, or four-engine, as long as a minimum of five thousand tons per month of key military supplies are transported from India to the interior of China, and efforts are made to expand this service as rapidly as possible. I assume that by your new recommendations denying us the four-engine transports you previously recommended, you have given the President the definite assurance for getting this flow of goods into China with other transport planes, substantial numbers of which must be sent.
>
> "I shall be grateful if I am informed in greater detail as to the number of transports you intend to send forward, and the accelerating schedule of tonnage which they will carry.
>
> "I hope we shall not repeat our last experience where 75 or more transports were directed to be sent forward early in February and only a small proportion has arrived for operation to date.
>
> "I review this unsatisfactory record because, in establishing an airline which will keep China from being cut off, these failures must not and cannot be repeated, as the Japanese will not give us time to make mistakes or experiments. It is a challenge to the American Air Force but, as the President said in his message to my people, a way must be found. It can be found if you will put the necessary men and materiel into the effort and keep them at it.
>
> "Finally, I beg you not to reply simply that Stilwell will undertake the responsibility because, unless provided with sufficient quantities of the appropriate planes, Stilwell cannot perform miracles. Only you can help us."

The American Volunteer Group's first reconnaissance missions, preparatory to meeting the Japanese Air Force in combat, took place while American ships and planes in Hawaii were still smoking from the enemy's sneak attack against the United States. For seven months thereafter, the Flying Tigers were almost the sole hope of the beleaguered Chinese ground forces, which for more than four years had been fighting desperate battles against the invading Japanese with little material help from the Allies. The AVG provided the first organized resistance in the air that the Japanese had faced since the beginning of the Sino-Japanese War in 1937.

At the same time, the AVG served as a proving ground for the revolutionary tactics and theories of Chennault, who had earlier recognized the impossibility of obtaining, in a short time, a sufficient force with which to meet the Japanese on equal terms in the skies over China. Thoroughly familiar with the limitations and advantages of the only fighters on hand – Curtiss P-40s – Chennault drummed into his pilots the rule that would help keep them alive: "If you take the best characteristics of your plane and fight with them, never letting the enemy fight with the best characteristics of his plane, then you can lick him."

Under Chennault's stern guidance the Flying Tigers hurled themselves at the enemy's overwhelming numbers. Between December 18, 1941, and July 4, 1942, they piled up the astonishing total of 247 confirmed air victories, taking a Japanese personnel toll conservatively estimated at 1,500 pilots, navigators, gunners and bombardiers. Even more amazing was the fact that at no time did the Flying Tigers have more than 55 planes capable of flight, planes which were never concentrated at one point because the tiny AVG force had a huge vulnerable area to protect.

Claire Lee Chennault was considered a rebel by his peers in the Army Air Corps because his unorthodox concepts as to the use of air power often clashed with the orthodox and standardized "school book" teaching of the U.S. military aviation schools of the time. He had won his wings in the Army Air Service in 1919 and served in fighter units in the States and Hawaii. He became well-known for his acrobatics and as the leader of the "Three Men on the Flying Trapeze," a trio that performed their precision aerobatic stunts in formation linked by ropes.

When Chennault was assigned as an instructor in pursuit aviation at the Air Corps Tactical School at Maxwell Field in Montgomery, Alabama he began to articulate his concept of fighter tactics. He published a book entitled *The Role of Defensive Pursuit* which was of more interest to Russian, German, and Chinese military aviators than those of his own service.

The Soviets offered Chennault a five-year contract to come to the USSR and teach his tactics to their air force but he refused, waiting and hoping that his ideas would take root in his own country. However, the hundreds of hours he had spent in open cockpit aircraft testing his theories took their toll. He was retired from the Army Air Corps in early 1937 at age 46 because of deafness; he also suffered from high blood pressure and chronic bronchitis.

Fearing that he was washed up as a pilot, he was surprised but pleased to be offered a two-year contract at $1,000 per month to be an advisor to the Chinese Aeronautical Commission. The offer had developed when a group of Chinese had been impressed by Chennault and his Flying Trapeze colleagues when they performed at the 1936 Pan-American Air Maneuvers in Miami. One of the Chinese was Mow Pan-tzu, who later commanded the Chinese Air Force under the name of Peter Mow. Chennault accepted the offer.

Leaving his family in Waterproof, Louisiana in the spring of 1937, he thought it would take only about three months to teach his tactics to the Chinese and train a cadre of pilots; he was sure he could return to Waterproof in time for the duck season in September.

While Chennault was a premier pilot and tactician, he was not experienced in politics, especially Chinese politics. By being totally honest and straight-forward about the true, sad condition of the Chinese air force that he found, he quickly earned the respect of Generalissimo and Madame Chiang Kai-shek. He was involved in planning the defense of Chinese airfields when the Japanese started their push inland from the coastal areas they controlled in their undeclared war with China.

Chennault did not return to Waterproof. He was made Director of Combat Training for the Chinese Air Force and in early 1941 persuaded the U.S. government to send him about 100 P-40s that were destined for Sweden but could not be sent there because of the war in Europe. Unfortunately, there were no pilots to fly them. But, with the advice of Thomas Corcoran, an influential banker, President Roosevelt was persuaded that pilots and ground crewmen of the Army Air Corps, Navy, and Marines could be released legally from their service commitments and fight for China as civilians. About 100 pilots and 150 mechanics were signed up and the First American Volunteer Group came into being. Although they would be flying as a unit of the Chinese Air Force, they would take their orders from Chennault. They would not lose their citizenship and would be paid $600 a month plus a bonus of $500 for each enemy aircraft shot down.

After their arrival, the Americans heard that the Chinese called the group "Tigers" and several pilots had seen an RAF squadron of P-40s with sharks' teeth painted along the nose of the plane. The AVG ground crewmen took brushes in hand and turned the noses of their P-40s into leering shark faces. In time they learned that the Japanese feared the shark as a symbol of evil, while the Chinese had considered the saber-toothed tiger of Fukien Province as their national symbol of strength. Thus, the Americans who had volunteered to fight for a nation half a world away from their homes became forever known as the Flying Tigers; the name was later applied to all who served in the original AVG, the China Air Task Force, and the 14th Air Force.

When the United States declared war on Japan, Chennault wanted to keep his fighter unit intact. On December 11, 1941, he posted the following "Statement of the War Situation" on the unit's bulletin boards and sent it to every squadron and department of the AVG:

> "All of you are aware of the murderous, unprovoked attack of the Japanese upon Hawaii, Midway, Wake, Guam, Manila, Hong Kong, Singapore, and other places last Sunday. You must realize that the United States is in this war now until the bitter end. You must also realize that the British Empire, China, Netherlands, East Indies, and other democracies are our friends and allies. Each of you must feel, as I do, the strongest and bitterest resentment over the cold-blooded murder of fellow Americans while Japanese envoys were pretending to talk peace with our government. Each of you must have silently pledged his utmost endeavor, even life itself, to the support of your government and its allies in the war to destroy the unprincipled beasts who are now waging worldwide battles for the destruction of all that we hold to be decent and good.
>
> "I, therefore, call upon you to render your best and truest service, so that this Group may accomplish the maximum of its efforts in the common cause. Personal desires and inclinations must be rigidly controlled and suppressed. Orders must be obeyed promptly and fully – half mea-

sures are also half disloyalty. Gossip, rumors, and unconfirmed reports must be suppressed. One of the objects of enemy propaganda is to wear the nerves of their opponents by spreading false reports; another is to encourage individuals to suggest better methods and better ways of doing things than the plan of the unit commanders; still another, practiced by Fifth Columnists, is to issue orders to individuals and small units countermanding the proper orders of higher authority.

"You must all fully realize that this war is grim reality, wherein life or death, victory or defeat are at stake. There is no place in such a struggle for childishness, carelessness or disobedience. Every man of you must settle down and play the part of a man with courage and intelligence.

"Finally, this is not a time for excuses. Your work must be done right and on time. When you are late, many others are forced to wait on you. Conserve your physical and mental strength as much as possible; take advantage of every opportunity to relax and rest. In this way only can you be certain that your body and mind will be ready when the crucial test comes."

The heroic record of Chennault's AVG is the first prologue to the story of the 14th Air Force. The second prologue was provided by the China Air Task Force (CATF), which was activated on July 4, 1942. This immediate forbear of the 14th Air Force was by this time composed of only 35 battered P-40s, most of them inherited from the AVG, and seven North American B-25 Mitchell medium bombers. The CATF was composed of the 23rd Fighter Group, the 16th Squadron on detached service from the 10th Air Force, one flight of the 9th Photo Reconnaissance Squadron, and several B-25s of the 11th Bomb Squadron of the 7th Bomb Group. There were no heavy, long-range Boeing B-17 or Consolidated B-24 bombers made available to CATF.

The other chief assets of the China Air Task Force were the highly efficient ground-observer warning net and the battle-tested theories of aerial warfare, both evolved by Chennault himself. The CATF, which was part of the 10th Air Force and responsible to the 10th's headquarters in India, pinned its hopes on the use of Chennault's clever air tactics to deny the Japanese complete air conquest of China until the Allies could bring up more planes and men.

Despite Chennault's apparent success in fighting the Japanese, he was the subject of intense discussion in Washington after a year of war in the dying days of 1942. On December 16, 1942, General Henry H. "Hap" Arnold, chief of the Army Air Forces, was briefed by an unidentified member of his staff on the situation in regard to the Tenth Air Force and the strained relations between Chennault and Generals Stilwell, commander of ground forces in the CBI, and Clayton Bissell, then commanding the 10th Air Force. It was a battle between vastly dissimilar personalities and military philosophies. Here are notes from that secret briefing:

"Generals Stilwell and Bissell reported that Chennault had five categories of personal shortcomings: (1) lack of administrative ability; (2) lack of appreciation of supply problems; (3) lack of discipline; (4) poor judgment in selecting key personnel; and (5) a tendency to take the part of the Chinese in controversies between General Stilwell and the Chinese.

"General Chennault has difficulty adapting himself and former AVG personnel to Army methods. He and they reason that by employing their own methods, they in the AVG and in the China Task Force were able to consistently defeat the Japanese in every encounter. Theirs is the easy, happy-go-lucky way. Army discipline and methods employed by Generals Bissell and Stilwell are distasteful, are considered unnecessary red tape. Chennault and his people would, we believe, lose their effectiveness if they were required to operate other than they do now, more or less as an air guerilla band. General Chennault told Mr. Wilkie that he required only 30 additional transports to supply the Air Forces of 110 airplanes with which he could drive the Japanese out of China. This illustrates his lack of knowledge of supply problems."

The report added:

"It is generally known that the British officers in India and Burma did not highly regard General Chennault and the AVG. In the eyes of these conventional people, the AVG was a motley organization. One British general described the AVG as 'louts' [who] even paint nude women on their aircraft.'"

Marine Lt. Col. James M. McHugh, naval attache at Chungking, disagreed with the appraisal of Chennault as summarized by the Air Force staff.

In a candid report to the Navy Department, he said:

> "With the exception of Chennault, American generals in China did more harm than good. They do not understand the Chinese nor properly appreciate their problems, nor have their confidence. Chennault was a superior fighting man who had the confidence of the Chinese and was capable of driving the Japanese out of China if he were given limited supplies and equipment and was not interfered with by General Bissell or Stilwell.
>
> "The outstanding fact about General Chennault is that he has succeeded in building and employing a very effective fighting force. Nevertheless, in damage done to the Japs' airplanes, installations and shipping, this unit's accomplishments compare favorably with units of considerably larger size...
>
> "Whatever General Chennault's shortcomings may be, he has definitely shown himself to be a leader. His men swear by him.
>
> "Of course, no one can operate 200 airplanes in China with the current gasoline situation. If and when this is corrected, it is believed that we would be justified in giving General Chennault a chance to do what he believes he can do, and wants to do."[2]

Despite the never-ending clash of personalities and the negative reports from Stilwell and Bissell about Chennault, the efforts and the feats of his Flying Tigers had become well-known outside China. His success at operating with the meager supplies he was able to get could not be denied. Two days after General "Hap" Arnold was briefed on the situation in China as noted above, he expressed the situation as he saw it in a December 18, 1942 letter to Chennault:

> "Needless to say I am very much pleased at the accomplishments of your China task force. What you and your men have accomplished is an inspiration to all of us. The effective manner in which you have utilized the limited resources available to you has caused special comment. I believe that no Air Force has done so much damage to an enemy with so little. We realize that only lack of equipment and necessary supplies has prevented you from accomplishing even greater things. We also realize that only by diligent effort, many hardships, and at great risks have your

units received the limited supplies that you have been required to operate with. General Bissell and other members of the 10th Air Force deserve highest praise for the work they have done in solving supply and administrative problems.

"We hope that in the not too distant future a land supply route to China will be opened. You realize, probably better than anyone else, what is necessary for the opening of supply lines, and you know how limited your resources will be for giving the air assistance necessary for accomplishing this task. Nevertheless, they must be reopened. The life of China depends upon it. The defeat of Japan depends upon it. You will have to continue, as you have in the past, using as best you can the forces available to you. If you can employ your augmented forces as effectively as you have to date, I have no doubt that you will accomplish your objectives.

"As you have often pointed out, we must take the air war to Japan and I know that to be your goal. Favorable reports of your relations with the Generalissimo and other Chinese officials reach me from time to time. As our operations in China increase, the closest cooperation and unity of purpose will be more necessary.

"It is very necessary, also, that all Americans in China present a united front. You can effectively utilize your contacts with the high Chinese officials to convey to them plans of action determined by General Stilwell, or higher headquarters, to be the soundest for the defeat of the Japanese in China."

Of the various stages in the development of the 14th Air Force, that belonging to the China Air Task Force (CATF) was the most memorable. Men such as Johnny Alison, David L. "Tex" Hill, Ed Rector, Johnny Hampshire, Jack Newkirk, Duke Hedman, Butch Morgan, and Bruce Hollaway were the pioneers in the history of the China-Burma-India theater of operations. Pitifully lacking in planes and supplies, they averted annihilation through improvisation, ingenuity and dogged determination. Outnumbered by the Japanese planes by a ratio of six to one, the battle-scarred P-40s sometimes took to the air as many as eight times a day. The pilots would alter their voices and give orders to imaginary squadrons to give the impression of superior force if the enemy was listening on the Tiger frequencies. The CATF was a "guerrilla" air force whose unorthodox methods and tactics baffled and angered the enemy. This handful of men and planes held its own until the arrival of a few additional planes on March 10, 1943.

The battle to get those planes had not been easy. There had been a dispute about priorities at the highest levels of the American, British, and Chinese governments. There was also a traditional conflict between the Army's airmen and ground officers. Specifically, it was the personal animosity between Lt. Gen. Joseph W. "Vinegar Joe" Stilwell and Generalissimo Chiang Kai-shek, and between Major General Clayton Bissell and Chennault.

In 1941, Chiang Kai-shek and his government had retreated inland to Chungking to escape the Japanese assault. When the Burma Road was cut in early 1942 and supplies could no longer be brought in from the south, Chiang had accepted General Stilwell as his chief of staff. Stilwell saw his job as fighting the Japanese on the ground but Chiang also had another enemy to worry about: the communists led by Mao Tse-tung. Chiang knew the communists would be there long after the Japanese were defeated and was reluctant to expend all of his men and supplies against the Japanese. This stubborn attitude earned Stilwell's scorn; he derisively referred to Chiang as "Peanut" and used words like "pigheaded," "ignorant" and "grasping" to describe him in conversations, staff meetings and letters to his wife.

Although Brigadier Generals Lewis H. Brereton, Caleb V. Haynes and then General Bissell were in charge of the 10th Air Force of which the China Air Task Force was a part, Chennault was the air advisor to Generalissimo Chiang Kai-shek, in addition to being the overall boss of all air units in China. Theoretically, in accordance with military protocol, Chennault was supposed to report to Chiang only through the 10th Air Force headquarters located in India. However, with Chiang's encouragement, Chennault insisted on reporting directly to the generalissimo without going through the normal military channels. It was this lack of control over Chennault that was the basis of conflict between Bissell, a straight-laced, stubborn administrator, who believed that proper paperwork was most important to fight the enemy, and Chennault, the individualist, who considered flexibility in the employment of air units was the key to success in battle. Bissell, a long-time friend of Arnold's, frequently conveyed his unhappiness with Chennault to Washington. Chiang, aware of this conflict, always sided with Chennault because he felt that Chennault was the only American truly interested in winning air battles against the Japanese rather than paper battles on the ground.

In January 1943, after the Allied landings in North Africa, President

Roosevelt and British Prime Minister Winston Churchill met at Casablanca to determine the American-British strategy for the future. It was decided that General Henry H. "Hap" Arnold, chief of the Army Air Forces, would proceed from Casablanca to China to attempt to mollify Chiang for not getting the supplies he wanted and brief him on the status of world operations. It had been acknowledged that everything possible would be done to build up the offensive of the British troops in India. If possible, Chinese troops would be employed with the British against the Japanese in Burma.

General Arnold commented in his memoirs: "It was agreed that I should take a message to Chiang Kai-shek, giving him an outline in most general terms of our plan for employment of troops and air forces all over the world. Our hope was to obtain a better understanding with the Generalissimo and thus get more Chinese troops into the Burma area; but no change was to be made in our Pacific policy."[3]

When Arnold arrived in Chungking, he met with Chiang and gave him a letter from President Roosevelt. The president wrote that he was "determined to increase General Chennault's Air Force in order that you may carry the offensive to the Japanese at once. General Arnold will work out the ways and means with you and General Chennault."[4]

In the ensuing discussion it became clear to Arnold that Chiang's confidence in Chennault was unbounded. Chiang could not see why Chennault could not be given complete charge of the entire Air Force operating in both India and China. However, Arnold did not believe such a command structure would work. The great animosity between Stilwell and Chiang was shared by Chennault. Chennault also had a personal dislike for Bissell who was, technically, Chennault's boss when it came to dissemination of assets from India to fight the war in China.

After more than a year of war, Chiang claimed he had received no cooperation from the United States after the AVG had been terminated. He said he had reorganized the Chinese Air Force and wanted it placed under American control and Chennault was the only one he would consent to handle it. Arnold summarized his impressions of the meeting with Chiang:

"1. The Generalissimo was not particularly interested in the Casablanca Conference nor in the Combined Chiefs of Staff, except where Burma and China were concerned.

2. He wanted a firm commitment for 500 additional U.S. planes at

a time he designated.

3. He would not listen to logic or reason when it came to logistics realities; that is, supplies coming in over the Hump.

4. He wanted to build up the Chinese Air Force in numbers, regardless of whether or not there was gasoline for the planes to use.

5. Regardless of his brilliancy as a military leader when he so completely defeated his opponents in 1925, he did not display the same genius or logic in thought now."[5]

It was the "logistics realities" that were the basis for not being able to support Chiang in the manner he wanted. It took time to build airports in India. The capacity of river boats along the Brahmaputra River and the railroad from Calcutta to Assam was extremely limited. In addition to the scarcity of airports, it was the gasoline situation in India that determined the volume of air cargo that could be hauled across the Hump for the air operations in China. All 100 octane gasoline used in the Hump flights or in China had to be freighted up the river, or up the railroad. Eighty-octane gasoline came in through a pipeline which paralleled the river. All gasoline destined for China then had to be carried by planes over the Hump. When it was hauled by a transport plane such as a C-46 or C-47, and gassed up for the return flight to India, there was not much left for Chinese aerial combat operations.

Another serious impediment to air combat operations in China was also the lack of suitable airports. Additional airdromes had to be built before there could be any substantial increase in the cargo loads that would be sent from India. While Chiang and Chennault blamed Bissell for their logistics problems and shortages, there was also a limit to how many aircraft could be allocated to the China theater while the Japanese were advancing toward India. General Arnold explains:

"What the situation added up to was this: Bissell was an excellent staff officer who carefully worked out every operation before he undertook it, or said he could not do it. Chennault had the originality, initiative and drive the Chinese liked; also, a knack of doing things in China that was possessed by few other American officers. He stood in well with the Generalissimo and Madame Chiang. On the other hand, General Bissell was not particularly liked by the Generalissimo. Chiang had made up his mind: Bissell had to go; Chennault must be put in command. What was I to do?"[6]

Chiang was specific about what he wanted from the United States:

1. An independent air force in China under Chennault, who would report directly to him.
2. Ten thousand tons a month of supplies delivered over the Hump. ("Excuses do not go," he said. "I must have tonnage.")
3. Five hundred planes sent to China by November 1943.

Arnold was in no position to promise these things. Fighting a war around the globe meant supplying men, materiel and fuel that did not yet exist, even after a year of war. And it was that last thousand miles over the most inhospitable territory in the world that prevented Chiang from getting what he wanted within the timetable he had set. In describing how difficult it was, General Bissell, chastised for mismanagement of the situation in China after a special probe by the Inspector General's Department, replied:

"From the base port of Karachi to the combat units in China is a distance greater than from San Francisco to New York. From Karachi, supplies go by broad gauge railroad, a distance about as far as from San Francisco to Kansas City. They are then transshipped to meter gauge and to narrow gauge and go on a distance by rail as far as from Kansas City to St. Louis. They are then transshipped to water and go down the Ganges and up the Brahmaputra, a distance about equivalent to that from St. Louis to Pittsburgh. They are then loaded on transports of the Ferrying Command in the Dinjan area and flown to Kunming – a distance greater than from Pittsburgh to Boston. From Kunming, aviation supplies go by air, truck, bullock cart, coolie and river to operating airdromes – a distance equivalent from Boston to Newfoundland. With interruption of this communications system due to sabotage incident to the internal political situation in India, you can readily appreciate that regular supply presents difficulties."[7]

At a meeting of General Arnold with Generals Stilwell and Bissell at Tenth Air Force headquarters in India on February 2, 1943, it was decided that the 308th Bombardment Group (Heavy), then in training with B-24s in the States, would be used for strategic operations out of China. A radiogram was immediately sent to Washington to set the administrative wheels in motion to order that transfer.

General Arnold returned to the States pondering what he had learned in China. In his memoirs, he labeled the problem as "theateritis" which meant that commanders in overseas theaters always made continued requests and demands for additional personnel and equipment, "regardless of the importance of the command in relation to others, regardless of the schedules worked out by the Joint or Combined Chiefs of Staff, regardless of production, and regardless of the effect upon other theaters." He added, "In addition, commanders with theateritis always suffered from the delusion that some mystic wave of the hand would bring about the impossible and secure thousands of planes overnight."[8]

Arnold returned to the States via India, Africa, Brazil and Puerto Rico. Upon landing at Borinquen Field, he met Colonel Eugene H. Beebe, who was waiting to go overseas with four squadrons of heavy bombers of the 308th Bomb Group. Beebe, instead of going to North Africa with four Consolidated B-24 Liberator squadrons – the 373rd, 374th, 375th and 425th – was told that he would proceed to India to join the Tenth Air Force under General Bissell at first and then prepare for a move to China. After Arnold left, Beebe briefed the squadron commanders still there on what General Arnold had said.

The basis for the decision to send a B-24 heavy bombardment group to China actually had its origin several months before Arnold's 1943 visit to China. It was contained in a lengthy letter to President Roosevelt, dated October 8, 1942, which Chennault sent via Wendell Wilkie, then on a world tour acting as a Special Representative of the President. Chennault's problems with the chain of command he detested were mounting daily. In the letter to the President, Chennault asked for a separate air force that would operate solely in China under his command. He said that Japan could be defeated and it could be done with a small air force "that in other theaters would be called ridiculous." He added that if he were given full authority as the American military commander in China, "I cannot only bring about the downfall of Japan but I can make the Chinese lasting friends with the United

States. I am confident that I can create such good will that China will be a great and friendly trade market for generations." He stated that he had the full confidence of the Generalissimo and the top Chinese leaders because "(a) I have been a winning general; (b) I have never lied to the Chinese; and I have never promised to perform more than I believed capable of performance."[9]

Chennault believed that he could accomplish the downfall of Japan if he were given "105 fighters of modern design, 30 medium bombers and, in the last phase, some months from now, 12 heavy bombers." He predicted that his loss rate would be 30 percent in fighters and 20 percent in bombers.[10]

The letter to the President gave more details about how Chennault proposed to accomplish his objectives if given free reign:

"Japan must hold Hong Kong, Shanghai, and the Yangtze Valley. They are essential to hold Japan itself. I can force the Japanese Air Force to fight in the defense of those objectives behind the best air warning net of its kind in the world. With the use of these tactics, I am confident that I can destroy Japanese aircraft at the rate of between ten and twenty to one. When the Japanese Air Force refuses to come within my warning net and fight, I will strike out with my medium bombers against their sea supply line to the Southwest Pacific. In a few months the enemy will lose so many aircraft that the aerial defense of Japan will be negligible. I can then strike at Japan from Chuchow and Lishui with heavy bombers. My air force can burn up Japan's two main industrial areas – Tokyo and the Kobe, Osaka, Nagoya triangle – and Japan will be unable to supply her armies in the newly conquered empire in China, Malaya, the Dutch East Indies, etc. with munitions of war. The road is then open for the Chinese Army in China, for the American Navy in the Pacific, and for MacArthur to advance from his Australian stronghold – all with comparatively slight cost.

"While engaged in these operations, I will maintain full ground installations for the eastern terminus of the ferry route in Yunnan, at Kunming, Chanyi, Yunnanyi, etc. If a really major swift aerial movement is made by the Japanese across their staging route into Burma, to attack the India-China air supply lines, then, acting on interior lines of air communications, I can move back and again be within the warning net which I have established in Yunnan, and meet the Japanese in the air over their

Burma airfields and then and there destroy whatever force they have sent against us.

"My entire above plan is simple. It has been long thought out. I have spent five years developing an air warning net and radio command service to fight this way. I have no doubt of my success."

Wilkie delivered the letter to Roosevelt who in turn sent it to the War Department where, as Chennault recalled in his memoirs, "it created a major scandal." It was considered just another of many requests similar to those the president had received from Chiang and Dr. T. V. Soong. When the Chinese learned that the Roosevelt-Churchill decision of December 1941 was to give first priority to the war in Europe, they had accepted it with good grace, according to Chennault. "But when the Casablanca Conference in 1943 indicated that action in Asia was so remote that top planners did not even include it on the agenda, the Chinese let out an anguished wail that carried clear to Morocco. Generals "Hap" Arnold and Brehon Somervell were dispatched from Casablanca to Chungking to sooth the Generalissimo with more promises. The Generalissimo bluntly demanded an air force of 500 planes under separate American command in China and a 10,000-ton monthly Hump lift to support them. Arnold promised to see what he could do. The Chinese were then well past the promise stage."[11]

In order to keep Chiang in the war, it was decided that he had to at least be given some indication that he was going to get what he asked for. Although Arnold had fought against Chennault having a command of his own subservient to Chiang, he ordered the activation of the Fourteenth Air Force on March 10, 1943, and Chennault's command was thus officially separated from that of Bissell's 10th Air Force. Seven days earlier, Chennault had been promoted to major general; Bissell as head of the 10th Air Force was also given two stars but outranked Chennault by two days.

It was this background of top-level wheeling and dealing that brought the 308th Bomb Group to China. In mid-March, 1943, the four squadrons of B-24s began arriving in India for assignment to Chennault. They were to be guinea pigs to test whether or not a heavy bombardment group, based in China but supplying themselves through India, could carry out missions successfully against strategic enemy targets such as airfields, railroads, supply warehouses, docks, and shipping.

Although Chennault wanted control over the Hump operation that brought him supplies so he could mount combat strikes, he was not to get it. General Stilwell, top U.S. Army officer in the theater and Bissell's superior, ignored a letter from Arnold that would have assured increased tonnage and the Hump supply route remained under the control of the dour-faced Bissell.

"With the activation of the China Air Task Force in July 1942," Chennault told the author, "I came under command of the Tenth Air Force, whose headquarters were at New Delhi, India. The Tenth AF was under the command of the Theater Commander, U.S. Forces, China, Burma, and India, Gen. Joe Stilwell, who maintained an advance headquarters at Chungking. Both the chain of command and communications between China, Burma and India were extremely unsatisfactory, and on March 10, 1943, the Fourteenth Air Force was activated under my command in China."[12]

The contentions between well-meaning, honorable men continued. Madame Chiang Kai-shek visited Washington to plead China's case in support of Chennault's plea for aggressive air action. President Roosevelt listened to the arguments of both sides and seemed to side with China's aspirations. Early in 1943, he had asked the Senate to ratify a treaty surrendering extraterritorial rights in China. He later asked Congress to repeal the Chinese exclusion laws which had harshly discriminated against Chinese immigration.

Although he had high hopes for China's future, the president was also aware that Chiang might seek a separate peace with Japan if he didn't get what he wanted. The military situation by early 1943 gave little cause for optimism. Stilwell called the Chinese army "underfed, unpaid, untrained, neglected, and rotten with corruption." However, he had ambitious plans to break through the land blockade, plans that were supported by General George C. Marshall, U.S. Army chief of staff. Stilwell proposed an Allied effort to recapture key areas of Burma and reopen communications from Rangoon to Kunming. British and Chinese forces in India would attack over the mountains from the west, Allied naval forces from the Bay of Bengal to the south. Stilwell would then send thousands of tons of supplies up the Burma Road to equip the Chinese armies. He would next launch a new land offensive to open a seaport in South China or Indo-China, thus enabling more supplies to get through so that the siege of China would be broken.

After listening to both sides, Roosevelt opted to support the Chiang-Chennault concept, rather than the Marshall-Stilwell plan.

"All of us must remember," he told Marshall, "that the Generalissimo came up the hard way to become the undisputed leader of four hundred million people – an enormously difficult job to attain any kind of unity from a diverse group of all kinds of leaders – military men, educators, scientists, public health people, engineers, all of them struggling for power and mastery, local or national, and to create in a very short time throughout China what it took us a couple of centuries to attain."[13]

Despite the empathy felt by the president and his general approval of Chennault's strategy, the forces of production, geography, and logistics worked against the Fourteenth getting the barest essentials to keep its planes in the air. Chennault was well aware of the obstacles ahead of him. General Arnold wrote a letter to him dated March 3, 1943:

> "Recently, you have been given the status of an independent commander of an Air Force. With this status comes, as you probably know, certain responsibilities which you must meet. These responsibilities involve not only normal matters of administration, supply, feeding, training, and operations of your command, but in your case other matters as well...
>
> "As a result of the reorganization, you will be placed in a position where great dependence will be placed upon your recommendations. You must make recommendations, for instance, as to when the Chinese units will be formed. These will include fighter groups, light bombardment groups, and perhaps you will also make recommendations as to when and if additional heavy groups are moved into China as a result of experiments being conducted with the 308th Group.
>
> "As I stated to you during my recent visit, everyone from the President on down is tremendously interested in your operations and all wish to build you up as rapidly as possible. However, we cannot afford to build you up more rapidly than your units can secure the where-with-all to make operations a success..."

Because of a breakdown in getting started to send supplies across the Hump to keep the squadrons in China operating, only 625 tons were delivered in the month of March 1943 and Chennault had to shut down his flying operations in April. Chennault explains: "Monsoon rains that deluged Assam in early April, a month earlier than usual, indicated the shoddiness of Bissell's airfield preparations on his end of the Hump. All but one of the six airfields constructed under his regime became a quagmire, useless for operations. Colonel [Edward H.] Alexander who had taken over as first Air Transport Command boss of the Hump in December 1942 was forced to operate all his transports and the 308th Bomb Group off the single hard-surfaced runway at Chabua – the only such runway in the entire Assam Valley. Hump operations slowed to a trickle. Of the 245 tons scheduled for delivery to the Fourteenth during the first ten days of April, only 45 tons reached China. I had no alternative but to suspend all combat operations until the supply situation improved."[14]

Chennault was ordered to accompany Stilwell to Washington in late April 1943, ostensibly to relay to the Combined Chiefs of Staff his plan for the air effort in China. While he was absent from Kunming, the Japanese took advantage of the supply shortage and raided the P-40 base at Yunnanyi. More than 200 Chinese coolies were killed; five P-40s and a C-47 were burned, and 11 P-40s damaged. A later raid on Kunming resulted in the deaths of two more Americans and the loss of the motor pool.

One of the purposes of the Washington meeting, called the Trident Conference, was for the Combined Chiefs of Staff to hear the views of Stilwell and Chennault and form the basis for future strategy in China. Chiang had insisted that Chennault accompany Stilwell to assure that Chennault's views would be heard. It was at the Trident briefings that Stilwell and Chennault argued extensively which showed the difference between a soldier's look at overall strategy and that of the airman. The official U.S. Air Force history explains:

"Stilwell and Chennault, in presentations broken at points by bitter exchanges, agreed only insofar as they both expected aerial operations of gigantic proportions to be mounted eventually against Japan from bases in China. Stilwell continued to argue that the Hump flights could never be developed to a point of removing the basic necessity for a land supply to China. Until the Ledo Road had been completed, he argued, Chinese land forces in Yunnan should be given the bulk of the air freight in support of their part in the reconquest of northern Burma, an operation which retained first claim in available resources. Chennault argued that the Burma campaign would be long drawn out and that China might collapse before its completion. Development of air bases in Assam should be given priority over the Ledo Road."[15]

The basic differences between Stilwell and Chennault are shown by a verbal exchange when they met with President Roosevelt. At one point in the discussions, the president asked Stilwell what he thought of Chiang. Stilwell replied: "He's a vacillating, tricky, undependable old scoundrel, who never keeps his word."

When Chennault was asked for his opinion, he replied: "Sir, I think the Generalissimo is one of the two or three greatest military and political leaders in the world today. He has never broken a commitment or promise made to me."

Chennault explained what happened next:

"On my last evening in Washington, I was busy cleaning out my desk at the Pentagon when a White House secretary called with word that the President wished to see me again. I postponed my departure one day and saw him again late in the afternoon. He wanted to know if I had everything I wanted from the conference. I assured him that if I got the supplies promised, the Fourteenth Air Force would do well. The President called for detailed maps of the China coast, and we went over my plans once again in great detail. He was greatly interested in just how we were going to do the job – what ports fighters would dive-bomb; which sea lanes the B-25s would sweep; the channels that could be mined by B-24s. Seldom have I had such an interested listener for my tactical expositions. Finally he seemed satisfied.

"Leaning back in his chair he said, 'Now I want you to write me from time to time and let me know how things are getting along.'

"'Do you mean you want me to write you personally?' I asked.

"'Yes I do.' he replied."[16]

Over the next 18 months, Chennault wrote a half-dozen letters to Roosevelt outlining his problems and proposed solutions and received encouraging notes in response. However, some of his letters to the White House were forwarded to the War Department. "For this alleged breach of protocol," Chennault wrote, "General Marshall never forgave me. To him it was convincing proof that I was intriguing against his old friend Stilwell."[17]

Chennault's arguments for more assistance eventually won with the help of Dr. T.V. Soong who presented China's official views to all who would listen in Washington. The development of the air cargo route over the Hump was given the highest priority and Chennault was promised the bulk of the tonnage. In addition to the 308th Bombardment Group (Heavy) with four squadrons of Consolidated B-24 Liberators, Chennault was also to be assigned a medium bomb group of B-25s but it would not be provided until the tonnage over the Hump reached 10,000 tons per month. Chennault's fighter units would be increased to two groups and the Chinese Air Force which would also be under Chennault's command, would receive 80 fighters and 40 medium bombers.

Problems with the construction of airfields in India prevented the Trident strategy from being carried out. The Air Force history reported:

"Rainfall, excessive even for a region notorious for its rains, greatly impeded construction; native laborers, panicked by Japanese bombings, fled the area in droves; construction equipment and vital materials failed to arrive on time...This meant that all the B-24s of the 308th Group, which hauled its own supplies to China, and eighty-odd other planes were using Chabua."[18]

It was a serious overall predicament of short supply that faced the 308th Bombardment Group when their planes and equipment arrived in India. There was not to be much improvement. The 308th would have to supply itself from the stockpiles that were beginning to mount in India.

Chapter 2

THE 308TH
COMES TO LIFE

C olonel Eugene H. Beebe; tall, handsome, charismatic, with a
Clark Gable mustache, was born in Utica, Nebraska on September 27, 1906. He served as a Private in the Idaho National Guard
and after graduating from the University of Idaho in 1928 with a
BS degree in mechanical engineering, immediately joined the Army Air Corps
at March Field, California as a Flying Cadet. He graduated from flying school
at Kelly Field, Texas in June 1929 and was assigned as an adjutant from
1930-1935 to the 1st Bombardment Wing at March Field commanded by
Lieutenant Colonel (later General) Henry H. "Hap" Arnold. When the Army
Air Corps was ordered to fly the U.S. mail in 1934, Beebe flew the route at
night between Reno and Elko, Nevada; Arnold was in charge of this sector.

During 1936 and 1937, Beebe was stationed at Wright Field, Dayton,
Ohio, first as a student in the Air Corps Engineering School, then as project
officer for bombardment aircraft. During this period, he had many additional contacts with Arnold at this time while the B-17 and B-24 were being
developed and tested. On a flight with Beebe to Panama in an early model
B-24C on loan for the trip from Wright Field, General Arnold was impressed
with the B-24's range and features as compared with the B-17.

When Arnold was assigned to Washington as Assistant Chief of the Air
Corps, he asked for Beebe to be transferred from Wright Field to Washington as his personal pilot and aide. From 1938 to 1942, Beebe flew Arnold
and other high-ranking Army officers, including General George C. Marshall,
Army Chief of Staff, and government civilians all over the 48 States and to
Hawaii and accompanied Arnold on other trips overseas, including once to
England.

After a trip to Hawaii in September 1941, Arnold reported that he was
unhappy with the Navy's apparent lack of defense preparedness that he ob-

served in the islands. He was quoted in the newspapers as saying that he "would have liked nothing better than to take a crack at Pearl Harbor from the air with all those ships lying at anchor." What Arnold also saw was the lack of unity of command in Hawaii. He remarked in his memoirs, "here the dismal idea of 'responsibility of the Army and Navy being divided at the shoreline' was as sadly evident as I had ever seen it. Actually, nobody was in over-all command and there was no over-all defense."[1]

It was Arnold's firm belief in the principle of unity of command that probably convinced him later that Chennault should not be allowed to operate by himself in China against a common enemy in the same relative geographical area without someone over him and his counterpart in India to mediate differences and make final decisions about strategy. Beebe was well aware of this ideological conflict. The controversy over how to wage the air war in the China-Burma-India theater did not help Chennault in his continuing effort to get the number of planes, personnel, and supplies he wanted to confront the enemy. In May 1942, Beebe traveled to London with Arnold and was privy to the strategy meetings Arnold held with Prime Minister Winston Churchill. It was this first of several similar meetings that shaped the future course of the air war in the European and China-Burma-India theaters.

Never having been assigned to combat during World War I, Arnold was sensitive about not having experienced any action and thought every officer should have a chance to practice his profession in wartime, rather than sit in an office somewhere. Arnold released Beebe from assignment as his aide in June 1942. In a letter to him, Arnold wrote:

"You probably know without my saying so, but nevertheless I do want to tell you that it was with honest-to-God real regret that I let you go. I thought about it for some time and finally decided that I would be selfish to stand between you and your first chance to put to test in the field your professional knowledge and training. I realized, too, the benefit which would accrue not only to yourself, but to the Army Air Forces as well, as a result of your being placed in a position of command where your skill and initiative could be used to the ultimate.

"I appreciate, Gene, more than I can ever tell you, the very able assistance which you have rendered me during the past four years and the loyalty and intelligent cooperation which you gave with unstinting generosity. Your engineering knowledge has been a constant source of strength to me, feeling as I did that I could always rely upon your judgment of any technical question that arose. Not once, I might add, was my faith in your judgment misplaced – not once did you let me down.

"As a matter of fact, Gene, at this moment I feel as if I have lost my right arm and I 'sorta' gather I am not alone in this feeling and the folks 'next door' [General Marshall's office] are just about in the same fix. However, we are all rooting for you and will follow your path in the future with the keenest pride."[2]

Beebe was transferred to the Second Air Force to train and organize heavy bomb groups. He was assigned to the 302nd Bomb Group and assumed command in July 1942. The 302nd was first an operational training unit using B-24s and later was a combat crew replacement training unit.

Meanwhile, the establishment of the 308th Bomb Group by the Army Air Forces was authorized on January 28, 1942, but it was not activated until April 15, 1942, at Gowen Field, Idaho. Concurrently, the 373rd, 374th, 375th, and 425th Bomb Squadrons were authorized and activated on the same dates and assigned to the 308th.

From April through July 1942, the unit was in the early stages of development and little training was accomplished. On July 28, 1942, all personnel, with the exception of four officers, were transferred to the 330th Bombardment Group. The 308th remained without its full complement of men until September 1942, when a new cadre was formed from personnel of the 39th Bombardment Group. Designated an Operational Training Unit (OTU), a home station was specified at Wendover Field, Utah, on September 29. Additional personnel were received from the 18th Replacement Wing and the Group was completely manned by November.

Meanwhile, the flying echelon of the Group and its squadrons was transferred to Davis-Monthan Field, Tucson, Arizona, on June 20, 1942, for initial training. On September 14, 1942, Beebe, now a colonel, was relieved of command of the 302nd Bomb Group and ordered to take command of the 308th. He immediately reported to Davis-Monthan Field and began to select his staff. Two weeks later, he flew to Wendover Field, Utah, with Major William S. Davis, Group S-2; Capt. Horace G. Foster, Group S-3; and Lt. John S. Szymkowicz, Group S-4. Four squadron commanders were appointed and also accompanied him. They were: Capt. Paul J. O'Brien (373rd); Capt.

Walter B. Beat (374th); Capt. Henry G. Brady (375th); and Capt. Robert W. Fensler (425th). The first group adjutant was Lt. Trimble B. Latting. At Wendover, Major William A. Miller was appointed Group Executive Officer; Capt. (Dr.) William P. Gjerde joined the unit as Group Surgeon.

Meanwhile, the crews had been chosen and assigned to all four squadrons for the first phase of their crew training. All the flying crews had completed their respective individual training schools – pilot, navigator, bombardier, radio operator, engineer, and gunner. Flight surgeons, all graduate physicians, were also assigned to each squadron after completing training in aviation medicine.

"I was stationed at Davis-Monthan Field at Tucson about September 1942," Dr. Gjerde recalled. "One day a handsome bird colonel came in and requested an eye examination. The next thing I knew I was assigned to a newly activated outfit, the 308th Bomb Group, as the group flight surgeon."

During the ensuing months, Gjerde was able to observe and assess Beebe's leadership qualities. "He was a friend to all of us," Gjerde says, "and I take pride in calling him my friend. I have roomed with him, taken trips out on the lake (near Kunming), played cribbage in the afternoon when he called me over, and gone on air and jeep trips. He is a man whose very being demanded one's respect and loyalty. It was very easy to do a good job under his command because he allowed freedom of action and at the same time was available for counsel and gave full support."

Gjerde organized a medical cadre consisting of a group dentist and eight enlisted men. Later, other flight surgeons arrived and were assigned one to a squadron. When the 308th arrived overseas, the group had 35 enlisted medics assigned. In addition to routine medical care, Gjerde and his men requisitioned medical equipment and examined the men to determine their fitness for foreign duty, then training, equipping, and preparing them. This included physical examinations, immunizations, supplying glasses, dental care, and giving lectures on personal health maintenance in various theaters of operation. Some men were found unfit for foreign duty and were rejected. The squadron commanders opposed the rejection of a few key men at first but, according to Gjerde, "strict adherence to standards proved wise later on. When overseas, the squadron which had been most strict had less illness and fewer men transferred from the organization for medical reasons at a time when replacements could not be obtained and personnel were all-important for combat duty."

Throughout the training phases, Gjerde and the squadron flight surgeons gave lectures and demonstrations on the care of combat casualties and prevention of diseases that might be encountered overseas. Combat crews were given instruction in the use of oxygen, the effects of high altitude and extremely cold temperatures and related medical subjects.

The 308th was required to complete three phases of training before heading overseas for combat duty. While the ground echelon was being organized at Wendover Field, Utah, the flying personnel remained at Tucson during most of October 1942 transitioning into B-24s and training combat crews under the supervision of the 39th Bomb Group. The month of October was spent at both locations processing incoming personnel and receiving supplies.

When the combat crews arrived at Wendover from Tucson around November 1st, additional B-24s were made available until a total of 14 were assigned to the group. Second phase training began immediately on a seven-day-a-week basis, day and night. Despite the intensity of the training, there were no fatal accidents.

Paul Tenello, a gunner with the 375th Squadron, wrote about that phase in his diary:

> "Boy, are we flying! Twelve hours on, 12 off, plus classes in plane recognition, first aid, machine guns, takeoffs and landings, cross-country trips. We fly to Idaho, Wyoming, Oregon, Colorado, Lord knows where."

Beginning on November 28, 1942, the group moved under heavy security from Wendover to the air base at Pueblo, Colorado, for the third phase of training. Most of the air echelon traveled in their own planes; the rest traveled by rail. This phase consisted primarily of long distance night and day bombing missions, with emphasis on the bombing. Combat conditions were simulated with crews being briefed on their targets and upon return being debriefed by group intelligence officers. While the flying crews practiced, the ground echelon packed equipment for overseas shipment and awaited orders to proceed to the port of embarkation.

The third phase of training was marred by a fatal accident. While on a training flight in formation on December 23, 1942, two B-24s collided in midair. One plane cut off a portion of the tail section of the lead plane which crashed into the bombing range near Pueblo and all aboard were killed.

Some of the men in the other plane parachuted; the pilot and two other crew members, finding that the plane was controllable, elected to return to the base at Pueblo and landed safely. It took several days to round up the ones who had bailed out. Tenello's pilot, Lt. John B. "Jack" Carey, flew over the wreckage and noted in his diary, "I caught myself crying for the first time since my mother passed away." In a notation for Christmas Day, he wrote, "Oh, boy. Sad."

When the third phase of training was completed at the end of December, the planes the group had used in training were turned over to other units which sent crews to ferry them away. The flying echelon took the train to Salina, Kansas, where all equipment for overseas movement to be flown with their aircraft was checked, packaged, and weighed. After a one-week leave, the crews returned on January 13, 1943, to find that their full complement of 35 new B-24Ds was on hand and ready to fly.

Colonel Beebe was concerned about the forecast of snow that would probably shut down operations at Salina and ordered, on short notice, all aircraft to proceed to DeRidder, Louisiana, on January 16th. The group's second fatal accident occurred on takeoff from Salina when a B-24 faltered and crashed. Five men were killed and one officer was so badly burned that he was unable to join the group. Others escaped with injuries and burns but eventually returned to duty.

During the flight from Salina to DeRidder, another B-24 became lost and ran out of fuel near St. Charles, Louisiana; the crew bailed out. The pilot was killed but the other nine men aboard parachuted to safety.

Capt. John N. Sherman, the pilot of *Maxwell House*, remembers seeing the aircraft he was assigned to fly parked on the ramp at Salina:

"There she sat with her tail low on the rear skid and her nose wheel off the ground. Somebody had loaded all the extra gear in the waist section and buckled it down. As they say now, the weight and balance was 'out of the envelope.'

"A day or two later on January 15, our group commander, Col. Eugene H. Beebe, assembled all and directed everybody to proceed to 'DeRidder, La. Air Base,' which no one had ever heard of before. Since most of the first pilots, including me, had the grand total of 20 some hours in the bird, this was no problem to us. We decided to find it on the chart after takeoff and so did the other crews.

"By this time it was raining and getting dark. The first B-24 took off from Salina and promptly crashed at the far end of the runway, sending up a large cloud of smoke. We were third or fourth in line for takeoff and when we were indicating about 80 mph, a convoy of 6x6 trucks started across the runway in front of us, which was no hazard, except the last one stopped right in the middle of the runway.

"This definitely was a hazard! Since we couldn't go over, under or stop, we went around the truck, slithering and sliding and off for the unknown DeRidder.

"We climbed the *Maxwell House* through the overcast to something around 5,000 feet on top with a full moon. It was a beautiful sight compared with the scene below.

"Our navigator, Selig Rothman, soon reported the chart location of DeRidder and before long we were in the general area although we could raise no one on the tower frequency. We later found out they didn't know we were coming. We landed over tall pines in a rain storm and later three or four other crews landed at DeRidder. The remaining B-24s landed all over the South, including Dallas, New Orleans, and other more obscure places. It took two or three days to get them all rounded up at DeRidder."

When all the aircraft finally arrived at DeRidder, it was found that they had a similar engine difficulty. Trouble with the engine oil lines developed because of the viscosity of the engine oil being used. When experts arrived from Tucson and Washington, the problem was solved by switching from winter- to summer-grade oil and overhauling each plane's oil system.

On January 20, 1943, Colonel Beebe flew to Morrison Field, West Palm Beach, Florida, to make arrangements for the group's arrival. From January 21st to February 15, most of the group personnel remained at Morrison while the aircraft were ferried to the depot at Mobile, Alabama, for thorough inspections and to have bomb bay gas tanks installed to give them extended range.

The unidentified historian for the group, with tongue in cheek, wrote of the "hardships" suffered at Morrison Field:

"During this time, all officers and men of the group aggressively fought the battle of Palm Beach, all with equal ardor, but some with

more distinction than others. Through some oversight in the War Department, no medals were awarded, but it is believed by some that time
and posterity may rectify this omission."

The group, now consisting of about 30 aircraft, started the journey overseas beginning on February 15th. The flight was made by squadrons scheduled one day apart with overnight stops planned at the following bases:
Borinquen Field, Puerto Rico; Trinidad; Atkinson Field, Georgetown, British Guiana; Belem and Natal, Brazil; Ascension Island; Accra, Gold Coast;
Maiduguri, Nigeria; Khartoum, Sudan; Aden, Arabia; Karachi and Agra,
India.

On February 18, 1943, General Arnold, returning from his visit to China,
told Colonel Beebe on Borinquen Field that the group was headed for China
and briefed him on the handicaps and hardships that the group was going to
experience there. He said the group would be headed for unique operations
in China as a result of the conference between Prime Minister Churchill and
President Roosevelt in January. He also said that the two leaders, along with
Generalissimo Chiang Kai-shek, would be anxiously awaiting the group's
arrival and would be observing their progress in fighting the enemy.

Beebe explained later that General Arnold's basic reason for sending
the 308th to China was far-reaching. The long-range Boeing B-29 Super For-
tresses would soon be in the inventory and Arnold knew, after his visit to
China, that there would be many problems to be solved. Arnold added that
the group would have to supply itself in China with bombs, fuel, etc. with no
help from the Hump transports. Beebe said later, "The idea being to find
out by experience how it might be best to use the B-29s which were about a
year away in time."

In a 1970 interview, Beebe reaffirmed that the basic reason for the 308th
being assigned to the CBI was because Arnold wanted to get preliminary
data for the future operation of the B-29s. "We had to supply ourselves from
India," he said, "just as the B-29s did later on. [My assignment] was to find
out what the logistic problems were and whether it was possible to do it. He
told me why he let me go (from assignment as his aide), and it's primarily
due, I'm sure, because of his experience in the first war."[3]

The choice of B-24s, with their capability to haul huge loads, was a good
decision. They could double as their own transports over the Hump and be
self-supporting because they could ferry their own heavy, bulk items such as

gasoline, bombs, and ammunition. In addition, the gunners could protect the aircraft from enemy fighters en route and, as will be seen, drop bombs on enemy targets instead of flying empty from China to India.

The flight for the air contingent of the 308th represented the first time that most, if not all, air crew members had ever been outside of the States. There would be at least a half dozen stops en route to India and all would be under conditions that no one had ever experienced before. It was to be a memorable flight for all.

Lt. Robert Stauffer, a bombardier assigned to the 375th Squadron, kept a journal of the *Katy-Did* on the flight to Natal, Brazil, which was piloted by Capt. John B. "Jack" Carey. His observations were similar to all those who flew this part of the route to China. Here are some excerpts:

"Our first stop was to be Borinquen Field, Puerto Rico. Our ship, named after Carey's daughter, Kathleen, was in perfect shape. The plane was loaded with spare parts and baggage until it seemed there could hardly be room for the crew itself. Our total weight was approximately 74,000 pounds and that first takeoff was ticklish. We all joked about it and no one realized how much worried everyone else was until we saw each other's faces relax and smile when the bumping of the runway suddenly stopped and we knew we were in the air.

"I decided to ride in the back end of the ship instead of my regular position in the greenhouse so the navigator would have plenty of room. Two of us in the nose at the same time always felt crowded, and with the baggage and machine guns it was too cramped to take for any length of time. I stood at the waist window watching the shore until it faded below the horizon. It would be a long time before any of us saw home again. There wasn't a man on the crew who wasn't eager to get into combat but just the same, there's a queer feeling inside of you when you know that last lingering look may be the last you'll have. Our tail gunner, just 19 years old, had kept his girl's picture unpacked and gazed at it silently for a few moments after land disappeared. Then suddenly the spell was broken and we settled down to the trip ahead.

"When the *Katy-Did* touched her wheels on the runway at Borinquen, it was the first time anyone in the crew had been outside the continental United States. Quarters and facilities there were more modern than on many fields we had seen before. We were there but a few minutes when word spread around of the amazingly low prices of cigarettes: sixty-five cents a carton. It was a problem to decide how many we would need because, although we would not be able to buy them in the combat zone except at exorbitant price, we had no idea how long we would be there.

"Another big attraction of Puerto Rico was as a source of a major rum supply. We finally decided against buying any liquor for ourselves, but some of the other crews bought as many as three cases. Some brands sold for as little as $13.50 a case. We received our first taste of the real tropics. It was indeed a mild and misleading taste for we found there none of the extremely damp and sticky climate or the vast hordes of insects we were to encounter farther south. We were confined to the post, so had no opportunity to visit any of the towns. The beach and gentle swell around the field looked inviting but swimming was out of the question because of a large population of sharks and barracudas. Before leaving all of us had our hair clipped short and threw away our combs. Where we were going looks would be unimportant. We were at Borinquen only 24 hours, then were off for Georgetown, British Guiana.

"We flew low over the jungles of French and British Guiana, but except for occasional flocks of birds there was little to break the monotony of this vast mass of trees. I couldn't help wondering what being forced down there would mean. It would be worse than the ocean.

"All that we saw of Georgetown itself was from the air, because here too we were confined to the field. We stayed at Georgetown overnight and at dawn were on our way to Belem. The field there had been built by the Germans before the U.S. entered the war and Brazil became our ally. The cooked food there was not too appetizing but this was made up for by larger quantities of fresh fruit. That night we met with swarms of mosquitoes and I slept for the first time under a mosquito net. We were now below the equator and got the first touch of heat but it was not as bad as I expected.

"We were given permission to visit the town of Belem provided we promised not to drink any water or eat any fruit.

"Belem is an unattractive town with only the post office and the largest hotel providing anything to see. We were stopped many times by small boys trying to sell us a night with their sisters at prices ranging from 10 to 75 cents. They had picked up a few choice phrases of gutter English to peddle their products. It is one of the few places in the world where you can get a shoe shine and a girl for 50 cents. Venereal disease, however, is found in 98 percent of the population. We were glad to push on a thousand miles down the coast to Natal.

"I found Natal to be the most disagreeable place we had yet visited. We could not go to town because of an epidemic of yellow fever, and we had to spend an extra day to give our planes a 50-hour inspection before making the long hop to Ascension Island.

"The food, except for the fruit, was bad and living quarters were cramped. Planes en route to every combat theater passed through in a steady stream, straining the facilities to the utmost. Shortly after getting in bed I found I was sharing it with innumerable ticks. In the middle of the night it rained and water splashed through the open window into my face. Closing the window meant shutting off the air, so I settled for the water.

"At a breakfast of powdered eggs and bacon I met an air transport pilot returning from China. His report on conditions there and on the way was anything but encouraging. Our quarters here, he said, were like palaces compared with what we could expect. Also, news here concerning our troops in North Africa sounded bad. Men returning from that area all told stories of heavy American casualties and strong German forces pushing our lines back. It was all very unexpected following the glowing newspaper accounts of our victories there. It was evident the Germans still had a great deal of fight in them, and no quick end to the war could be seen. The American people were taking too much for granted in expecting the war to end soon. Their toughest fighting was not yet begun."

The diary of Paul Tenello, a gunner on *The Little Flower*, picks up the story:

"Ascension Island. Just a dot in the Atlantic. We made it OK. Volcanic. Not a level spot on the whole darn place. Just the runway and it ends at the end of a cliff.

"I climbed down to the water's edge and I climbed up again. The wind blows awful. To hell with this place. Feel sorry for the permanent party here. Believe me, I'm sweating out the takeoff. I got to reach the war. No use dying in the ocean!"

Emerald B. McNeer, a radio operator on the *Rum Runner,* also recalled the stopover at Ascension:

"February 23, 1943. Landed on this God-forsaken volcanic upheaval after a pretty uneventful first leg on our hop across the pond. J.P. Murphy's crew turned back with a dead engine just out of Natal.

"The runway is tricky with a hump in the middle making it seem shorter than it really is. Dust is terrific.

"Tent quarters are furnished and the chow is excellent. Washing facilities are poor. Movies are shown at night with the audience sitting on sand bags on the side of a hill. Service crews are good but repair parts are practically nil."

The planes that had accumulated at Ascension departed on February 25th, flew loose formation and reached the African coast after about eight hours of flight. 100 hour inspections were carried out on all the aircraft in preparation for the remaining long haul to India. Next stop was Accra, British West Africa. Tenello and several others went to town but the "smells on top of smells" were so bad that they returned to base on the next bus. Tenello commented, "Some of the men have let their beards and mustaches grow, and shaved their heads. Look like a bunch of pirates. I think we're getting careless in our appearance. Maybe the constant flying is becoming a strain. Tempers are short."

In subsequent notes, Tenello wrote that "The women don't wear anything above the waist and all the children run around bare! The native guards are at least seven feet tall, no fooling. The turbans add another foot. Wrap leggings and sandals."

The planes continued to Nigeria. The *Katy-Did* had supercharger trouble and was delayed. Lt. Albert N. Keene's plane had to return to Maidugure after being airborne for three hours with engine problems. Although the flight to India was carried out by most of the aircraft without serious mishaps or long delays, one B-24 remained behind for several days at Natal for an engine change. Another, piloted by Major Robert Fensler, the 425th Squadron commander, had hydraulic failure and had to land at Georgetown, British Guiana, without brakes. The aircraft was damaged as Fensler groundlooped it trying to stop but no one was injured and all of his crew proceeded in other airplanes. The plane was eventually repaired and later joined the group as a replacement. John B. Carey, CO of the 374th, was another who had to make an emergency landing. He lost his No. 3 engine and landed at El Fasher, Sudan, for repairs.

Jack L. Pierson, a bombardier with the 375th, remembers the trip across the Atlantic in the *Bad Penny* from a different perspective. At Natal, Lt. Watts, the navigator, got sick and was left there. Pierson was "elected" navigator:

> "Ascension Island, a fly speck in the ocean was our next destination and I, as a dumb bombardier, was supposed to get us there. I told Henderson [the pilot], if he [didn't keep the squadron in sight], our goose was cooked. He did. Our next leg was to Accra on the Gold Coast of Africa. I did not think I could miss Africa, so I curled up in the nose and took a nap. The faint outline of the Gold Coast came into view. It was a sight I'll never forget. Upon landing the first thing I saw was a sentry standing on a termite mound. He was in a tropical uniform and his muscular body glistened in the sunlight.
>
> "Our next leg took us to Maiduguri where we ate delicious food and found the British living the good life. One officer had a cheetah for a pet, and many of them owned Arabian horses. In the town, leprosy was rampant and beggars stretched stumps toward us beseeching the Americans to help them, and we did so."

Except for storms across the Atlantic and dust storms over Africa, most of the individual crew members completed the trip without individual physical problems; however, one man was hospitalized in Aden, Saudi Arabia, for jaundice and did not rejoin the group. Several had bouts with dysentery in varying degrees after reaching India.

One unidentified plane had engine trouble over the Atlantic and began losing altitude. When a water landing seemed imminent, the pilot ordered all movable cargo that they could get their hands on thrown overboard. The crew responded and the loss of weight enabled the aircraft to maintain level flight; it continued to Ascension Island where it was delayed briefly for repairs. The group historian commented wryly, "Fortunately, for some inexplicable reason, none of the crew could get their hands on any of their personal equipment or luggage, so none of it was lost. It is rumored that organizational equipment did not fare so well."

The aircraft that Capt. Gjerde was flying in as a passenger lost power on two engines when oil lines broke over the Indian Ocean, and both had to be feathered. His plane limped into a small emergency landing field in the Sultanate of Salalah on the southern coast of the Arabian peninsula. They remained there several days until repairs were made and then caught up with the group at Agra.

The aircraft continued to Agra, India, where all were thoroughly inspected before proceeding. Emerald McNeer tells what happened to the *Rum Runner* after departing Agra:

> "Crew ten led the squadron off the field in a gale of hen shit only to have the oil temperature on No. 4 engine run up 45 minutes out and the *Rum Runner* turned back. Oh, unhappy day!
>
> "On landing she fell out from several feet and the tail skid hit with a hell of a wallop. Results: skid broken, bulkhead torn. Delay: two days. Naturally, having a few odd moments at hand, we drew a few items and, ah, borrowed a few. We're to be self-supporting, it says, or 'Hap' said. He didn't make any stipulations (just in case your conscience calls for a little rationalizing)."

Meanwhile, Colonel Beebe left immediately for Karachi and New Delhi, headquarters of General Bissell and the 10th Air Force. While the planes were en route to India, it had been decided that the 308th would be based around Kunming in order to put the squadrons within range of Japanese airfields in East China and also to be in position to pound strategic targets in Indo-China, depending on the pace of combat and the advances made by the Japanese ground forces.

Beebe returned to Agra on March 7th, with aeronautical charts for the flight from India to China. The next day, Beebe and the four squadron commanders left on a week's trip to Chabua, India, which was to be the western terminus for the 308th's operations, and thence over the Hump to Kunming to determine the status of the airfields there that the group was to use.

Meanwhile at Agra, the 308th flight crews were preparing to fly the Hump to begin their sojourn in China. "While we were at Agra," Capt. Gjerde recalls:

"We kept a 308th member on guard on each plane 24 hours a day with strict orders that none of our supplies were to be touched without specific orders from Colonel Beebe. Some of us flew to a base near Calcutta and were treated to a final weekend R&R by going to the Grand Hotel. The trip was made memorable medically by picking up about 20+ cases of amoebiasis, after I had given them a special lecture about not eating anything other than cooked food. The beautiful salad carts pushed around the large ornate dining room were too tempting.

"We then flew up to Chabua where we refueled, had a cold bacon sandwich on bread with weevils and then took off for our initial trip to Kunming. I had been reassigned to a 425th plane because they were to go into the Kunming field where the group headquarters was to be located. The sad event of this trip was the initial 308th loss of a crew to the Hump. Major Bob Fensler, C.O. of the 425th, never arrived."

Despite many days of searching, no trace of Fensler's plane, *The Pregnant Swan* with ten men aboard, was ever found. When it was evident that Fensler was lost, Captain William E. Ellsworth assumed command of the 425th. It was at this time – March 1943 – that the China Air Task Force (CATF) was deactivated and the 14th Air Force came into being. From about March 10th to March 20, 1943, while waiting for the signal to proceed to China, the 425th staged at Pandavasewar, the 373rd at Chekulia, and the 374th and 375th at Agra. Meanwhile, a small contingent was assigned to man the rear echelon at Chabua, India, and a forward echelon was sent to Kweilin, China.

On and shortly after March 20, the entire flying echelon flew over the Hump into the Kunming area. The 425th was to be stationed at Kunming; the 373rd at Yanghai, 48 miles northeast of Kunming; and the 374rd and 375th were to operate from Chengkung, 12 miles southeast of Kunming.

While the flying echelon was flying eastward to the group's ultimate destination, the ground echelon, under the command of Major David B. Lindsay, remained at Pueblo, Colorado, and awaited orders. Their days were filled with calisthenics, hiking, formation marches, tent pitching practice, and target practice. Everyone was given practice shooting the .45 caliber pistol, .30 caliber rifle and .50 caliber machine gun. All were given six-day leaves of absence between January 6th and the 22nd.

The ground echelon left on four troop trains for California on February 7th and arrived at Camp Stoneman on the 10th. The group historian commented:

> "After being processed there, we were ready for our world tour. As a part of the processing, each man turned in a perfectly good pair of four-buckle overshoes, which we were advised we would not need because we would be issued rubber boots – which (by 1944) we ain't seen yet."

On February 14th, the group embarked on a ferry boat at Pittsburg, California, for a trip down the river to San Francisco to board the *USS West Point*, reportedly then one of America's fastest and finest luxury ships. Already aboard were members of other units, including about 165 nurses. Altogether, there were about eight thousand Army personnel aboard. The *West Point* left the next day.

"The first day was uneventful," the historian reported:

> "Though all aboard were a little nervous because of the submarine menace. The announcement that the ship was to make the voyage without convoy was hardly calculated to allay the fears of the passengers.
>
> "Despite the fact that the trip was made mostly in calm weather, many became seasick soon after sailing. It was not unusual to see men and nurses standing in line for chow for 30 minutes or more, then, just as they reached the dining room door, have to make a dash for the nearest bathroom or bucket. Sometimes they made it, and sometimes they didn't but they always tried. Halls and stairways required frequent moppings."

At 5 a.m. on February 18th, naval gunners, without prior notice to the passengers, began target practice. Passengers hastily donned life jackets and waited in their rooms in complete darkness for orders to abandon ship. "Thereafter target practice in the early morning was a frequent occurrence," the historian commented, "but never again did it make the impression on the passengers that was made on that first morning."

On March 7th, Sgt. Charles Willard of the 425th Squadron died of unreported causes and was buried at sea the following day. A soldier, not a 308th member, also died a few days later. A member of the 425th was operated on successfully for appendicitis during the voyage which was otherwise uneventful for the remainder of the trip.

The *West Point* arrived in port at Wellington, New Zealand, on February 28 to exchange mail and then proceeded to Melbourne, Australia, where all personnel were given shore leave for eight hours. Without giving details but implying that at least two officers had departed from the expected decorum while ashore, the historian commented that two captains, "by pure coincidence, of course," were appointed commanding officers of the ship's latrines, "and, at the 'suggestion' of Col. Lothrop (the troop commander), spent the rest of the trip attending to their new duties."

The *West Point* crossed the equator twice during the voyage to India. On the first crossing, elaborate Neptune ceremonies were held and all Army personnel were given Neptune and international dateline cards. "Many of them were also given peculiar haircuts, egg massages, etc." according to the official 308th history. "Quite a few of the initiates ate standing up for several days."

The ship arrived at Bombay on March 19th and the 308th's contingent boarded the *HMSS Rajula*, a World War I British steamer which was a much smaller ship than the *West Point.* It departed March 23rd for Karachi in a convoy of 14 freighters and transports, one cruiser and two destroyers. Manned mostly by Indian sailors, the food was not acceptable to American stomachs and many of the 308th's personnel were sick en route.

On March 25th, the sea-weary 308th personnel offloaded and proceeded to Malir Cantonment located about 15 miles from Karachi. From there, in groups of about 20 men each, they moved by train via Lajore, Calcutta, and then northward into Assam province to Chabua. The trip for each group usually took from ten to seventeen days, with interminable delays and confusion. Some men did not leave Karachi for several weeks. Karl Hartung, a 308th communications specialist, remembers that he didn't reach China until July 13th.

The official history tells of the train trip to Chabua:

> "Dining cars were unavailable except for the first day of the trip, and during the remainder of the time it was quite a problem to get palatable food. The water problem was solved by drawing boiling water from the locomotive, letting it cool in stone jars which were carried aboard, and then filling the canteens from the jars. Sometimes food was obtained at

native cafes, or catering services along the railroad, but for the most part the men lived on canned corned beef, hard-tack, and similar Army rations."

The 308th was not ready to go to war yet. When the *USS West Point* arrived at Bombay, most of the group's ground equipment was only three days out of Los Angeles aboard the *USS Fred Morris*. It did not arrive at Calcutta until May 7.

Meanwhile, the flying personnel were flying from Chabua, located at the base of the Himalayas. It had a hand-built mile-long runway which had excellent drainage. The mess halls, operations building, and crew quarters were new. It was to be a base which many would see in the months ahead as their aircraft returned for supplies, ammunition, and bombs.

Sgt. Paul Tenello's diary records his first full day after arrival in China after flying the Hump:

"Guarded the plane last night. We started unloading the plane this morning. I can't believe it carried so much. The bomb bays are loaded right to the top. The back, right to the tail. Thank goodness. Now we can move around again. The bomb bay doors have been boarded and secured since Salina. The lower hatch where the ball turret belongs is empty for the first time in so long. Got my 50 cartons of cigarettes out. Also my rum. Wish I'd bought whiskey.

"Haven't the slightest idea when the ground crew will catch up. Someone started the rumor that the ship with the rest of the equipment has been torpedoed.

"There's a bunch of Chinese kids hanging around. Red-cheeked. Very healthy-looking and curious. The little ones' backsides are slit; front, too. They relieve themselves just anywhere.

"The hills all around us are terraced. Rice paddies. Wherever you look you see graves. The hills are clustered with mounds. The sky is just beautiful. Have never seen sky like this. All shades of greens, pinks, yellows, with fine black streamers. Just like a delicate marble. The air is so rare; it reminds me of Pueblo. I think I'm liking all this."

For all of the 308th crews, the first crossing of the Hump was an experience they would never forget. Lt. Vince Olson, a pilot with the India-China

Wing (ICW) of the Air Transport Command (ATC), recalled how he later got involved in flying with the 308th:

> "Some of us ICW-ATC types were sitting around in the large straw-roofed basha at Tezpur on a dark, wet winter night in 1943 when a messenger came walking through with a call for volunteers. The mission was supposed to be secret. It was no trouble to pry out the details, however.
>
> "The 308th Bomb Group was being transferred to China. They needed a couple of experienced Hump pilots to show them the way. Apparently their pilots had never flown the rock pile and they felt that they might need a little guidance at first.
>
> "I can still see, as if it were yesterday, the bare interior of the old basha that night. A single cord with a dim electric light on it hung down from a dank rafter. The usual poker game was going on in one corner, a booze party in another.
>
> "What would prompt ATC pilots to volunteer for what appeared to be combat duty? Today, at the age of 56, I think we were crazy, but in those days we were young and filled with bravery and energy. I was one of the first to volunteer, and I was accepted.
>
> "A few days later the little band of volunteers arrived at 308th headquarters. When the C.O. interviewed us he found to his delight that we had all been in attendance at Tarrant Field, Fort Worth, Texas, (a B-24 training base), and at least on paper we were bomber pilots.
>
> "The 308th had been hitting both Rangoon and Mandalay and in the process had suffered some casualties. Ergo, we ATC pilots were their replacements. We found that instead of flying the Hump as check pilots and instructors we were riding into combat on regular bomb missions.
>
> "Our service with the 308th lasted about one month. As far as I remember we did our job well and I firmly believe this was the only time in the history of the war that ATC pilots were assigned to combat units.
>
> "Ironically, the worst missions were the transport flights to China. Typical of a non-transport combat outfit, the 308th insisted upon adding the cargo on top of a full military load of guns, ammo, gunners and bombs. The result was a murderous combination of flying tank, battleship and cargo liner, using up 6,000 feet of runway, 500 feet of overrun and light scattered bamboo at the end for takeoff."

When the flying personnel arrived in Kunming, they began to realize what General Arnold meant when he told Colonel Beebe about the conditions in China, and he, in turn, had relayed to the troops. Dr. William Gjerde explains what he found:

> "We were housed in old Chinese barracks in the main compound bordering the Kunming field where we remained for several months until our new barracks and headquarters building were completed. The most memorable part of this stay is that we were crowded into these primitive buildings which were infested with rats and bed bugs and, of these, I believe the latter were the worst."

Over the next two and one-half years, Dr. Gjerde stayed with the 308th and remarked that its operations were different from most other U.S. units. "The Chinese had complete charge of our housing, mess, water supply, laundry, barbers, etc.," he said:

> "The medical department had, as in most military units, the responsibility for sanitation and health; thus had close contact with the Chinese in regard to mess and housing. We, so to speak, lived off the land because there was no way to transport rations. We watched the food for sanitation and the water supply which was obtained from surface wells and boiled. Even then, cultures were often contaminated by the time they got back to the place where the water and food was consumed.
>
> "In all of China, we had only a station hospital. We could not afford a general hospital or care for patients requiring extended care. We had all the regular diseases and injuries plus many diseases most of us had never encountered before. Even with all these problems we had a remarkable health record."

George Plantz, an engineer gunner on the crew of the *Shootin' Star* of the 374th, commented on the living conditions he encountered:

> "Our quarters and buildings were the product of many hands and crude tools. Mud bricks were formed and baked in the sun to provide external structures. Poles, straw matting, and hempen rope were the materials used to make bunks for the interior. The niceties and refine-

ments that some of us had known were supplanted with crude, make-shift showers, toilets and messing facilities. The only American items were our clothing, a few personal things, and, of course, our reason for being there: the lumbering B-24s bristling with guns and turrets armed with munitions and bellies full of bombs. Yes, even the gasoline to run the engines of war had to be flown in from India.

"So what the 308th's personnel found upon their arrival in 1943 wasn't quite like some of the other theaters of war where all the materiel needed to wage a war was stockpiled and a never-ending flow of supply ships backed up the effort. In China, everything that was needed had to be flown over the Hump from India and the highest priorities were aircraft parts, gasoline and munitions. If there was ever an inch to spare in a crowded and overladen airplane, a few extras in the form of a can of beer, carton of cigarettes or a tube of toothpaste would loom up and it was Christmas in July."

A large number of supply flights over the Hump were necessary before a single B-24 could get into the air on a combat mission. The last 500 miles of a 12,000-mile supply line was a critical bottleneck but it could have been worse. The B-24s had the advantage of carrying their own supplies directly to their operating bases. The supply runs made by the Air Transport Command's base terminated at Yunnan, the northern terminal. Anything destined for the other bases in the interior had to come from there 400 to 700 miles by rail, barge and truck, a trip that sometimes took as long as eight weeks. And that was under ideal conditions that were "seldom experienced" according to General Chennault.

Chennault explained the difficulties the 308th's B-24 units experienced at the end of the most complicated supply line of the war:

"Our supply problems were beyond the comprehension of anyone who had not actively wrestled with them...It was more than 3,000 miles from western India supply ports to our targets on Formosa. It was as though an air force based in Kansas was supplied from San Francisco to bomb targets from Maine to Florida...To drop a ton of bombs on Shanghai, it was necessary to deliver 18 tons of supplies to an Indian port. The total cost of delivering gas from Indian ports to advanced China bases was actually six times the gas received."[4]

Although the flights over the Hump were sometimes more dangerous than combat, some crew members didn't mind. Evans Kranidas, a radio operator and gunner in the 425th, said he and others looked forward to them for a number of reasons. The flight was usually only a six-hour mission, compared to the 8 to 10 hours of combat missions. The tanks in the Liberator's bomb bay used to haul gas left room to hold other scarce supplies like beer and Spam.

"We stuck the beer up in the bomb bay and after flying at 26,000 feet over the Hump," Kranidas explained, "it would be nicely cooled when we got back. Everybody knew when a Lib was due back from the Hump.

"The guys in Europe didn't like Spam but for us it was a link with home. We knew how much effort went into getting it over those mountains; besides, we got tired of water buffalo. The cooks tried to camouflage it by making it into hamburgers, stew and steaks but..."

From the time of its arrival in China throughout the month of April, the aircraft from the four squadrons were engaged primarily in making supply runs between Chabua and the bases at Kunming. About seven trips were made daily. By May 1st, the group had accumulated about 100,000 gallons of gasoline and nearly 200,000 lbs. of bombs in 500- and 1,000-lb. sizes.

Although the base at Chabua seemed to be in fairly good shape, the other airports in India from which British and American air units were supposed to operate were in a sad state. On April 30, 1943, General Henry H. Arnold wrote to Field Marshall Sir John Dill, the British representative in charge of logistics in India:

"General Chennault, who has just arrived in the United States, has reported to me that the movement of supplies into China over the India-China air route has been reduced to marked degree as a result of conditions of the airdromes in Assam. Rains have softened the fields, necessitating that all aircraft remain on runways and taxi strips. The hard surfacing of runways, taxi ways and hard stands is of such light construction that they are breaking up under the weight of C-87 and B-24 type aircraft. This condition has been aggravated by a softening of the dirt underneath runways as a result of rains.

"Some time ago I requested you to take action that would ensure the early completion of new airdrome facilities in Assam. This you kindly agreed to do. I should like to ask now that you do whatever is practicable to expedite the construction of these new airdromes, and take immediate action to provide a force of airdrome maintenance personnel of sufficient size to keep existing airdromes in Assam in a constant state of repair. Unless this is done the present rate of shipment of supplies into China cannot be maintained, much less expanded."

In the beginning, the ferry route over the Hump used by the 308th was the direct route which required flying the B-24s at altitudes from 20,000 to 25,000 feet. This meant flying through nearly continual bad weather and severe icing conditions. Later, the route was changed to a more southerly course, making a turn at the junction of the Nmai and Mali Rivers, about 20 miles north of Myitkyina, a Japanese base. Thus, for a considerable portion of the trip, the flights would be over Japanese-held territory. However, most of the crews preferred this route rather than the higher mountains which they considered more hazardous than possible interception by Japanese fighters.

On April 3, 1943, *The Bad Penny,* was lost with all on board. It, along with *Katy-Did, Battling Bitch* and *Little Flower,* was returning to Chengkung from Chabua. All encountered wing icing and Lts. John Carey and Robert F. Burnett in the *Katy-Did* reported they almost lost control because of it. About one and a half hours after departure, the pilot of *The Bad Penny,* Lt. James H. Henderson, radioed that he was returning to Chabua but gave no information about the difficulty he was experiencing. Nothing further was ever heard from the plane or the five men on board.

On April 9, another plane, named *Thumper,* piloted by Lt. Morris E. Heald, was lost on a ferry flight from Chabua to Chengkung. It crashed in a bamboo thicket about ten miles from the field at Chabua, killing all six men aboard. It was last seen spinning down out of an overcast without its tail assembly. A native was killed by the falling wreckage.

A freak ground accident occurred at Chabua on April 24th. A DC-3 was taking off when the pilot lost control and it ploughed into a parked B-24. The impact cut completely through the Lib's fuselage directly behind the wings. One man was sleeping in the tail section. As the official Group history wryly notes, "He was scared as hell but unhurt."

On the same day, another B-24, the *Betty G,* crashed about six miles from Chabua while making an approach. The apparent cause was a long power-off descent from about 20,000 feet through an overcast. The carburetors had probably iced up because the engines would not respond when the throttles were pushed forward for the level-off and landing. Three men were killed; three others were seriously injured.

It was at this time that General Chennault was called to Washington, along with General Stilwell. Brigadier General Edgar E. Glenn was left in command of the Fourteenth. After Chennault left, there were reports that Japanese planes were seen near Kunming but no bombs were dropped. On April 26, enemy planes raided Yunnanyi. Out of the 25 P-40s on the field, five were destroyed and eleven were damaged. A C-47 was burned. More than 200 coolies working on the runway and two Americans were killed. This success probably encouraged the Japanese to launch a raid on Kunming.

The Kunming airfield had been bombed several times in 1941 from low altitudes. The intruders were not intercepted because there were no fighter planes on the field at the time. On December 18, 1941, they bombed the field again. The next day, Chennault sent ten P-40s to Kunming to wait. On the 20th, the Japs sent eight bombers to attack the field and all eight were intercepted fifty miles from Kunming and shot down. No more attempts were made to bomb the field until Chennault left for Washington in April 1943.

A large enemy raid on Kunming occurred on April 28. It was April 29 in Washington, the Emperor's birthday, when Chennault heard that the personnel of the 308th got their first taste of what it was like to be bombed on the ground. Twenty Japanese twin-engine bombers, accompanied by about 21 fighters, approached from the southwest at 11 a.m. The bombers dropped anti-personnel fragmentation bombs and a few incendiaries. Most of the bombs fell on a Chinese village west of the field killing about 60 Chinese and burning a number of houses.

Two bombs fell near the control tower and plotting room on the field, killing Col. Don Lyon, director of operations for the Fourteenth Air Force. General Glenn was wounded but remained on duty; he immediately radioed information about the raid to Chennault who had just arrived in Washington. Chennault later wrote, "I was ready to head back for China an hour after I received Glenn's radios describing the bombings. Instead, I spent more than a month in a seemingly endless round of conferences, dinners, cocktail parties, speeches, sitting for portraits and a bust, and turning down a dozen authors who wanted to write the story of my life."[5]

The P-40s had been alerted about forty minutes ahead of the raid and shot down a confirmed eight enemy fighters and two bombers. Eight others were counted as probables. Stung by this reception, the Japanese returned on May 15th with a greater number of aircraft than had previously been seen in this area: thirty-six twin-engine bombers and about forty fighters in a tight formation. Approximately 200 bombs were dropped.

The defending P-40s had about forty minutes warning - plenty of time to get airborne. The bombers were completely surrounded by Zeros and the P-40s were not able to get to the altitude of the top cover of enemy fighters. However, the two forces engaged in a running gun battle and the early interception probably caused the enemy bombers to drop most of their bombs short. When the pattern of the 200 bombs was analyzed, almost all of them would have covered the entire field if they had not been dropped prematurely.

The P-40s knocked down a confirmed thirteen Zeros and two bombers, and probably shot down eight more Zeroes and two bombers. None of the P-40s was lost.

The damage from the raid was remarkably small, considering the number of bombs dropped. One B-24 on the ground, which had just arrived, received a direct hit and was destroyed. The crew had been out of it for about five minutes when it was hit. A B-25 in a revetment was also demolished. A Chinese training plane burned as a result of the explosion of a Russian bomb which was lying near a tent of the 425th Squadron. Four other tents and some office equipment of the 425th were lost by a direct hit. Miraculously, none of the personnel of the 425th, crouching in foxholes, were hurt. However, there were a few casualties among Chinese civilians in the village west of the field.

While this raid represented a temporary setback to the 308th, it had already been battle-tested in the air. All four squadrons had participated in a raid on Hanoi, French Indo-China, the Group's first mission.

Chapter 3

BAPTISM OF FIRE

May 4, 1943, was a red letter day in the history of the 308th. Its four squadrons, with a total of eighteen B-24s led by the group's commander, Colonel Eugene H. Beebe, participated in a combined mission to the Hanoi-Haiphong area in French Indo-China. It was the Group's first combat experience. In addition to the Liberators, the 11th Bomb Squadron sent up nine B-25s and the 23rd Fighter Group launched about fifteen P-40s. Major Everett W. "Brick" Holstrom, one of Jimmy Doolittle's Tokyo Raiders, led the B-25s and Colonel Bruce K. Holloway, the P-40s.

The force departed about 8:30 a.m. and proceeded directly to Loa Kay, then downriver to Hanoi in a deliberate attempt to draw Jap fighters into the air. The target was clearly visible in good "contact" weather. The B-25s, with fighter escort, bombed a cement works and installations at Haiphong before pulling away for the dash home.

Beebe, leading with the longer-range B-24s loaded with 500- and 1,000-lb. bombs, pulled away from the B-25s near Hanoi and continued in a southeasterly direction over water to bomb the Samah Bay Airport, a coal yard, storage and barracks area, harbor installations, and wharf areas on the south coast of Hainan Island. P-40s strafed the target area following the bombing and on the return flight destroyed two locomotives and strafed a supply train.

The enemy was taken by surprise. There was no interception and very little anti-aircraft fire. Large fires and destruction were evident after the bombing; an underground fuel storage area erupted with the largest fire. The official Air Force history reported, "The first heavy bomber mission by the Fourteenth Air Force was a success."

Sixteen of the eighteen B-24s landed at the squadrons' respective bases at Kunming, Chengkung, and Yangkai. One ship, piloted by Lt. John H.

Keene of the 375th Squadron, had engine trouble before reaching the target area and flew the rest of the mission with one engine feathered. Since so much of the flight was made on three engines, he ran short of fuel and had to land at Yungning. Keene and his crew returned the next day.

The other B-24, piloted by Lt. D. L. Willis of the 373rd Squadron, also ran short of fuel because the fuel transfer system failed to function and gas could not be transferred from the bomb bay tanks to the wing tanks. The entire crew had to take to their parachutes near Amichow, about 150 miles from Kunming. All bailed out but one man was killed when his chute failed to open; eight of the nine survivors returned to their base within three days; T/Sgt Stanley Marshall, unable to join up with the rest of the crew, arrived seven days later.

Four days after the first mission, the group geared up for another combined mission with the B-25s and P-40s. Again led by Colonel Beebe, the target was the Tien Ho Airdrome near Canton, China. The B-25s were assigned to bomb the airport, while the 16 B-24s targeted the barracks and storage areas nearby. P-40s would fly top cover. The approach route to the target area was planned for the B-24s so that if any of the bombs overshot the target, they would hit the airfield.

Leaflets were dropped on the bomb run over the target and most were believed to have fallen in Canton. They showed the Chinese and American flags with Japanese characters which said, "The planes are coming!"

One flight of three ships from the 374th made a second run before dropping their bombs. This flight encountered eleven to fifteen enemy fighters and three were confirmed as shot down. Sgts. Harold A. McQuate, Edward J. McCon, and Israel Blumenfeld were credited with these victories.

A number of enemy fighters were encountered by the P-40s, led by Colonel Clinton D. "Casey" Vincent. Thirteen enemy planes were confirmed as shot down; one flight of the B-24s, led by Capt. W.G. Adler, of the 374th Squadron, was credited with three fighters confirmed and two others damaged. There was considerable anti-aircraft fire over the target but it was low and ineffective. One of the B-25s experienced a premature detonation of the bombs in the bomb bay; it caught fire and crashed into Canton. There were no survivors.

From the standpoint of damage assessment, the raid was judged more successful than the previous one. Large fires were started; smoke was visible for more than an hour after the planes left the target area. Two days later, the smoke was still so heavy over the target area that a reconnaissance plane could not get any photographs. As the group historian commented, "The crews were all elated over the success of their first two missions, and were genuinely sorry to have to return to the routine business of ferrying bombs and gasoline over the Hump."

The Japanese retaliated after these attacks on their installations by launching a massive attack on Fourteenth Air Force headquarters at Kunming on May 15. The enemy attack force of thirty bombers and forty fighters met little resistance. As one historian declared, "Only the inaccuracy of the Japanese bombardiers saved the base from complete destruction."

Other raids against the Fourteenth's bases followed during the rest of the month which were accompanied by enemy land offensives toward these locations. They moved near Changsha and dangerously close to Hengyang, one of the principal forward bases of the Fourteenth.

As the enemy forces advanced toward the wartime capital of China, Chennault's assistance was requested and he agreed to send the B-24s against them. The bombers were used to fly at low level and strafe Japanese troops massing at the Yangtze River gorges.

Inclement weather hampered all American missions and presumably also kept the Japanese on the ground. However, English-language leaflets reportedly dropped by at least one Japanese plane on May 15, 1943 dared the Americans to fight. They said:

"To the Officers and Men of the United States Airforce:

"We express our respects to you men who have taken great pains to come to the interior of China.

"We of the Fighter Command of the Imperial Japanese Airforces take pride in the fact that we are the strongest and best in the world.

"Consequently, we express our desire as sportsman to hold a decisive battle with you in a fair and honorable manner.

"We then can best prove to you the spirit and ability of our airforce.

"With hearty best wishes for a decisive battle.

"The Fighter Command of the
IMPERIAL JAPANESE AIRFORCE"

On May 28th, the 308th was visited by Capt. Eddie Rickenbacker,

America's top scoring ace of World War I. He talked with the personnel at Kunming, Chengkung and Yanghai and gave them his assessment of the war effort at home and in other theaters. Although he predicted a long war, he gave an encouraging picture of the equipment that the 308th could expect to have assigned to it during the next year.

During the latter part of May 1943, Japanese troops began a drive west and north from the Tungting Lake area with the announced intention of taking Chungking, China's capital city. Chiang was alarmed and urgently requested support from the 14th Air Force to bomb targets at Ichang. Though it hardly looked like a proper mission for the 308th, Major Walter B. Beat, commander of the 374th Squadron took six planes from the 374th and three from the 425th to Chengtu, along with five transports with ground personnel, equipment and supplies. On May 29th, the nine planes departed from there to bomb Ichang. No fighter opposition or anti-aircraft fire was encountered and all planes returned safely.

The next day, Ichang was attacked again. Although on both occasions, the crews did not see targets of much value, the Chinese reported that it was successful. Again, no enemy aircraft rose to make an interception.

On May 31st, all nine planes took off again with Kingmen Airdrome as the primary target but a solid undercast made it impossible to bomb. Led by Major Beat again, the formation turned toward the secondary target: Ichang. Meanwhile about twenty Japanese Navy Zeros came up to greet the bombers and were met by Col. John R. Alison with a flight of P-40s flown by one other American pilot, Charlie Tucker, and seven Chinese pilots. After a running ten-minute battle, the P-40s, low on fuel, peeled off for home. Years later, Alison recalled that mission vividly because he was nearly shot down:

> "I knew where Ichang was because I had flown over it once before and it was a very active base. When we got into the area, there was cloud cover but there were some holes in the clouds. Beat called me and said, 'Johnny, what do you think?' I said, 'Well, I don't know.' He said, 'Do you think we can go down through that hole?' I said, 'Before you take that formation down through that hole, I'm somewhat familiar with the terrain, I'll go down and take a look and see what the weather is under the clouds.'
>
> "So I started down with Tucker on my wing. Now, the Chinese didn't speak any English and I didn't speak any Chinese, but somehow the

Chinese pilots had enough sense to stay with the bombers. We were at 15,000 feet and the top of the clouds were at 9,000. Before I got to the top of the clouds, Japanese fighters started popping up through them. I don't know how many but there were lots of them. They could outclimb us and were passing me going up.

"I got in behind one fighter and I hit him. I could see my tracers exploding on the side of his airplane. He turned over and went straight down through the clouds. I claimed him as a probable.

"As I got near the bombers, I came up on another one, and as he turned, I hit him and he exploded. There were three of them and how they got up there so fast, I'll never figure out but they came in toward the bombers from the side and above. There was also one coming up from underneath and I saw him. I pulled the nose of the airplane up and just held the trigger. I really didn't expect to hit any of the three coming in but I thought the fact that I was firing at them might be able to divert or turn them. I thought I could finish this before the guys from down below got within range but I didn't and one of them got a lucky first blow. His shots started to pepper me from the rear.

"I called Charlie Tucker but he couldn't see me. I said, 'Charlie if you don't help me, I'm gone.' I know there was a tone of terror in my voice because those bullets make a lot of noise when they hit the armor plate behind you. A Chinese pilot came in and shot him down but I thought he was going to kill me in the process.

"I thought the airplane was about to shake apart. I didn't know it but the bottom half of the rudder was still hanging on by the wire cables and was fluttering in the wind. The left rudder pedal went all the way forward and the right one all the way back and that's when I knew something bad had happened. I didn't know the rudder was off until I got back to base. Four bullets had hit the center post of the rudder and I'm sure there were hundreds of others around. I don't know how many times the airplane was hit but all of the gas tanks were punctured; however, since they were self-sealing, they closed right up.

"I was able to get the gear down and land the airplane at Kunming but both tires had been shot out and I stood the airplane on its nose as I skidded to a stop. When I looked at the damage, the rudder was hanging down on a piece of cable. My armor plate had been hit a number of times and one armor-piercing bullet stuck in the armor plate right between my shoulder blades."[1]

As the B-24s reached the target area and found they were able to bomb visually, they were also met by about forty Zeros. During the bomb run and while heading home, the bombers engaged in a running shootout. Twenty Zeros were claimed that day and five probables. There were no losses for the 308th but there was minor damage to three Liberators.

The Japanese were forced to withdraw their advance units and on June 2, Radio Tokyo announced the suspension of the operation. The raids on Ichang resulted in much praise from Chinese and American authorities. Laudatory telegrams and letters were received from high military and civil Chinese authorities. One from the Provincial People's Political Council of Kiang-hsi Province was typical of the others:

> "During the recent great campaign in West Hupeh and North Human Provinces, you have gained majestic prestige by many admirable feats and you have dealt hammering blows at the enemy. The crushing onslaught of aggression has been dammed up and final victory for the United Nations thus assured. Ravished by your grand success, we are hereby sending you our grateful congratulations."

By June 1, the Japanese were in retreat all through the area from Tungting Lake to Ichang. As they pulled back, P-40s took a heavy toll of the fleeing troops. The official history comments:

> "American army men believe that the shooting down of the large number of enemy planes on May 31st was one of the biggest factors in turning the tide in favor of the Chinese, since this not only gave the Chinese an effective air umbrella, but at the same time deprived the Japanese of the very planes with which they intended strafing the Chinese forces."

During the next few days, the 425th's planes returned to Kunming and the remaining six of the 374th were sent home to Chengkung on June 10th. The 308th historian reported:

> "During their last few days (at Chengtu) they spent most of their

time making personal runs to the Chinese toilet, and lamenting the absence of American toilet paper. When they finally returned to Kunming and Chengkung on June 10th, practically all of the crew members, from commanding officer to lowest buck private, were suffering from acute malfunctioning of the rectal intervalometer. Loads were dropped in salvo over the rice paddies all the way from Chengtu to Kunming, and crew members stood in line waiting for access to the only bombsight."

June marked the beginning of the monsoon season in southern China. It rained intermittently for five days, then on June 6th, the skies let loose with more than six inches of rain in six hours. When morning came, the airfield was a veritable lake, all slit trenches were overflowing, and the tents near the headquarters building had collapsed. The film storage pit under the photo tent was filled with water which damaged cameras but only a small amount of film that was sealed in containers was lost.

The weather prevented much flying but on June 8th, a mission was scheduled to bomb a Japanese convoy reported to be in Haiphong Harbor. Seventeen ships from the 373rd, 375th and 425th Squadrons carried a total of 60 1,000-lb. bombs but the formation encountered a heavy overcast and thunderstorms before reaching Haiphong and were unable to attack the primary target. Three planes from the 425th, unable to find a suitable alternate target, returned to their home base with all bombs aboard, a practice that was considered dangerous but necessary because the bombs were so valuable and in such short supply. In other theaters they would have been jettisoned.

In the months following, many of the 308th's heavies would return to their bases with full or partial bomb loads. Although most of the bombs and fuses made in the U.S. were usually reliable, those made in Russia or China were not and could explode from the impact of a hard landing. It was always up to the pilot whether or not a landing with bombs aboard would be attempted.

The other fourteen aircraft bombed targets of opportunity and met no enemy fighters. The seven Liberators from the 375rd bombed Gia Lam Airdrome at Hanoi, scoring hits on the runway and the building area. The planes of the 373rd scored hits on ships and damaged several others. The railroad yards, a power plant, and the Haiphong docks were also attacked and damaged. The sinking of a large Japanese transport was the highlight of the mission. The B-24 of the 373rd that accounted for the sinking made six passes, the last one at 1,500 feet and strafed the deck as it roared past.

The monsoon rains hit in earnest the balance of the month of June and, since it appeared that no combat missions could be scheduled for a while, all squadrons went back to the Hump run. Stores of gasoline, bombs, and supplies were accumulated for use when better weather could be expected.

There were 151 Hump ferry trips to Chabua that month. In one week – June 20 to 26 – in which fifty-six round trips were made, over 327,000 pounds of payload were carried, including 32,000 gallons of gasoline. More could have been carried if the facilities at Chabua had been capable of handling and loading more planes. On a number of occasions, planes were held up at Chabua because of a shortage of fuel there. The only incident at Chabua occurred when a B-24 was damaged because its brakes locked; it struck an ambulance and ran off the runway.

Despite the fact that the bad weather did not improve during July, nine combat missions were flown, in addition to the Hump flights. At the beginning of the month, the group was advised that shipping would be given first priority for targeting. As a result, eight of the nine missions were against shipping or dock installations.

Planes from all four squadrons took part in missions on July 8th to Haiphong where they met heavy anti-aircraft fire. Several B-24s suffered minor damage from shrapnel. While all aircraft returned that day, one plane, *Mudfish*, piloted by Lt. Arthur D. Karp of the 425th, struck a large steam roller on takeoff which was just off the end of the runway. The impact shattered the nose gear and left the nosewheel hanging in the slipstream. Karp continued on the mission but found that he had to get rid of the nosewheel because the drag on the plane increased the load on the engines which, in turn, increased his gas consumption. Any attacking fighters could see that the plane was a cripple. Although the plane was flying at 17,000 feet, T/Sgt. Ferguson volunteered to try to cut the demolished wheel loose from the ship.

Ferguson worked with screw driver, hammer, and fire ax while the plane was en route from Kunming to Hanoi. Just as the plane reached the outskirts of Hanoi, he suspended himself by his arms over the open hole and jumped repeatedly on the wheel. It finally broke loose and fell off. Karp continued the bomb run. Over the target area, a piece of shrapnel broke the windshield in front of Lt. Jones, the co-pilot, but no one was hurt.

After the planes had returned over friendly territory, Karp explained their situation to the crew and discussed the best means of getting the plane home. No one expressed a desire to bail out, although without a nose wheel, a crash landing was the only other alternative.

About three-quarters of an hour from Kunming, Karp had the crew, except himself and Jones, move all equipment possible to the rear of the plane. Bombsight, ammunition, parachutes, and all loose equipment was moved aft to take the weight as far away from the nose as possible. After burning off gas so as to have minimum fuel aboard on landing, the crew members wrapped themselves in heavy flying equipment to cushion themselves from the landing shock. Karp brought the aircraft in smoothly and cut the engines just before the main wheels touched down. The plane made a perfect landing, settled on its tailskid and dragged to a stop without injury to anyone or any further damage. For this outstanding example of airmanship, Lt. Karp was awarded an Oak Leaf Cluster to his Air Medal; Sgt. Ferguson was awarded the Soldier's Medal for heroism.

Another group mission for the 308th – the fifth – was another sea search which was launched on July 10, 1943. The objective was to bomb targets of opportunity in the Haiphong-Hongay area. Breaking off individually from the group formation when no targets could be spotted, several B-24s picked the largest ships they could see and scored some hits. Direct hits were also scored on a smelter, docks, warehouses and a railroad yard. There was no damage to any planes, and no injuries to personnel.

Between July 11th and July 27th, 1943, planes from the four squadrons went on four sea searches and bombed ship and land targets at Haiphong, Dalong Bay, Kunlong, Hon Cay, and the Samah Bay area. Several planes also dropped down to low altitudes to strafe ground and sea targets of opportunity. There was some opposition from fighters or anti-aircraft fire and many hits on targets were observed. Propaganda leaflets in the French language were dropped by a few of the aircraft.

On the mission to Samah Bay area on the 27th, one plane lost an engine over the target; nearly out of gas, it successfully crash-landed at Kunming. The bombardier, Lt. H. M. Thomas, wounded in the right leg, bailed out over the Kunming airport as a result of a misunderstanding. When the pilot, preparatory to landing, ordered the navigator out of the nose, Thomas misunderstood the order to mean to bail out and jumped successfully from an altitude of 500 feet. He received credit for downing one attacking enemy fighter.

During this mission, the formation was attacked by twenty-five or thirty Zeros and engaged in a running gunfight for about thirty minutes. The bombers' gunners accounted for fourteen confirmed victories and six probables.

Another plane landed at Nanning to obtain medical assistance for Lt. Christopher H. Williams, a bombardier, who was seriously wounded in the groin. He had lost so much blood that the pilot landed there to get him to the medics quickly. After the flow of blood was stopped, he reboarded his plane and took off again for Kunming where he was taken to the station hospital. Crew members in other planes also suffered wounds but none were considered as serious as Williams.

Shipyards and installations at Hong Kong and Kowloon were the targets of the July 29, 1943 mission. On this date, the 308th lost its first plane due to combat action. It was a new one which had a ball turret installed and it was believed that the added weight may have contributed to the plane's engines burning more gasoline than the older planes. Capt. William Chenowith, the pilot, and Major Schultz, co-pilot, ordered the rest of the crew to bail out before they attempted to land at Yangkai. Fifteen miles before reaching the field, the engines quit and Chenowith tried to land in a rice paddy. Chenowith, Schultz, and a Chinese officer, acting as a spare co-pilot, were killed. Those who jumped received minor injuries.

On that same day, another Group B-24 was lost during a test hop at Chabua and four enlisted men were killed.

The month of August 1943 was what the group historian called "a rather unsuccessful month." Out of five missions completed, six planes were lost as a result of enemy action; one crashed on the return trip from Kweilin after a mission had been completed the previous day, and another was so badly damaged that it had to be salvaged after its return to Kunming.

There were heavy losses of personnel that month, totalling fourteen officers and thirteen enlisted men killed; nine officers and nineteen men were reported missing and never returned. However, considerable damage was inflicted on the enemy's ground installations and personnel, which was confirmed by Chinese intelligence sources. A total of seventy-six enemy planes were destroyed in the air, twenty-four probably destroyed and others damaged.

There were two group raids on Hankow during August, a hotly contested target area which was beyond the round-trip range of the B-24s. The plan was to land at Kweilin for refueling before returning to the Kunming bases. On the first raid that was launched on August 21st, fourteen B-24s of the 374th and 375th squadrons hit docks and warehouses at Hankow. Major Walter Beat, C.O. of the 374th led the mission with his flight; Major Henry G. Brady led the 375th flight. They were to be accompanied by B-25s and P-40s but attacking enemy fighters prevented their joining in the mission. The escort had been delayed defending Hengyang against thirty-three Zeros.

An intense air battle developed and two B-24s were lost over the target. More than sixty enemy fighters (one estimate was that there may have been as many as 100) descended on the formation. Even so, the bombers were undeterred and there were many direct hits on the docks and warehouses and large fires were left burning. "Hank" Brady related many years later what happened that day in an issue of the *Jing Bao Journal*:

"For three days, an unusual frontal system with low clouds, rain and fog hung over Chengkung and most of southwestern China as well as the eastern slopes of the Himalayan Mountains.

"The flight crews had been briefed and just sat around playing cards, or reading, or sleeping, while eagerly and nervously waiting for a weather change.

"Our mission called for 14 B-24s from the 374th and 375th to assemble over Chengkung, fly to Hengyang where we were to pick up a formidable fighter escort and proceed to bomb the warehouses and dock facilities along the Yangtze at Hankow.

"Hankow was a most important target since the Japanese used it as a central base for the training of fighter pilots, and we did not anticipate this mission as a milk run. There was no doubt in our minds that we would have to fight our way in and then fight our way out.

"The day was beautiful with a bright sun, blue skies and just a few patches of stratus clouds.

"We received our weather clearance and I recall the big, bulky, bomb-loaded B-24s taxiing for takeoff in single file like a herd of elephants in a circus following one behind the other.

"In the lead aircraft, Bruce Beat, the C.O. of the 374th B.S., with George Bell, his A Flight Commander, in the right seat. Phil Adler, the 374th's operations officer led the second flight.

"In the 375th, I often flew with Jack Carey, the A Flight Commander, as we wanted two first pilots in the lead aircraft. Jack, however, was on temporary duty in India, and I don't recall who flew with me that day. It was probably Leon Bogan or Jack Keene. Ed Ballenger and Bob Stauffer, our squadron's lead navigator and bombardier, were on board my plane.

"As we approached Hengyang with every man scanning the skies, it was soon apparent that there were no escorting fighters aloft to protect us over Hankow.

"Bruce Beat made two lazy circles over Hengyang and from what we could see, it was apparent that the field had just been bombed and strafed by the Japanese.

"Our worst fears had been realized. We all knew during those three days of waiting that Japanese spies in our midst undoubtedly knew as much about our impending mission as we did, and the defenses of Hankow were ready and waiting.

"As we circled, I could imagine the thoughts going through Bruce Beat's mind. He had three options: (1) Land at Kweilin or Hengyang, if possible, and wait for a fighter escort; (2) Abort the mission and return to Chengkung; (3) Proceed to Hankow without escort.

"Bruce opted for number 3 and headed for Hankow. I do not believe that he received any radio instruction as we were trained to maintain radio silence on combat missions and the odds were that during the just-completed Jap raid on Hengyang, the control tower had probably been destroyed.

"So on to the target and long before Hankow was in sight we were hit by a swarm of Zeros. Suddenly Beat's plane went into a steep dive and he was followed by most of the 374th's planes who probably thought that Bruce was executing a combat maneuver.

"Our squadron maintained altitude since I was convinced that Bruce had gone into that steep dive for other reasons than a maneuver. Our fears were confirmed as it became apparent that Bruce was on fire and with a Poof! his plane exploded.

"We proceeded to the target through the hornet's nest of Jap Zeros and scored direct hits on our target due to excellent navigation by Ballenger and superb bombardier skill by Stauffer.

"We lost altitude purposely as we left the target so that our top gunners would have a better shot at the Zeros who were hitting us mostly with a frontal attack. Our gunners were firing like crazy and I'm sure that we had a couple of aces as a result of the battle, but we were too busy firing at new targets to follow up on old ones.

"The last time I saw the 374th planes, their formation was scattered and the Zeros were all over them. I was told that one of their planes piloted by a Capt. Murphy tacked on to our squadron rather than descend with Beat and bombed the target with us.

"Both squadrons – or what was left of us – landed at Hengyang to assess damage. All planes had been hit and some had suffered severe damage.

"Since Bruce Beat had been killed, I was now senior officer and I was instructed by the acting commander of the Fourteenth Air Force Eastern Headquarters to survey the damage to both squadrons and prepare to return to Hankow the following day. I reported that only five B-24s were in shape to fly another mission. The mission, therefore, was scrubbed.

"Next day, while flying to Chengkung, I received a radio call to land at Kunming and report to General Chennault. I was met by Col. John Neal, the Fourteenth's operations officer, and we proceeded to Chennault's office. Neal repeatedly told me, 'the Old Man is hard of hearing so speak up when you describe the mission.'

"Chennault was informal and friendly, as always, and listened carefully and attentively to all the details I could report, often cupping his hand behind his ear in order to catch every word. When I finished, he asked, 'Why did you elect to proceed with the mission without fighter escort?'

"I told him that the decision was Major Beat's as mission leader but if I had been the leader, I would have done the same thing.

"The next afternoon Colonel Beebe, group C.O., told me that photo reconnaissance showed a direct hit on our target and that fires were still burning. He congratulated our crews on excellent bombing and stated that many, many Zeros had been shot down. He did not tell me that the 373rd and 425th squadrons were scheduled to hit Hankow again the following day, this time with fighter escort.

"I heard later that the 373rd had to abort and the 425th continued alone and lost five out of seven aircraft on the mission. The lead aircraft had again been shot down and the group lost its operations officer, Major Race Foster, and the 425th C.O., Major Ellsworth.

"Thus ends the 375th's participation in the 308th's group mission to Hankow. We had fought a hell of an air battle going in and away from the target, had scored a direct hit on the primary target, and shot down a large number of enemy planes. My recollection is that the 374th and 375th later received the Presidential Unit Citation for our part in the mission."

Two weeks later, a group intelligence team learned through the Chinese network that the damage included 1,000 barrels of gasoline, destruction of a gas depot and destruction of an enemy navy headquarters where Japanese and puppet government officials were holding a meeting. A number of high-ranking Japanese military personnel were killed.

The battle with the fighters had lasted twenty-seven minutes during which the Liberator gunners shot down fifty-seven enemy planes confirmed, thirteen probables and damaged two. High scorer was Staff Sergeant Arthur P. Benko of the 374th with five. Staff Sergeants Jonas C. Unruh, a tail gunner, and E. H. Kemp, radio operator with the 375th, both of whom were killed in the action, scored four each. The crew on one plane of the 375th was credited with shooting down fourteen enemy planes as it was attacked viciously by a number of Zeros.

Benko, of Bisbee, Arizona, who was destined to become the all-time high scorer of all the gunners in the Fourteenth and possibly the entire Air Force, was a former Arizona pistol and skeet champion and had won the state rifle championship at Fort Huachuca. He had done a lot of hunting as a youth and had a love of firearms. One of his favorite diversions was what he called "ink shooting" which was done by throwing tin cans in the air and firing at them without using gun sights.

Said the modest Benko, "My Dad taught me to shoot, and it certainly paid off. There were so many Zeros in the air that I just picked them off one at a time as they came at our ship. I gave them a lead and then a couple of bursts. I shot at nine Zeros altogether. One Zero pilot bailed out and I could see that he was wearing shorts. It must have been hot for him in more ways than one."

One plane of the 373rd, named *Je Reviens*, piloted by Lt. Robert H. McMurray, was severely damaged when a shell blasted into the cockpit and struck him in mid-body. While three Zeros continued the attack, Lt. Alfred D. Hansen, the co-pilot, took over. The enlisted members of the crew were Sgts. Jonas C. Unruh, Carl D. Fox, Melvin W. Harlow, Charles H. Brown,

Alexander M. Blamire, and E. H. Kemp. Lts. William W. Hanley, navigator and Lt. Milton A. Eheman, bombardier were the other officers on the crew.

With two engines out, the ailerons shot off, bomb bay doors stuck open and the instruments destroyed, it didn't appear that the plane could survive. However, Hansen was able to bring the plane in between two hills and barely clear a high tree before he crash-landed the plane on a sand bar at Tanlon.

Sgts. Kemp and Unruh died in the crash; several members of the crew were wounded and injured, either in the fight or on the crash landing. Lt. Robert H. McMurray, the pilot, died during the night. The three were buried in Chinese coffins near the crash site; their graves were marked for subsequent removal later.

Lt. Eheman remembers the August 21st Hankow raid vividly, as do a number of those of other crews. His experiences of hospitalization, evading capture and returning to his base are indicative of what many other crews had after bailing bail out or crash-landing in enemy-occupied China. They also tend to reveal the difficult conditions under which the 308th had to operate. Here's his story:

"Prior to take off I checked the bombs and installed my bombsight. As we approached Hankow, we began to be attacked by Japanese fighters. I got off some shots at one of the fighters but it veered off out of firing range. I saw, from the right hand corner of the nose plexiglass, Hanley shoot down one of the fighters. It had been flying on our right side out of firing range, when just before we got to the anti-aircraft fire it decided to attack the nose of our aircraft. When it made its turn, it turned into Hanley's line of fire. He blew it up.

"I got off my gun and on the bombsight. As we approached I could see the black with red center bursts of anti-aircraft fire. Since Mac (the pilot) had killed almost all the drift while maintaining position as tail-end Charlie on the right side of the formation, it took little correction to pick up and hold on our target for a few seconds which was long enough to drop our ten 500-lb. bombs.

"Shortly after dropping our bombs an anti-aircraft shell knocked out our No. 3 engine. Since we couldn't feather the prop, we couldn't keep up with the formation. We immediately tried to get into some clouds but they were thin and we had cover for only a few minutes. Just as we got there we lost another engine and we were picked up by some enemy fighters. When we ran out of clouds, a fighter zoomed in on us and before any of us could fire he fired a 20mm shell into our aircraft. It got part of the plexiglass in the upper part of the nose and part of the flight deck on the pilot's side of the aircraft.

"I was smashed against the navigator's desk by the force of the air coming through the hole in the nose. I had pieces of shrapnel in my head. The force of the air ripped parts of my clothing off, tore my gun out of its holster, and took a ring off a finger on my left hand. My gun belt which had various items of first aid medication in it remained intact.

"As soon as I got over being half knocked out I began popping sulfa pills in my mouth, drinking water and putting sulfa powder on my wounds. Quite a bit of blood came from my head but there weren't any gaping hopes in my skull. It was bloody but not holey.

"Hanley was busy firing his gun although he had been hit in the leg with shrapnel. Staying flat on the floor, I got the nose gun but I couldn't handle it. I worked my way back to the navigator's desk and sat on the floor with my back against the drop-leaf of the desk.

"By this time we were on the deck and Hanley screamed in my ear that I should prepare for a crash and that the plane was being flown by Hansen; Mac and Brownie were wounded and out of action. I couldn't stand so I remained backed up to the navigator's table.

"With only the outboard engine on the pilot's side operating by this time, Hansen put the plane down on a sand bar. For a few seconds it looked like we were home free until a big hump in the sandbar got in our way. When we hit it, the plane was crushed and broke apart. The .50 caliber gun in the nose ripped across my lower legs taking flesh and bone out of the left leg and flesh out of the right. When the plane stopped, I was buried under part of the nose up to my pelvis.

"As soon as we stopped those who were capable of moving began to try to help the wounded and injured out of the aircraft. Just as they got started they had to hit the deck and get out of sight, or act dead, because a Jap fighter was down on the deck and coming at us. He didn't shoot but he did a vertical roll when he got directly over the aircraft. As it turned out he was spotting our location for a Jap patrol that was in the area. A Chinese patrol had seen us coming down and being aware of the Jap patrol had intercepted them and soon we could hear the ground fire.

"Although the fire fight was nearby, people began to come out to us on the sandbar. At that point we didn't know if they were Japanese or Chinese. They were Chinese guerrillas and they began to help dig us out. Some of them teamed up with Hanley who, although wounded in the leg, went all out in getting me out, and also helping the others to get out. All the while this was being done, we could hear the gunfire.

"When they finally got me free, they popped my 'chute and made a litter out of some of it. Six of the guerrillas carried me across the narrow stream that abutted the sandbar. After we crossed the stream I was put on the litter someone had made out of bamboo poles and wild grass.

"Then the guerrillas transported both of us and the dead to an abandoned monastery. Mac died that night. He had been seriously wounded in the groin and had to be cut out of the plane. All that could be done for him was try to keep him out of as much pain as possible. When our men went to get medical supplies from the medical box, they found it had been rifled. There was no morphine in it so we all gave the morphine that we carried on our gun belts for use on Mac. It would alleviate the pain while he was bleeding to death.

"We passed the three coffins as we left the monastery the next evening and the guerrillas started our trip back to friendly territory. We traveled all night for the next two nights until we arrived at a Chinese Army camp. They had no doctor but they had saline solution so we cleaned our wounds with it. We used pieces of parachute for bandages. We still had some sulfa powder so we sprinkled it on our wounds."

When the group arrived at another army camp, the guerrillas were dismissed and Chinese troops took over the job of getting the crew back to Changsha. Eheman continues:

"Our next stop was at a Chinese Army Field Headquarters. They had an elderly doctor there and although his hands shook when he picked up one of the few instruments he had, as soon as he got close to the wounds, his hands stopped shaking. He removed the dead tissue and cleaned the wounds with an antiseptic which smelled like sheep dip. He had a splint fashioned out of tree bark for my left leg. The parachute came in handy again as bandages.

"I stayed in the infirmary that night and one of the medical orderlies kept me awake picking pieces of plexiglass and shrapnel from my scalp. I had a burr haircut so he had no trouble seeing them. He had a pair of tweezers and when he got hold of one of the pieces, he would giggle all the while he was pulling it out.

"...On the eighth day after our crash, we were greeted with a parade through the village where the Chinese Army had what was probably a staff headquarters. We were given flowers and were greeted by some high ranking officers and their families. Just before entering the village, young boys dressed in what looked like Boy Scout uniforms got the job of parading us through the village. There were soldiers on white horses leading the parade. I was on the litter following directly behind the cavalry. When we got in front of a large crowd they started firing firecrackers. I expected to get kicked out of the litter and thrown into the crowd. I guess the horses were deaf because I seemed to be the only one shook up.

"We were given some presents. I think some people got slippers. I was given a black cane. It was well-made and looked like it had a lacquer finish. It had some Chinese lettering on it which in English meant 'May you always climb higher.' I never got to keep it because somewhere in my travels from one hospital to another, it disappeared.

"When we got through the crowd we continued our journey toward Changsha. We hadn't gone very far when we were met by a Dr. Flowers and his nurse, Sister Kenneth. They had traveled continuously for two days to take care of us. Dr. Flowers, with the help of some of his Chinese assistants, operated on me out in the open in the field where he met us. One of his assistants gave me chloroform for an anesthetic. It knocked me out and along with other sedatives, I didn't wake up until two days later when we arrived at the British Red Cross Hospital in Changsha. When I came to, I felt my body to see what was missing. I was surprised that I still had my left leg, although it was in a cast.

"I got to talk with some of the crew before they started their trip to Hengyang after Dr. Flowers had treated their injuries. I also met some crew members from some planes that had bombed Hankow a few days after we did. In particular I remember a Lt. Schuermann from Philadelphia. He was the navigator on his plane and he bailed out when they were hit. In a very excitable voice he told me how he was shot at by the Jap fighters after he had parachuted out of the aircraft, and how his 'chute got caught in a tree and the fighters continued to fire at him. That was rough.

"In the ten days since we were shot down, I couldn't eat. All I could handle was boiled water. I lost about 30 pounds. I felt like I was oozing through the hole in my pelvis bone. Dr. Flowers had me injected with glucose after the operation in the open field and they continued this procedure, along with giving me glucose liquid to drink until I could eat solid food.

"Dr. Flowers and his assistant operated on me twice while I was at their hospital. They would clean the wounds and put on a new cast on my leg up to the hip. After each operation they put me in bed and propped the foot of the bed higher than my head. They had given me a spinal anesthetic and told me that this was the proper procedure to keep me from having severe headaches. They also tied the bottom of the cast to the foot of the bed to keep my leg in a safe position.

"After the first operation while I was still tied in bed, the Japs came over and bombed some boats moving in the river. The hospital staff went up on the roof to watch the bombing and the Chinese went to the basement to escape the bombing. As soon as I heard the bombs bursting I tried to get out of the bed so I could get under it. I found I was too weak and with my leg tied to the bed I couldn't move anyway. The bombing didn't last very long and the staff members returned to their posts. The doctor then took some shrapnel out of my right hand.

"Between the first and second operations, the Chinese made me a pair of crutches. When I was strong enough, Doc Flowers had me learn how to use them. He told me I couldn't leave the hospital until I could walk from the second floor to the first floor. I wasn't very strong but I made up my mind that I wasn't going to waste any time learning how to use them so with the help of two young Chinese men I started immediately.

"I got along very well with the staff personnel although at times I had difficulty understanding their English. They had Scottish and Irish accents and it took me a little time to get accustomed to their brogues.

"When I finally reached the point where I could keep my food down they stopped feeding me glucose through my veins. They put me on four meals a day. These small but adequate quantities got me started. Sometimes the Chinese cooks would sneak to me some 'moon cakes' for dessert. A U.S. Army sergeant who operated a radio up in the hills nearby visited me several times and brought me some No. 10 cans of fruit. He also left some cigarettes that tasted good with a meal.

"From time to time I had some visitors. I met missionaries from various religious groups. I remember especially a Canadian priest. He had spent considerable time in the States. He liked sports so we had plenty to talk about. He also liked to smoke American cigarettes. We discussed the war and the hoped-for (very soon) peace.

"One day Dr. Flowers told me it was getting close to the time for the Japs to move in and confiscate the rice crop being grown in the area. He said I would have to leave very soon. The next day he operated on me for the second and last time in the hospital. He cleaned the wound and put on an extra-heavy cast up to the hip, with a walking heel on it. I couldn't walk without the crutches but I walked with more stability with the walking heel.

"Dr. Flowers and his staff were all heroes. They were living under the gun constantly. They were to treat civilians only but anyone who was ill was a civilian to Dr. Flowers.

"When I left for Hengyang, I still had some of those cans of fruit so I told Dr. Flowers to use them. He would join me at night sometimes and we'd eat some of the fruit. About a year later when I was in the Valley Forge General Hospital in Pennsylvania, I met a Major Bell, C.O. of a fighter squadron who had gone down near a lake north of Changsha. I told him about the fruit I had left there for Dr. Flowers. He said it was still there when he got there and it had never been touched.

"On October 3rd, an American intelligence officer arrived to escort me to Hengyang. He had a Chinese motorcycle with a sidecar and driver to take us to the Changsha dock where we were to board a boat. The driver had one speed: wide open. The sidecar wasn't very deep and it was small. To fit into it my left leg with the heavy cast had to sit on top of the sidecar. I was propped up so I wasn't too uncomfortable. At the speed the driver maintained I expected to spear some pedestrian or become a part of a pillbox sitting in the middle of the street. The intelligence officer yelled at the guy in Chinese to slow down but he just kept on going wide open.

"I was helped on to the boat. My first thought was what a great bombing target. I don't know how long we were on that boat but we finally arrived at a port where I went from the boat to a train. The car we got on was made by the Pullman Co. The engine was the type used to shift railroad cars into their proper position in our railroad yards. It moved about five miles per hour.

"I don't know how long it took us to get to Hengyang but that was our only stop. I remained overnight at the Army air base there and the next day boarded a C-47 for Kunming. After two passes at the field, because they wanted to give me a soft landing, they set it down OK.

"On October 4, 1943, I entered the Kunming Station Hospital. I was to remain there until they could get transportation to take me to Chabua, India. While there, my leg began to drain through the cast. The odor wasn't very pleasant. We put oil of wintergreen on the cast to try to overpower the stench.

"On October 10th, Major [Henry G.] Brady, my C.O. visited me and presented me with the Purple Heart.

"...I spent my last night in the infirmary or a room near it at Chengkung before boarding a C-87 for Chabua. There were two other passengers on board. They were going to India to trade food with the British and take it back with them. I didn't smoke on that plane. The gasoline fumes were heavy. It was a tanker going back for another load of gasoline for the fighters and B-25s.

"We couldn't get into Chabua so the pilot put the plane down on one of those metal airstrips out in the jungle. I was given a bunk in a basha which was guarded by sentries. I asked if the Japs were near us. They said no, they were there to guard us against wild animals. I was picked up by an ambulance and taken to the 20th General Hospital. The staff consisted of many nurses and doctors from the University of Pennsylvania's Medical School.

"I was put in an officer's ward where there were several other patients. Since the hospital was maintained under blackout conditions, the shutters had to be closed tight at night. Some of the patients complained because the stench from my draining leg was heavy. They wanted the shutters open. I requested that the medical officer in charge have me moved to some isolated area. He refused.

"The next day I was operated on by a Major North and a Captain Frazier. They removed the cast and proceeded to scrub the leg. They didn't need to use an anesthetic on me because I had no feeling in the leg. I sat up and watched them clean the exposed bone and inside the leg. They put on a new cast and opened the front of it so the leg could be treated daily. I was put on sulfa and told that I would have to drink loads of fluids. Some people have very bad side effects from sulfa; the only side effect I had was loss of appetite. I was still 20 pounds underweight so the nurses were constantly trying to make me eat. When I got stronger they allowed me to stop using the bed pans and urinals. I still couldn't navigate too well on crutches but I always made it to the latrine.

"Soon I was assigned to a smaller basha close to the operating room. All around the basha they had gullies for rain water. When the monsoons came, there were constant downpours. I had to walk on a board to cross the gully into the basha. Although I still walked with crutches I could navigate on the board but halfway across the board on one occasion the board broke and I went into the gully vertically. I was hurting. The orderlies got me out and into bed. That night I was running a temperature so was put back on sulfa.

"While a patient in this basha we had an air raid alert. The orderlies put us on mattresses under the beds. I could hear anti-aircraft fire in the distance but never learned where or what if anything was hit. Our basha was near the building with the Big Red Cross on it. What a target for the Japs."

Eheman was returned to the States in January 1944 and was eventually retired for disability. For a number of years he had small pieces of shrapnel periodically removed from his head and arm; pieces of bone were removed from his left leg.

The other loss on this mission of August 21, 1943 was the B-24 flown by Major Walter B. Beat who was leading the 374th's formation. When the enemy attack came, the fighters seemed to converge on the leader and his B-24 was hard hit at the beginning of the attack. When last seen by other crews, it was descending on fire and blew up over the city of Hankow. Two or three men were seen jumping from the plane before it exploded. Other crews reported that those who jumped were repeatedly strafed by the enemy fighters as the parachutes descended.

As the planes departed the target area, approximately forty enemy fighters, faster than any seen previously, attacked and four B-24s were lost. Three others landed at Kweilin but on the following day, when returning from Kweilin to Kunming, one of these crashed in bad weather. Two men escaped serious injury when they were thrown clear; ten others died, including two passengers.

Sgt. Anthony Tricoli, a flight engineer on *80 Days*, kept a diary of his China flying experiences. His entry for August 21, 1943, reads just as he wrote it in his shirt pocket size notebook:

"Saw Hankow from 15,000. We were 14 B-24s. Were attacked just over target by about 150 Zeros. We didn't have umbrella escort. We had a tough time. Our ship and one of the others were the only ones to drop their bombs. I believe the other was *The Goon*. Lead ship, *Rum Runner*, was shot down. Major Beat, our CO, went down in it with the rest of the crew. A few were able to bail out but were gunned by the yellow rats. It seems the bomb bay tank exploded, trapping everyone else on the flight deck. The reason for this catastrophe was due to missing our fighter escort. Tail gunner on *Thundermug* got it. Jerry and I helped take him out of the turret. Poor kid. Our ship got five Zeros. I got three and Lt. Robinson and Odie got one each. There was a little ack-ack. It was a tough battle with all those Zeros. I saw them plain as day. We also lost one of the 375th's ships *Je Reviens* (French for I will return). Our operations officer, Capt. Adler, got it bad as pilot in *Hot Nuts* and Lt. Murphy got a bad shoulder as pilot in *Escalator*. They were forced to land at an auxiliary field. After we had a running battle for about 1/2 hour with the Zeros they left us. Forty minutes after we left Hankow B-25s and 40s, along with 38s moved in for low level bombing and strafing on the two airfields. They did plenty of damage to the Zeros which had landed to refuel after leaving us. We land and stay at Kweilin. Took off in morning for home (Chengkung). Was 15 min. out of Kweilin and we blew a cylinder and had to land on three engines. The ship will be there for a while due to the cylinder. Col. Beebe, our Group CO was there to check. He's a swell guy. He took our loss bad. Main personnel of ship stood at Kweilin to await repairs. We returned with the Col. on his ship. He's a good pilot. On inspection our ship didn't have a scratch on it and those Zeros were in plenty close. I suppose it isn't my time yet. That's the closest I've been to it. The attack was from above. We imagine they were tipped off somehow. They were just waiting for us."

The August 21, 1943 mission to Hankow did not go unnoticed in New Delhi. General Stilwell, not known as one to praise flying units lavishly, sent a message to Chennault on August 26:

"The 308th Bomb Group is to be highly commended for their fine performance over Hankow, China on August 21, 1943.

"Despite engagement by more than 50 Zeros, the bombing mission was carried out without fighter escort.

"The report of 35 confirmed fighters shot down with the loss of but two of ours, indicates that the crews possess a superb fighting spirit as well as a high state of training.

"Congratulations and special commendation should be given to S/Sgt Arthur Benko for his performance in shooting down four Zeros, repeating results of his last engagement with the enemy. He shows expert knowledge of his guns combined with cool and careful timing of his shots."

Another raid on Hankow was staged on August 24th by fourteen planes from the 373rd and 425th Squadrons. The seven planes of the 373rd were forced to turn back because of weather but the rest from the 425th proceeded to a rendezvous with fighter escort over Hengyang and then flew to the target. Two or more planes bombed Wuchang, a city en route to Hankow, by mistake. However, much damage was caused at both cities. In the ensuing forty-five minute fight with about forty enemy fighters, four B-24s were lost and the remaining three badly damaged. The 425th gunners claimed seventeen confirmed victories and ten probables. S/Sgt. L. Kne, a tail gunner, shot down two enemy planes before he was killed.

On the planes lost, ten men were able to bail out and return later to their bases. Several others were known to have been strafed by the enemy fighters as they descended helpless to the ground. One of the engineer-gunners, T/Sgt. W.H. Gieseke, died the next morning and was buried at Hsieng Ling. An after-action intelligence report noted that Gieseke "jumped but was strafed while descending. His feet were virtually shot off."

On the planes that did return from this mission, Major H.G. Foster, group operations officer, was killed by an explosive shell; seven enlisted men suffered wounds and fractures. Of the seven planes that had departed Kunming, only two returned. With a third of its strength lost or grounded, the 308th avoided central China and returned to unescorted missions over Hong Kong and French Indo-China.

Valuable lessons were learned during these missions and the report made by the intelligence officer after interrogating the returnees summarized his observations that were passed along to the crews:

"(a) Practically all who jumped were strafed. They think it best not to pull the string at high altitudes.

"(b) Men cannot get into the turrets while wearing jungle kit on parachute harness. Therefore, several men did not have chutes on when needed. They recommend that this kit be removed from the harness of those men working in tight places.

"(c) More medical supplies (particularly gauze and tape) should be in jungle kit. Also more morphine for use of badly wounded.

"(d) They think big jungle knife is unnecessary, but that there should be a smaller knife, attached to the harness so it could be used, if necessary to cut free from the parachute.

"(e) White parachutes make a good target. Several men were strafed after landing.

"(f) A step is needed to make it easier to get out of top hatch.

"(g) The bomb bay tanks are a hazard.

"(h) The Chinese farmers and coolies accepted money and trinkets. Guerrilla troops and regular troops were very helpful but refused to accept pay.

"(i) The "Pointee-Talkies" were very useful. They should have an additional phrase enabling the user to inquire about the presence of any other American airmen.

"(j) Well-meant delays and entertainment by the Chinese make the trip more difficult for wounded men. They think Chinese authorities should be requested to instruct guerrilla and army troops to return American airmen with all possible speed."

The *Jing Bao Journal* editor, in the February-March 1992 issue, commented that "probably the bloodiest but most successful missions by the 308th Bomb Group, were the two directed at the warehouse and dock areas at Hankow in August 1943." Of the seventy men on the raids, more than fifty were killed, injured or missing.

Nearly two years later, on May 26, 1945, the mission of August 21, 1943, was acknowledged by a General Order that was issued from the 14th Air Force headquarters by General Chennault commending the group for outstanding performance of duty in action on that fateful day. The order said:

"After a portion of the Group's aircraft had flown the Hump to India and back to bring in sufficient gasoline and bombs for the missions, fourteen of the Group's B-24 planes took off on that date to attack the dock and warehouse area at Hankow, China, the most important supply and communication center in the interior of China by the Japanese. When the fighter escorts' base was attacked by the enemy just before takeoff time, the gallant crews of the 308th Bombardment Group (H) elected to carry out their attack unescorted. As the bombers neared the target, 80 Zero interceptors dove upon the formation and a furious battle ensued. For twenty-seven minutes the interceptors pressed a determined attack. Only after the 308th Group crews had shot down 57 enemy fighters, probably destroyed 13 and damaged two, did the enemy break away and flee. Two of the bombers were shot down by enemy fire and all of the others were damaged. Although the battle continued over the target and intense anti-aircraft barrage was encountered over Hankow, the bombers scored a perfect bomb pattern along the entire length of the dock area. Extensive destruction was caused among dock installations and warehouses, and direct hits were scored on a Japanese Navy headquarters, killing three Japanese Army generals, four colonels and one Navy commander. The exceptional heroism, gallantry, determination and esprit de corps demonstrated in the face of overwhelming enemy odds reflect the highest credit upon the 308th Bombardment Group (H) and are worthy of the heroic traditions of the American military service."

Major Henry G. Brady led a formation of 373rd, 375th, and 425th planes from Yanhai, Chengkung, and Kunming to bomb the Kowloon docks at Hong Kong on August 26. On the return trip, one plane developed engine trouble and, in order to lighten the load, the crew threw out all loose equipment and eight men jumped. Lt. F. C. Keish, pilot, and Flight Officer H. B. Tyra, co-pilot, elected to stay with the plane and were able to land it safely at Kunming.

The men who jumped gathered together at Silinhs and intended to hike to Kunming. However, after contacting the headquarters at Kunming, they were advised to remain where they were and await an airdrop of supplies which were parachuted on August 30th. The group left for Kunming on horseback, except for S/Sgt R. L. Berkowitz who had broken his foot in the landing and was carried in a sedan chair by Chinese prisoners. Next was a bus ride from Loli to Poseh where they were met by high Chinese officials, including two Chinese generals. Apparently, the Chinese had not seen American airmen before and treated them royally with eight meals that had many courses. A concert was held in their honor, with one American song that the men recognized: "The Last Rose of Summer." When the men left for Nanning by boat after two days of celebrating, many Chinese cried. At towns along the river, grateful villagers gave the men meals of rice, chicken, and fish; at one stop they were presented with a carved bust of the Generalissimo.

A mission on August 31st was made by 16 B-24s from the 373rd and 375th Squadrons against the Gia Lam Airdrome and the Cobi barracks east of the airdrome. Nine planes from the 373rd were to bomb Cobi as a diverting action, while the seven planes of the 375th were to bomb the airdrome with fragmentation bombs. Immediately after, fighters were to divebomb the dikes surrounding Gia Lam in an effort to flood the airport. The 373rd was over the area on time but could not bomb because a large thunderstorm was directly overhead. Although the flight descended to 6,000 feet, the target could not be seen and all aircraft returned home with their bombs.

The 375th's planes bombed according to plan and reconnaissance photos taken afterward showed hits were scored on hangars, aprons, and building areas. French intelligence sources later reported that fires burned long after the raid and that large gasoline stores were blown up. Colonel Beebe wrote a letter to the 375th's C.O. commending his squadron for "the accuracy of bombing attained on the mission over Gai Lam Airdrome on 31 August 1943. Pictures of this bombing show that severe damage was caused to buildings and a high probability that damage to personnel was extensive."

Chapter 4

THE NEUTRALIZATION OF HAIPHONG

Although the monsoon season is normally over in China by September, the 308th was able to mount only two regularly assigned missions during that month because of the weather; both were to the Haiphong area. However, group planes flew the Hump on ferrying trips for bombs and gas and took advantage of the route to bomb Japanese installations en route to Chabua. On ten different days, 21,000 lbs. of bombs were dropped by forty-one planes on Myitkyina, Tengchung, Lukow, Nawlong, Htawgaw, Lungling and Mangshih. The bombs were mostly Russian- or Chinese-made 100-lb. types. With the exception of one nine-plane raid on Tengchung and one eight-plane raid on Myitkyina, all of the Hump bombing was done by flights of from one to three planes.

The first September group mission to Haiphong was of fifteen planes from the 373rd and 374th Squadrons. On the 14th, the 373rd flight of seven, with a large cement plant at Haiphong as its target, had to return to base because of weather but the 374th was able to split up with one flight of four aircraft attacking a dry dock area and the remaining three bombing a freighter. Many hits were scored on the docks and smoke could be seen rising to 4000 feet as the bombers departed. No fighters rose to the challenge but anti-aircraft fire was heavy although no hits were made.

Since the cement plant at Haiphong had not been bombed, a mission for six of the 373rd planes was scheduled for the next day. One plane had to abort but the remaining five proceeded to the target without fighter escort. This time enemy fighters were waiting at high altitude and about 50 of them attacked out of the sun. Three of the B-24s were shot down over the target area within minutes. Twenty-eight men were lost in the combat action, although one plane with a crew of ten was able to limp into friendly territory before bailing out.

The tragedies did not end there. One plane that had carried on a running fight with the Zeros crashed just 200 yards from the field at Kunming. The crew of the only plane to land safely, piloted by Capt. Leroy D. Cunningham, was credited with shooting down ten enemy fighters and eighteen probables. Although reports were never available from the other planes, it was believed that they had also scored some victories over enemy planes.

It was during September 1943 that the Kunming airfield received its third attack from Japanese bombers since the arrival of the 308th. On the morning of the 27th, twenty-seven enemy bombers, escorted by a number of fighters, attacked the field dropping a large number of bombs which strung out across the field. One Curtiss C-46 transport was destroyed and several others received hits by bomb fragments. Cars, trucks, a vehicle repair shop, several buildings, and the gas station were destroyed. One fragment came through the roof of the 308th headquarters and landed within a few inches of the adjutant's desk. There were no reported injuries to personnel.

Twenty-four P-40s and three P-38s intercepted the incoming bombers at 20,000 feet. It marked the first time that P-38s were mentioned in 308th intelligence reports. However, the first six P-38s had actually arrived in July, along with newer P-40K and M models.

The new month of October brought better weather than had been seen since the previous April. Nine scheduled missions were carried out and ferrying aircraft bombed targets on thirteen flights over the Hump en route to Chabua. Of the nine scheduled combat missions, one was a two-day sea sweep with an overnight stop at Kweilin. The other eight were all to the Hanoi-Haiphong area. As a result, the port of Haiphong was virtually neutralized as a port of entry for French Indo-China and Burma.

As could be expected, most of the missions were intercepted by enemy fighters. The land targets ranged from the airport at Gia Lam to the cement plant, docks, and railroad yards at Haiphong and a zinc smelter at Quangyen. Instead of frontal attacks, however, the Japanese pilots directed their fire at the rear aircraft in the formations. An attack by the 375th resulted in a commendation letter from Colonel Beebe for "the accuracy of bombing" on the mission over Haiphong on October 1, 1943. The pictures of the bombing show extensive damage in the target area. Many direct hits were observed in barracks, gas storage, warehouses and power plant areas.

On October 2, Sgt. Arthur Benko was credited with shooting down seven Japanese fighters. His guns jammed twice during the mission but he was able to clear them. He said he thought the fight had lasted only a minute but it was actually forty minutes. He told reporters that he had never worked a turret so fast in his life.

A sea search around Hainan Island was disappointing. As planned, six planes of the 425th Squadron circled Hainan Island and landed at Kweilin on October 3rd; then the next day, they took off from Kweilin, retraced their route around Hainan Island in the other direction and landed at Kunming. No hits were scored on the ships sighted.

On October 7th, the cement plant at Haiphong was finally knocked out by ten B-24s. The intelligence report notes: "The formation was attacked by about 12 Zeros. Three were confirmed destroyed, and eight were damaged. One of those confirmed was being pursued by a P-38 when it came across the bomber formation so that the B-24 gunners could shoot the Zero off. Sergeant Bates, one of the B-24 gunners, obliged. After the fighters landed, the P-38 pilot called the squadron to express his appreciation."

Those participating in a raid on Htaw Gaw on October 23rd were commended by Colonel Beebe "for being on the alert for enemy attacks which materialized at a most unexpected time with a result of no damage to our ships or personnel, and also accurate bombing of a difficult target." He especially commended Captain Lunt for his leadership of this formation and for the manner in which he made the required reports.

Howard H. Morgan, a pilot with the 375th, comments on one mission to Hanoi that he flew in October 1943:

"The Hanoi missions were considered the most devastating in terms of enemy opposition, loss of our crews and aircraft. U.S. and Chinese intelligence was of great importance. Fighter cover often made the difference between a defeated purpose or successful results. Missing either of these elements and a bombing mission would be in serious trouble going in on a well-fortified target.

"The 374th and 375th were scheduled for a mission to the Gia Lam Aerodrome one day in October. It was to be a milk run without fighter escort. We had been there before and we thought our intelligence information was accurate. We had no reason to doubt it since our previous challenge attracted only some inaccurate anti-aircraft fire. On this day, everything seemed right: no cloud obstruction to interfere.

"We were at the I.P. as scheduled at 18,000 feet and on the target at

1300 hours. We broke off target on a shallow descent picking up plenty of speed. It all looked like duck soup when suddenly, everything went haywire. It was later estimated that we were hit by more than 50 Jap Zeros which were all over us like a blanket and coming at us from all sides and angles. I'll never understand how they got there so fast without being noticed. I never heard any warning as no one broke radio silence, at least for the moment. My gunners never got off a shot on the first two attacks.

"I told my co-pilot, who was a replacement on his first mission, to scan and identify the positions of the oncoming fighters. At that point, communications completely broke down. Our intercom was cluttered with 'Bogie coming in right, high then low; straight in and going under...' etc. I think every gun position had something to shout about at the same time. I remember demanding some discipline on the intercom: 'Shut up and watch!'

"I was flying No. 3 on Capt. Brady's right wing as he led the squadron. When the attacks began, I tucked in so tight that I may have obstructed the fire of Brady's waist gunner. The attack continued for about 15 minutes. Most of them came in from the 12 o'clock position about 20 degrees high in an attempt to destroy the lead aircraft.

"I'll never forget one of those fighter passes. This guy came in head-on at 12 o'clock level. He never varied and kept coming. I can still see those 20mm cannons in rapid fire which looked like two giant camera lens shutters blinking right at me. Every time, a blink would produce an over-size orange. He held his course at us so long that I felt myself scootching to the right over my seat pack. I thought this guy was a Kamikazi idiot. He never pulled up but bore right over our wings and between the two fuselages. Bullets and shell fragments ripped holes through the side and upper wing surface. I'm certain the self-sealing gas tanks prevented a fatal explosion.

"I was surprised that the Jap Zero carried such fire power. Checking with our intelligence staff later, I found that the fighters we encountered were Mitsubishi A6M Zeros, Sen-Zekes, a Jap fighter which was flown by the elite pilots of the Imperial Navy. They were equipped with two 22mm cannons and two 7.7mm machine guns. It was the first carrier-based fighter that outperformed corresponding land-based fighters. I don't know if those that attacked us were carrier- or land-based but they were certainly all over us like flies on sh-sh-sh-sh-ugar.

"Our crew experienced no casualties that day; however, three planes were lost."

When the effect of the October raids was analyzed, it was found that much damage had been done to the targeted installations. French sources reported over 1,200 enemy casualties. A truck depot, Japanese munitions stores and a bridge were damaged; the cement plant and zinc smelter were put out of business.

The Hump combination bombing/ferry missions continued with a total of forty-four sorties being flown on nine different days with 31,000 lbs. of bombs dropped on five or more targets. In most instances, the damage done could not be easily observed, since the targets were small and the bombs used were only Russian or Chinese 100-pounders. However, ground sources reported that on a raid on Lungling, 300 Japanese soldiers, 100 civilians, and 100 horses and mules were killed. Enemy casualties at Tengchung were reported as high as 800.

During the late summer and fall of 1943, B-24Js, with better forward-firing firepower by virtue of the installation of new nose turrets, began to arrive for use by the Tenth Air Force. The Tenth was concentrating on Rangoon as a primary target because intelligence estimates showed that 40,000 tons of shipping passed through the port and ran up the Rangoon River daily. A number of the J models were subsequently assigned to the 308th, although on early missions, some gunners were disappointed in the new nose turrets until they got used to them.

November 1943 was marked by the promotion of Colonel Beebe to Brigadier General on the 11th and his transfer to Lord Louis Mountbatten's staff in New Delhi. To a man, the members of the 308th didn't want to see him go. General Chennault presented him with the Distinguished Flying Cross for his combat missions and leadership during the 308th's baptism of fire and he proceeded to his new assignment. His successor was Colonel William P. Fisher who took command and promptly outlined a heavy schedule of group combat operations.

Colonel Fisher was not a newcomer to combat. A 1934 graduate of North Carolina State College with a degree in mechanical engineering, he entered the army as a flying cadet and was graduated from flying training in June 1935. In March 1940, he was assigned to Hawaii where he was commanding officer of the 78th Pursuit Squadron flying P-36s and P-40s. In May 1941, he became operations officer for the Hawaiian Air Force and in September took part in the epochal flight of nine B-17s from Hawaii to the Philippines. He was appointed C.O. of the 28th Bomb Squadron of the 19th Bomb Group at Clark Field when the islands were invaded by the Japanese and was wounded during the first Jap bombing attack on the morning of December 7.

At the time, the early model B-17s had no tail gun position so they were vulnerable from attacks from the rear. According to Bob Dykstra of the 308th, "Colonel Fisher had the back part of the fuselage cut off and a gunner placed back there with a submachine gun." Fisher took the 28th from Bataan to the island of Mindanao in the southern Philippines in January 1942 where the squadron fought on the ground for more than two months against the Japanese army until they were overwhelmed. In February 1942, Fisher flew to Java and was assigned as commander of all allied fighters in East Java. When Java fell, he was evacuated to Australia and then returned to the United States. He was sent to China in July 1943 and assumed command of the 308th in October 1943.

Colonel (later Brigadier General) Fisher had been awarded the Distinguished Flying Cross for "extraordinary achievement in a flight of bombers from Honolulu to the Philippines in the latter part of 1941." He was cited for displaying "skillful airmanship and accurate knowledge of the highly technical details in the successful execution of the flight."

Just as Colonel Fisher assumed command of the 308th, the Japanese sent two fighter squadrons into northern Burma to attack the Hump transports. On October 13, avenging enemy fighters shot down three of them. On the 27th, two formations of freight-hauling B-24s were attacked. Their intelligence sources had intercepted a secret itinerary for Lord Louis Mountbatten and his staff that would take them over the Hump to China in early November. Chennault explains what action he took:

"The 308th successfully executed one of the best deceptions I ever perpetrated against the Japanese. Jap fighters were bagging two and three unarmed transports a day and playing hob with transport crew morale when I hit on an idea to stop them. A.T.C. was still using the C-87, a transport version of the Liberator. A few days before Mountbatten was due in China, I ordered Colonel Bill Fisher to send the 308th well south of the regular transport run on their supply trips to India. They were to fly a loose, ragged formation and carry extra ammunition for their guns.

"Sure enough, Jap fighter pilots swallowed the bait, mistaking B-24 bombers for C-87 transports. They barreled in for the kill with more enthusiasm than sense. The 308th gunners held fire until the Japanese were well within range and then blasted with their powered gun turrets. In three days of this masquerade across the Hump, the 308th shot down and damaged 18 fighters, virtually all the operational strength of the two harassing squadrons. Mountbatten's plane crossed to China unmolested, and the Hump remained clear of enemy fighters for five weeks."[1]

Chennault gave more details in 1957 correspondence with the author:

"Early in October 1943, the Japanese pushed two squadrons of fighters into north Burma and began attacking the airfields in Assam and shooting down transports over north Burma. Tenth AF was helpless. It had no radar and could not organize an Observer Corps warning net such as I had in China. At this time a good many C-87 transports (cargo version of the B-24 Liberator) were being used as tankers over the Hump, and the Japanese fighters took particular delight in hitting them – probably because they made such a spectacular fire.

"The Japanese fighter fields and their operating area were beyond the range of my fighters, and I was greatly worried because of the reduction in tonnage of supplies arriving in China and the possibility that transport operations would be completely terminated. In conference with the group commander of my B-24 group, it was decided that squadrons of heavily armed B-24s would be flown in tight formation and low altitude over the area known to be occupied by the Japanese fighter squadrons.

"Since their arrival in China, the B-24s had been obliged to lift their own supplies such as fuel, bombs, food and equipment from Assam to China. They usually made these ferry flights individually or in small units. Therefore, their planned employment as Japanese fighter-destroyers did not depart from normal procedure except that they would fly by squadrons, in tight formation, at low altitude, on a course a hundred miles south of the usual transport route, and would carry extra belts of ammunition for all guns.

"The first B-24 squadron took off the following day and was jumped by a full squadron of Japanese fighters whose pilots undoubtedly thought they were attacking unarmed C-87s. Holding their fire until the enemy was in close range, the B-24s cut them down rapidly with their massed fire. Arriving in Assam, the B-24s refilled their ammo belts and gas tanks but took on no additional loads.

"Upon their return flight the next morning, the second Japanese fighter squadron attacked with the same eagerness as the first had – and with the same result. It was assumed that the lone fighter seen leaving the combat the previous day had not made it back to his field to spread the word about the false C-87s.

"This combat ended Japanese fighter attacks on Assam airfields and transports crossing north Burma. Transport deliveries rose rapidly and the service did not have to be suspended. The cost, according to my recollection, was one man killed, two or three wounded, one B-24 shot up badly, and several others damaged slightly.

"This employment of B-24s as fighter-destroyers was the only occasion on which I was ever able to prove the old bombardment theory that daylight bombers do not require fighter support. It was a situation where the plan had to work. If it had failed, I would have lost a squadron of heavy bombers, my supply line from India would have been severed, and I would undoubtedly have been transferred to a nice, safe job as supply officer in the Zone of Interior.

"Despite the phenomenal success of this unusual method of employing B-24s, I was criticized severely, both in Delhi and Washington, for improper employment of bombardment aviation. However, I did not permit this criticism to restrict my exercise of individualism whenever I thought the situation warranted it throughout the remainder of the war."[2]

During the first half of November 1943, the 308th continued to operate from China and carried out five regularly assigned missions. The first mission of the month hit the Kowloon docks at Hong Kong on November 3rd with twenty-one aircraft from all four squadrons. Because of the weather, no bombs were dropped but one aircraft was hit by anti-aircraft fire over Canton. When it fell behind the formation, it was heavily attacked by about thirty Zeros and two engines were knocked out; however, Lt. Herbert W. Oglesby, the pilot, was able to continue on course toward Kweilin. About two miles from Hsingping, the remaining two engines quit at 6,000 feet and the entire crew bailed out successfully. The other B-24s were also attacked but returned home undamaged, with four enemy planes confirmed, one damaged, and one probable.

Howard H. Morgan of the 375th, recalls another November mission to mine Hong Kong harbor and bomb the Kowloon docks that month with seven aircraft of his squadron. The 374th Squadron was to bomb the docks from altitude after the 375th departed the harbor:

"Timing was of the essence. The moon was bright and shiny over the target area. One aircraft from our squadron aborted and the six remaining flew loose formation to the staging area about 50 miles southwest of the target at about 12,000 feet. We had been given extensive briefings for this mission. In fact, each crew included a U.S. Navy officer who knew about the type of mines we were carrying that night. These were not the usual smaller type but were about ten to twelve feet long and the maximum girth that would fit. The Navy officer was to arm the mine just before being dropped.

"It was midnight when we deployed. We broke formation at one minute intervals with all navigation and formation lights out. We retarded our throttles to reduce the glow of the turbosuperchargers at the exhaust end of the engines and slowed our speed to 150 mph as we entered the harbor area. I believe I was third to break. The six aircraft had a similar pattern but we were to drop the mines in a string throughout the run. The moon was so bright that we could see the surrounding hills and the gateways between them.

"Our navigator, Lyndell Highley, was to signal the release point to bombardier Al Monitto. I am certain we were on target. It seemed to me that I was looking up at the lighted portholes of the large ships as we slipped by them. We maintained 50 feet over the water throughout the run until we began our ascent.

"The mission was a complete success. We surprised the enemy and didn't see any blackouts or enemy fire. We were happy that the Navy was pleased with our performance that night.

"All aircraft dispersed and lost contact with one another on the return flight. The weather was very poor at Kweilin. Only a couple of us landed at Kweilin, others landed at alternate bases and there may have

Sharknosed Curtiss P-40s of Chennault's Flying Tigers are guarded by a Chinese soldier. (USAF photo)

Crew chief J. R. Hill points to score of Japanese planes downed by Col. Robert L. Scott of the 23rd Fighter Group. The original Flying Tigers rarely had more than a dozen fighters available to intercept enemy bombers. (USAF photo)

The crew chief of this P-40 decided to paint the nose differently from others. Belly tanks extended the range of the P-40s but not enough to escort the B-24 Liberators of the 308th to distant targets. (USAF photo)

140076

Major General Claire L. Chennault (hands behind back) talks with his fighter pilots before a mission. Well-liked by his men, he perfected methods of attacking Japanese planes that enabled his Flying Tigers to exact a high ratio of enemy planes compared to losses of P-40s. (USAF photo)

After his arrival in China in 1937 Chennault perfected an air raid alert system that gave the 14th Air Force plenty of warning of approaching enemy planes. He watches their progress on the map held by Lt. Col. Robert Breitweiser as Major C. H. Whitaker and Sgt. A. L. Jones look on. (USAF photo)

The "21 Curves" on the Burma Road between Chanyi and Kweiyang, China. When it was captured by the Japanese, the only route of supply was by air over the Hump from India to China. The 308th bombed the Burma Road in mountainous areas on several occasions causing land slides that interrupted Japanese ground traffic for days. (National Archives photo)

Thousands of Chinese coolies were used to construct airfields for the Americans in China. Large rocks were laboriously broken into pebbles by old men, women and children. (National Archives photo)

Chennault, dubbed "Old Leatherface" by his men, loved to play baseball and usually pitched. Here he awaits his turn at bat near his headquarters in Kunming. (USAF photo)

More than 100 Chinese coolies pull a cement roller to level an airstrip somewhere in China. The strips were usually well-drained and could support heavily loaded Boeing B-29 Superfortresses. (USAF photo)

Officers of the 308th Bomb Group enjoy a meal at their mess hall in Chungking. Meals were prepared by Chinese cooks under the supervision of an American officer and a Mess Sergeant. Note "blood chit" on the back of one crew member that identifies him as an American who came to China to fight the Japanese and asks the Chinese to assist him. (USAF photo)

Officers originally assigned to the 308th enjoy dinner at Wendover, Utah in November 1942. Colonel Beebe, group commander, is second from left facing camera. (Photo courtesy John S. Szymkowicz)

A Curtiss C-46 lands at a Flying Tiger base. Several types of transports flew the Hump to supply the 14th Air Force, including C-87s and C-109s, cargo variants of the B-24. However, nearly all combat supplies such as fuel, bombs and ammunition for the 308th Bomb Group were flown in the group's own B-24s. (USAF photo)

"Homesick Susie" departs for a bombing mission to a target deep in enemy-held territory soon after arrival of the 308th in China in 1943. (Photo courtesy Milton H. Werner)

All B-24 maintenance and repair work on 308th planes was performed in the open. Here a Liberator that had bellied in is having its No. 3 engine removed at Chengkung. (Photo courtesy Sandra Beebe)

Colonel Eugene H. Beebe, commander of the 308th Bomb Group, receives the Distinguished Flying Cross from General Chennault at Kunming in November 1943. (Photo courtesy Sandra Beebe)

Eugene H. Beebe smiles broadly after being promoted from colonel to brigadier general. He was transferred from command of the 308th to serve on the staff of the Supreme Allied Commander-in-Chief Lord Louis Mountbatten in India in November 1943. (Photo courtesy Sandra Beebe)

Right, after his return to the United States, General Henry H. "Hap" Arnold presented General Beebe with the Legion of Merit and the Air Medal for his service in China. Beebe had served as Arnold's pilot and aide for several years before assuming command of the 308th Bomb Group. (Photo courtesy Sandra Beebe)

Pointee Talkie booklets were issued to air crew members as part of their survival equipment. The questions in English and Chinese were on left hand pages; answers on right hand pages. However, they were not useful if the Chinese were illiterate. (Booklet courtesy Howard H. Morgan)

POINTIE TALKIE

中美協力爭取勝利

Before using, show the Chinese to whom you want to get an idea across the Chinese text at the top of the opposite page. Then for your question, point to the Chinese writing on the same line as the English language idea you want to put across. In reply, the Chinese will point to the phrase he wishes to use as an answer. All questions are on left-hand pages; answers on right-hand pages.

I. FINDING AN INTERPRETER

1. Is there someone here 這裏有人能夠講 who can speak

English?	英文
French?	法文
Spanish?	西班牙文
German?	德文
Italian?	意大利文？

2. Will he come here? 他將要來這裏嗎？

3. Shall I wait here for him or shall I go with you? 我在這裏等他或者我同你一道去呢？

(2)

親愛的中國朋友們：

我是美國軍官，到中國來，幫助中國抗戰，但是，我不會講中國話，倘若我問你甚麼話，指着這本書上左邊的問話，希望你指着右邊的答語，很正確的答覆我。

有	1. Yes.
沒有	No.
我不知道	I don't know.

他要來	2. Yes.
他不來	No.
我不知道	I don't know.

| 請等他 | 3. Please wait. |
| 請你同我一道來 | Please come with me. |

(3)

---

4. I shall wait here for him. 我在這裏等他。

5. I shall go to speak with him if someone will escort me. 假使有人送我，我將要去同他談話。

6. Can I speak to him within the next 在五分鐘內我能同他講話嗎？
   5 mins?
   ½ hour? 在半點鐘內我能同他講話嗎？
   1 hour? 在一點鐘內我能同他講話嗎？
   to-day? 今天我能同他講話嗎？

7. Please get me someone who speaks English. 請替我找一個能講英文的人來。

8. Is there someone else here who can speak English? 這裏有沒有別人能講英文呢？

9. Please get me on the phone someone who speaks English. 請你替我找一位能講英文的人來聽電話。

(4)

4

HEADQUARTERS 308TH BOMBARDMENT GROUP, AAF
Office of the Commanding Officer
APO 627

May 5, 1943.

SUBJECT: Operations and Intelligence Summary of Mission No. 1.

FROM : Colonel E. H. BEEBE, Commanding Officer.

TO : Commanding General, 14th U. S. Air Force, Kunming, China.

1. Three ships, 425th Squadron - Three ships, 375th Squadron - Six ships, 374th Squadron - Six ships, 373rd Squadron, departed 0830, Kunming, May 4th, bombing mission on SAMAH AIRPORT, HARBOR, and installations at HAINAN ISLAND, returning 1640 to 1650.

2. Good contact weather over target. All eighteen ships bombed from 18,200 to 18,900 feet altitude, with 500 and 1000 lb. bombs, totaling 63,000 lbs. of bombs.

3. All bombs dropped on or near their specified targets. Particularly large fuel storage on NE edge of runway ✱ ✗) which caused large heavy fuel fire, dense clouds rising almost immediately to about 5,000 feet and was seen by our ships 40 minutes or about 100 miles away. At least four bombs on runway, 1,000 lb. bomb believed on intersection. Fires started at oil farm and coal pits on point East of harbor. Several hangars and other installations destroyed.

4. No enemy interception. Light ineffective AA fire over HANOI on way to target and only about two ineffective bursts observed over target.

5. Two or three 400 to 500 foot boats and other boats in harbor bombed. No definate hits or near misses observed. One very large vessel starting headway out to sea in outer harbor was not successfully bombed.

6. Ship No. 24237, Lt. J. H. KEENE, pilot, made most of trip and bombed with three engines, landing successfully, out of gas, at YUNGNING. Ship No. 24143, 1st Lt. D. L. WILLIS, pilot, lost from returning formation in heavy overcast. Last reported at 1530 at coordinates 22° 50' N - 104° 45' E at about 1,900 feet headed on 310°, believed probably bailed out or landed at WENSHAN about 50 miles NE of reported position.

7. All bombs dropped in train at about 200 feet intervals except in few cases of mechanical difficulties dropped in salvo. Bomb doors on two ships required operation by hand. Intervelometer failed on three ships, two of which were worked by hand causing over bombing of their targets. Other ship made second bomb run bombing successfully.

EUGENE H. BEEBE,
Colonel, Air Corps,
Commanding.

Eugene Beebe, then a colonel, led the group's first combat mission to bomb Samah Bay, harbor and installations on Hainan Island. His one-page report is a classic in military reporting of a significant action against enemy targets. (Copy of order courtesy of Sandra Beebe)

A study in contrasts as a Consolidated B-24 roars over primitive animal-drawn carts at a Chinese base shared with C-46 and C-47 cargo planes. (USAF photo)

A Liberator of the 308th departs from a base near Kunming which it shared with a P-40 squadron. (USAF photo)

Bombs were stored in revetments for use by fighters and bombers of the 14th Air Force. The 308th hauled its own bombs and ammunition from India across the Hump. (USAF photo)

It was a rare sight to have members of the 308th headquarters in full uniform in the officers' mess hall at Kunming. This was a dinner given by the 373rd Squadron honoring Colonel Beebe while he was still the 308th's commander. He is shown third from left at head table. Major Paul O'Brien on his left was squadron commander. (Photo courtesy Sandra Beebe)

Doug Ogilvie, a flight engineer with the 375th Bomb Squadron, donned his old 1940s A-2 jacket and cap and posed at a B-24 gunner's waist window during a Stateside air show in the 1990s. (Photo courtesy Doug Ogilvie)

Engine changes were performed in China and at the base in Chabua, India. When hoists were not available, mechanics used available materials to remove, repair and replace them. (Photo courtesy John S. Szymkowicz)

T/Sgt. Arthur J. Benko, top aerial gunner in the CBI theater and possibly the entire Air Force, is credited with destroying 18 Japanese planes. A member of the 374th Squadron, he is shown after he had scored his ninth victory. He later had to bail out over a target area and was captured. Intelligence sources reported that he was tortured and killed by his captors. (Photo courtesy Malcolm Rosholt)

The 375th's coffee shop at Chengkung. (Photo courtesy Ed Opheim)

"Ole Baldy" met an ignominious end on July 17, 1943 when the pilot buzzed boats on the Brahmaputra River in India too low and hit the water. The catwalk and bomb bay gas tanks were torn out and four men riding in the rear were killed. Four crew members and two passengers survived. (Photo courtesy Ed Opheim)

The "Georgia Peach" poses with the ground crews of the 375th Bomb Squadron at Chengkung. (Photo courtesy Ed Opheim)

Members of the 373rd Bomb Squadron pose outside the new recreation hall at Yangkai. (Photo courtesy M. F. Johnson)

The crew of the "Battlin' Bitch" pose beside her between bombing missions. Front row, (l to r): Lt. Leo M. Miller, co-pilot; Lt. Leo S. Behrens, bombardier; Lt. Fred E. Sweeney, navigator; Capt. Howard H. Morgan, pilot. Rear row, (l to r): S/Sgt. David G. Schultz; T/Sgt John F. Cummings; S/Sgt. William V. Austin; S/Sgt. Richard M. Griggs; T/Sgt Frank W. Martin; S/Sgt John J. Mulligan. (Photo courtesy Howard H. Morgan)

The crew of the "Battlin' Bitch" is briefed informally before a mission from Chengkung. Note "blood chits" on the jackets of two of the men. (Photo courtesy Howard H. Morgan)

"The Battlin' Bitch" lost an engine en route to bomb an airdrome at Haiphong. The crew voted to continue on three engines. They dropped their bombs on the target but ran short of fuel and landed at Nanning. (Photo courtesy Howard H. Morgan)

The 308th planes had many accidents during their tour in China. When this B-24 of the 375th settled back on the ground during a takeoff, the No. 3 propeller came through the cockpit and severed Lt. John McBrayer's left leg. (Photo courtesy Howard H. Morgan)

There were no casualties when "Little Flower" piloted by Lt. Gene Leslie blew a tire on takeoff from Pandagar, India. (L to r) Lts. Leo Miller, Jack Keene and Ken Weiman view the damage. (Photo courtesy Howard H. Morgan)

been a bailout or two. Highley got us within range of the direction finder, the only nav-aid at Kweilin. The ceiling was solid overcast at about 800 feet. Remembering the cone-like terrain around Kweilin, I crossed the DF at 5,000 feet and made a tight spiral down until I broke through right over the base and landed without incident."

A new type of mission was assigned on November 11th: Bomb the Burma Road. The objective was to cause landslides and block the road. Six B-24s were dispatched and twenty 1,000 lb. bombs were dropped; later reconnaissance photographs showed that the road was blocked for at least the next five days.

The next day, an eight-plane raid was laid on with six planes from the 374th assigned to bomb a Haiphong chemical plant while two planes of the 425th, in a diversion action, were to lay mines in the ship channel. The target area was completely covered by clouds so all of the 374th planes and one of the two carrying mines returned with their loads intact. However, Captain Harry H. Musinski went down through the overcast and laid all four of his mines in the harbor from an altitude of 200 feet. This act earned him a commendation from General Chennault.

On November 15th, with Musinski's success as encouragement, another diversionary night mission was laid on with a total of 20 B-24s. Fourteen were to bomb Kowloon harbor and docks as a diverting action, while six planes of the 375th laid mines in the sea lanes.

The results were disappointing, although five of the mine-laying planes did an excellent job bombing in the clear moonlight. Only five other planes dropped their bombs on the land target, the rest and one of the mine-layers brought their loads home. It was intended that all planes land at Kweilin after the mission but because of bad weather, five planes returned to their home fields, thirteen landed at Kweilin and two crashed en route to Kunming. The crews of both planes bailed out successfully but Lt. Malcolm S. Sanders and T/Sgt Arthur J. Benko, the 308th's top scoring gunner, landed in Japanese-held territory near Shiuhing and were believed captured.

Another crew, flying in *The Goon*, with the exception of the Capt. S. J. Skousen, pilot, T/Sgt. A. L. Flaherty, engineer, and T/Sgt W. J. Novak, radio operator, bailed out when two engines failed and the third seemed about to go. Among the seven who bailed out was Capt. James S. "Jack" Edney, who was along as an observer. As Skousen struggled to keep the plane airborne, the third engine was finally persuaded to produce enough power to make a controlled approach and Skousen landed the plane safely at Kweilin.

On November 16, two B-24s accompanied by a fighter escort of 26 P-40s and P-51s, newly introduced in the theater for the use of the Fourteenth, took off from Kweilin for an attack on Kowloon. Eleven bombers found the target; the twelfth plane received a hit from anti-aircraft fire and left the formation. It was promptly attacked by Zeros but managed to escape when two P-40s came to the rescue. Although all planes were to return to their respective fields in the Kunming area, this one landed at Kweilin for repairs.

The information gained by those who bailed out and returned to safety with the help of the Chinese led to observations which were reported to the 308th headquarters by Capt. John W. Watson, intelligence officer of the 374th:

"People contacted assured our men that help can be obtained in any locality in that area (Canton) by any American soldiers attempting to return to home base. Feeling of local people toward Japs is hatred, but not fear; feeling toward Americans is of highest respect.

"Japs consider one of the greatest offenses is to take currency out of occupied territory. Penalty is death.

"About bailing out, when necessary to jump, first have period of getting ready, then all bail out quickly to avoid scattering. Make decision, act promptly.

"Greatest needs - Pointee-Talkees - Mae West - compass - rations - water bag - map of China - currency (rupees are of no value in forward areas in China) - something to clean gun.

"Suggestions - Carry silk from parachute (invaluable) - helpful if pills to relieve dysentery can be in jungle kit - take tooth brush and extra pair of socks. Always be prepared for emergency.

"Important to have location of missionaries for they provide marvelous aid. Crew expressed view that information concerning location of missions is more valuable than information regarding temporary landing fields.

"Chinese people proved themselves great friends. Exhibition of kindness and willingness to sacrifice are outstanding in views of our men. The American soldier (and nation) can well afford to cultivate these people.

"Chinese will get the American soldier out when treated with respect and courtesy. But they are quick to resent unkind remarks and officiousness.

"Monies carried in money belts were for most part fully expended. The money belt when tied tightly about the waist is not lost when parachuting."

As these raids against strategic targets were being carried out, President Roosevelt had decided that new leadership was required in the CBI theater. In June, the Generalissimo had been informed that Major General George Stratemeyer would be sent to the theater to command the Tenth and Fourteenth Air Forces. However, before he left the States, Stratemeyer was instructed not to interfere with the special relations between Chiang Kai-shek and Chennault. Therefore, Stratemeyer would have only advisory authority over the Fourteenth. At the same time, to reduce the friction between Chennault and Bissell, Chiang asked the President to transfer Bissell out of the theater. This was done and Major General Howard Davidson was assigned to replace him.

On July 28, Stratemeyer was designated Commanding General, Army Air Force Units, India-Burma Theater and Air Advisor to the Asiatic Theater Commander. He was responsible for direct control of the Tenth Air Force and for supply and maintenance of the Fourteenth Air Force and protection of the Hump route. Meanwhile, General Stilwell was given the title of Commanding General of the U.S. Army Forces in the China-Burma-India theater and as such was in direct command of all American ground troops, whether in India, Burma or China.

At the same time, Lord Louis Mountbatten was designated Supreme Allied Commander-in-Chief, with Stilwell as Deputy Supreme Commander. Mountbatten would have no control over American-trained Chinese ground forces except through Stilwell in his capacity as chief of staff for the Chinese army. In reality, this meant that ultimate authority rested with the Generalissimo.

General "Hap" Arnold realized that this command structure was unwieldy and wrote to General Stratemeyer. "This command setup and your relationships with Generals Stilwell, Mountbatten, and Chennault are somewhat complicated," he said, "and will have to be worked out to a great extent among yourselves. We feel that it can be made to work efficiently. The success of this complicated command setup depends in a great measure on personalities. If a true spirit of cooperation is engendered throughout this command, it will work. If the reverse is true, it is doomed to failure."[3]

There was a shock ahead for Chennault when Stratemeyer told him that he would not receive any increase in Hump tonnage; in fact, he would receive less. He was also informed about Operation Twilight, the Allied plan to place B-29 Superfortresses in China under a separate command for the purpose of launching raids against the Japanese islands in 1944. This was a blow to Chennault because he visualized that he would be the leader of future aerial assaults against the enemy's homeland.

When General Stratemeyer analyzed the situation after his arrival, he had his staff plan what the official history calls "one of the most significant series of missions ever executed in the CBI theater." He proposed that the two air arms of the British and American forces collaborate in a number of attacks intended to destroy completely the most vital installations in the Rangoon area. He suggested to Chennault that the 308th be moved to India temporarily to add numbers to the effort. Chennault agreed.

On November 18, 1943, the 308th group received orders to proceed to India on temporary duty with all available planes and crews. Two squadrons, the 373rd and 425th, went to Pandaveswar and the others to Panagarh where the 7th Bomb Group was located. By doing this, the ground crews of the 7th could assist in maintenance of the 308th's aircraft.

The 308th's planes, about nine from each of the four squadrons, arrived at the two Indian bases by November 24th. While there, enough new B-24Js were added to bring the total number of aircraft assigned to each squadron up to nine B-24Js and three or more B-24Ds per squadron. A total of 15 B-24s of the D series were retained by the group as a reserve for combat missions but thereafter were used primarily for ferrying trips across the Hump.

The basic strategy for the joint missions was to be accomplished in a series of six missions with B-24 and B-25 aircraft, escorted by P-38s and P-51s, to attack targets in the Rangoon area with a maximum number of aircraft, in two waves. One wave from the 7th Bomb Group was to hit locomotive shops at Insein; the 308th, in company with the 490th Squadron of the Tenth Air Force, would bomb fighter airfields. RAF bombers would bomb railroad marshalling yards at Mahlwagon at night and the American bombers would attack the same targets the next day.

The weather did not cooperate. On the takeoffs of the first wave before daylight on November 25th, two B-24s of the 7th Bomb Group crashed and all on board both of them were killed. As the 308th's historian writes, "The other squadrons of our group were being briefed only a few hundred yards from the scene of (one) crash, and consequently the frequent explosions served to thoroughly disrupt the briefing."

Of the twenty-four planes of the 308th that took off that morning, seven had to return because of engine, oxygen, fuel, or other troubles. When the remaining B-24s were to pick up their escorts over Ramu, the fighters could not find them in the overcast and the bombers proceeded alone but were unable to attack. The second wave encountered the same conditions and also abandoned the primary target area. However, attacks were made on secondary targets: an airdrome at Zayatkwin and the city of Akyab Town.

While circling to find an opening through the overcast, one B-24 of the 7th Bomb Group sustained a hit by flak and later crashed. Several B-25s attacked successfully; two P-51s were shot down. The results were disappointing but later attacks on Insein had excellent results with about 70 percent of the target area destroyed. However, four P-51s, two P-38s and three B-24s were lost. One of the B-24s landed in the water off the coast and nine of the crew were rescued by friendly forces.

On November 27, the first day's assigned targets were attacked and the bombers were met with an increasing number of enemy fighters. The Air Force history describes the action:

"When the planes of the 308th arrived and were ready to begin their bomb run, the attacks experienced by the 7th Bomb Group in the first wave were repeated by a slightly smaller number of aircraft, estimated at about 25 Zeros and Oscars. Sometimes enemy fighters came in three abreast, all concentrating on a single plane. At other times they approached in a string, each plane making a pass and pulling away to allow the next in line to come in. The lead plane of the 308th was shot down on the first pass, just before the bomb run, and the plane which took its place was badly hit during the run. Attacks persisted after bombs were away, enemy pilots singling out cripples; but the P-51s finally arrived in time to offer some protection on the return, losing one ship in their brief participation.

"Bombing results of this costly mission were largely unobserved because of the continuing fighter attacks during the bomb run, but the pattern was believed good. American losses, however, were appallingly high – six B-24s and one P-51 destroyed and five B-24s seriously damaged."[4]

Sgt. Anthony Tricoli, flight engineer in the 374th, recorded his view of events in his diary that day:

"Was up at four and left on a group mission to Rangoon. Both groups, 56 B-24s, 4 P-38s and 5 P-51s. Formation was lousy. I watched the 7th Bomb Group go over the target and saw the dog fights. A P-51 and a B-24 went down. It's not so nice to see. We got over the target a few minutes later and were intercepted by about nine Zeros. I did get a shot at one. Yes, just one. It was on the tail of a P-38 and I tried to help the fellow with no results. The formation was in my way. The Zero got the 38. Another Zero came from nowhere and passed me so close that I could see the gold fillings in the pilot's teeth. Another 24 went down in the bay with two engines shot out. Our squadron lost a ship and crew. It was their first mission. They were a new crew. Too bad. They rescued the men that went down in the bay."

Two of the lost B-24s were from the 308th; four others were damaged. The 308th's survivors claimed six victories, three probably destroyed, and one damaged. Lt. N. J. Kellam, pilot of a 374th plane, and his crew bailed out successfully. A few days after his plane was listed as missing, a Radio Tokyo broadcast stated that all ten men were prisoners of war.

On November 29th, 27 B-24s of all four of the 308th's squadrons joined with planes from the 7th Group and 11 P-51s to attack the Bobataung wharves at Rangoon. Much damage was done but most of it was not in the specified target area.

The joint attacks continued on December 1 with thirty B-24s of the 308th led by Major Paul J. O'Brien. They were joined by twenty-eight B-24s of the 7th Bomb Group and both formations attacked storage and warehouse areas at Insein. At Ramu, they picked up an escort of P-38s and P-51s. The 7th's planes were in the lead and were attacked by an estimated forty to fifty enemy fighters in a fight that lasted for seventy minutes. Evidence of the bitterness of the battle is shown by the quantity of .50 caliber machine gun ammunition expended: 35,450 rounds. The 7th lost five bombers and had nine damaged. The 308th lost five B-24s. Nine fighters were claimed shot down, five probably destroyed, and many damaged.

When the 308th arrived in the area the formation was disrupted as O'Brien's ship was attacked by more than twelve Jap fighters and burst into flames over the target; none of the ten men aboard escaped. Five other bombers were damaged, one so badly that it had to land at Chittagong. Bombing results on the target area were poor although many fires were started. The 308th's gunners shot down six enemy fighters and damaged one.

One item of interest in the fighter interception was noted in the mission report: "After leaving the target, two Oscars passed over one of our bombers, rolled over on their backs, and released about one hundred flat pieces of white metal, about three inches long. None fell on the bomber. It is presumed that these objects were incendiary leaflets." This maneuver, whatever it was supposed to accomplish, was never repeated.

On December 4th, twelve B-24s of the 374th and 375th Squadrons departed their respective bases for a night mission to lay mines ("peanuts") in the mouth of the Salween River below Moulwein. All planes returned safely. The next day, twelve more B-24s flew another mine-laying mission to the Rangoon Estuary and the mouth of the Salween River near Green Island. This was the last of the 308th's scheduled missions dispatched from the Indian bases.

All 308th personnel were given a two-day leave to visit Calcutta before returning to China. The 308th's historian tells the story:

"Since the full complement of planes was not required for the last two missions, the crews began going into Calcutta about the second of December, so that not more than 75 or a hundred officers and men would reach the city during the same period. By staggering their visit in this manner, it was possible for the city to withstand our visit, as well as the first Japanese bombing in 11 months, which seemed to be timed for our visit. One group of Americans, including this historian, were in Firpo's getting a last fill of ice cream before setting out for Pandaveswar when the bombs began dropping over near the riverfront area."

Everyone returned to China between the 5th and 10th of December. On the trip across the Hump, one flight of planes was attacked by two Zeros and one 425th plane was considerably shot up. Lt. G. C. Pratt, a co-pilot, received bullet wounds in one leg and S/Sgts. Meaney and M. A. McGee received minor wounds.

It was acknowledged by post-mission analysts and historians that the objectives of these joint missions with the 7th Bomb Group were not fully accomplished. The absence of sufficient fighter support was noticeable even on the first missions. As a few fighters were lost from day to day, the inadequacy of the escort became more and more pronounced, until on the last daylight mission flown, only a half dozen planes were available as escort for the two groups of bombers. However, the fact that the RAF, Tenth, and Fourteenth Air Forces had participated in a jointly planned mission was a good omen for the theater. The cooperation between the 7th and 308th Bomb Groups was, as Air Force historians stated later, "beyond reproach."

When the Group returned from India, they found a heavy schedule awaiting them. Those who arrived first were off on another combat mission. During the month of December, nine bombing missions were flown from the Kunming area.

The first assignment for planes from the 373rd, 375th, and 425th was to attack the railroad yards at Hanoi and twelve B-24s were dispatched on December 10, 1943, although two had to return to base. The remaining ten hit the target and, although many fires were started, only about ten hits could be seen on the rolling stock which was the primary target.

On the night of the 11th, aircraft that had flown to Kweilin from India, earlier in the day, left to attack hangars and repair shops at Hankow Airdrome. The crews could not ascertain the damage inflicted because of the glare of searchlights and ground haze. However, intelligence sources later revealed that over 200 Japanese police and twenty-three high Nipponese and Wuhan puppet officials were killed. One crew that had to turn back before reaching Hankow, salvoed their bombs on Wuchang Airdrome which was on the escape route.

Although all planes returned safely, one plane, with its left landing gear tire blown, ran off the runway and crashed. Four men, including the pilot, Capt. J. C. Keene, were injured.

The next day, nine planes were sent back to the Hanoi marshalling yards for a night attack and again, results were disappointing as far as hitting rolling stock was concerned which was the primary objective. However, ground reports indicated considerable damage to the railroad station and surrounding buildings; there were many casualties, especially among the French and natives. Shortly after this mission, many civilians began evacuating the Haiphong-Hanoi area.

This flight was not without loss of aircraft. Lt. Donald P. Lackey and his crew of ten, lost and running out of fuel, bailed out. All returned safely to their home base on December 20.

Next was a mission of twenty-nine B-24s and twenty-eight P-40s from all four squadrons to attack the airdrome at Namsang on December 18. Three days later, thirty-two B-24s, led by Major Robert F. Burnett, attacked marshalling yards at Chengmai, Thailand. The results were very encouraging. "Photographs taken during the mission showed exceptionally accurate work," the official history reports, "with very many direct hits on the yards and along the warehouses on each side." All of the factories in the vicinity of the railroad station were completely destroyed, and the light plant was damaged to such an extent that the city was without electricity for seven days.

There was an air raid on Kunming on the 22nd with nineteen enemy bombers and about thirty Zeros in the formation. Sgt. Tricoli's diary reports:

"Our Forties were up but didn't intercept until the eggs were dropped. They claim four bombers and three Zeros. There wasn't much of a dog fight. They dropped plenty of bombs and they sure did make lots of noise. It seems the bombers let something like puffs of smoke out of their tails. From the ground it appears to be our ack-ack. The fighters claim it's a protection against our fighters. They claim they'll drop airborne troops on Xmas Day. I wonder?"

On December 24, 1943, another large formation of 29 B-24s from all four squadrons departed Kunming, Chengkung, and Yanghai to attack Tien Ho Airdrome. However, the lead plane mistakenly made its run on White Cloud airdrome, a satellite field, and made many hits on the runways and revetment area.

Three minutes before reaching the target area, the formation was jumped by fifteen or more enemy fighters which damaged five bombers, one seriously. One B-24, named *Johnny Doughboy*, of the 374th Squadron with eleven men aboard, was hit before reaching the target; it started smoking and the right landing gear dropped. The plane peeled off to the left, went into a flat spin and was heading down when last seen. At least three and possibly as many as six men were seen to bail out; some of the parachutes were strafed by enemy fighters on the descent.

One of those who bailed out was Lt. Charles M. Swanson, an aerial photographer, who was not on flying status and therefore received no extra flying pay and had no obligation to go on the mission. In his diary, he tersely described what happened on that mission:

"Up at 6:00 a.m. and good breakfast, air raid alert at 7:45 a.m. and we went to hill near planes. We took off at 11 a.m. with 250# bombs, in group formation of 23 bombers, 30 fighters, 17,000 feet on last wing of group - led us to White Cloud auxiliary (supposed to bomb Tien Ho) and just before we reached, we were hit - started down and out of control, sharp bank to left, diving, left landing gear down, #2 engine smoking, smoke and heat coming from front (2 Zeros had hit from 12 o'clock shortly before). Bail out at 1 p.m. Plane started screaming down. I jerked cord from wall and flipped camera up, went out camera hatch at once and pulled ripcord - plane continued on down fast - Culps jumped next, then Humphries, then Lee, then Giebel, then Boone out nose and either Anderson, Meltect or Berman (one) also jumped. Two dead on ground in chutes from Zeros strafing. Rest were still in plane when it went on down in flat spiral spin and crashed and burned.

"I landed in mud hole, got out of chute, walked toward some Chinese people; one man came with me and we cut chute out of bush away from chords. He carried it and we walked to a house - a Chinese told me to go with this first man and to remove my clothes. I did this and removed pants, flying suit and leather jacket, giving all to Chinese here. I was glad to see [Wallace] Culps and [Al] Giebel join me and we three and the guerrilla went to small village near hill and hid rest of day in brush, where we were fed rice and tea, with some greens cooked with meat. At 5:00 p.m. it was getting dark and so we went out to path and I put on old pair of blue pants (had black shirt and old straw hat, coolie type). Kept gun cocked in hand for a while until it was real dark. We walked until 8:30 p.m. and stopped at a village where we were joined by six guerrillas all armed; stopped here to eat again, went on one hour to a mud cabin on a mountain side quite far up. To bed on floor, parachute beneath us, one blanket over us (partly)."

For the next ten days, the group was guided by Chinese guerrillas and military escorts to Kweilin. En route, they were honored with a parade and food as they passed through small villages. On one occasion, believed to be at Tsungfa, they went to bed exhausted at 6 p.m. but were awakened at 9 p.m. and told to get ready to leave because Japanese spies had seen them and enemy forces were too close for safety.

Although not a flyer, Swanson was later recommended for the Distinguished Flying Cross for a number of hazardous missions he flew "beyond the call of duty."

Sgt. Wallace Culps, one of the crew members, was interviewed by *The Houston Press* about the December 24 mission after he returned home:

> "I landed about 100 yards from Sgt. Al Giebel, our ball turret gunner, and both of us crawled into a ditch while the Jap planes sprayed us with their guns. After dark we crept into a village where we found our photographer, Lt. Swanson."

Culps told the reporter that their only hope of escape from the searching Japanese rested with the Chinese. He was asked if he could trust the Chinese because some might be Japanese sympathizers or spies.

"Trust them?" he said. "Why they would die for any American – one did for us." He explained that when they arrived at a small village at daybreak on January 1st, a Chinese peasant hid them in his hut, but was spotted by a Jap soldier.

"To give us time to go out the back way," Culps explained, "that brave Chinese stood in the front door refusing admission to the Jap. They bayoneted him."

Meanwhile, *Johnny Doughboy* had not crashed and the personnel left in the badly damaged plane had no injuries; the plane headed back toward Kweilin, the intended destination. However, en route, one engine lost its propeller; when another engine began to falter, the pilot Lt. Roger F. Haley, gave the order to bail out. No one heard the order except the navigator, bombardier, and co-pilot in the nose of the aircraft because the interphone had been shot out. They left through the nose hatch. After they left, the weakening engine picked up again and Lt. Haley, with the assistance of his engineer, and with an escort of other B-24s that dropped back with him, was able to bring it and the remaining crew members back to Kweilin. The three who had bailed out landed in friendly territory.

The gunners on planes of the 373rd claimed twelve victories and eight probables; the 374th, seven victories and two probables.

Since the Tien Ho airport had not been bombed as briefed, twenty-three B-24s left Kweilin on Christmas Day to attack it. Four planes failed to form up with the others and another had engine problems; all five returned to Kweilin. Meanwhile, the other planes again mistakenly bombed the satellite field and were attacked by from twenty-five to fifty enemy planes. An intense battle ensued that lasted for about half an hour, during which 308th gunners destroyed seventeen enemy fighters, probably destroyed seven and damaged six.

One bomber was lost with eleven men aboard. It crashed a short distance from the target area and it was thought that surely all would have been captured if any were able to jump and survive the bailout. Of the eleven men on the plane, six bailed out but one was seen being strafed and was probably killed during the descent. Miraculously, the five survivors returned safely later, all with interesting stories to tell.

When they bailed out, the plane was almost directly over the Japanese airfield and during the descent all believed they were going to land on the field itself. However, the wind took them from one to three miles away. T/Sgt Dan W. Lee had a very narrow escape when he landed only about 250 yards from where the plane crashed. Within a few minutes the area was full of Japanese soldiers.

Lee hid in a hole surrounded by tall grass and stayed there until dark; Japanese soldiers came within ten feet of him a number of times but he was not detected. After dark he crawled farther into nearby hills and spent the next day (Christmas) hiding. He moved higher into the hills the next night and after being almost forty-eight hours without food or drink, he walked into a small Chinese village where he met some friendly Chinese guerrillas.

The four other survivors also avoided capture and the five were finally brought together at Kukong by friendly guerrilla forces and from there made their way to Hengyang and finally to Kunming. All five had evaded capture from well within the Japanese lines and emerged into the friendly area wearing the garb of Chinese peasants. They were high in their praise of the many guerrilla fighters who had helped them avoid discovery.

To close out the 308th's operations for 1943, the group ran what proved to be one of its most successful strategic missions thus far. Twenty-nine B-

24s departed their respective bases without fighter escort to attack railroad marshalling yards at Lampang, Thailand. Four planes turned back with mechanical difficulties but the remaining twenty-five bombed the primary target. The crews reported huge fires and secondary explosions as they departed the area. Photos taken two days later showed direct hits on the tracks, 250 buildings, including the roundhouse and locomotive shed, destroyed and there was much corollary damage on surrounding buildings.

Although a number of enemy fighters were seen, they seemed reluctant to attack such a large force and only a few passes were made. All of the 308th's planes returned safely; none were damaged.

"So successful was the raid," according to the 308th's history, "that it received much favorable comment throughout the theater." It was reported that Lord Mountbatten was especially impressed when he learned that several months' worth of supplies for two enemy task forces had been destroyed.

During the last half of 1943, the Fourteenth Air Force had been slowly changing from a band of guerrillas into a highly specialized striking force that began to take a toll of the enemy's two most valuable military assets: planes and merchant ships, the latter being the most vulnerable to attack. The smallest of the numbered Army Air Forces, the Fourteenth had the largest territory in which to operate and attack the enemy.

Chennault had divided China with the Chinese Air Force so that the Fourteenth was responsible for everything south of the Yangtze River. During 1943, his meager fleet of fighters, medium bombers and the heavies of the 308th had attacked from Burma east to Formosa and from the Yangtze south to the Tropic of Cancer. Meanwhile, Lt. General Shunroku Hata, commander of the enemy's China Expeditionary Army, ordered an aerial offensive against American installations to be followed up with a massive ground offensive in east China in the spring of 1944.

Although the 308th had a difficult time getting started because of the supply shortage and monsoon weather, it had built up an impressive record, especially when it is realized that all gas, bombs, ammunition, and other supplies had to be flown over the Hump in the unit's own planes, thus making it necessary to fly about three Hump flights for every combat mission.

By year's end, a tally of flights showed the group had flown 1,331 round trips from China to India and brought in an average payload of 6,934 lbs. per trip. The total poundage was over 7.8 million lbs., including 863,000 gallons of gas and 25,000 gallons of oil. In addition, more than 1100 passengers had been carried across the Hump; many more had been transported between bases in China.

The group had flown fifty-one regularly assigned bombing missions and dropped 2,393,000 lbs. of bombs. In addition, the group's planes had dropped 85,620 lbs. of bombs on enemy installations during the Hump ferry runs. Although the bombs on these missions were small 100-pounders of Russian or Chinese manufacture and damage was relatively light, these flights served to give the bombardiers practice as well as harass the enemy.

After checking and rechecking the claims of enemy aircraft shot down, probably destroyed or damaged, analysts concluded that the year-end score was impressive. The group's gunners had destroyed 203 enemy planes in the air, probably destroyed seventy-eight, and damaged twenty-eight. Exact figures for those destroyed on the ground were not usually available but it was known from intelligence sources behind enemy lines that twenty-eight or more were destroyed on the ground by 308th bombers.

In India, operating with the 7th Bomb Group, the 308th had flown a total of six missions, hitting Mingaladon and Zayatkwin airports, Botataung wharves, Insein railroad shops and storage dumps, and laying mines at Moulwein and in the mouth of the Salween River.

The damage by the 308th to enemy installations was also assessed and it was found that the ports of Haiphong and Hanoi as ports of entry for Indo-China were virtually shut down and enemy shipping and coal loading at the Hongay and Campha ports were seriously disrupted. Bombing attacks on shipping resulted in the sinking of six ships for a total of approximately 42,000 tons and the damaging of others estimated at 32,000 tons.

The damage to the enemy during 1943 was not accomplished without considerable personnel losses to the 308th. Sixty-six men who were initially listed as missing in action returned to their units. All had bailed out and walked back, many from behind enemy lines in occupied China. The final count at the end of the year showed the Group had sustained the following casualties:

	Officers	Enlisted Men
Killed in Action	24	31
Missing in Action	23	37
Prisoners of War (Known)	5	4
Permanently Hospitalized	7	20
Died (Not the result of combat)	10	14

The losses included the Group Operations Officer, Major Foster, Squadron Commanders Major Robert W. Fensler and Major William W. Ellsworth of the 425th Squadron, and Major Walter B. Beat of the 374th. Major E. G. Schultz, Assistant Tactical Executive for the Group, was also killed. Unfortunately, more tragedies were to follow as the 308th continued to fight without adequate logistical support.

Chapter 5

JANUARY TO JUNE 1944

Late in 1943, Allied successes in other theaters encouraged Chennault to hope that more resources would be coming his way so that he could extend the Fourteenth's reach and attack the Japanese supply lines with greater vigor during the coming year. He drew up a comprehensive plan that would depend on increased tonnage coming over the Hump and improvements in the overland supply line between Kunming and Kweilin. His plan called first for continued but much heavier strikes against merchant shipping and the Japanese air force. He would then launch long-range bombing attacks on the enemy home islands from bases in eastern China.

Between January and June 1944, Chennault's plan of action was to concentrate on targets in the western sector of China when weather frequently rendered eastern bases inoperative. From July to the end of the year, he hoped to intensify attacks launched from eastern bases. To carry out this strategy, he estimated that he would need six fighter groups, two medium bomb groups, and three heavy bomb groups.

The Japanese were gathering their ground forces on the mainland when 1944 began to make the greatest land offensive of the war. Their assignment, as Chennault saw it, was to knock the Fourteenth Air Force out of the war in China and more than a million and a half enemy troops were tasked with the job of doing that by mid-summer. The overall strategy objective was to bring about the eventual collapse of Chiang Kai-shek and all resistance in China.

When it was learned that the Japanese were marshalling their forces for the offensive to begin in April 1944, Chennault felt the entire Allied strategy in the China-Burma-India theater was totally misdirected. He explains:

"Ever since Stilwell trudged out of Burma in the spring of 1942, he had burned with a consuming desire to march back at the head of a victorious army that would wipe out the stain of his humiliating defeat. The Burma campaign became an obsession with Stilwell, which he pursued relentlessly without any regard for reality."[1]

It was at this point that Chennault learned the details that were being worked out in Washington for sending the very long-range (VLR) bombers – Boeing B-29 Superfortresses – to China with fighters to support them. However, to his dismay, the units would be directed from Washington and would not be under his command. The first production models of the B-29s rolled off the production lines beginning in July 1943 but so many modifications were needed because of design deficiencies and engine problems that production and delivery to combat units was slowed down.

President Roosevelt had promised Chiang that the B-29s would be in China by January 1944 but the earliest seemed to be April. Exasperated when he learned of the delay, the president wrote to General Marshall and offered another solution to keep the promise. "The worst thing is that we are falling down on our promises to China every single time," the president wrote. "I do not see why we have to use B-29s. We have several other types of bombing planes."

Even if the B-29s had been available on time, the bases in India and China were not yet ready to receive them. General Arnold set a March 1, 1944, deadline and sent General K. B. Wolfe to India and China to find out what the problems were. When Wolfe arrived in India in January 1944, he checked first at Calcutta.

"We wanted runways," he reported later. "We found a bunch of Indians making mudpies."

What he saw were thousands of Indian native laborers trying to remove 1.7 million cubic yards of earth in wicker baskets. What was needed was heavy construction machinery like bulldozers and steam shovels and skilled men to use them. The solution was to transfer to the airport sites a battalion of black American construction workers who had been working on the Ledo Road. To their great credit, they turned the situation around in a very short time and built five concrete runways at Calcutta, each 8,500 feet long and ten inches thick which were needed to accommodate the heavy Superfortresses.

Wolfe proceeded to Chengtu, 1,200 miles closer to Japan. He found progress there but under conditions that amazed him.

A quarter of a million Chinese male and female coolies were building, literally by hand, four runways 8,500 feet long and nineteen inches thick. Old men, women and children were crushing large rocks into smaller pieces and then breaking these up into pebbles with hammers. The small stones were moved to the runway layouts in wooden wheelbarrows and buckets hanging on shoulder poles.

When the rock bed of a runway was finished, thick tung oil was spread to coat the stones and then ten-ton rollers packed them down. The rollers had to be pulled by hundreds of workers who sometimes slipped and were crushed into the runways because, once moving, the rollers were nearly impossible to stop in time.

Any plans that Chennault might have had to carry the war to Japan itself would not have precedence over the overall plan to attack Japan with B-29s from first, bases in India, then from China. He was not to have any control over the B-29s or the bases. The only consolation that Chennault had was that at least the second half of his strategy to bomb Japan from China was going to be carried out, albeit not under his command or with his aircraft. However, although disappointed in not having control over the B-29s, Chennault found that the news was not all bad. Two squadrons of B-25s and another of P-40s were added to the Fourteenth, which netted a gain of eighteen P-40s and thirty-three B-25s for him to employ as he saw fit. He also won minor concessions in that improvements were promised for the land supply line between Kunming and Kweilin.

Chennault decided to take advantage of the invitation that President Roosevelt had given him earlier to write directly to him whenever he felt the urge. Since Chennault had promised that by January 1, 1944, the Fourteenth would have crippled a significant number of enemy aircraft and sunk half a million tons of shipping, he wanted the President to know why those promises had not been kept. He wrote:

"We have not been given the tools to do the job. Furthermore much of the good fighting weather has been irretrievably lost. If the air offensive had been launched on schedule, its first phase, establishment of air superiority in southeast China, would already be completed and the second phase, further softening of Jap airpower and hitting sea communications, would now be in progress. The time would be in sight when occupation of our bases nearest the coast would be feasible and the third phase, including long range bombardment of the Japanese Islands, could begin.

"Actually, it has not been possible to launch even the first phase due to continued weakness in fighter planes...We have succeeded in defeating the Japanese repeatedly only because of the courage, aggressiveness, and determination of our air and ground crews. At this time in the war, American combat units should not be forced to fight against such superior odds as the Japanese possess in China."[2]

Chennault also wrote a letter on July 2, 1943 to Harry Hopkins, personal confidante of the president:

"Numerous disappointments have thus far threatened the launching of the China air offensive and now threaten to postpone it altogether...After trying to form the most impartial judgment possible in my situation, I feel that postponement of the China air offensive will be downright tragic.

"I am ready to pledge my reputation, such as it is, that the return on the investment will cripple the enemy's total airpower and weaken the sea communications on which his whole system of conquest depends."

While Chennault was still operating his meager air force on a shoestring, there had been command changes in the theater which were not to his liking. A new combined headquarters had been established at New Delhi in the fall of 1943 known as the Southeast Asia Command under Lord Mountbatten. It was to this command that Brigadier General Eugene Beebe was assigned.

"This joint Anglo-American enterprise was a monument to military boondoggling," Chennault said in his memoirs. The good news to him, however, was the fact that his nemesis, Major General Clayton Bissell, had been sent home to the States and was replaced by Major General George Stratemeyer as commander of the Tenth Air Force.

There was no cessation in Chennault's effort to deprive the Japanese of their lines of supply into the occupied areas of China with his own forces when the new year of 1944 began. Although continuing to be hampered by gas shortages, the 308th flew a total of fourteen combat missions during January 1944. Two were from high altitude, one was mine-laying, one a combination bombing and mine-laying, and ten were low altitude sea sweeps against shipping.

Laying mines was relatively new to the USAAF at this phase of the war. Mines are underwater explosive devices that are meant to damage, sink, or deter the passage of ships. Known as "weapons that wait," they were seldom seen at work by crews of the planes that dropped them into harbors and sea lanes. They lay in wait for a ship to strike them and usually do not explode with a flash of fire or loud blast. They explode underwater and the pressure blasts against the hulls of metal ships can cause huge holes and leaks.

Developed by the U.S. Navy, mines began to gain acceptance in both the Navy and Air Forces as effective weapons beginning in 1943. The 308th, as well as B-24s of the Tenth Air Force and, later, the B-29s of the Twentieth Air Force, laid mines from the Tonkin Gulf to the Yangtze River from 1943 to 1945. Their purpose was to disrupt ship traffic going to and from the major ports such as Takao, Shanghai, Canton, and Hong Kong. The mines used by the 308th were airlifted over the Hump and readied by a detail of Navy experts at Kunming. The first use of the mines by the 308th occurred on October 18, 1943, when a single B-24 dropped three mines in the harbor at Haiphong. This was followed by a raid on land targets on November 12 to the same target area.

Lt. Col. John S. Chilstrom, a historian who has studied the history of mine-laying, noted: "This operation demonstrated the potential of even a small number of mines to destroy and disrupt shipping. The first mines sank a merchant ship and the second mining another. A ten-ship convoy then refused to enter the port, but as it diverted to Hainan Island, Fourteenth Air Force planes attacked it and sank six ships. Afterwards, no traffic larger than junks approached Haiphong.

"Elsewhere, at General Claire Chennault's insistence, Fourteenth Air Force aircraft laid mines along the Yangtze River between October 1944 and May 1945. The effect was to block Japanese steamers from supplying troops fighting inland. The results so pleased Chennault that he remarked, 'The aerial mine has done more to stop the Japanese drive north from Canton than any other weapon.'"[3]

Jack Keene, a 375th pilot, described one of his mine-laying missions:

"We had two 2,000-pound mines that were to be placed near Hong Kong in the area of the Kowloon docks. The mines had a salt water soluble fuse which, after being submerged for about an hour, would become armed. Navy personnel briefed us for the mission with these warnings: Do not release mines above 250 feet as they would become buried in the mud. Release only where instructed and do not release if not positive of position so the Navy could chart them. We were cautioned to be alert for cables that the enemy may have strung between some of the islands.

"The mission was intended for when there was a good moon but no way could you see a cable at night, no matter how bright it was. Flying that low over the water we just had to avoid flying between islets which we thought were close enough to be capable of cable connections. As if this weren't perplexing enough, there were patches of low hanging white puffy clouds throughout the area – some of which had rocks in them. This was the most vexing mission imaginable and, after darting in and around the Hong Kong harbor area for an hour and a half trying to locate the proscribed drop area, we had to carry our mines all the way back to Kweilin."

After the initial mine-laying successes in late 1943, the 308th's Liberators dropped mines with ever-increasing frequency as the reader will see. As the mine-laying results were analyzed in China and in Washington, it was believed that mining Japanese ports was often more economical than bombing to dislocate the flow of supplies at any one time.

The first group mission of 1944 for the 308th was to the Lampang railroad yards on January 3, 1944. Escorted by only two P-38s, twenty-eight B-24s reached the target and made a run over the area in formation. The weather was eight-tenths to totally undercast and some of the crews were unable to see the target at all, while others caught only fleeting glimpses. Five planes returned without dropping their bombs. However, those that did got excellent results. One plane accidentally salvoed its bombs when the bomb bay doors were opened. Later photographs showed that these bombs landed squarely on the Lampang airdrome.

About January 8, the flying echelon of the 373rd flew to Kweilin to remain for two or three weeks and launch sea searches and mine laying when weather permitted. On January 10th, a sea search turned up no targets. On the 11th, mines were dropped in the ship channel off Hong Kong and later reconnaissance showed a 325-foot ship sinking in the channel.

On the same day, Colonel Fisher led a raid to Takao, Formosa, with eleven aircraft. It was a mission that was aimed at a vital focal point for Japanese air and naval strength and would be repeated many times by the 308th. There were at least thirteen major airports at and near Takao, three repair depots, and an additional twenty-three airports from which bombers could be operated. One flight of eight Liberators, which Colonel Fisher led, had an aluminum plant as their target. The other eight, under the command of Capt. John B. "Jack" Carey of the 373rd, were to lay mines in the Takao harbor. Good results were reported; one ship was seen sinking shortly after the run. Carey tells about his part in the mission:

"I was flying the *Katy-Did* as the lead aircraft of the mine laying element. We planned to rendezvous as soon as we got out of the weather which was forecast to be about the China coast in the Amoy area. The weather was much worse than forecast and by the time we got to the coast, I was convinced that everyone else had gone back to Kweilin. We decided to proceed and at least put three mines in the channel. We broke out of the weather about halfway across the Formosa Straits and proceeded at about 500 feet.

"When we arrived at the Formosan coast about 20 miles south of our target, some of the bombing diversion (about six or seven aircraft) had arrived and alerted the defense forces and dropped their bombs on the aluminum plant. At this point the searchlights and flak were directed at the high altitude boys and we got halfway across the bay when they discovered us and all hell broke loose. First a searchlight caught us and then tracers from shore fire were heavy. We dropped down over the water until the waist gunner reported spray coming in his window. We discovered then that the searchlights could not lower enough to get us in focus. They would raise the lights and drop them down to the stops and still couldn't get us. This was somewhat comforting, except the absence of light allowed us to see the tracers better. We headed for the channel and the bombardier readied for release.

"We had studied a topographic relief map of the area and knew we had to pull up and turn left after we released the mines in order to avoid a hill where the channel made a turn. We released the mines in the middle of the channel and I started a left climbing turn when there was a loud explosion sound and some debris hit the windshield. The navigator said we hit a tree on the hill that we were trying to avoid. The aircraft seemed to be okay so we proceeded to Kweilin.

"We had a repeat of the bad weather on the way home and a tired crew finally landed at our base. On inspecting the aircraft after landing we found broken twigs in the wheel wells and green stain on the props, leading edge of the wings, and in the landing lights.

"The flight was productive. About ten days later, a P-38 recon aircraft took pictures of a cargo ship submerged in the middle of the channel."

No personnel were lost on this mission, although four members of one crew bailed out ten miles from Kweilin when it appeared that the landing might be unsuccessful because of the weather. Another plane, piloted by Lt. Frederick C. Keish, became lost and its entire crew was reported missing for several days but eventually everyone returned to the home field after bailing out near Lanping. Two men returned on January 24. The other six members remained in Lanping for several days where they received supplies dropped from a C-47 transport. They then proceeded by horseback and on foot to Wayao where Captain Wilcox and a rescue party met them in two jeeps. No one had been seriously injured in the jump but all suffered considerably from the cold before supplies could be dropped to them.

On the night of January 12, seventeen planes of the 374th and 425th Squadrons took advantage of a full moon to make a night attack deep into Thailand. The target was the Bangsue rail marshalling yards on the north edge of Bangkok. Fourteen planes found the target and bombed it with explosive and incendiary bombs. Photos taken the next day showed no damage to the railroad yards but the main passenger terminal, a cement plant, and seven other buildings were burned out. Inside the city, fires were started which could be seen for thirty minutes by the bomber crews after their planes left the area. No enemy aircraft attacked the formation.

On January 13, two planes of the 373rd at Kweilin departed on a sea sweep of the waters from Hainan Island to within sight of Luzon Island in the Philippines. No worthwhile targets were sighted. The next day, two more planes of the 373rd made a similar trip and sighted two large ships which were promptly bombed and strafed. Both were believed sunk. A similar two-ship flight left the next day from Kweilin for a search of the waters along the French Indo-China coast and south of Hainan Island. One of the aircraft, with ten men aboard, could never be contacted again and was still missing a month later.

Sea searches were continued on January 18 and 19 without results. Then, on the 20th, two B-24s were searching south and east of Hong Kong at low altitude and were hit with small arms fire. Capt. Richard D. Furbush, pilot of a 425th plane, was wounded in his right hand and left arm while the co-pilot, Lt. Byron, suffered flesh wounds in both legs. Despite his own wounds, when Furbush's injuries prevented him from handling the controls, Byron took over and brought the plane back to Kweilin.

Two-plane sea searches continued on January 21 and 22. After the latter mission, the planes of the 373rd were replaced at Kweilin by those of the 375th under the command of Capt. Irwin Basen who led an attack on the 24th. This flight was intercepted by a single Zero; the bombs were salvoed in order to take evasive action.

While only two planes were lost on combat missions in January 1944, there were other heavy non-combat losses. Five planes were lost on January 25 on a routine ferry flight to Chabua from Kunming and Chengkung. The weather, reported as sufficiently high at Chabua at takeoff time for the return flight, closed in upon arrival in the Chengkung area. One plane crashed there killing all aboard except two men, Sgts. Donald L. McQueen and George M. Keefauver. Two planes crashed after the crews bailed out and two others were reported missing. One of the missing planes, piloted by Major Harry H. Musinski, had twelve men aboard, including Lt. Charles H. Mortimer, the 425th's flight surgeon. The other missing plane had eight men aboard.

The crew of one of the aircraft that later bailed out had reached Chabua and circled until the gas ran out. All crew members landed on or near the field. The 308th historian reported:

> "Some members of the crew complained that fate was by no means impartial. Lt. Cates landed in the hospital yard and was promptly 'rescued' by two attractive nurses; Lt. Werner, who landed less than half a mile away, fell in a tea plantation and had to be satisfied with the ministrations of a group of ultra-brunette tea pickers. Lt. Thomas, making his third jump since coming to China, landed in the yard of the parachute department and promptly lost his parachute to the officer-in-charge. The rest of the crew, in casting about for some suitable recognition of Lt. Thomas's frequent jumps, have recommended for him an Oak Leaf

Cluster to his gold tooth, a tooth which replaces one that he knocked out with his knee on his first jump."

The six men in the other crew that bailed out crashed in the Dinjan area. All returned safely to base a short time later.

There were three bombing missions, seven sea sweeps, and two mine-laying missions during February 1944. All were flown without fighter escort. Twenty-three aircraft made a night attack on Bangkok on February 5 but only five got through the weather to the target area. Those that failed to find the target bombed an airdrome on the Mekong River and a town called Nagorn Nayok. One dropped its bombs through the overcast and later reports indicated that a large number of enemy troops were killed in a small town about 100 miles northeast of Bangkok. Two planes became lost and the crews bailed out successfully over Central China with only minor injuries reported.

On the same night of the Bangkok raid, two planes led by Capt. Lunt went on a sea search and spotted a convoy of ten vessels escorted by a destroyer. In the following attack, three 2700-ton ships were sunk and three others of the same size damaged. Two smaller ships exploded from direct hits and sank. Small arms fire from the cargo ships and flak from the destroyer were encountered but only a few minor holes were found in one of the planes.

Sea searches were launched on February 6 and 7 but both were unable to locate any targets. The mission on the 6th went along the coast line from Hong Kong north to the Tonkin Gulf. The other proceeded east and south from St. John's Island.

A precedent-setting night mine-laying mission by five planes was carried out to Shanghai on February 10 with the planes departing from Kweilin. It was the first time that an offensive mission had been sent as far as the Shanghai area on China's east coast. The next night, more mines were dropped at Takoa, Formosa. A sea search on the 12th was fruitless.

On the 13th, a group mission of twenty-four planes led by Colonel Fisher and Major Robert F. Burnett of the 375th was sent to bomb the railroad shops at Vinh, French-Indo-China. The group history reports that "This mission was about as nearly perfect as any mission could be." At least 95 percent of the bombs landed on the small target; those that didn't landed in a phosphorus plant nearby. Later ground reports indicated the target was completely destroyed.

On the same day, a sea search was made south of Hong Kong without results, followed by another on February 18 that patrolled from Hong Kong north to Formosa with no significant sightings.

On the 19th, the search by four B-24s in two flights was successful. Two cargo ships and a destroyer that had just left a port on Formosa were attacked; both freighters were sunk.

On the final mission of the month, which took place on February 29, twenty-three B-24s attacked storage and warehouse areas at Yochow. A rendezvous was made with a flight of twelve B-25s and the combined flight proceeded to the target area. Weather was overcast over the target so that the planes had to descend through the clouds to make the bomb run. Although they failed to make the initial point, good results were obtained. There was no fighter opposition but heavy, accurate anti-aircraft fire was encountered and three of the 308th's planes were damaged slightly. Three men received minor injuries. All planes returned safely.

Gasoline shortage continued to plague the 308th during March 1944 at bases in China and at Assam, the supply point, because it was being diverted to support forces in India. At no time was it possible to send a maximum number of planes to Chabua or Jorhat for gas; consequently, only twelve combat missions were scheduled. Most sea searches were with two or three planes each.

On the night of March 10, eleven B-24s departed Kweilin and bombed the docks at Kowloon, Hong Kong. The plan was to use flares to light up the area but they did not function as planned, probably because the fuses were delayed too long, and the crews found it difficult to see the target area. Although all planes returned safely, only about half dropped their bombs.

On a search on March 19, two "Sniffers" (radar-equipped planes) left Kweilin on different courses. At the end of the mission they intended to land at Suichwan, preparatory to going out on another mission. One plane, piloted by Lt. Glenn A. McConnell of the 373rd, sighted a Kawanishi four-engine flying boat on radar off the southwest coast of Formosa. The gunners attacked it in a running gun battle and sent it splashing into the sea where it sank immediately. In the fight, three crew members, including McConnell, were wounded. McConnell, not seriously hurt, elected to return to Kweilin. The plane had been damaged to the extent that its radio compasses were inoperative and a hydraulic line was severed. Sgts. Peter S. Maholick and

Jonas C. Holley entered the bomb bay and salvoed the bombs. Despite the damage, McConnell landed without difficulty.

The other plane discovered two freighters on its search and strafed it thoroughly while dropping four bombs. It landed at Suichwan as briefed.

On March 27, two other crews sighted a four-engine flying boat and also shot it down after a running gun fight in which both B-24s participated. The planes were piloted by Lts. W. K. Smith of the 425th and Lt. Laurence of the 374th; Sgts. William A. Bracy and William J. Taylor of the respective squadrons were credited with the kills, although a number of gunners fired at the target plane before it landed on the water and burst into flames.

On March 30, Colonel Fisher set out on a sea search in the Samah Bay area of Hainan Island in a single B-24. Unable to find any shipping, he made a bomb run on a cotton mill at Nam Dinh at 250 feet and all six bombs landed squarely on the main building. Debris was blown as high as the plane and later reports confirmed that it was completely destroyed and casualties were extremely heavy.

Another single-plane sea search was flown at the same time by Lt. Robert J. Nolan and his crew. They attacked a 300-foot ship at 250 feet but the bombs failed to release. As the plane passed by, the ship was strafed thoroughly but the plane was also damaged; as it pulled away, a column of smoke was seen rising between midships and the bow. A second run was not made because the pilot, co-pilot, and navigator had sustained minor wounds and the extent of the damage to the B-24 was not known. Nolan landed without further difficulty.

During April 1944, the group flew eighteen combat missions that departed from the fields at Kunming, Chengkung, and Yankai, the home fields, but also from Liuchow, Kweilin, Suichwan, and Chengtu. On or about April 23, most of the combat staff and ground personnel moved to Chengtu, in anticipation of bombing operations in support of Chinese ground forces resisting the advance of the Japanese in the Yellow River sector. They returned to the Kunming area bases later in the month.

Of the eighteen missions flown during April, seven were bombing missions against specific targets, eight were low-level sea searches and attacks on shipping, two were mine-laying, and one was a combination of mine-laying and bombing. Meanwhile, the shortage of supplies to continue operations against the Japanese buildup for the spring offensive was worsening. Whereas Chennault had asked Stilwell for between eight and ten thousand tons, he was actually receiving only six thousand. Realizing how serious the situation was, Chiang Kai-shek asked Stilwell to divert B-29 stockpiles for Chennault's use but Stilwell refused. The generalissimo then appealed to President Roosevelt who also refused the request after checking with the War Department. The rationale: "It is our view that the early bombing of Japan will have a far more beneficial effect on the situation in China than the long delay in such an operation which would be caused by the transfer of these [B-29] stocks to Chennault." The 308th and the rest of Chennault's air force would have to continue to supply itself or do without.

A mine-laying mission of April 3rd to Haiphong by three Liberators of the 425th Squadron was the first attempt to lay mines in daylight. Since it was intended to bomb visually under an overcast, the mines were not laid accurately because of low visibility. However, the canal and the Song Bac River entrance were believed blocked effectively.

A daylight raid on April 6 on Kiungshan Airdrome on Hainan Island was reasonably successful and no enemy fighters attacked the formation of seventeen planes that reached the target area. However, anti-aircraft fire was encountered and several B-24s were damaged.

On a sea search the next day, Lt. Alfred W. Ritter and his crew bombed two small ships but upon completion of the mission they were unable to find Kweilin because of malfunctioning compasses. When the fuel was exhausted, the crew bailed out near Hengyang. All crew members returned within three days; Lt. Bernstein and S/Sgt John N. Costello received minor injuries on the bailout.

The April 8 mission, scheduled to attack Samah Bay without fighter escort, was changed to attack a secondary target at Hanoi when information was received that thirty-nine Japanese fighter planes had been flown to Samah Bay. Although the fifteen planes reached the target area, they had to drop their bombs on the lead bombardier because of the weather and were not sure of results. Ground reports later indicated that much damage was inflicted upon enemy forces. Hits were reported on enemy barracks, the puppet government headquarters, a supply area, and an estimated 300 enemy casualties were sustained.

Two "Sniffer" planes departed from Kweilin on separate courses to make a sea sweep on April 18, 1944. One plane, piloted by Lt. Glenn H. McConnell and with eleven other men aboard, did not return. It had been shot down near Hong Kong. Chinese sources later reported that two men had gotten out of the plane after it crashed in the water and were captured. Another was said to have been killed by gunfire as he descended in a parachute. The fate of the other men was unknown.

On another two-plane sea search on April 21st, Lt. Portyrata's plane was intercepted by two enemy fighters near St. John's Island. Although both were shot down, the B-24 suffered extensive damage and two men were wounded. Despite one tire being shot out and one engine feathered, a safe landing was made at Kweilin.

An epic mission was flown by three planes from the 374th Squadron and four from the 425th on April 22-23. They went to Liuchow for staging on April 21. The next day they left at noon and planned to be over the target area which was a harbor at Cape St. Jacques near Saigon late in the evening so that the return trip over enemy territory would be made after midnight. Of the seven planes that departed Liuchow, one had to abort before reaching the target area because of the weather but bombed a railroad bridge southwest of Vinh with excellent results, knocking two spans into the water. The other planes made individual low level attacks and destroyed six large ships, one of them a tanker, and one naval vessel for a total of 40,000 tons of shipping. Although the planes caught some intense small arms and anti-aircraft fire, the only casualty was T/Sgt Anastasio M. Contreras who received a severe wound in the upper arm from an explosive shell. "Considering the forces involved, this was probably one of the most successful missions the Group has performed," according to the 308th's history.

A few days after this mission, General Chennault received a congratulatory message from Admiral Nimitz in Hawaii:

HEARTIEST CONGRATULATIONS. THE SHIPPING DESTROYED BY YOUR AIR FORCE ON ITS ATTACK 22ND THIS MONTH ON CAPE ST. JACQUES CAN ILL BE AFFORDED BY THE JAPS.

On April 25, a force of twenty-seven Liberators, led by Lt. Col. James Averill, and escorted by ten P-51s, hit rail and highway bridges north of Chengshien. The next day, twenty-four B-24s, escorted by ten P-51s and twelve of the first P-47 Thunderbolts to arrive in China, attacked Chungmow.

On an unsuccessful mission to bomb a bridge on the Yellow River near Chengmou on April 29, a flight of twenty-four B-24s, escorted by ten P-51

Mustangs and twelve P-47 Thunderbolts, returned to the takeoff point at Hsingching. Four planes landed before receiving instructions to the contrary. The others were ordered to return to their home fields. All crews had been instructed not to land with their bomb loads on board because they were Chinese-made bombs and had fuses which might be unsafe. These instructions were given because a few days earlier some of the bombs had been dropped "safe" during practice runs but had exploded when they hit the ground.

Unfortunately, several of the planes that jettisoned their bombs had dropped them on a Chinese village and six Chinese were killed. To atone for this regrettable incident, every officer in the Group and four Squadrons contributed 400CN each and every enlisted man gave 200CN to the families of the victims.

There were other tragic incidents during the month. On April 4, Capt. John Z. McBrayer of the 375th lost a leg in a plane crash at Chengkung. On the 16th, Lt. Herman F. Ridenour of the 373rd was killed in a crash near Yangkai. He had left Chabua on a ferrying mission and the plane developed engine trouble as it approached Yangkai. He ordered the eight men aboard to bail out but then had insufficient time to bail out himself.

The losses were indeed heavy. Seven crews were lost. Eight planes were downed on sea searches, two on Hump resupply flights and one on a land target mission. However, the squadrons claimed a total of 39,400 tons of shipping sunk and an additional 16,000 tons probably sunk.

One of the heaviest attacks was made against the docks and shipping at Saigon by planes of the 373rd, 375th and 425th Squadrons. In a night attack, nine of them bombed the target area but five could not find it in the smoke and darkness and elected to bomb Haiphong and the airdrome at Cat Bai. On the return, the crew of Lt. R. M. King's plane, with one engine shot out, bailed out safely; three men of the 10-man crew suffered minor injuries.

After a mission to Chabua, six B-24s were given an assignment on May 6 to bomb the Burma Road and cause land slides with thousand-pound bombs on the trip back to Chengkung. Two were able to find the road through an overcast with unobserved results while the others returned to their home base without bombing, thus converting the bombing mission into a ferry trip.

On May 11, a bombing mission was scheduled in reverse with five planes assigned to make another attack on the Burma Road while flying from

Chengkung to Chabua. This time the bombs were well-placed and the road was closed for several days. "This was considered a very successful mission," the 308th's history reports, "since it effectively interrupted the flow of supplies to the Japanese in the Salween front just as the Chinese offensive in that area was getting under way."

Other combat missions to and from Chabua were flown in mid-May. The targets were Mangshih, Tengchung, and Lungling, all with good results. It was on a May 19 sea search mission that a plane was lost during an attack on a convoy in the South China Sea. Lt. Walton encountered intense fire from a destroyer when he made a run on a freighter and his plane was hit before he could drop his bombs. It was seen to hit the water and explode by the crew of another plane on the same mission that was able to damage one of the ships. There were no survivors from Walton's ten-man crew.

Sea searches on May 19 and 20 were more successful. A nine-plane mission on the 20th found a large convoy and accounted for six freighters and one destroyer sunk. However, three B-24s were shot down and crashed in the water near the convoy.

On the return flight, the crews of two more B-24s were forced to bail out but all crew members returned safely. However, everyone on Capt. Chester H. Bohart's crew was wounded; it was reported that their plane was full of holes when they left it and it was pure luck that allowed the plane to limp to the coast and over friendly territory with two engines out and a third slowly losing power. The group history tells more:

> "The plane suffered many hits from the guns on the destroyer; in addition to many holes caused by machine gun fire, what is believed to have been a five-inch shell came through the waist of the plane. The shell which hit the waist cut the rudder control cables and trim tab cables, and knocked out the interphone. The plane continued its run, despite its condition, and sank a large freighter. Gun fire from the freighter shot the nose turret doors off the plane. Immediately upon completion of the bomb run, Lt. Duffey went back to the waist and succeeded in splicing the rudder control cables. He and Sgt. Elder then busied themselves rendering first aid to the wounded. At the time all the damage was being sustained by the plane, it was flying in the midst of the enemy convoy and at an altitude of less than 200 feet. Nevertheless, the crew managed to get it back over land before it was necessary to bail out.

"Before bailing out, Sgt. Yelton's parachute was pulled and blossomed in the plane, so that it was necessary for Sgt. Elder and Lt. Duffey to re-pack it for him, but when the time came to bail out, it served its purpose.

"Sgt. Elder, after bailing out, had another remarkable experience. After jumping from 8,000 feet, he descended until very near the ground, then was caught in an updraft between two mountains. This was repeated several times, and when he finally landed, he reported that by actual timing on his wrist watch, he was in the air one hour and ten minutes."

One crew on a three-plane sea search to the Tonkin Gulf on May 26 was not so lucky. It was never heard from after takeoff. The next day, Lt. Kenneth S. Starcher and his nine-man crew were killed shortly after takeoff from Lingling in bad weather.

There were several non-battle casualties suffered that month. On May 19, a plane from the 375th Squadron, returning from Chabua lost two engines and attempted to land on a small fighter strip near Ledo. In the ensuing crash, the plane was wrecked and five of the ten men aboard were killed.

On May 25, a 373rd plane took off from Yanghai on a routine flight to Chabua. It was last sighted by another crew which had been flying in formation with it about fifteen minutes from Chabua. It had appeared to turn off course and was never seen again. Lt. Robert M. King, the pilot and eight others were killed, including Capt. Thomas H. Clare, a chaplain from the 341st Group, who was flying as a passenger.

According to the group history, "May 1944 will be remembered by the Group as a month of heavy losses, of successful sea searches, exceptional turnover of personnel, the arrival of new LAB (Low Altitude Bombing-equipped) planes with radar equipment, and perhaps, as the beginning of the Japanese drive in Central China."

While the 308th was carrying out its missions as best it could, the situation on the ground would signal a new strategy for the Fourteenth. Beginning in the spring of 1944 and continuing through most of the year, the Japanese launched Operation Ichigo. It had three major objectives: (1) denial to the Fourteenth Air Force of all bases in central and eastern China, particularly those along the Peiping-Canton-Hanoi railway corridors; (2) establishment of an overland line of communications and supply between Manchuria in the north and Indochina in the south, as a means of partially compensating for the tremendous losses being sustained in ocean shipping; and (3) over-throw of Chiang Kai-shek and withdrawal of China from the war. During these Ichigo operations, the Japanese employed large forces, concentrating them in the Yellow River bend area, in the environs of Hankow, and around Canton. Opposing Chinese armies, although superior in number, were hope-lessly outclassed in training, equipment, provisions, morale, and with one or two exceptions in leadership, and were almost totally ineffective throughout the campaign.

It was up to the Fourteenth Air Force to single-handedly take on both the Japanese air and ground forces. Although Chennault's meager forces frequently thwarted Japanese aggression schedules, they could not contain the enemy advances for the simple reason they could neither assemble suffi-cient forces nor even supply adequately those on hand.

One of the bright notes during this period for the 308th Bomb Group and other bomb groups in other theaters using B-24s was the development of radar equipment that was combined with electronic equipment called magnetic anomaly detection (MAD) to provide a new capability for the heavy bombers. Crews were selected and units called Sea-Search Squadrons were formed to test and perfect the equipment in conjunction with the highly secret Norden bomb sight. Training was conducted in using the equipment for low altitude bombing (the LAB system) and high altitude bombing which was called the H2X system. The former was installed in the then-new B-24Js for use against surface craft, usually at night; the latter was mostly used by B-17s against land targets in Europe.

The B-24s were to fly at low altitudes, considered a dangerous practice at first because of the large size of the B-24s which made them more vulner-able to defensive fire and the dependence of the electronic equipment on an adequate power supply. The risk was enhanced by flying at these low alti-tudes under cover of darkness. Although several planes might be dispatched on a mission together, they would, by necessity to avoid collision and false radar echoes, make their attacks alone, each carrying 500 lb. bombs which would be dropped from 1,000 feet or less. After experimentation, it was found that the best method of attack was to release three bombs on each bomb run.

The development of LAB equipment for the B-24s was one of the best-kept secrets of the air war and vastly improved the economy of operations. In the early part of 1944, a group of B-24s was assigned to Langley Field,

Virginia, where pilots and bombardiers underwent special training. Using specially-equipped B-24s with the plexiglass noses blacked out, the pilots and bombardiers were taught to fly at very low altitudes and bomb targets anchored in the Potomac River without seeing outside the aircraft. This was accomplished by combining the top secret Norden bombsight with a small auxiliary radarscope in the nose of each bomber. The small scope was connected to a large radarscope located in the middle of the plane. Substituting radar traces on a screen for the cross hairs of the Norden sight, runs could be made on targets at sea in total darkness.

The arrival in China of about thirty new B-24s with special radar bombing equipment was to mark a new era of bombing capability for the 308th. Lt. Col. William D. Hopson, a pilot who had flown civilian aircraft since 1929 and was a military pilot with the Arkansas National Guard since 1930, had been called to active duty as a captain in September 1940. He flew antisubmarine missions from Maine after the war began and later trained B-17 and B-24 crews in the use of the newly-developed low altitude radar bomb sight; he was considered the Air Forces' foremost expert on its use.

The first flight of about twenty LAB-equipped B-24Js arrived in China in May 1944 under Hopson's command. In addition to the installation of low altitude radio altimeters, a newly-developed drift meter that was especially reliable at low altitudes, plus the latest radar, the J models had additional gas tanks installed in their bomb bays which gave them more than fifteen hours of range if cruise control techniques were followed. Since they were to fly at extremely low altitudes, the belly turrets were removed.

It was Hopson's theory that if the B-24s would bomb at 400 feet, instead of the 1,200 feet they were bombing from initially on their sea searches, their accuracy would improve by 300 percent. Since it had never been tried before, there was much grumbling among the pilots because of the added danger of more accurate anti-aircraft fire. However, Hopson's reply was that if a ship could be hit on the first run by surprise, no second run would be necessary.

While normal bombing missions against land targets were continued through June 1944 with mixed results, it was a month of successful sea searches. The Group was just beginning to use the LAB planes with trained crews and the results achieved were gratifying; heavy losses were inflicted upon an already hard-pressed Japanese merchant marine fleet. Of the 197 combat sorties flown that month, seventy-one were search sorties which accounted for sixteen enemy vessels sunk for a total of 53,100 tons; five were probably sunk and ten were damaged. In addition, mining operations were conducted against harbors at Takao and Canton.

As the squadron bombardiers gained expertise with their radar and LAB bombing equipment and flying at night, more flights found enemy ships attempting to supply enemy forces through coastal ports. Taking off in flights of two to five planes and flying to the sea areas within 200-300 miles off the China coast where convoys were reported, they were able to locate them despite the haze, fog, and darkness. On some missions, when targets could not be found on the water, the crews were encouraged to seek and bomb land targets and harbor areas. Although fighter opposition was light to nonexistent, almost all aircraft, flying at low levels over convoys could expect antiaircraft and small arms fire from the ships.

The strategy for using the radar-equipped B-24s was to stage three or four of them from each of the four squadrons from an advance base near the city of Liuchow in the eastern part of Kwangsi Province. A detachment commander was designated to take charge of this provisional squadron.

When shipping was being reported sunk by the radar-equipped LAB Liberators at a much greater rate than the Fourteenth had ever achieved, Edward G. Menaker, one of the radar officers assigned to Group headquarters, was asked how it could be ascertained that the claims made by the crews were accurate. His reply:

"These claims were based on what the flight crews reported. Sometimes, looking out the windows of the plane, they could see the flash of the bombs exploding and possibly what type of ship they were attacking. Intelligence officers at the interrogation of the crews did their best to assess what had actually happened, trying to correlate what the crew members reported with what they were able to determine from other intelligence reports of ship movements, etc. I set about formulating standards and criteria for assessment of results.

"To do this, I met with the officers of the small Navy detachment which served as liaison with Fourteenth HQ. Our crews were already instructed in the various types of Japanese merchant and war vessels, as they were in the types of enemy aircraft. The Air Forces and Navy already classified positive results of attacks as 'sunk,' 'probably sunk' or 'damaged.'

"Now how could we tell after attacking a previously invisible target what that target was and what happened to it? We discovered fairly soon that isolated rocks in the sea gave radar reflections similar to substantial ships. So did the sails on sampans.

"Suppose the flash showed that a 500-pound had hit a ship directly. Is it sunk, probably sunk or damaged? The bombs we used had delay fuses, 2-second delay, I believe. This was to give them time to penetrate to the interior of a vessel before they exploded. The Navy people were willing to estimate the result of a hit by such a bomb on various types of ships. They also estimated that a near miss by one of those bombs would at least cause damage to any ship. Based on our collective, conservative opinions, we arrived at the following set of standards:

"1. If a target disappeared from the screen after an attack, and the radar was still working properly as indicated by the presence of other targets still showing, sea scatter (the broad indications at the shortest range of the radar scope, resulting from radar reflections from the water and waves), it was sunk.

"2. If the target suffered a hit or a near miss and was identified as of a type which would be sunk if it sustained a direct hit or a near miss, whichever was appropriate, but the plane had to leave the area after a few minutes without seeing it disappear from the screen, it was probably sunk.

"3. If the target after visual identification was one which the Navy could not be sure would be sunk by one or more such bombs – such as warships – and it did not disappear from the screen, it was counted as damaged.

"We did not communicate these standards to the flight crews. We simply had the interrogating officers, radar and intelligence people, ask the crews the pertinent questions about the nature of the target, where the bombs landed, how long they stayed in the area, what other targets they saw on radar, how long the targets remained on the screen, etc. The intelligence officer then drew the appropriate conclusions."[4]

After flying a number of missions, Hopson drew up a procedure for crews to follow which Menaker cited:

"1. If the autopilot was working, all bomb runs were to be made on autopilot. Many pilots were incensed. They believed they could fly manually better than any autopilot, and at low altitude they considered relying on the autopilot dangerous and foolhardy. Hopson responded by saying that a properly working autopilot could do a better job of holding the plane straight and level than he or any other pilot could, and it was necessary to achieve maximum accuracy.

"2. Searches would be conducted at whatever altitude was appropriate to get maximum range from the radar. Once a target at sea was determined, the pilot was to descend and make his first run at an altitude of 400 feet. He could use his own judgment about altitude, up to 2,000 feet, on subsequent runs. If he had identified the target as a war vessel, the 400-foot requirement did not apply.

"3. Our weather information was so meager we had no reliable knowledge of the barometric pressure. So to insure safety when descending so low it would be necessary to calibrate the barometric altimeter from the radio altimeter for local conditions; but was the radio altimeter reliable enough to trust the crews' lives completely to it? Therefore, we established the following procedure: Pilots were to descend to 2,000 feet as shown on the radio altimeter. That was its upper limit and still high enough to be pretty certain of not hitting the water. They were then to set the barometric altimeter to the same 2,000 feet, by changing the pressure setting.

"4.While descending to bombing altitude of 400 feet they were to let out the trailing-wire radio antenna, which was a few hundred feet long. The reel for that antenna was in the interior of the waist of the plane, and the gunner on the end of the antenna who let it out was to keep a hand on it. The weight on the end of the antenna was sure to hit the water before the plane if it descended too low because the radio altimeter had provided a wrong reading. Although I never heard of a plane having its antenna hit, going that low at night so far from home was still a risky procedure. Nevertheless many crews made all their runs at 400 feet; some went as low as 100 feet.

"This was a demanding – and hazardous – requirement, but this was the collective judgment of the responsible commanders. Everything about the operation was risky, even above the normal risks of wartime bombing operations: Airplane maintenance was carried on under primitive conditions at the end of the supply line, with everything having to be flown in over the Himalayas; weather was very changeable, with sparse data on which to base forecasts; terrain was daunting with mountains west of Kunming going up to 25,000 feet and the Kunming area itself sitting on a 6,000-foot high plateau; communications were minimal; and the threat of Japanese bombing always remained. So these additional risks seemed worthwhile in order to have the best chance of achieving the best results."[5]

The number of Hump missions by the 308th had decreased during the month of June 1944, although intra-China missions increased to provide support of the Forward Echelon at Kweilin from where most of the sea searches were now being flown. Four planes and two crews were lost in combat. Three officers were injured when their plane, returning from Chabua on a routine flight, landed without brakes and ran into a deep ditch off the end of the runway.

On June 2, three B-24 "Snoopers" departed on a search to the Yangtze River between Nanking and Hankow. The crews were instructed to use their radar equipment and bomb from a low altitude. All three planes bombed ships of different sizes and were met with heavy and light defensive machine gun fire which damaged each plane. However, T/Sgt E. F. Timme was the only crew member wounded.

An eighteen-ship formation of B-24Js, accompanied by twelve P-40s from Yunnanyi, departed Kunming on June 5th to bomb barracks and supply installations at Lashio. The target area was well-covered with bombs. The only casualties occurred when a nose gunner suffered face lacerations from falling bomb clustering bands of the plane ahead. The plexiglass on the nose and upper turrets of another plane was smashed and the gunner was injured from the same kind of debris.

On that same day, seven B-24Js returning from Chabua bombed military installations and supply dumps at Namkhan en route to their home bases in the Kunming area. Three others left the next day with the same assigned target. Much damage was seen on both flights; there was no fighter opposition.

Sea searches with the LAB equipment continued for the rest of the month. On one mission on June 9, no ship targets were sighted using the radar so the B-24 piloted by Lt. L. H. Abbott climbed to 2,000 feet and bombed the docks at Swatow by radar. No fighter opposition was observed on these flights and it was clear that the enemy never realized that the B-24s could use radar to bomb targets in almost total darkness.

One mission to the Yangtze River ended in tragedy for its pilot, Lt. William H. Wallace. Finding no shipping, he tried to return to Kweilin but was unable to land there because of weather and tried to reach Kunming. The plane ran out of gas and the crew had to jump. Wallace was killed on the bailout; the other seven men made it without injury.

There was more tragedy on June 13 when Lt. Swett, after refueling at Suichwan, took off shortly before midnight for a sea search to the Upper Yangtze Valley. The plane struck a mountaintop soon after takeoff but did not crash at that time; Swett turned back to the field but the plane was so badly damaged that it could not be landed safely. The crew bailed out; Flight Officer F. S. Brock and S/Sgt W. A. Buckman were killed in the jump.

Three other planes were dispatched to Canton Harbor, the Formosa Straits and the Lower Yangtze Valley sighted and sank one freighter and damaged two others.

With their longer reach and radar capability, the B-24Js were scheduled for more sea sweep missions. However, on June 15 and 18, 24J models from all four squadrons were sent to Canton and Yochow to bomb storage and supply areas, railroad shops and an arms factory at night. The results were mildly favorable and there was no fighter opposition. On the latter mission to Yochow, one plane crashed twenty-five miles west of Chanyi because of failure of two engines. Lt. Pat Moeller and the crew of *Impatient Virgin* bailed out successfully with only minor injuries.

Lt. Clarence L. MacDonald, bombardier, told what happened in a letter to his parents. It was typical of many bailout stories:

"About an hour out from our home base, No. 3 engine ran away. It made an awful noise. [Lt. Myron A.] Currie, the navigator, looked at me and I looked at him and simultaneously we reached down and fastened the leg straps on our parachutes. The engineer came down to the nose and said we were going back. So Currie and I went back to the flight deck. Pat and Neal were struggling with the controls to keep the *Virgin* in the air, but we were losing 500 feet a minute. Pat gave the order to salvo the bombs and throw everything out possible to lighten the ship, but it was to no avail. Soon [Sgt. Charles] McCarty, the engineer, turned around from his position between the pilots and said, to [Sgt. Martin] Rintz the radio operator, 'Radio in our position and hit the silk.' 'Hit the silk.' What a saying! It sure sunk in.

"I leaned down and opened the bomb bay doors. I turned around to see Currie falling from the plane. My thought at the time was I wanted to land near him, for he was the navigator. So, without a minute's hesitation I stepped onto the six-inch catwalk, paused a second and jumped for the ground. Luckily for us the ground was visible, for we had been flying through a warm front. (Front-heavy clouds with rain.) As I fell through space I turned about 10 somersaults, straightened out my body to stop the somersaults and pulled the ripcord. At first the chute didn't open and I tore at it with my hands and finally the silk blossomed out and gave me the jolt of my life. But now I was floating along very easily, drifting earthwards. I looked around me and saw three chutes below me. I looked back up and saw the old *Impatient Virgin* flying along. It didn't dawn on me until about three minutes later what I had actually done. Soon the ground appeared close to me. I remembered now, I have to keep my feet together and roll when I land in order to absorb the shock. But just as I was about to hit the ground, my chute side-stepped and threw me in sideways and sprained my right ankle.

"As soon as I hit, I called out for Currie and found him right away. My ankle was awfully sore and made walking very hard. Soon we found [Sgt. Lauren] Rittenour, tail gunner, and the three of us started out towards the plane which had cracked up. We hadn't gotten very far before it turned dark. We got into a rice paddy which was surrounded on three sides by an eight-foot ditch and it had water in the bottom of it. I couldn't make it across the ditch and it was too dark to see anything and we had no flashlight. So all we could do was sit down and wait for dawn. So we did and no sooner had we sat down than it started to rain. It rained all night and we got soaked. We had two chutes with us and we pulled them over us but it was to no avail. In about five minutes we were sitting in four inches of water. We just sat there. The three of us huddled up close together to keep warm but we couldn't keep from getting cold. So we shivered all night. Nine hours we sat out there in the darkness and rain waiting for dawn. Being dark, I couldn't read my Bible like I wanted to, but I said over verses of Scripture and sang a few hymns to myself. At last dawn came.

"My ankle was so swollen that I couldn't walk on it. Currie and Rittenour had to drag me. At first we sank into mud over our shoes. I never saw such mire in all my life. It was awful. Then we finally sighted a Chinese village. The only way to get there was to wade a small creek. The water came up to our waists. So wade it we did. When we arrived at the village I made signs that I was cold and wanted to go to a fire. So they took me inside and built a fire right in the middle of the floor. This sure felt good. I took off the biggest part of the wet clothes. The reason I say the biggest part of the wet clothes is because the whole village of men and women were all crowded in one room to look at us. So, of course, with the women around I was rather bashful. But anyway I got most of the clothes dry and had one of the little kids wash out my socks and wash off my shoes. I had a couple of pieces of Chinese peanut brittle in my pocket and I passed these out to the little kids and they sure enjoyed it. Then I asked for hot water and put some applications on my ankle which made it feel a lot better.

"Then they brought us some eggs and we had them hard-boiled, and, boy, they sure did taste good. They sure treated us swell. They had never seen a gun or wrist watch. These things fascinated them. They couldn't understand how we got there at all and we had an awful time explaining.

"Soon we started out for the 'fye' which is the word for airplane in Chinese. As we asked the direction they showed us, we started out. They started jabbering in Chinese and didn't want us to leave and we couldn't understand why. But we soon found out. Neal [Phelan], the co-pilot, was there and had slept in the village all night. He had been out looking for us. So the four of us started out for a four-mile hike to the plane. I had an old Chinese fellow helping me up the mountain and he wasn't satisfied unless I was putting all of my weight on him. He was certainly a big help. All this time we were without water.

"At long last the plane came into view, or at least what was left of it. That plane was scattered over twenty acres. There was scarcely a piece left that was bigger than two square feet in size. It must have hit the ground at about 300 mph and really blew sky high. When we arrived, Pat and all the rest of the boys were there as was also a Lt. Miller of the Air Service command, and a Lt. Lee, a Chinese doctor. We were most glad to see them.

"They brought a jeep to within two miles of the plane. I rode in an ox cart for those two miles and then got into the jeep. All this time the Chinese who had been helping me was walking alongside of the cart and keeping the flies off me with a tree branch. I gave him a thousand dollars (Chinese money) and, boy, was he happy!

"So we got into the jeep and drove over some roads that were practically impossible to get over. We had to ford rivers and lakes and upon approaching the middle of one lake which had a road under the water, we came to a place in the road that was washed away. We nearly capsized the jeep and had to leave it there and go to another one not very far away. Of course, this necessitated some more wading with a sore ankle.

"When I think of some of the mountains this Lt. Miller navigated in a jeep and at night, I don't see how he ever found us. But he had us in about fifteen hours. I can't describe the places he had to come through to get us. It was awful. And he did it at night. He left a party they were having to come get us.

"Finally we arrived at the ambulance and it sure was a welcome sight. We all piled in and in about an hour we were at the base hospital. The doctor looked at my foot and said he thought that no bones were broken but it was a very bad sprain. He said he thought Rintz had a broken bone in his foot and put a cast on it and said he was sending us to the hospital at our home base and we were to have X-rays made as soon as possible. So the next day a B-25, belonging to a general, was up after us and we were on our way back home. The bath we finally got at the air base was the most wonderful one I have ever had.

"Upon arriving at our home base, X-rays showed I had a broken ankle and Rintz had the sprain."

On June 18, 1944, Japanese ground forces captured Changsha, a major rail center that was an en route stop on the way to Fourteenth installations in eastern China. Before the end of the month they had reached Hengyang which the Chinese were determined to hold. As preparations were being made to defend the city, Vice President Henry Wallace arrived in China on June 20th to survey the China situation for the president. As a result of his visit and meetings with Chennault and Chiang, Wallace took with him to Washington a revised edition of Chennault's plan to defeat the Japanese by the end of the year, provided he received the supplies and reinforcements he needed. The result was not what either Chiang or Chennault had hoped. On July 4, the Joint Chiefs of Staff rendered a strange statement to refute Chennault's plan in their reply to the president about Chennault's ideas:

> "Our experience against both the Germans and Japanese in theaters where we have had immensely superior air power has demonstrated the inability of air forces alone to prevent the movement of trained and determined ground armies. If we have been unable to stop the movement of ground armies in Italy with our tremendous air power, there is little reason to believe that Chennault, with the comparatively small air force that can be supported in China, can exert a decisive effect on Japanese ground forces in China. The more effective his bombing of their shipping...the more determined will be the Japanese thrusts in China."

What the JCS was referring to was Chennault's insistence on scheduling missions for the B-24s which were paying off with success by the attacks on ships supplying the occupying enemy army. To prove his point, sea sweeps were scheduled during the rest of June to show the growing capability of the 308th to destroy enemy shipping.

Fourteen sweeps during the final days of June resulted in a large number of ships sunk and damaged. Mine-laying missions to the harbors at Takao on Formosa and Hong Kong were also successful. On the Hong Kong missions, two-language leaflets were dropped by the B-24s which said:

> "This leaflet is dropped by aircraft of the United Nations.
>
> "Every day now, more and more planes will fly over Japanese-occupied countries wreaking vengeance on the Japanese invaders. We are getting stronger every day. Already the Japs are retreating in the Solomons, New Guinea, and the South Seas. We are destroying their planes and sinking their ships. Five of their aircraft carriers are at the bottom of the sea; their names are *Kaga, Akagi, Hiryu, Soryu, Ryukaku.* The Allied air force in China grows more deadly every day. The United Nations will never forget the sufferings you have endured, the rape of your womenfolk, the loss of your houses, the confiscation of your goods, and the humiliations forced upon you by Japanese beasts.
>
> "But keep your spirits up; side by side with your brothers of the

Chinese Army, we shall come back to Hong Kong."

Many of the sea searches were launched from Erh Tong for night missions using the LAB equipment. The mission of June 18 accounted for the only loss. A B-24 "Snooper" piloted by Lt. Col. A. Pohan took off from Erh Tong for a Yangtze River search from Yochow to Hankow. No contact was ever made after takeoff and the crew was reported missing.

Other sea searches that month encountered heavy anti-aircraft fire but no aircraft were damaged severely. A single B-24 of the 425th Squadron, piloted by Lt. Jay E. Levan, operating from Liuchow on a sea search, encountered a huge blip on the radar screen. The bombardier, Lt. John D. Shytle, triggered off two 1,000-bombs on what turned out to be a large cruiser. Probably thinking that the bombers couldn't see them in the darkness, it was cruising with lights out. After the bombs exploded, the cruiser lit up with heavy anti-aircraft fire. Levan made two more bomb runs at low altitude and then pulled away to watch while the ship caught fire. Levan queried his crew: should they try one more run? It was decided to do so because the ship was so big. But just as they lined up for the fourth attack, the huge vessel rolled over and sank.

A bombing mission to Hankow on June 24 by twenty B-24s, while very successful in bombing docks and shipping in the harbor, resulted in the loss of a B-24 from the 324th Squadron piloted by Lt. Henry Portyrata. Although there was no fighter opposition, intense anti-aircraft fire was encountered which may have caused the loss of the plane and the six-man crew. A second attack on Hankow took place on June 26 and many fires were started that could be seen eighty miles away; large secondary explosions were reported by ground observers.

By mid-year, Allied advances had been made in all theaters. On June 6, 1944, the invasion of the European continent had begun. General Hap Arnold attended a Combined Chiefs of Staff meeting in London at that time to discuss the progress of the war in France, Italy, Burma, the Southwest Pacific, the Pacific, China, and Russia. One of the subjects brought up was the increase in traffic over the Hump in China. The Air Transport Command had transported 11,000 tons during June and it seemed that 14,000 tons would be possible in July.

In his memoirs, Arnold commented: "We discussed future operations in North Burma; also, cargo-plane requirements for the British troops near

Imphal. All these problems were much easier to solve than they would have been six months or a year before, because we were getting real airplane production now; in fact most of the theaters were becoming saturated, and the demands for airplanes were being met everywhere."[6]

While that may have been so in other theaters, Chennault did not see the significant increase in the tonnage he received. By the summer of 1944, the Japanese massive land offensive to divide China in two and subjugate each part separately with thousands of troops, reached its full fury. Bent on a war of devastation and plunder, they burned entire villages and murdered the fleeing men, women, and children. The basic objective was to overrun the forward bases of the Fourteenth with ground troops.

In May, a squadron of B-25s based at Liangshan had to evacuate; by July 1, the base at Hengyang was abandoned. As Chennault noted in his memoirs, "During the battle of Hengyang in the summer of 1944, the Sino-American combination was well on the way toward another disastrous defeat from lack of supplies. The Japanese were never able to take an American air base in China so long as air and ground forces had sufficient supplies to keep fighting."[7]

As the days progressed, it was clear that the Japanese seemed to be achieving their objectives. The official Air Force history relates the situation as it was in July 1944:

> "Moving southward in at least six distinct lines of attack the Japanese refused to pile up before fixed points of resistance, by-passing each prepared position of the Chinese and leaving only enough strength behind to contain the defending garrisons. They used almost every conceivable means of transportation in their advance, and their speed and tactics tended to throw the defenders into a panic. Within a few days the various penetrations had consolidated into three main drives, one directly southward from Yochow toward Changsha, and one on each side, directed at points south of Changsha on the Hsiang River.
>
> "As the summer approached, it was all too evident that a crucial battle was at hand, a battle upon whose outcome hung the future of air operations in east China."[8]

Chapter 6

JULY TO
DECEMBER 1944

The Japanese Ichigo offensive was in three phases: (1) the Honan-campaign between April and June 1944; (2) Hunan campaign from May to August, and (3) the drive to Liuchow from September to November. Hengyang fell in August and by early November, the remaining Fourteenth bases, including the ones at Kweilin and Liuchow, had fallen. Despite the loss of bases, Chennault's small force of fighters and bombers had taken a heavy toll of troops and supplies, but they could only delay, not defeat, the enemy. The toll, however, was sufficiently high to make the Japanese victory a hollow one and forestall the possibility of drives on Kunming and Chungking.

Japanese commanders after the war attributed at least 75 percent of the total resistance in China to the Fourteenth Air Force, which in 1944 received monthly supplies adequate to support less than one infantry division. While the nimble fighters flew most of the sorties between May and December 1944, the 308th's B-24s flew as much of their share as possible, despite the shortage of fuel and bombs.

Beginning in the spring until the end of 1944, the ground strategy for the Japanese had been clearly defined. They were driving west from Canton and southwest into Indo-China and had severed East China from West China with consequent isolation of East China bases at Hengyang, Lingling, Kweilin, Luvchow, and Nanning, and thus establishing a continuous line of communication and supply from French Indo-China to North China.

Despite the setbacks to his own strategic plans, Chennault was determined to continue his attacks on the enemy's supply lines while they advanced toward Hengyang during the summer of 1944. Despite the overwhelming numbers of the enemy, the Chinese put up a fierce resistance because of the city's strategic location along the Hankow-Hanoi axis along the main line of communication between Indo-China and Japanese-occupied China. Control of Hengyang was essential to the Japanese if they were to continue to sustain their armies in China. The battle for Hengyang became one of the major confrontations between the opposing Chinese and Japanese ground forces during the war.

The Japanese began their attack on Hengyang on June 28, only about a week after capturing Changsha. Chennault called on his fighters and bombers to stem the invading tide.

During July 1944, the 308th flew a total of twenty-six missions. Unfortunately, almost all of the Fourteenth's aircraft had to be grounded between the 12th and 24th because of a fuel shortage. However, thirteen of the missions attacked ground targets, eleven were sea searches, and two were laid mines. A total of 12,300 tons of shipping were claimed sunk, plus a 350-foot light cruiser; a 75-foot submarine was probably sunk. The attacks on ground targets, with one exception, were made in an effort to give air support to Chinese ground troops aligned against the Japanese offensive south of the Tungting Lake area. Those missions included attacks on Sinshih, Palachi airdrome, two on Yochow, two in the Canton area, two on Wuchang and four on Changsha, which only a few weeks before had been an Allied base. The single mission not directly connected with the Japanese offensive was an attack on Samah Bay which was being used extensively by the enemy in their shipping between the Empire Islands and the Philippines and Dutch Indies.

The 308th's mine-laying missions, both to the Canton area, were also calculated to impede the movement of supplies to the Japanese forces threatening to move north from the Canton-Hong Kong area to join up with the column moving south from Changsha and Hengyang.

During the month, the Group's Forward Echelon moved from Kweilin to Liuchow in order to make more room at Kweilin for fighter planes needed to stall the advance of the Japanese. This move proved to be a decided advantage to the Group since the longer runway and better approaches to the field at Liuchow made it possible to take off on sea sweeps with heavier bomb loads.

On the plus side of the ledger for the Group during July, more than 827,000 lbs. of bombs were dropped on land targets and three enemy aircraft were destroyed, with one probable. The tonnage sunk on sea searches, previously mentioned, was also encouraging. On the minus side, however, one B-24 was lost on land target missions and six during other operational flights. Another was lost on a sea search. Eighteen men were killed, eight injured and one was listed as missing.

It was on the evening of July 8, 1944, that the first 308th plane was lost that month. Piloted by Lt. R. P. Aldridge of the 373rd Squadron, the crew of eight had to bail out five miles from Kunming. The target was the military area near Chungshan University at Canton. Another ill-fated mission took place on July 12th. With the Paluichi Airdrome as the target, one plane each from the 373rd 374th Squadrons crashed on takeoff from Chengkung. Eleven crew members were killed; four survived but were seriously injured.

The next loss of a B-24 occurred on July 17 after a raid on Changsha with twenty-two aircraft. The crew of Lt. Bigelow had to bail out south of Mengtze on the return trip. All returned to Kunming within four days except Lt. Bigelow, who was listed as missing.

On another raid to Changsha, the crew of the plane piloted by Lt. J. P. Burkett had to bail out and did so successfully without serious injury. They returned to Kunming six days afterward. In addition, the plane with Major Horace S. Carswell, operations officer of 374th Squadron, as pilot, bailed out in the vicinity of Tsuyung when the weather closed in over the Kunming area and the plane ran out of gas.

One of the raids that month encountered more aggressive fighter opposition than on many previous missions. It was on a twenty-four-plane flight, accompanied by P-40s from Chihkiang, to bomb military stores and railroad facilities at Yochow that about fifteen enemy fighters identified as Zeros, Hamps, Oscars, and Tojos attacked as the B-24s left the target area. Three enemy fighters were observed being shot down by the escorting P-40s. Gunners of the bomb group claimed three probables.

On the morning of July 27, twenty-six B-24s departed from their bases in the Kunming area for a joint operation with B-25s and fighter cover of P-38s to bomb Samah Bay. The plan was for the B-24s to bomb from high altitude (15,000 feet), while the B-25s were to attack shipping the harbor area at low levels. Rendezvous was to be made with the B-25s and P-38s at Nanning.

The mission proceeded as planned and twenty-five B-24s bombed the target area. Apparently without any attempt at levity, the group historian recorded that the last plane of the last element also dropped about eighty beer bottles to add to the noise of the attack, intending to draw anti-aircraft and ground fire away from the B-25s. The target was well covered. Eight large fires, believed to be burning fuel, and many smaller fires were observed by departing aircraft. Columns of black smoke rose to 5,000 feet and could be seen nearly forty miles away.

Just after bombs away, the formation was attacked by ten to fifteen enemy fighters. In a running fight that lasted twenty minutes, the P-38s gave excellent protection, although the rear elements of the formation received the heaviest attacks with passes from all directions; however, the enemy fighters never pressed their attacks and no damage was received by the B-24s. Five attacking aircraft were seen to crash into the water. B-24 gunners claimed one confirmed, one probable, and one damaged.

When the radar-equipped aircraft were flight-tested and ready for bombing from extremely low altitudes, Lt. Col. Hopson volunteered to "try masthead bombing at night with an approach on instruments" and put his theories into practice on July 27, 1944. That night, he sank three enemy vessels and damaged one in four attacks without damage to his B-24. He received a commendation from General Arnold and the Distinguished Flying Cross. The citation read:

> "The success of the mission, plus the fact that no damage was sustained by the attacking aircraft, removed all crew opposition to the plan and very low altitude bombing became standard procedure with a very noticeable increase in effectiveness."

During the first month of LAB operations, an average of 90 tons of shipping was sunk per mission.

The final mission of the month was an unsuccessful sea sweep by one aircraft piloted by Lt. Stricker. On the return to Liuchow, confusing bearings were received from ground stations and the crew had to bail out near Kichang when the fuel was gone. Several crew members received minor injuries but all returned to Liuchow on August 5.

Weather in the target areas and at the home bases plagued the 308th's mission planners in August 1944. There was a sharp reduction in operations against land targets and Hump flights but there was an increase in sea searches and intra-China ferrying trips. The twenty-one sea searches during the month were particularly successful and clearly justified the continued use of low level radar. Confirmed sinkings for August totaled 69,000 tons, including the converted Italian liner *Conte Verde*, which was sunk at Shanghai in a daring single-plane moonlight attack by Lt. Col. William D. Hopson and his crew on August 8th.

On the day that Italy surrendered to the Allies, the *Conte Verde* was moored in the middle of the Whampoo River at Shanghai. The crew had scuttled it to prevent it from being used by the Japanese. The Japanese had raised it, however, and intended to convert it into a small aircraft carrier. A daylight mission, with some fifty enemy fighters and a large number of anti-aircraft batteries nearby, would have been unwise but it was an ideal mission for a LAB-equipped B-24.

The Distinguished Flying Cross that Hopson received acknowledged in the citation that "he was the pilot of a heavy bombardment aircraft that sank an 18,000 ton enemy vessel on the night of 8 August 1944. The ship was at anchor in a heavily fortified enemy harbor in China, defended by both aircraft and ground installations, and the weather at the home base was exceptionally adverse. Knowing these facts, Lt. Col. Hopson volunteered to go on this mission. The target was approached at low altitude making it difficult to recognize check points. As a result it was necessary to pass over the vessel a second time when direct hits were scored, sinking it."

In addition to the sea searches, there were five successful attacks on land targets, seven mine-laying missions, and one combination bombing and mining attack. Four aircraft, three of them in combat, and three crews were lost during the month. Twelve enemy aircraft were confirmed as destroyed and three others were believed damaged. Meanwhile, Hump flights and intra-China ferry flights continued.

One of the outstanding missions of the Group took place on August 3, 1944, when twenty-three aircraft, led by Lt. Col. Jamie Gough, commander of the 425th Squadron, flew in a group diamond formation to attack the railroad yards at Yochow. An excellent run was made from the initial point and more than thirty-one tons of bombs landed in the target area. The official mission report states: "All squadrons report that this is the most accurate concentrated bombing on a correct run that we have ever done with a full group formation."

The formation was attacked by about fifteen enemy fighters but they were not aggressive due to the protection of the escorting P-40s. The B-24 crews claimed one fighter confirmed, one probable and three damaged. Minor damage was suffered by some of the B-24s but all aircraft returned safely.

On a mine-laying mission to Victoria Harbor at Hong Kong and the estuary at Canton with nine LAB and three J model B-24s, one plane failed to return. The pilot of the nine-man crew that was lost was Lt. E. P. Mitchell. The mission report states: "Although the weather forecast was not ideal for the type of precision navigation and flying required for the exacting operation of laying mines, the mission was ordered nevertheless because this was the last night for more than two weeks that the moon would be in a position to permit the low altitude flight necessary in laying mines."

The entire crew of a 375th plane piloted by Lt. R. Bachelor bailed out near Yunnanyi after a successful twenty-three-plane mission to Changsha on August 11th. Five crew members received minor injuries on the bailout but all returned to base four days later.

There was one mission of twenty-two B-24Js against Yochow on August 14 that was aborted by all planes when a solid overcast from the ground to 15,000 ft. was reported.

When another mission was assigned to attack Yochow, twenty-four B-24s left their respective bases on the morning of August 29, rendezvoused with fighter cover at Chihkiang and proceeded to the target area. About five minutes before reaching the bomb drop point, the formation was attacked by twenty-five to thirty enemy fighters that had been alerted and were apparently waiting at altitude. One B-24 was seriously damaged and six others were slightly damaged in the ensuing melee. Flight Officer Carmichael was killed by a 20mm shell and four others were wounded. Despite the fury of the attack, the B-24s dropped their bombs anyhow. The P-40s shot down at least two of the attackers and B-24 gunners claimed eleven confirmed, two probables, and one damaged.

Lt. Swart, the pilot of the plane that was seriously crippled, was able to maintain control, although there was a fire in the right wing tank which was discovered after the plane left the target. When it was found that Sgt. McCoy had a serious bullet wound in the head, Swart elected not to have the crew throw the wounded man out with a static line attached to his ripcord before their own bailouts; he decided to attempt a landing at the home field. Sgt. Rutz gave McCoy first aid and succeeded in stopping the bleeding. When the wing fire increased in size, Swart elected to try a landing at Chihkiang. Although the nose wheel would not extend, Swart made a successful controlled crash and the rescue personnel at Chihkiang put out the fire. For his superior airmanship in bringing the plane in, Swart was recommended for the Silver Star.

There were two separate missions scheduled against Takao, Formosa, for August 31. The first was to sow mines in the Takao Harbor with four low-flying "Snoopers." This run was successful and there was no difficulty. However, on the second mission, eleven planes that were dispatched to bomb shipping after dark in the inner harbor experienced intense anti-aircraft fire; searchlights made target identification difficult but the target was well-covered and a number of ships were left burning. Smoke and fire could be seen seventy miles away. A number of enemy night fighters were encountered but their attacks were not considered particularly aggressive and they scored no hits on the surviving Liberators.

Of the eleven B-24s that participated, a plane piloted by Lt. N. B. Clendenen of the 425th and one by Lt. G. H. Pierpont of the 375th failed to return and were listed as missing.

In mid-August, a B-24 piloted by Lt. Jaye Leven, participated in a mission that made the newspapers in the States. His bomber delivered three damaging attacks that blasted a Japanese cruiser and sent it to the bottom. The time over the target area lasted one hour and forty-eight minutes. After making the three attacks, Leven asked the crew if they should make a fourth run since the target was still afloat.

"We were a little leery about making the third run," Leven recalled. "We knew how tough it is to tackle a warship. We held a hurried crew conference and decided to stick it out until something gave out – either our bombs or that ship.

"I consulted the bombardier," Leven said. "'Well, what do you think, John?' I asked."

The bombardier, Lt. John D. Shytle, who had 51,000 tons of shipping to his credit since arriving in June, responded with an eager, "Let's plaster hell out of it!"

Tech. Sgt. Harry A. Niess, one of three communications specialists aboard, chimed in: "She's sure hard to sink, but let's go after her again."

"We can't pass up a chance to sink part of the Japanese navy," said co-pilot Lt. William R. McCaffrey. The other crewmen all voted in favor but before starting the fourth run, the cruiser was seen to disappear off the radar screen. "Its sinking," Colonel William Fisher, the 308th's commanding officer, told a reporter, "was one of the finest achievements of the war. It proves what teamwork can do," he said.

During the month of August, the battle for Hengyang had continued and the city fell to the Japanese on August 8. At the beginning of September the invaders started their advance from Hengyang toward Lingling. The advance could not be delayed or halted because of the Fourteenth's inability to provide sustained air coverage for the bases at Lingling and Kweilin, the next stops along the railwayline from Hankow to Hanoi. It seemed probable that these bases would also fall next. It became the painful duty of Chennault's engineers to destroy the airfields. On September 4, the buildings at Lingling were set on fire and the runways were blown up. Ten days later, the field at Shaoyang was also destroyed.

Chennault considered the situation extremely serious but he received no sympathy from Stilwell when he asked for help in the form of supplies. Stilwell considered the situation hopeless. Instead, he wanted to reorganize China's army under his command and give them the priority for supplies. As an old soldier who had never been convinced that air power was essential to win wars, he refused to approve any increase in tonnage for Chennault's units.

Chiang Kia-shek was convinced now that Stilwell was in favor of sacrificing East China in favor of winning Burma back from the Japanese. He decided to demand that Stilwell be replaced. Sensing this, Stilwell flew to Kweilin on September 14 to inspect the situation there and remained satisfied that there was no need to apply "band-aids to open wounds" by giving Chiang additional support. He felt that Kweilin would become "another rat trap" when he learned that the Chinese were going to retire inside the city's walls. He then conferred with Chiang who remained firm in his belief that Stilwell must go. In a message to President Roosevelt, Chiang said he would "have to ask for his resignation as chief of staff of the China Theater and his relief from duty in this area."

Meanwhile, Stilwell, thoroughly convinced that the airports at Kweilin would be the next ones lost, ordered the destruction of the three fields there which were being used by the 308th. Army engineers complied during the night of September 14. They buried and detonated bombs in the taxiways while Air Force personnel burned the buildings. The need for replacement fields required the construction of new ones for the fighters and medium bombers to begin northwest and west of Kweilin.

Because of the critical need for more tonnage, Chennault's supply allocation had been increased during July but these supplies, because they had to be driven overland from the ATC bases after landing in China, would not reach the forward bases until September. Meanwhile, the Japanese had begun the march toward Lingling and there seemed little chance of halting the tide.

Unaware of the deep hostility between their leader and his superior, the men of the 308th had improved their techniques of low level attacks by the B-24s on shipping with the radar-equipped planes. Used experimentally during the previous three months, this type of low level flying "was phenomenally successful in September," according to the Group history. Thirty-two vessels totalling 104,800 tons were sunk, plus one 268 ft. destroyer. Additional shipping probably sunk included 7,500 tons of merchant freighters, plus a 400-ft. naval vessel. Mine-laying missions also continued. One aircraft and its crew were lost on the low level attacks.

Bombing of land targets continued with over one million pounds of bombs dropped in eighteen missions. Hump and intra-China flying also continued at a mild pace with over 70,000 lbs. of payload carried.

In September 1944, another new mission was assigned to a few pilots of the 308th. They were to act as "ferrets" and determine the location, quality, and extent of Japanese radar. The 375th's Lt. George E. Uthe, pilot, and Lt. Stephan J. Koss, co-pilot, with navigator Lt. Theodore Pulich, and two electronic counter-measures experts, Capt. Robert R. Perry and Lt. Claud C. Pinson, flew ten-hour missions to Yochow, Hankow, Canton, Hong Kong, and the Liuchow Peninsula. Their job was to pinpoint the locations and types of enemy radar encountered, and log their pulse strength, time of operation, and operating frequencies.

One of the unusual bombing missions of September was an assignment for all four of the 308th's squadrons to bomb bridges along the French Indo-China coast between Tourane and Haiphong. Each squadron was to bomb two railroad bridges with flights of three planes to attack each bridge. However, the 373rd's planes at Yankai were unable to take off because of weather.

The planes of the other three squadrons attacked bridges at Giap Nhat, Quang Tri and Trach. However, high hills near the bridges made low level attacks difficult. Only one of the bridges attacked had one span destroyed but all planes did considerable strafing of railroad stations, cars, and locomotives found near the bridges. All planes returned undamaged to their bases.

On the afternoon of September 11, eighteen B-24s from three squadrons departed from Kunming bases to bomb two areas in Wanling which contained extensive stores of fuel, ammunition, and other supplies together with barracks and repair facilities for motor vehicles. Seventeen planes reached the target area in javelin formation. Two squadrons of eleven planes bombed one area with about 60 percent of the bombs on the target, causing fires, secondary explosions, and many direct hits on buildings. The other squadron had difficulty locating the target area because of the cloud cover and dropped only 15 percent of its bombs directly on the assigned target area. However, they got many hits on buildings and believed much corollary damage was done.

One plane of the 425th Squadron, piloted by Lt. H. F. Weber, had to leave the formation just after the Group assembled over Kunming. Weber radioed that, for some unknown reason, he could get only about 25 inches of mercury worth of power out of his four engines. He and ten other crew members men bailed out near Yanghai with only minor injuries.

A flight of nineteen Liberators on September 15 was assigned to bomb military stores and buildings at Hengyang. However, as they proceeded on course, they ran into solid weather and the formation had to break up. The formation leader, realizing there was little likelihood that the formation could reassemble, ordered all planes to return to their bases. However, three of the planes did not hear the order to turn back and flew to the target area individually through the overcast and found the weather suitable for visual bombing. They dropped their bombs from 12,000 and 10,000 feet and had excellent results. There was one massive explosion and large fires were observed. Black and gray smoke rose from the center of the target area.

A successful sea sweep by two B-24s on this date could be called typical of this time period and the post-mission report is presented here to show what many sea sweep crews experienced on their missions:

> Two (2) B-24 Snoopers took off from Liuchow in late afternoon of 15 September 1944. Both intercepted freighters 50 miles southwest of St. John's Island and sank two (2) 200-foot vessels and one 250-foot vessel. Of these Capt. Levan in Plane No. 782 scored one visual direct hit and two near misses on the 250-footer on three runs and by radar observed it disappear in three minutes. Lt. Cashmore scored two visual direct hits on each of the 200-footers and observed them disappear in the scope from eight to thirty minutes. All three ships are confirmed

sunk. Time was approximately 1915 hours. Two additional freighters were intercepted 50 miles south of Hong Kong and sunk by both planes. Capt. Levan sank a 200-foot vessel with one visual direct hit and two near misses and watched it disappear in the scope in two minutes. Lt. Cashmore, Plane No. 788, sank a 250-foot freighter with two direct hits; saw it make a secondary explosion and burn and disappear from the scope in 15 minutes. Both vessels are confirmed sunk. Radar in both ships worked perfectly. Weather was good. All 24 bombs were expended on the five confirmed ships. Lights of Macao, Hong Kong and Kowloon were very distinct and numerous. No sweeping was done beyond the point south of Hong Kong where the ships were sunk.

Plane No. 782, Capt. Levan, crossed the coastline on course and let down to 3000 feet, picking up one blip. Two unsuccessful runs were made on it and the third was good; blip disappeared in three minutes. The second ship appeared 20 miles away which at seven miles turned out to be a target-sized blip and a small blip or sampan. Bombs straddled the vessel, with the middle bomb a direct hit. The blip disappeared in two minutes, with the sampan remaining. Bombs were dropped three in a train in each case, and no gunfire came from the ships.

The first run was made on a blip at 1843 hours, heading of 150 degrees, altitude 600 feet, boat headed 170 degrees, all bombs 100 feet short. At this point Plane No. 788 was picked up on scope as he appeared to make a run on the vessel. This later turned out to be the other plane's run on a ship eight miles to the north. A second run was made on the same vessel at 1902 hours, 260 degrees heading, ship about the same, altitude 1000 feet. Bombs dropped short on the right side about 50 feet. No damage was claimed. A third run was made at 1913 hours, 260 degrees heading, ship headed 250 degrees, altitude 1000 feet. Bombs straddled the ship; the second bomb hit just aft of midships. At six-mile range, the blip disappeared about three minutes after bombs hit. All hits were visual. The fourth run was made (21 35N-115 30E), one blip being located there. It was seen from a distance of 20 miles and at eight miles was seen to be a larger blip and a small blip or sampan. A run was made on the larger blip, a 200-ft. freighter at 2019 hours, heading of 55 degrees, ship headed 145 degrees, no gunfire. Bombs hit center and straddle of vessel. Blip disappeared in two minutes while sampan remained fast. Boats did not appear to be moving enough to make a wake and it was too dark to identify the vessel. Two other blips were seen at this time about 20 minutes away. Plane returned on same route with no further observations.

Plane No. 788 found its first blips at 18 miles distance, attacked and sank a 200-foot vessel eight miles north of Plane No. 782's first kill and another 20 miles farther east with equal success. The first boat was quite heavily loaded and looked like a Fox Tare Charley; the second did not show up well. both were hit with two direct hits each and disappeared in eight and 30 minutes respectively. Three bombs were dropped on each run at 600 feet altitude. First run was made at location (21-04N-112 08E), time 1847 hours, heading 260 degrees, boat nearly the same. One bomb was short, one on stern direct and one amidships; i.e., two visual hits. This vessel had used some sort of white signal blinker light before the bomb run, the only lights seen on this sweep. The blip disappeared from screen after circling for 30 minutes.

Ship was 200-foot freighter. A third run was made at (21 24N-114 13E), two blips being located from 12 miles away. A run was made on one, time 2019 hours, heading 250 degrees, bow to stern, bombs 50 feet to one side. No damage was claimed. A fourth run was made on the same ship, 250-foot freighter, time 2034 hours; a secondary explosion was seen, also dark smoke. In 15 minutes the blip disappeared from screen. The tail gunner saw its rounded stern and wide beam.

A sea sweep on September 16, 1944, by two planes was not so successful for one of them. After departure from Liuchow on sweeps of the South China Sea and the northern Formosa Strait, one plane claimed two vessels probably sunk while the crew encountered heavy fire from an accompanying freighter and a naval vessel. The other plane, flown by Lt. R. S. Throgmorton and a crew of six, delayed on takeoff by tire trouble, was told of the interception by the other plane and proceeded to the area. The radio operator later reported that they had found a mixed convoy of three vessels. It is assumed that the convoy was then attacked but it was the last message received from this aircraft. Other sea sweeps by Snoopers during the rest of the month were effective although a few missions netted no targets and the aircraft returned with their bomb loads.

As the number of planes available in commission increased and lucrative targets were found, the total of ship-hunting missions assigned to the

308th increased proportionately. The encounters with defensive fire from the vessels attacked also increased, although no more aircraft returned with their bomb loads.

One bombing attack on the Hankow and Wuchang warehouse areas was particularly successful during the month. On the 22nd, a group mission of twenty-four B-24s was scheduled to hit the area after dark. The formation was broken up as it approached Hankow which was enveloped in a heavy haze. Consequently, most of the planes bombed on individual runs and dropped their eggs all over the area causing many fires and explosions which could be seen as far as 100 miles away. There was no fighter interception and few searchlights were sighted during the attack.

The success of the mission against Wuchang was noted in a special report dated November 1, 1944, which was received from the Chief, Operations Division, Chinese Commission on Aeronautical Affairs:

On the night of September 22, 2130 hours, three Allied planes attacked Wuchang, dropping a great number of bombs in the vicinities of Wuchang Wang-tai, the Shang Toa Normal School for Girls, the Army Surveying School and the munitions storage to the right of the gasoline dump of the 1st Spinning Factory. Two gasoline dumps and eighteen munitions store houses were destroyed. The above mentioned places were guarded by enemy troops of the 1616th Unit.

Stored there were large quantities of important munitions and gasoline, sufficient for four months' use. It was the Central China ammo storage of the enemy. There was also a large number of newly-made shells, torpedoes, mines, land mines and bombs. More than one thousand enemy engineers were in the underground chambers putting together weapons when our planes arrived to bomb. Casualties were, therefore, very heavy. Formerly, there were five heavy caliber land mines there. Three have been destroyed and the other two exploded as the result of this bombing. Flames and reports of explosions continued until 0400 hours the following morning. All places around Hankow and Wuchang felt the tremor. Fragments of shrapnel were flying in every direction. The enemy admitted that their losses are incalculably heavy. It is also reported that five hundred enemy trucks were also destroyed by the bombing.

During the rest of the month, successful raids by the 308th against other land targets were made on the Burma Road, Fukow railroad yards, Tien Ho airport near Canton and the Samshui military storage area. On this latter attack of September 28, it was planned that twenty-six planes from all four squadron would participate; fighter support was to be given by twelve P-51s. One plane, piloted by Lt. Robert F. Hochrein of the 373rd Squadron, crashed on takeoff and the bombs exploded on impact, killing seven men and injuring three other crew members. Another plane had to abort, leaving twenty-four planes to continue the mission.

A rendezvous with fighters was made at Nanning and the formation and a very effective ruse was employed by directing the mission as if the target were to be Hong Kong, thereby drawing enemy fighters away from the real target and delaying their contact with the group by some thirty minutes or after the bombs were released. Actually, the target area was 22 miles east of Canton.

The planes made their bomb runs on headings from 320 to 340 degrees, from altitudes of 9,400 to 10,000 feet. It is believed that 60 percent of the bombs landed within the target area. Two large explosions and heavy gray smoke were observed after leaving the area.

About twenty-five minutes after leaving the target area, the escorting fighters reported nine Zeros. Two made passes from above and went through the formation. The others concentrated on the planes of the 374th, the last squadron in the formation. The P-51s prevented any concerted attacks and believe they destroyed one or two enemy planes. The formation returned to their respective bases with minor damage to three aircraft.

The largest formation of the month took off on September 30 for a raid on the Tien Ho Airport near Canton. Twenty-nine aircraft departed but extremely bad weather prevented some from finding their targets. Fourteen dropped their bombs on identifiable targets while others salvoed their bombs over enemy territory when towering thunderstorms prevented their seeing any targets of opportunity and they were running out of gas. Seven planes returned their bombs to their home bases. The official mission report summarized: "It is believed that those planes that bombed the primary target accomplished some damage, but no fires were observed and the mission was considered unsatisfactory due to weather."

Despite the occasional disappointments, the month of October 1944 found the group setting a new record for enemy naval vessels sunk. In addition, the 308th located 407 surface vessels and reported their positions to the U.S. Navy. These reports were the first evidence of an impending naval battle off the Philippines.

Enemy forces were forging south from Hankow and north from Canton at that time to overrun more U.S. airfields. It became more urgent than ever to try to stop them from being resupplied. The month also marked the beginning of day and night reconnaissance flights by the 308th conducted with full crews but without bombs. Armed sea searches also located two large Japanese task forces en route to the Philippines and three destroyers and one cruiser were sent to the bottom. On October 19, a reconnaissance of the South China Sea discovered another task force consisting of an aircraft carrier, a battleship, two cruisers and two destroyers. Still another task force was located about 400 miles from Hong Kong. These flotillas were believed heading for the Philippines where the Allied invasion had just begun. This was the first evidence of the enemy reacting to what would eventually be the enemy's loss of the Philippines to MacArthur's forces.

The statistics show that 755 sorties of all types were flown during the month, including Hump and intra-China flights, mining, bombing of land targets, and anti-shipping attacks. No enemy aircraft were shot down but five B-24s and three crews were lost. In addition, three men were killed during a bailout and three others in a crash after the rest of the crew had jumped.

It was on the second mission of October that a Liberator piloted by Lt. Bonning had difficulty on a sea sweep mission of the South China Sea and the Formosa Strait. After departing from Liuchow on October 2, the crew sighted no shipping so they attacked a secondary ground target which was the warehouse and dock area at Amoy. After the bombs were dropped, he headed for Liuchow via Kukong as briefed. However, the homing station at Kukong was not operating so Bonning took up a heading for Liuchow on top of a solid overcast. Unable to get any bearings, he tried to head for Kunming but radio failures prevented communication with any ground stations. Running low on gas, Bonning ordered the crew out. The plane crashed about 65 miles east of Chengkung. Most of the crew landed close together. Bonning and two other crew members were injured; all returned to their base five days later.

The next day another B-24 sweeping the same course and sighting no shipping also bombed Amoy and became lost trying to return to Liuchow. This crew, led by Lt. P. Destiche, also bailed out when two engines cut out from fuel starvation. However, the bodies of three men were found in the aircraft after it crashed. The report of the mission said: "At the time of the crash, they were either attempting to bail out or were trying to fasten 'chute straps. Perhaps one of them had difficulty getting a buckle fastened and the other stayed to help." It took the survivors of this crew six days to walk out. In both cases, much help was received from the Chinese who welcomed them at various stops with meals and official receptions by the townspeople.

On the next day, another B-24 crew had to salvo the bombs and bail out when the fuel could not be transferred from the bomb bay tanks.

Missions on October 5th and 9th sowing floating mines in the Yangtze River north and south of Hankow were particularly successful. Both used LAB equipment exclusively to place them precisely. The objective was to have the mines float downstream and explode when they collided with shipping.

One of the major land targets during the month was the White Cloud Airdrome at Canton. Twenty-eight B-24s, in a formation led by Major James S. "Jack" Edney, left their bases on October 15 and rendezvoused with thirty-five to forty fighters which afforded excellent protection since none of the enemy fighters attacked. The objective of the mission was to destroy enemy aircraft as they sat in a revetment area. Of those observed, seven or eight were destroyed as the bombardiers toggled off their loads from 17,000 feet. Some bombs landed short but there was much collateral damage; some fires and secondary explosions were observed.

A mission by one of two Snoopers on October 15 met with great success. One of them flown by Major Horace S. Carswell and Capt. Don Armstrong attacked a convoy and destroyed a cruiser and probably sank a destroyer. This mission is covered in detail in a later chapter.

Meanwhile, for three days, U.S. Navy carrier planes hit Formosan ports which caused the Japanese to reroute their shipping across the South China Sea to Hong Kong and Kowloon.

A high altitude raid was made on October 16 to the Kowloon docks at Hong Kong by the 308th. It was made in conjunction with a formation of B-25s that skip-bombed anchored ships. P-51s dive-bombed and P-40s flew top cover. The object of the B-24 bombing was to strike at the Kowloon docks and draw attention of the enemy fighters and anti-aircraft gunners away from the B-25s that were to go in at low levels to attack shipping in Victoria Harbor. The ruse was successful. There was heavy ack-ack over the target area but due to excellent fighter cover, no determined enemy fighter passes were made at the B-24 aircraft; however, three Liberators received minor damage from anti-aircraft fire. In one of the most precise missions of the war, 90 percent of the 308th's bombs hit the narrow target (1,000 x 3,500 feet). Many direct hits were observed on the nearby buildings, wharves, and facilities. Fifteen cargo vessels were sunk or damaged. In addition, the largest Japanese ship repair facility in the area sustained major damage.

The success of the mission was due to the exceptionally close formation "that even made me nervous and I had flown a lot of formation," Major Harvard W. Powell, then commander of the 374th, recalled. And it was the skill of Foster Davidoff, the lead bombardier, that accounted for the placing of bombs on the extremely small target area. "To him, without a doubt, goes all the credit for the bombing accuracy on that mission," Powell told the author.

The next loss of aircraft occurred that same day when Lt. Beadle and another bomber piloted by Lt. Johnson took off on the 308th's first reconnaissance mission without bombs. Beadle reported the position of a large group of ships and returned to base successfully. However, Johnson lost an engine while off the China coast and had difficulty finding his way home. The crew bailed out successfully 45 miles northeast of Liuchow and all returned to their base within three days.

Sea searches and extended-range reconnaissance flights without bombs were continued during the rest of the month. On the early morning of October 26, two B-24s took off from Liuchow on reconnaissance missions and sighted a number of ships in convoys. One large convoy appeared to be heading for the Philippines and the other to Hong Kong. That afternoon and evening, four radar-equipped B-24s took off from Liuchow to attack one of the convoys. This mission, which resulted in Major Horace S. Carswell, Jr., receiving the Medal of Honor, is described in detail in another chapter.

With enemy shipping increasing, the reconnaissance missions were proving their value. Sightings were reported to the U.S. Navy and the 308th planned for more mine-laying missions to Victoria Harbor and other port areas.

The reporting of enemy convoys by the 308th enabled the Navy to seek them out and successfully attack them with submarines. Admiral Chester W. Nimitiz, commander in chief of naval operations in the Pacific, sent a radio message from Hawaii to Chennault who relayed it to the C.O. of the

308th on November 4, 1944:

"Admiral Halsey, Commander of the Third Fleet, says: 'Please express my appreciation to Chennault for cooperative efforts of Fourteenth Air Force searchers and the value of their information.' At same time, I wish to extend my sincere thanks for outstanding cooperation by your forces on this as well as other occasions that have played important roles toward Japan's final defeat."

The official Air Force account entitled "Report on Fourteenth Air Force Activities, 4 July 1942 to 31 October 1944" summarizes the accomplishments of Chennault's air forces and the importance of the 308th's role at the end of this period as follows:

Shipping, basically important in Japanese economics was constantly attacked on the China coast and on the Yangtze and other important rivers. Hong Kong and other harbors of lesser importance were bombed. The figures in enemy shipping destroyed and damaged reached impressive totals. Laying of mines in coordination with the Navy, in enemy-controlled waters was an important feature of Fourteenth Air Force activity...

The Fourteenth Air Force opened what might be called a new front. It swept the East coast of Indo-China, the Gulf of Tonkin, the South China Sea and the East China Sea with its planes. Japanese shipping became one of its major targets. Much of the shipping between Japan and its Southern Empire has been thrust toward the China coast by mounting Allied naval power in the Pacific, and was passing through the Formosa Straits and the South China Sea. Lightnings and P-40s dive-bombed and skip-bombed transports and tankers. Mitchells concentrated on low-level skip-bombing and strafing attacks on ships anchored in harbors. They swept the coastal sea lanes with 75mm. cannon employed at deck level, and with bombs and machine guns. Liberators attacked at high level and also developed their own type of low level skip-bombing attack. This campaign against shipping caused the Japanese to resort to night shipping and in June 1944, Liberators specifically equipped for low altitude night bombing made their appearance and began to take their toll of Japanese shipping which mounted steadily in total tonnage sunk as well as in tonnage sunk per sortie. In September alone 108,700 tons of shipping were sent to the bottom with an average of 1,600 tons for every two and one-half pounds of bombs expended. By October, fighters and bombers had sunk 620,000 tons of Japanese merchant shipping and had probably sunk or damaged 520,000 tons. In addition, a total of 13 Japanese naval vessels, ranging from cruisers to gunboats were sunk and 2,419 boats under 100 feet in length destroyed.

In October 1944, the [U.S.] carrier strikes against Formosa were supported by the Fourteenth's strike against Hong Kong. Reconnaissance missions were flown for the Navy before and after the naval battles in the Philippines. Liberators of the Fourteenth were officially credited by Admiral Nimitz with first sighting the Japanese naval force steaming northeast to engage the American fleet.

River sweeps, particularly on the Yangtze, were made using bombs, cannon, bullets, and rockets. After dive-bombing and skip-bombing the larger vessels, smaller craft were then strafed. Mines were laid by planes in rivers and harbors, and later reconnaissance established the operation as successful.

Sea searches and armed reconnaissance missions of the 308th, now usually in units of two aircraft, continued in November as this seemed to be the most profitable role for the Liberators in terms of destruction of enemy targets. A change in bombing tactics was inaugurated when the direction of attack on enemy vessels was made at right angles to the longitudinal axis of a target. This was tried in an attempt to determine if success could be achieved by flying a true course from an easily located initial point with the bombardier synchronizing on the line formed by water and land in the moonlight. As the 308th historian noted, "This scheme utilizing the line of demarcation between the Yangtze River and the city of Hankow proved disastrous for Jap installations on the Hankow waterfront."

There were 643 sorties flown during the month of November. One aircraft was lost on a combat mission and four were counted as operational losses, three of them on intra-China ferrying missions. Most combat missions of the month were sea searches, armed reconnaissance searches or night strikes on convoys. During a November 9 night strike on a six-ship convoy near Hainan Island, bombs were dropped on two runs over a destroyer which was seen to sink within fifteen minutes. Minor hits were sustained on the B-24.

The right landing gear on "Chug-A-Lug" would not lock down because of damage caused by enemy fire after an April 1944 raid. Lt. Milton H. Werner of the 425th landed it without injury to the crew. (Photo courtesy Milton H. Werner)

Maintenance on the "Doodlebug" is carried out in a revetment at one of the 308th's bases in China. (Photo courtesy Hubert A. Krawczyk)

General Chennault at his desk in Kunming. He was proud of the bombing record of the 308th's squadrons and commended them for "exceptional heroism, gallantry, determination and esprit de corps demonstrated in the face of overwhelming enemy odds." (National Archives photo)

B-24s score hits on a railroad marshalling yard at Hanoi, then French Indo-China. (Photo courtesy of John S. Szymkowicz)

Above, A Liberator of the 425th drops 250-lb. bombs on an airdrome at Canton, China. (USAF photo) Below, It's "bombs away" on a target area at Hengyang, China from a B-24 of the 425th. (USAF photo)

"Shootin' Star" drops out of formation suffering from battle damage after a raid on the Samah Bay-Hainan mission of July 20, 1944. (Photo courtesy Howard H. Morgan)

The *"Battlin' Bitch"* ended its days at Tezpur, India after her nose and right landing gear were wiped out in a landing accident. The B-24 had been converted to a C-109 to haul gasoline to China. (Photo courtesy Howard H. Morgan)

Col. William P. Fisher, C.O. of the 308th from November 1943 to October 1944, cuts a birthday cake at a party given for him by the group staff. (Photo courtesy John S. Szymkowicz)

A Japanese light bomber, probably using fragmentation bombs, destroyed this B-24 and damaged three others on a base used by the 425th Squadron. Beyond runway on the hillside is the hostel and storage buildings. All were destroyed when the base was evacuated in November 1944. (Photo courtesy Donald N. Armstrong)

Controllers plot the courses of 14th Air Force fighters in the fighter control section at Kunming. Note aircraft status board in the background. (USAF photo)

Communications and operations personnel of the control section of the 312th Fighter Wing track fighters assigned to bomber escort missions or attacks against enemy targets. (USAF photo)

親愛的中國朋友們：

廣州是中國革命的策源地，沒有廣州精神就沒有新中國

可是自從日寇佔領以後，廣州人民失去了一切自由，過著

暗無天日的生活。

日寇不但奴役廣州人民，而且利用廣州飛機場、工場、

輪船、碼頭、火車、堆棧、作為侵擾中國內地的根據地和搾

取中國物資的口岸。

現在日漸強大的美國在華空軍決定隨時推毀這一切

供給日寇作戰的設備，但是大家知道凡是愛國的中國人都

是美國最好的朋友。二百年前美國人第一次來到中國就是

到廣州，所以我們決不願意傷害中國民衆。

不過，飛機在空中投彈掃射，不容易看清誰是敵人誰是

朋友，為了你們生命財產的安全，我們不得不奉告大家趕快

遠遠的避開一切上述軍事、工業和運輸的設備。

美國在華空軍敬告

堅持廣州精神！

勿與日寇鬼混！

Propaganda leaflets in Japanese were dropped on target areas in an effort to "lower Jap fighting ability by suggesting that their American opponents are men of sentiment and feeling." Note USAAF aircraft symbol at bottom of message printed on rear of drawing. (From Office of War Information files, May 1945.)

Leaflets were created and dropped to call attention of the Chinese to the blood chits worn or carried by American flyers. They were asked to assist downed American flyers and help them back to their own lines. One theme was "Who helps a friend is helped by a friend." (From Office of War Information files)

Routine maintenance was performed in revetments to reduce the chance of damage from Japanese air raids. Here three members of the 375th clean propeller domes. (L to r) Jack Safford, Ramon Miranda and Morris "Buck" Buckmiller. (Photo courtesy Howard H. Morgan)

"80 Days" cruises in formation toward a distant target with all guns manned and ready. (Photo courtesy Jeff Ethell)

The crew of the 373rd's "Zoot Chute" pose for the camera simulating an informal briefing by the pilot. Note electrically-operated nose turret on B-24J. (Photo courtesy John S. Szymkowicz)

GREETINGS FROM YOUR FRIENDS

This leaflet is dropped by aircraft of the United Nations. Every day now more and more planes will fly over Japanese-occupied countries wrecking vengeance on the Japanese invaders. We are getting stronger every day. Already the Japs are retreating in the Solomons, New Guinea and the South Seas. We are destroying their planes and sinking their ships. Five of their aircraft-carriers are at the bottom of the sea; their names are "Kaga", "Akagi", "Hiryu", "Soryu", "Ryukaku". The Allied air force in China grows more deadly every day. The United Nations will never forget the sufferings you have endured, the rape of your womenfolk, the loss of your houses, the confiscation of your goods, and the humiliations forced on you by Japanese beasts.

But keep your spirits up; side by side with your brothers of the Chinese Army, we shall come back to Hongkong.

你們的朋友向你們致意

這張紙是從同盟國飛機上投下來的。

現在盟國的飛機飛過日本佔領區，一天要比一天多，向日本侵略者報復。我們的力量一天比一天大。日本人在所羅門羣島，新幾內亞和南洋一帶，已節節敗退，他們的飛機被擊毀，船隻被擊沉。他們有五條航空母艦：——"Kaga"、"Akagi"、"Hiryu"、"Soryu"、"Ryukaku"。已被擊沉。在中國的盟國空軍實力日加維厚。盟國從未忘記你們所忍受的痛苦，你們的婦女被姦淫，你們家室被破壞，你們的財物被沒收，以及日本人給予你們的各種侮辱。

但你們要鼓起勇氣來，我們就要和中國軍隊的弟兄們並肩重來香港了。

GREETINGS FROM YOUR FRIENDS

Dear Brothers and Sisters,

We grieve that you are having such a bitter time. But keep your hearts up. Resist. Side by side with your brothers of the Chinese army, we are coming back to Hongkong.

The population and industrial power of China, Britain and America are infinitely greater than that of Japan. Japan shall never enslave and monopolise Asia.

Japan has lost the power to advance. She has been defeated in the Solomons and in New Guinea. During the month of October, for example, she lost 630 aeroplanes alone, and had huge naval losses. The Allied air power is growing relentlessly. In Russia, the Germans are dying in tens of thousands and special detachments have had to be prepared to prevent Germans from retreating.

The day of liberation is coming.

Resist the Japanese devils in every way until that day comes.

It will be a glorious day for you and a fearful one for the oppressors. Japan will crawl and grovel for mercy, and China and her Allies will be Japan's judge.

Hold on, brave comrades.

Your affectionate friends,
The Governments and Peoples of the United Nations.

你們的朋友向你們致意

親愛的兄弟姊妹：

我們的艱苦的日子非常使我們戚愛。我們希望你們能鼓起勇氣來抵抗。我們將要和中國軍隊的弟兄們並肩回到亞洲來了。

中英美的人民，中英美的工業力量比日本大得多，日本絕不能作亞洲主人，絕不能在亞洲獨霸。

日本已喪失了您的前進力。在所羅門羣島，在新幾內亞，他已完全失敗。去年十月一個月間他就損失了六百三十架飛機，海軍方面損失也很大。同盟國的空軍實力不在生長。在蘇聯，德軍的死亡以萬計，德方派員組織了特別部隊阻止德軍潰退。

解放的日期已不遠了。

你們要從各方面抵抗日本鬼子，直到解放日來臨為止。

那日是你們的光榮之日，是侵略者恐懼之日。日本將如此俯伏求饒，中國及同盟國將宰割日本。

勇敢的朋友，抵抗到底。

你們的朋友，同盟國各政府和人民上。

Morale-building leaflets in Chinese were dropped during 308th missions to inform the populace of the progress of the war. (From Office of War Information files)

GREETINGS FROM YOUR FRIENDS

Dear Chinese of Hongkong,

This message is being carried by Allied planes. They come once more with greetings and a message of admiration from the United Nations.

You are constantly in our thoughts. We know your sufferings and your courage.

We have all passed through hard days of defeat and retreat. But the tide has turned, and, side by side with your brothers of the Chinese army, we shall come back to Hongkong. Resist the Japanese devils until that terrible day for them arrives.

We have good news for you. The Australians have almost occupied the whole of New Guinea. The Americans have beaten the Japanese in the Solomons. The Chinese Army has won back the "bomb Japan" cities in Chekiang. The Allied air forces have smashed the great Kailan coal mines in Hopei Province. The British have swept Egypt of the Germans and Italians, and almost the whole of North Africa is in Allied hands. Italy talks of withdrawal from the war, and the Russians captured 51,000 prisoners in three days in their glorious advance.

Soon the Japanese will be thrown back into the sea. Be of good heart. Your descendants will remember nothing of this nightmare except the courage with which you faced it.

Goodbye — we shall bring you greetings again.

Your affectionate friends,
The Governments & Peoples of the United Nations.

你們的朋友向你們致意

留港的親愛的中國人民：

這封信是從盟國的飛機上落下來的，這是同盟國第二次向你們感敬，致意。

我們時常在想到諸君，我們知道諸君所受的苦楚，我們知道諸君的勇敢。

我們大家都經過失敗退卻的苦日子，但現在局勢已經轉變了，我們就要和中國軍隊的弟兄並肩回到香港來了。你們要抵抗日本鬼子，他們所懼怕的那一日快來了。

我們給諸君帶來好消息；澳洲軍隊差不多已將新幾內亞全部佔領，美國軍隊已把所羅門羣島的敵人打敗，中國軍隊已克復浙江各縣，可以直接轟炸日本了，盟國空軍已擊毀河北省之開灤煤礦，英軍已將德金軍逐出埃及，北非全岸差不多都在聯軍之手了，意大利有要求停戰的消息，蘇聯軍隊三日之內俘虜德軍五萬一千人，這成光榮的戰果。

不久日本人也要退歸海上。諸君應鼓起勇氣。你們的子孫肥不得今日的這場噩夢，只會記得你們的英勇。

再見，不久我們還要來向你們致意。

你們的朋友，同盟國各政府和人民上。

Ground crew of the 375th Bomb Squadron poses on and under the wings of "Georgia Peach" at Chengkung in 1944. (Photo courtesy Malcolm Rosholt)

A group mission shows Liberators of the 308th in loose formation somewhere over occupied China. (Photo courtesy Malcolm Rosholt)

This damaged P-51 Mustang, destroyed on the ground before the fighter squadrons evacuated Nanning air base, was shot full of holes by the occupying Japanese. A sign placed on it by the overconfident enemy troops, said: "This happens to all American planes that come over our bases." When the enemy left in May 1945, rejoicing Chinese ripped the sign down. (USAF photo)

General Chennault studies the latest aerial reconnaissance photos of targets on China's eastern front in early 1945. (L to r) Col. John O. Neal, 14th AF operations chief, Brig. Gen. Edgar E. Glenn, chief of staff, and Lt. Col. Joseph M. Murphy, intelligence officer, look on. (USAF photo)

Generalissimo Chiang Kai-shek and General Chennault pose for photographers when the former visited 14th Air Force headquarters in Kunming. (USAF photo)

General Joseph "Vinegar Joe" Stilwell meets informally with enlisted men in their recreation hall before he departed China. He had been ousted after a long dispute with Chennault and Chiang Kai-shek over conduct of the war. (National Archives photo)

General Chennault greets General Albert C. Wedemeyer upon the latter's arrival in China in October 1944. Wedemeyer replaced General Stilwell as top U.S. commander in the China-Burma-India theater. (U.S. Army photo)

Movie star Pat O'Brien chats with General Joseph "Vinegar Joe" Stilwell before the latter's departure from China. A number of movie celebrities visited the theater in 1944 and 1945 to entertain the troops. (National Archives photo)

Actress Jinx Falkenberg shares a laugh about her short snorter bills with Col. John G. Amstrong, 308th Group commander from October 1944 to July 1945. (Photo courtesy John S. Szymkowicz)

Dual language poster and English language newspaper announce the surrender of Germany to Chinese civilians in May 1945. Note the hanging figure of Mussolini. Illiterate Chinese depended on drawings to convey the message to them. (National Archives photo)

After receiving orders to return to the States, General Chennault was awarded an Oak Leaf Cluster to the Distinguished Service Cross by General Wedemeyer. He had just been awarded the Order of the Blue Sky and White Sun by Generalissimo Chiang Kai-shek. (National Archives photo)

The 308th group staff poses for an official photo in 1945. (L to r, front row) Major John S. Szymkowicz, S-4; Lt. Col. Hightower Smith, Operations Officer; Col. John G. Armstrong, Group C.O.; Lt. Col. William Hobson, Deputy C.O.; Major Jones C. Laughlin, Flight Surgeon. (Photo courtesy John S. Szymkowicz)

The Chinese were grateful for the assistance rendered by the Americans during World War II. This memorial to pilots and crew members killed in the war was erected and dedicated in May 1993 at Nanjin, China. (Photo courtesy Embassy of People's Republic of China)

Each year on the Saturday before Memorial Day, many former members of Chennault's 14th Air Force meet at an Arlington National Cemetery amphitheater for a memorial ceremony. Afterward, they walk to General Chennault's grave nearby to pay tribute to their leader. Here Mrs. Chennault and Senator Ted Stevens (R-Alaska), who served in the 14th, pose beside his tombstone at the 1994 pilgrimage. (Photo by C. V. Glines)

Gaunt allied prisoners of war at Aomori camp near Yokohama cheer rescuers from the U.S. Navy. U.S., British and Dutch officers and enlisted men were released on August 29, 1945. Glenn A. McConnell was one of the 308th's combat crew members who was imprisoned here briefly. (National Archives photo)

An official portrait was taken after Carswell was promoted to major in April 1943. He received the Distinguished Service Cross posthumously for a strike against a Japanese task force eleven days before his fatal mission. (Photo courtesy Peter M. Bennethum)

Horace S. Carswell, Jr. as a Flying Cadet in 1940. A graduate of Texas Christian University at Fort Worth, he was nicknamed "Stump" because he resisted opposing football players like a tree stump when they tried to plunge through his position. (Photo courtesy Peter M. Bennethum)

Carswell at his desk at a Stateside base before transferring to China with the 308th. (Photo courtesy Peter M. Bennethum)

A tired and unshaven Carswell was photographed by Lt. Col. Harvard W. Powell, 374th Squadron commander, just as he returned to the base after a bailout in July 1944. (Photo courtesy Brig. Gen. Harvard W. Powell)

On October 15, 1944, Major Carswell chose to fly with this crew of the 374th on a night mission in a B-24J. Front row, l to r: T/Sgt. Emory Lusk, aerial engineer; S/Sgt. John Nolan, nose gunner; S/Sgt. Ferney Kunkle, radio operator; S/Sgt. Reginald Leonard, tail gunner. Top row, l to r: Lt. Nolan Klepinger, bombardier; Carswell, aircraft commander; Lt. Carlos Rickertson, co-pilot; Lt. Alfred Withiam, navigator; Capt. Donald Armstrong, pilot; T/Sgt Vincent Zeyak, radar operator. (Photo courtesy Peter M. Bennethum)

THE UNITED STATES OF AMERICA

TO ALL WHO SHALL SEE THESE PRESENTS, GREETING:

THIS IS TO CERTIFY THAT
THE PRESIDENT OF THE UNITED STATES OF AMERICA
PURSUANT TO ACTS OF CONGRESS APPROVED MARCH 3,1863
AND JULY 9,1918, HAS AWARDED IN THE NAME OF CONGRESS TO

Major Horace S. Carswell, Jr., Air Corps, U.S. Army

THE MEDAL OF HONOR

FOR
CONSPICUOUS GALLANTRY AND INTREPIDITY INVOLVING
RISK OF LIFE ABOVE AND BEYOND THE CALL OF DUTY
IN ACTION WITH THE ENEMY

over the China Sea, on 26 October 1944

GIVEN UNDER MY HAND IN THE CITY OF WASHINGTON
THIS   28th   DAY OF January   1946

SECRETARY OF WAR

Certificate of the Medal of Honor awarded posthumously to Major Carswell for his final mission on October 26, 1944.

A number of missions with the radar-equipped B-24s were now being made at the request of the U.S. Navy to the Tonkin Gulf area. When armed reconnaissance missions were scheduled, the bombs were usually dropped on land targets of opportunity if no suitable water targets were located. Three naval vessels were sunk and two damaged; a total of 26,100 tons of enemy shipping was sunk with another 11,000 tons damaged during the month.

The first group mission of the month occurred on November 16 when 23 B-24s left bases in the Kunming area for an attack on the motor pool and military storage area at Changsha. P-40 fighter cover was provided but no enemy fighters were sighted. However, heavy anti-aircraft fire was encountered and four planes received minor damage.

One of the planes lost on a routine intra-theater supply flight was the *Monsoon Maiden*, piloted by Lt. Robert F. Revard, with four other crew members aboard. They departed Kunming at night for Suichwan to transport gasoline, RDX bombs and .50 caliber ammunition. The base was under attack by Japanese bombers when they arrived so the plane was redirected to Kanchow, a nearby fighter strip.

When they dragged Kanchow to check the condition of the field, they found the strip very short for a bomber with a full load of explosive materials. They were able to land the *Maiden* but had to pop the parachutes of Sgt. John Turner, flight engineer and Sgt. Ray Daniels, radio operator, out the waist window and anchored to the machine gun mounts to get more braking power on the short strip. The fighters at Kanchow, which had been out of gas, bombs and ammunitions, for over a week got back into the air and flew fifteen sorties with the load the *Maiden* and crew had brought that night.

On the return trip, the *Maiden* got lost. Although Revard and Lt. Len Gelhaus, the co-pilot, thought they knew where they were, the navigator, thinking they were near Kunming, suggested they drop down to take a look but as they descended, they immediately picked up flak. They had flown over a field, previously held by the Fourteenth but which was now the Jap-held base at Hengyang.

As they pulled up and away, Daniels tried to contact Kunming but had no luck. Sgt. Turner went back to check the equipment and found that the radio and gas lines had been hit by flak over Hengyang. A short time later they could smell gasoline and were concerned that a spark of any kind, such as their parachute snaps hitting anything and making a spark, could blow them up. The bomb bay doors were open for ventilation. From the amount of air traffic in the area, they believed they were near Kunming but there was a thick undercast. A decision had to be made. A letdown in the mountainous area surrounding Kunming without any radio guidance would be impossible.

With the gas leaking, the gauges were inaccurate and they didn't know how much fuel was left in the tanks. Revard decided the crew should bail out. Daniels was the first to jump, Turner was next, but Lt. T. Lopez, the navigator, was hesitant so Gelhaus went out, with Lopez following. Revard put the *Maiden* on autopilot and followed them out. As he started to jump, one engine quit, apparently out of gas. The *Maiden* went into a spiral, and the centrifugal force kept Revard on the catwalk. He finally shoved himself but as he dropped, the plane kept coming toward him, one time even spilling his chute. He saw it finally hit the ground and explode.

The flight could easily have turned out differently. Turner and Daniels, having used their chutes at Kanchow for braking the B-24 on the short strip, almost decided not to take new ones with them when they left. Revard insisted they do so. His order saved their lives. All five returned to Kunming after a few days of wandering. They had been led to safety by many Chinese who provided food, shelter, and guides. None would accept any payment. The Pointee-Talkee aids proved useful in getting the Chinese to understand what the Americans wanted.

A twenty-two-plane raid was made on Hankow on November 22nd which was considered successful. No enemy fighters rose to intercept the formation and ack-ack fire was ineffective. Two days later, Hankow was attacked again by a large formation from all four squadrons of the 308th. Again, the attack was successful. There were many secondary explosions which lasted for some time; smoke and flames rose to 3,000 feet and were visible for seventy miles after the planes left the target area. The flashes from secondary explosions could be seen as far away as forty miles.

During this period, more leaflets were dropped on Hong Kong to build up the morale of the citizenry. Here's what one of them said in English and Chinese:

GREETINGS FROM YOUR FRIENDS

Dear Brothers and Sisters,
We grieve that you are having such a bitter time. But keep your

hearts up. Resist. Side by side with your brothers of the Chinese army, we are coming back to Hong Kong.

The population and industrial power of China, Britain and America are infinitely greater than that of Japan. Japan shall never enslave and monopolize Asia.

Japan has lost the power to advance. She has been defeated in the Solomons and in New Guinea. During the month of October, for example, she lost 630 aeroplanes alone, and huge naval losses. The Allied air power is growing relentlessly. In Russia, the Germans are dying in tens of thousands and special detachments have had to be prepared to prevent the Germans from retreating.

The day of liberation is coming.

Resist the Japanese devils in every way until the day comes.

It will be a glorious day for you and a fearful one for the oppressors. Japan will crawl and grovel for mercy, and China and her Allies will be Japan's judge.

Hold on, brave comrades.

Your affectionate friends,

The Government and Peoples
of the United Nations

The second non-combat loss of the month occurred on a supply run between Suichwan and Chengkung on November 26. Lt. Stanley F. Marek, four crewmen, and two passengers were forced to bail out when they became lost and ran out of fuel near Hsingi, about forty miles east of Kumning. All reached the ground safely except Marek who sustained fractured ribs. They returned to Chengkung on December 4.

Group bombing missions against the Gia Lam railroad yards at Hanoi were flown on November 27 and 28, both escorted by P-51s. In both cases, the bombing was accomplished by squadrons against an extremely narrow target 700 feet wide. The lead bombardier aimed for deflection and range, with the second and third squadron bombardiers aiming for range only. The target was completely covered on both raids. No fighters came up to intercept but antiaircraft fire was heavy with concentration on the squadron that came closest to flying over the target area on the second day as it had on the first. Although several planes were hit with shrapnel, there were no casualties on either raid. Many secondary explosions and fires were observed as the planes left the area.

During the final month of 1944, the 308th continued to coordinate its missions with the Navy. Routine reconnaissance and mining activities were carried out in addition to land bombing and strike assignments. As in the previous month, Hankow was the priority target and the warehouse and waterfront areas were hit strongly.

There were 609 sorties flown during the month with an increased tonnage scored against enemy shipping. Nearly 38,000 tons of merchant ships were sent to the bottom and an additional 22,600 tons damaged. Two aircraft were lost on a combat mission and three more on non-combat flights.

One of the land targets assigned during the month was a railroad bridge at Pengpu which was attacked on December 3. Five planes left Liliang and all found the target. Four bombed the bridge with one direct hit on a span.

Another aircraft loss occurred during a twenty-five-plane group raid in December against the warehouse and waterfront area of Hankow on December 10. The plane piloted by Lt. Erving E. Beltz was last heard from by other planes in the group when he radioed to say one engine was shot out and he planned to land at Chihkiang. However, the crew had to bail out before reaching the field; two men were injured.

Unlike other missions against Hankow, this group raid was made in the dark of the moon. However, pathfinder planes carrying incendiaries and using radar as a navigational aid were able to light up the target sufficiently for other planes to synchronize their drops. Fifty-five tons of bombs were unloaded from altitudes of 7,000 to 9,000 feet. The target was well-covered; many fires were started and there were many secondary explosions.

On the morning of December 17, nine B-24s took off from Liliang to attack naval shipping that had been sighted in the inner harbor at Cam Ranh Bay by a B-24 reconnaissance on the day before. The attack was in elements of two and three planes each, there being a time interval of about one hour between attacks. One plane turned back due to mechanical trouble; of the remaining eight, three attacked twelve vessels which were variously described as large merchant vessels or naval ships which could have included battleships and cruisers. No hits were scored on the ships by any of the planes; several planes dropped their bombs on a military camp and warehouse area with unobserved results. The after-mission report said tersely: "The mission was unsatisfactory due to weather."

One combat loss occurred during a sea sweep of the South China Sea and Formosa on December 18. The aircraft departed Suichwan but was not heard from after takeoff. No trace was ever found of the plane or its ten-man crew.

Enemy attacks over a target area were always expected but during this period the Japanese were also attacking American bases. On the night before Christmas 1944, the *Time Will Tell*, piloted by Lt. Mitchell J. Salares, was assigned with two other aircraft to ferry gas from Kunming to Suichwan, an advanced base for the B-25s. Leland Miles, the crew's navigator, tells what happened as they approached Suichwan:

"It was a solid undercast all the way and when we arrived over the field, each ship peeled off in turn and dropped beneath the undercast. As we came out we recognized the river on which the field was situated and started to home in over the runway with our radio compass. We flew beyond the river for ten minutes and began to suspect the radio compass was wrong. We turned around, switched on our emergency IFF and were soon told by the ground station that we were 35 miles northeast of the field and to fly a course of 200 degrees. Since we were already flying 180 degrees, we had only to alter the heading slightly to come over the field.

"From the experience, we learned two valuable lessons. First the Japs had their own radio station a short distance north of Suichwan with a frequency only 2 kilocycles off our own. We had been homing on a Jap beacon and had we continued to home on it we would probably have run into a trap of flak or fighters or both.

"Second, we learned that the advanced base had a remarkable radar plotting outfit which locate you and give you a heading very quickly.

"Since we wanted to get back in time for the Christmas program, we cheated a little and saved time by cutting south of Chanyi. Our ETA was 2120 and we came between the Kunming and Chengkung light beacons a minute or two later. Mitch [Salares] cleared to the tower and we turned on our downwind leg. Merle [Peck, the co-pilot] got set to lower the landing gear. Suddenly, as if a giant had rubbed them out with a single sweep, every light winked out, and all that was left was the outline of the lake and a long, light patch that was the runway. We circled for 45 minutes until the gas gauges read less than 100 gallons. Chris [T/Sgt Jack J.

Christenson, radio operator] had been hounding the radio station to give us permission to land, and now he told them we would have to land or else. They replied that a "three ball" alert was in progress, and that Jap planes were suspected circling in the vicinity waiting for a chance to strike. They finished their message with some very heartwarming words: 'Fly one mile south of runway. In exactly three and one-half minutes we will flash on runway lights to give you a chance to line up and come in.'

"Sure enough, magically the lights came on. We banked into our final approach and started dropping toward the runway. The runway lights went off. Salares quickly switched on his landing lights. The runway lights blinked on once more just before we hit. We rolled down the runway, brakes squealing, swung onto a taxi strip, and cut the engines. [S/Sgt. George P.] Clark, with whom I had landed in the plane, and I were out of the plane before the last props stopped turning. Salares, Peck, Christenson and [T/Sgt. Stanley R.] Rudisell were already over two hills and into a slit trench.

"We discovered next morning only 80 gallons of gas remained in our tanks when we landed. That was enough for perhaps an hour and a half of flying."

One of the contentious issues Chennault faced in the final weeks of 1944 occurred when he tangled with Major General Curtis E. LeMay, chief of the Twentieth Air Force, who was sending his B-29 Superfortresses against strategic targets in Japan. For months, Chennault had wanted an all-out incendiary raid against Hankow, the largest Japanese supply base in China, using the B-29s in conjunction with Chennault's B-24s, B-25s, and fighters. LeMay balked because he thought Chennault's B-24s could do the job by themselves. General Arnold, who maintained control from Washington over LeMay's missions, supported LeMay but General Wedemeyer intervened and asked for one full-scale attack to be authorized on Hankow. His request was approved by the Joint Chiefs of Staff in the Pentagon.

On December 18, eighty-four B-29s dropped fire bombs from above 20,000 feet on Hankow, reducing most of the city to charred rubble. Thirty-three of the 308th's B-24s, in the largest group mission it ever flew, targeted the airdromes in the area, while the B-25s dropped fragmentation bombs and strafed at low levels. After the B-29s struck, the smoke was so thick the B-25s had to fly on instruments. Chennault's P-40s and P-51s, flying top cover, shot down sixty-four enemy fighters.

The results of the Fourteenth's attack were considered uncertain because the targets could not be identified by photo analysts through the smoke, although much damage was wrought among the barracks and administrative buildings south and east of the intended target area. There was no damage to any B-24s and all landed safely at their respective bases.

Nevertheless, this combined raid had been an historic mission for the theater, with more than 200 planes in the air at one time. Fires in Hankow were said to have burned for more than three days. Chennault said the raid was so devastating that it "destroyed Hankow as a major base." But the raid was to represent more than the destruction of these particular military targets. It proved the value of incendiary attacks against the flimsy wood, fire-prone structures that were typical of the cities of the Orient. Even though he had been reluctant to schedule such a mission, General LeMay did not forget the damage his Superfortresses had inflicted. He wrote in his memoirs that the fire-bombing of Hankow was instrumental in his later deciding to use low-level fire bomb attacks on Japanese homeland cities.

The final mission of 1944 for the 308th was a four-plane Snooper strike on December 31 over the waters of the Tonkin Gulf and the South China Sea in the Hainan area. One plane had to turn back early and another crashed. It was last heard from after reporting its position fifty miles from Kunming. The other two aircraft attacked vessels and claimed one sunk and one probably sunk.

Next to maintaining air superiority over China, which was a requisite for any of his bombing operations, General Chennault made Japanese shipping the primary target for the Fourteenth Air Force throughout the rest of the war. He explained his thinking at the time:

"From our China bases we flanked two of Japan's critical watery arteries through which economic lifeblood flowed to the Empire – first, the Yangtze, key to all Japanese supply in China; and second, the Formosa Straits and the South China Sea, through which raw materials of the conquered territories flowed to Japan. Two prime sources of high grade iron ore, Shihweiyao on the Yangtze and Hainan Island, were within range of our fighters and medium bombers. Fighters and cannon-carrying B-25s swept the Yangtze from Nanking to Ichang, destroying shipping from sampans to ocean-going freighters. The Yangtze was mined with sonic, magnetic, and floating mines until the river was closed to metal ships above Nanking. Two B-25 squadrons in East China, by refueling at Suichwan, could sweep across the Formosa Straits and far out into the South China Sea, skip-bombing the tankers and freighters carrying oil, bauxite, coal, lead, manganese, and rice to Japan.

"One detachment of the 308th was based at Kweilin and Liuchow to fly long-range sea search missions as far as the Philippines and locate shipping for Navy submarine strikes. These Liberators knocked out enemy radar stations in the Pescadores and Pratas Island, dueled with four-engine flying boats on antisubmarine patrol off Formosa, and mined the harbors of Formosa and the China coast. The entire strength of the 308th was thrown against the Hong Kong-Canton port areas. B-25s from Yunnan bases swept the Tonkin Gulf and pounded the Hainan iron-loading ports of Bakli and Samah Bay. Despite increasingly bad weather we struck 78,000 tons of enemy shipping in January 1944 and certainly sank 56,900 tons. In February we hit 100,000 tons and sank 65,000 tons. This was at a time when total Japanese shipping losses in the Pacific were averaging 175,000 tons a month. With our tiny force we were accounting for nearly one-third of the total bag of Japanese shipping.

"I was so optimistic over these dividends on our minute ivestment that I wrote the President again and boosted my promise of Trident. I assured him that if we ever actually received our long-promised 10,000 Hump tons per month, I would now guarantee we would sink between 175,000 and 200,000 tons a month instead of the 150,000 tons I had promised in Washington."[1]

While the haggling about the future conduct of the war in China continued at the highest U.S. levels, the Japanese dedicated thousands of troops to subjugating all of East China in accordance with their Ichigo plan. Liuchow was the first major Fourteenth base to go. It was evacuated on November 10. The other forward bases that were overrun included Hengyang, Kweilin, and Nanning. These were followed by the loss of Suichwan and advance fields at Kanchow, Namyung, and Kulong. At the end of the month, it was thought that the next city to be overrun would be Kweiyang, followed by Kunming.

Chennault's plea for increased tonnage still went unheeded in India. Stilwell continued to insist on having command of the Chinese armies, including the Communists, and giving them priority for supplies. While Chiang Kai-shek was willing to have an American commander in China, as far as he was concerned, it could be almost anyone except Stilwell.

President Roosevelt had sent a letter to Chiang saying he was promoting Stilwell to four-star rank and recommended "for your must urgent consideration that you recall him from Burma and place him directly under you in command of all Chinese and American forces and that you charge him with full responsibility and authority for the coordination and direction of the operations required to stem the tide of the enemy's advances."

On August 6, 1944, Stilwell was promoted to full general. The promotion did not impress Chiang and he was adamant: no matter how many stars Stilwell wore, he would still have to go. President Roosevelt finally gave in and decided on October 18, 1944, to have him recalled. He was replaced by Lt. Gen. Albert C. Wedemeyer, then on Lord Mountbatten's staff, who would have command of all U.S. troops in China. That is, all except the Fourteenth Air Force, much to Chennault's relief.

Wedemeyer was an excellent choice who found it possible to deal with the Chinese and was able to begin to create a Chinese army equipped with American arms and supplies. When he took over the American forces in China, the Fourteenth Air Force had a personnel strength of 17,473 men. There were 535 fighters, 109 medium bombers and 47 heavy bombers – the B-24s of the 308th – in the inventory. There were thirty-six combat squadrons which had been organized into two composite wings, a Chinese-American Composite Wing (CACW), and a fighter wing with two groups. Their respective assignments were divided into support of the Hump route and southwest China; support of Chinese ground forces along the Hankow-Canton railroad; the combat area of Central China; and the interdiction of railroads of North and East China. The 308th Bomb Group and the 409th Bomb Squadron of B-25s were to focus on attacking the railroads. However, by the time this reorganization took place, the Japanese had occupied almost all of Eastern China.

Stilwell remained in the theater for only two days after his orders were received. A tough, profane soldier of the old school, he wrote in his diary: "...the Peanut offers me China's highest decoration. Told him to stick it up his —."

Stilwell was subsequently made commander of Army Ground Forces in the U.S. in January 1945; six months later he was transferred to take command of the Tenth Army on Okinawa which was poised to invade Japan. Never a proponent of air power, Stilwell was to find that the B-29s and two atomic bombs made the invasion unnecessary.

In his memoirs, Chennault wrote:

> "I was not sorry to see Stilwell go...Stilwell's abrupt exit cleared the way for the first effective top level Sino-American military cooperation of the war. So marked was the change, that less than six months after Stilwell left, Wedemeyer and his chief field commander, Major General Robert B. McClure, had forged a genuine Sino-American ground army team on a basis that Stilwell contended was impossible."[2]

For Chennault, Stilwell's departure was a definite victory in the political battle between them. With him gone, Chennault hoped for improvement in the supply situation. Although he had the confidence of General Wedemeyer, he no longer had the support of Generals Arnold and Marshall in Washington. He didn't realize it immediately but his own days in China were numbered.

While he had maintained a position of command above Chennault, Stilwell also had differences of opinion with Lord Louis Mountbatten on the conduct of the war in Burma; in addition, his planning for future ground operations in China was continually opposed by the Combined Chiefs of Staff.

Stilwell's stubborn refusal to acknowledge Chennault's concerns about Japanese offensives in East China has never been fully explained. Stilwell had continued to the last to refuse to increase airlift tonnage to keep the Fourteenth in the air in sufficient numbers to make a significant difference. As a result, the 308th had to continue flying the Hump for its own battle supplies.

When the last page of the 1944 calendar was turned, the combat record of the Fourteenth was impressive, despite the conditions under which it had to operate. In trying to stem the tide of the Japanese ground forces in East China, Chennault's planes had killed an estimated 33,450 Japanese troops, destroyed 494 planes and had positively sunk nearly 650,000 tons of enemy shipping.

While the job of interdiction of shipping off the coast would still be carried out by planes of the 308th, it was decided that the fighters would be assigned more of the action against land targets in the weeks ahead. There was less opposition from enemy fighters and the P-51s, with belly tanks and by exercising good cruise control techniques, could fly nearly 2,000 miles. It was no fault of the 308th that a number of P-51s could fly many more sorties against ground targets than the B-24s with their high gas consumption; operations analysts concluded that about fifty fighter missions could be launched against ground targets on the gasoline that it took for the B-24s to make several sea sweeps. However, the value of the B-24s was their ability to seek and destroy enemy shipping many miles from shore and thus do much to prevent the resupply of the Japanese army.

Chapter 7

THE YEAR
OF VICTORY

N ew Year's Day, 1945, marked the beginning of the 308th's third calendar year in China. By this time, the Japanese had seized all of the north-south rail line from Hankow to Canton, then pushed eastward and had taken the Fourteenth's East China airfields at Suichwan and Kanchow. But loss of territory was nothing new to the Chinese; they had been giving ground to the enemy since 1937. Evacuation and demolition of the laboriously constructed airfields and the necessary destruction of precious supplies was a bitter blow to them as well as the Fourteenth.

Although Chennault's men were driven from one base to another, operations against rail lines and freight yards, supply depots, airfields, moving troops and river shipping were carried on as much as fuel, weather and supplies would permit. The Chinese intelligence net proved invaluable to locate vulnerable enemy locations that should be attacked. When enemy river and rail shipping assembled, the Fourteenth was advised and the targets assigned to the 308th and the other medium bomber and fighter units that were within range to hit them.

The enemy suffered from these attacks and could never fully use the lines to supply their advancing troops. So complete was the Chennault strategy that Japanese air units dared not attack in daylight and their last inland bombing attack against Kunming was in December 1944. American air power had fulfilled its purpose of gaining air superiority, at least to prevent attacks on this important city. The Fourteenth could now concentrate on bombing enemy land targets.

By the beginning of the year, a few flying and some non-flying personnel of the 308th had returned to the States and there was optimism that this was the year the Japanese would be driven out of China. By the end of February

1945, nearly all of the original LAB crews had been replaced by others who had been trained more completely before being transferred overseas. The lessons learned by the original crews had been transmitted Stateside and the crews following had been able to take advantage of their experience. The LAB and radar equipment had improved and the 308th was ready to continue to add to its past glory as American forces slowly pushed back the enemy in the entire CBI theater.

Under General Wedemeyer's direction, a counter-offensive was planned beginning in December 1944 which was labeled Operation Alpha. It called for a three-phase operation designed to hold the line at Kunming and then push the Japanese back until they were forced to relinquish their newly-won areas in east China.

Phase I of Alpha involved using Chinese ground forces to make contact with enemy forces in south and southeast China to slow their advances toward Kunming. Chennault's aircraft would be used to interrupt supply convoys. Phase II would require Chinese troops to be transferred from India to China while the Fourteenth continued to harass the enemy's supply routes. Phase III would require the Fourteenth to carry the war to the enemy in east China by destroying land communications and continuing to interdict supply routes.

The operations orders for the Fourteenth included continuing to use the 308th's B-24s for reconnaissance and sea sweeps against enemy shipping in coordination with the U.S. Navy, as well as sorties against land targets. The sea sweeps had been exceptionally successful. Between March 1944 and January 1945, the Liberators had sunk 395,342 tons of Japanese shipping and probably sent another 109,315 tons to the bottom.

However ambitious was the plan, the problem of supply for the Fourteenth remained the same. The B-29 project, which was getting favored treatment from Washington, received the highest priority and consumed a large percentage of the tonnage flown over the Hump. Wedemeyer was adamant: the B-29s would have to leave the CBI. They were not making the contributions that was expected of them and were not helping to defeat the Japanese in China.

The base at Chengtu was closed to B-29 operations and the stocks of fuel and supplies were transferred to the Fourteenth. Although Chennault had less than 300 aircraft at his disposal when the Japanese had started their offensive into east China, at the beginning of 1945, there were nearly 700 aircraft now available and, with the B-29s leaving for new bases at Tinian and Okinawa, the fuel was on hand to fly them.

Capt. William J. Hession, intelligence officer assigned to the 425th Squadron, wrote a frank, secret commentary at the beginning of 1945 which is printed here verbatim. It expresses a rare candid observation about the time and place it was written:

"As the new year dawns, officers and men of the 308th Bombardment Group, together with the rest of the world, look forward to 1945 as a year of victory. The 308th will commence its third year of operations in the China Theater in 1945. An attempt will be made in the following pages to present a faithful account of how men of this organization work, fight, live and die in contributing their small part to the total war effort in the Far East.

"It would be a simple matter to rise to the heights of rhetorical hysteria in describing the heroic and glorious adventures of our gallant soldiers fighting far from home for the principles of democracy and freedom. But to gloss over the failures, the mistakes, rebuffs, heartaches, ennui, the squalid living conditions, the pettiness and vice, would be to distort historical fact. Our mass of over 2000 human beings is representative of a perfect cross-section of American society, blessed with the many sterling qualities which had made our country unique among nations, and cursed with the frailties, selfishness and viciousness found among human beings wherever they are gathered. We have the craftsmen, the tradesmen, clerks, mechanics, barbers, cooks and bakers; students, teachers, artists, lawyers, doctors, and businessmen; thoroughly honorable men, potential criminals, and ordinary men. We have welded into an arm of the service (essentially most of us are still civilians) a heterogeneous assortment held together by the regulations and customs of the army and the strong personality of our commanding officer, a gifted and professional soldier.

"It would doubtlessly be inspiring to a reviewer of this document in some remote future year, to read how we were aflame with the sacred fire of patriotism, engaged in a holy crusade to assist the oppressed and to destroy the oppressor. In some cases, this is the truth, but in many others the men are fighting because they had no other choice. They are here to do a job as quickly as they can. Lofty motives have been traded for common sense principles. The majority of airmen are absorbed with the thought of getting in their required combat hours and returning to the United States. The ground men speculate on just what rotation will bring them home. These purely selfish motives are engendered by our humane method of warfare, and the system goes far in maintaining the morale and efficiency of our citizen-soldiers. As a rule, assignments are performed with alacrity and initiative which typifies the American soldier. The heroism of our fliers is a simple matter of records.

"Although we have been indoctrinated to say nothing about our allies, we may take advantage of the secret classification of this document to give some indication what our men really think of the Chinese. They have commented in the picturesque language of the GI on the lack of national unity and cohesive purpose, jangling discord and the old world inefficiency of the people. They have been victimized by the clever efforts of Chinese merchants, bullied into paying inordinately high fees by coolies. They have been amazed at the outright treason when natives would collaborate with the Japanese in lighting guiding beacons in the vicinity of our bases on the occasions of enemy air raids. On the brighter side, the soldier has found the average Chinese a hard-working, happy and friendly individual who, in spite of staggering physical burdens, cheerfully accepts his rugged lot.

"This year's outset saw the Jap blockade-induced black market still functioning. A thin trickle of U.S. goods sold and resold at fabulous prices. The ratio of China National Currency, commonly known as CN, rose to 700 to 1 with promises of going higher. American cigarettes brought $10 to $12 a carton, depending upon the brand (the Chinese have a preference for Camels and Phillip Morris). Tightening regulations reduced U.S. Army participation in these activities to a minimum.

"Organized vice flourished in most communities with the usual pull between the chaplain and the surgeon. The former urging men not to fall morally; the latter how to fall sanitarily. The incidence of venereal disease in the 308th remained relatively low.

"The effect thus far of a semi-monastic existence has not resulted in warped personalities as predicted by some psychologists. Army discipline, teamwork, fairly good food, and a well-planned recreational program, have bolstered the mental and spiritual well-being of the individual.

"To a man the group begins the new year with hope generated by healthy optimism that it will produce complete and final victory over the enemy on all fronts."

The air of optimism among the men of the 308th when the year began was also expressed by the anonymous 308th historian:

"Officers and enlisted men alike were well quartered and despite the handicaps of continued adjustment to Oriental customs and minor inconveniences, morale was high. The day room shared by the men of the 425th and the 308th served triple duty as a coffee shop, recreation hall and motion picture theater. The cinema was well-patronized three times weekly, preceded by a 15-minute digest of the military situation. It might be added that the day room also doubled in brass as a palace of fortune where those inclined to court Lady Luck were obliged by an enterprising group of 425th enlisted men who conducted the course of the rattling ivories and backed the Black Jack. The 'syndicate' as it was termed, managed to divert the flow of currency its way in a painless, efficient, but none the less, honest and friendly manner.

"The well-rounded recreational program included soft ball, volley ball, horse shoe pitching, and tennis, plus a modest and repressed share of elbow-bending, for the most part hampered by the inconsiderable flow of alcoholic beverages into this theater.

"Group officers, comfortably ensconced in their living quarters adjoining headquarters, prepared for a more rugged existence in tents as the first faint rumors of a portended move northward made itself felt. This rumor later materialized into fact and preliminary preparations for a group movement to Chengtu were arranged."

At the beginning of 1945, Group headquarters and the 425th Squadron were still located in Kunming. The 373rd operated from Luliang, while the 374th and 375th squadrons had their headquarters at Chengkung.

There were few bombing attacks against enemy shipping during this month and only two merchant vessels were sunk. Over thirty mining missions were flown to the Yangtze River and Hong Kong harbor with unknown results. However, during every twenty-four hours, four planes from the group took off at six-hour intervals on unarmed reconnaissance sorties over the South China Sea, Formosa and the Gulf of Tonkin.

A total of 338 sorties were flown by the 308th's forty-six aircraft in January 1945. These missions were not flown without loss of life. The first tragedy of the month occurred on New Year's Day when a plane piloted by Lt. R. W. Smith ran into difficulty after being hit by anti-aircraft fire during a bombing attack against enemy shipping. The crew bailed out in French Indo-China. Fortunately, the majority of the crew members, through the help of a super-secret guerrilla organization, made their way home successfully. Four of the ten men aboard, including the co-pilot, Lt. F. D. Padgett, were either captured by the enemy or died on the bailout.

On January 10, a B-24 of the 425th crashed on takeoff after losing an engine. The plane burned and two crew members died after being pinned under the top turret which tore loose in the crash. Seven other crew members suffered second- and third-degree burns.

A B-24 of the 374th was lost on January 12. It departed from Luliang on a routine sea sweep of the South China Sea and did not return. It was piloted by Lt. John W. Carmody.

Although only a few missions were flown against land targets, one of them was a very successful twenty-seven-plane assault on the Hankow military storage area on January 14. Fighter opposition was ineffective and anti-aircraft fire was lighter than expected; however, six planes received minor damage. Thirty-five P-40s and two P-51s provided escort. One enemy fighter was shot down.

On the morning of January 18, twenty-nine B-24s of the four squadrons of the 308th attacked Hong Kong but it was not a good day for bombing because of two layers of clouds which obscured most of the ground. Approaching the target area and preparing to bomb, the lead plane of the last squadron in the formation had a malfunction of the bomb release mechanism causing its bombs to be released prematurely. Five other planes following dropped their bombs on the squadron leader; all bombs were believed to have landed in the water. The formation spent an hour in the Hong Kong-Canton area hoping that the area would clear but it didn't. Those that still had bombs left dropped them on what they believed to be the airdrome at Canton but accurate observation was impossible.

On the return from this mission, an aircraft of the 375th ran out of gas. All crew members, except the pilot, bailed out successfully and eventually returned safely to base. Lt. Ernest G. Swart, the pilot, last to bail out, jumped from an altitude of only about 250 feet. Although his chute opened, he was fatally injured on impact.

On the same day, four men were injured on a bailout from a B-24 near Kunming in what was reported as a "non-battle casualty." On January 22, two others were injured when bailing out of a plane near Chengkung.

Hong Kong was again the target for a thirty-plane unescorted group mission on January 22nd. When the docks, the primary target for the mission, could not be seen through the clouds, the Royal Navy Yard, which was to have been the target for the next mission, was visible so the decision was made to attack it. Although three B-24s had to abort, there were no casualties and the target area was well-blanketed.

On January 28, returning from a routine reconnaissance mission to the Tonkin Gulf, the crew of the 375th led by Lt. S. J. Bobek, had to bail out after fourteen hours of flight when radio communication was lost. All crew members landed successfully near Hingi and made contact with friendly Chinese farmers and guerrillas. They were taken to the headquarters of the U.S. Army's 45th Division liaison team and returned to Kunming on February 13.

The docks and storage area at Hong Kong were again the targets for a successful multi-plane raid on January 30th.

The interdiction raids against enemy supply routes and storage areas forced the Japanese to attempt to curtail the Fourteenth's air activities by capturing the remaining bases in east China. Since they did not have control of the air, they decided to launch a vigorous ground assault late in January 1945 without air power. One main target was Suichwan, located behind Japanese lines and defended only by a motley army of Chinese survivors of the previous battle for Hengyang. The field was overrun in February, causing the Fourteenth's units to withdraw from its east China bases.

The month of January 1945 saw another loss of a 308th aircraft on the Hump flight to Chabua. One crew, led by Lt. Col. William H. Smith of the 425th, with Major Harrison L. Marshall as co-pilot, ran into difficulty with heavy icing in a thick overcast when the aircraft's antenna snapped off. With no radio communication and having overshot the valley, Smith ordered the crew to bail out. The crew of five, with four passengers, including Lt. P. J. Tom, a Chinese Army liaison officer, landed in the unsurveyed territory in the Naga Hills among headhunters that, although mostly allies of the Americans, still practiced their specialty among their own tribes. However, despite minor injuries to three of those aboard, including Marshall, they all returned safely with the help of the theater's Air Rescue Service. Their return had not been without adventures with the natives. The official "Bail-out Report" describes what happened:

"All were assisted by the Naga tribesmen, reputedly head hunters, whose tattooed faces, matted long hair decorated with bones, ears dangling with large ornaments, and slight Mongolian features, presented a fearsome aspect. These people, scattered in small villages of less than 100, are clad only in loin cloths, carry primitive axes and dated firearms. They have a language of their own, understand no English and a little Hindustani and rarely venture outside of their own territory.

"These semi-savages were helpful in most instances when they understood they were to be compensated for their efforts. In the case of Major Marshall, who approached a village at dusk after endeavoring to attain aid from two tribesmen whom he met on a nearby trail, they displayed outright hostility, and with threatening gestures and hostile movements of their spears and axes, literally chased the major from the village. On his second day, however, the major approached another village wherein the inhabitants were more friendly. Evidently drum signals had gone out from various points advising tribesmen that a number of American airmen were down in the area.

"Lt. [S.S.] Richmond, [the navigator] proved one of the most fortunate of the group. After some hard travel down a jungle stream, he reached a village he describes as Longhai, on his second day out. He was brought to another small village, Tenhai, where he encountered Capt. Morrone, Capt. Tom, and Sgt. Rhodes. Ghurka troops from Wakching, summoned by runner, brought them to the last named village where they were aided and fed through kindly ministrations of the Indian doctor, Dr. Boro, who spoke English and who succeeded in getting them to Borjan, via bamboo chairs and bearers."

The other men eventually also returned to Chabua with similar experiences. They made several suggestions to help others who might find themselves as guests of the Naga tribesmen:

1. Equip crews and passengers with money belts, jungle kits and maps when flying the Hump. Medical kits containing iodine were also

recommended.

2. Natives should be approached in daylight hours with gifts in hand.

3. Since the natives were not familiar with American money, they appreciate silver rupees and articles of clothing as gifts.

4. The standard machetes in the jungle kits were inadequate. Four out of five of them broke when used to hack through the heavy jungle undergrowth.

The month of February saw a revision in operations and strategy because of the changing military ground situation in China. Japanese troops initiated a strong offensive action aimed at allied positions and air bases in western China. The 308th was ordered northward to bases in the vicinity of Chengtu. The move was required because of the advances being made by Japanese troops aiming at allied positions and air bases near Chengtu. Locating there gave the B-24s an advantage in shortened distance to the target areas.

The move to Chengtu began February 8. In the unemotional language of the movement order, the men were advised to "take all items desired for their personal comfort."

First priority equipment and personnel were flown in the B-24s and some C-47s of the Air Transport Command, a distance of 411 air miles. Motor convoys followed over the torturous dirt roads through the rugged mountains, a distance of 805 land miles. The group historian commented, "the convoyites gained a true insight as to the habits and customs of the population of inner China and were treated with kindness by our Oriental allies. However, the system of overcharging with a disarming smile was not entirely abandoned."

The continuing success of the radar-equipped B-24s was encouraging and it was decided to establish the 308th Bomb Group Radar Control Center at Kunming to keep track of reports of enemy ship sightings and control the dispatch of missions against them. Capt. Elmer E. Haynes was put in charge of the center. A U.S. Navy liaison team was assigned with Lt. Cmdr. F. Marvin Plake as head of the team. He explained the reason why Navy personnel were assigned:

"A bomber on the hunt must often fly for hours over monotonous stretches of water – something many an Army pilot did not anticipate when he entered the Air Forces.

"In our liaison work, we chart the sightings of enemy shipping made by both Army and Navy observers; we help determine the ships' routes, so the air crews will more readily find the targets; and we try to help the Army men better identify and describe what they have seen when they come back.

"Identification of craft is often peculiarly important. That is an essential part of the Navy man's training. Most of us attached to an Army Air Force unit have done our time at sea. We know most of the weak spots in various types of ships.

"Shipping strikes have been a major assignment for most of our Army Air Forces in the Pacific ever since the war began. The Japanese octopus lives on two-way circulation. Manufacturers and troops must flow down the tentacles from the home islands; raw materials like oil, rubber, rice, must flow steadily back to the homeland. Interrupt this circulation, and decay of the organism sets in."[1]

A mission on February 1st, dispatched from Kunming, was typical of those where liaison with the Navy paid off. It had been learned that there were two enemy ships grounded off the French Indo-China coast; consequently, they were attacked and sunk by six of the 308th's B-24s. Three other ships were sighted and presumed damaged.

Again, there was loss of aircraft and personnel during the month. On February 5, Lt. George C. Turpyn and his ten-man crew from the 375th, were reported missing on a reconnaissance flight over the Tonkin Gulf. Icing conditions were encountered and the plane could not be climbed to more than 21,500 feet. No. 4 engine was putting out only half power, then the propellers of Nos. 1 and 3 engines began to run away and could not be feathered. All bailed out successfully but Turpyn and three others, last to leave the plane, landed near Chaotung in an area controlled by unfriendly Lalo tribesmen. The others were gathered together by a Chinese guerrilla leader but not without two of them being ransomed for two Luger pistols when they landed on the Japanese-held side of the Yangtze River.

While the other men were eventually returned to their base on February 23rd and 24th, Turpyn and the other three who had landed separately made contact with the natives individually three days later. The interrogation report tells the story:

"During the these first two days, the tribesmen were most unfriendly and the treatment accorded each man was similar in most respects. In each case, when the flier showed the tribesmen the Chinese identification flag, it was taken from them and never returned. In the same manner, the pointee-talkees were taken from the men. Although initial contact was made with individuals or groups of two or three, it was not long before at least six of the tribesmen gathered around a particular airman, whereupon they proceeded to relieve him first of his gun (on the pretense of wanting to examine it), then his valuables, watch, rings, identification bracelets, and the contents of his pockets, money belt, and jungle pack. When more of the late arriving tribesmen wanted a souvenir, the men were stripped down to their underwear and shoes. The tribesmen were armed either with spears or rifles of an ancient model; besides their acquisitive habits, they were unfriendly in attitude, and unconcerned for the welfare of the fliers. It was cold in this region and the men suffered from the loss of their outer clothing.

"Lts. [George C.] Turpyn and [Samuel W.] Royse [copilot] found each other on the morning of the first day and shortly thereafter were located by three of the tribesmen. After taking their .45 cal. automatic pistols, the natives seemed nervous and undecided as to what to do. The three of them were armed with rifles and Turpyn and Royse got the idea that the hill men were going to murder them. The conclusion was reached and while the three were in a conference a short distance away, Turpyn and Royse ran for cover in different directions. They both got away, Royse following a rocky gulch. He was pursued by just one of the natives. From time to time, the native fired Royse's .45 and the bullets pinged on the rocks near him but he managed to get away without injury. The next day, both he and Turpyn were surrounded by bands of six or more natives and they subsequently met in a small village on 6 February. Their treatment during this period was not particularly bad, except that they were relieved of their clothing and all equipment.

"The experiences of Lt. [Carlton R.] Lutterbei [navigator] and Sgt. [Daniel J.] Nalivaika [gunner] were not much different except that they did not attempt to escape. In the town, on February 6, there was a tribal chieftain who was able to exercise some control over the natives and some of the clothing was returned to the men.

"The four fliers were taken to the next town where they had an interpreter and several guards. It snowed and the men remained there for the next seven days. On February 15 and 16, they traveled to the headquarters of friendly guerrillas and on the 17th were given horses for the trip to Chiao Chia. Supplies were airdropped to the men here. They crossed the Yellow River and traveled to Chaotung which they reached on February 28th. They arrived in Kunming on March 2."

Lt. John W. Chambliss, the intelligence officer who interrogated the men, made some recommendations in his report:

"Try to evade all contact with individuals in the hills. Climb a mountain and locate a town. Make for this town in the late afternoon to arrive shortly before dark. On meeting the townspeople, give the Ding Hao sign and point to yourself. This indicates that you are a chief or an important person. Attempt to get to the head man of the town because he usually has some small sense of consideration for the comfort and welfare of the downed flier.

"Keep your gun hidden at all times and don't fire it except as a possible distress signal in the case of an injured man."

On February 11, a 373rd B-24, piloted by Lt. Glenn B. Taylor, developed engine trouble during a strike against shipping off the coast of French Indo-China. The crew bailed out but only one member was ever found. On February 27, another 373rd plane crashed ten miles south of Luliang, killing all eight men aboard.

During the month, ten strike missions were flown against enemy shipping in the waters off French Indo-China and the Gulf of Tonkin. An additional ten reconnaissance flights were made to the same general area. Seven mine-laying missions were laid on to the Yangtze River.

By late February, the Group had settled into its new environment and missions were immediately begun against Japanese railroad and supply centers. The 308th was placed under the operational control of the 312th Fighter Wing for strikes against the centers that were rallying points for the advancing Japanese ground troops. Group headquarters and the 375th were set up at A-1, an air base near Hsinching. The 425th and 374th operated from A-3, a base near Kwanghan, about eighty road miles away. The 373rd operated from Luliang, north of Kunming, to maintain a force that would continue attacks on Japanese shipping. All of the radar-equipped B-24s were assigned to this squadron and a detachment, designated Detachment No. 1, headed by Lt. Col. William P. Hopson, was set up at Kunming to facilitate administration and work closely with the Navy. Detachment No. 2 was established at Chabua, India, to train new crews.

During the month, the 373rd at Luliang received credit for fourteen Japanese ships sunk, two probably sunk and four damaged.

Two years of duty for the 308th overseas had been completed by February 1945 and the first contingent of non-flying personnel received orders to return to the States on March 15. At the same time, replacements began to arrive in small numbers after preliminary training and briefing in India.

The Group historian commented wryly on conditions at the base near Hsinching:

"The general morale of group personnel was at a low ebb in the first weeks at A-1. Climatic conditions were partially responsible. Although the Chengtu Basin is one of the most fertile spots in the world, gray skies and a low overcast are prevalent more often than not. Group enlisted personnel quartered in a barracks of disintegrating plaster and crumbling cement floors promptly named their incommodious habitation the 'upholstered sewer.' Droves of bewhiskered rats (king size) boldly competed for space. During the day the rodents remained aloof in their quarters on the top side of a matted bamboo ceiling. By night, they launched an average of fifty or more sorties, mainly of a foraging nature. Carelessly stowed candy bars were considered toothsome delicacies. Brother rat would daintily expectorate the paper and bore into the chocolate with all the hunger inspired by untold generations of chocolate-starved China rats. The story goes around that a cannibalistic rodent loved raw white flesh and satisfied his craving by chewing off a few joints of an unsuspecting GI's index finger. The GI was supposedly heavily fatigued after a bout with Chinese jing bao juice. This raid is unconfirmed, however, and our historian warns against accepting it as fact."

In March, the 373rd continued its offensive operations against enemy shipping in the South China Sea with 108 sorties. Close coordination was maintained with the 312th Fighter Wing, also stationed in the Chengtu area. Eight merchant ships were sunk and eleven others damaged. The remaining three squadrons continued to attack railroads. Although handicapped by weather and the slow movement of supplies to their bases, excellent results were achieved in raids against rail facilities at Shihshianchuang, Tsinan, Chengsien, Anyang, and Kafeng. The enemy offensive was temporarily stalled when Liberators knocked out a span of a Yellow River bridge.

On the morning of March 8, thirty-four B-24s left bases in the Chengtu area for a raid against the North Railroad Yards of Shihchiachueng, China. The mission was escorted by fighters that made rendezvous over Hsian. The mission did not go as briefed. On takeoff, one plane struck two Chinese crossing the runway against the red light at Hsinching, causing a dented left stabilizer and a broken hydraulic line. Because of hazy weather conditions, only half of the planes made assembly with the group leader. The pilots were briefed to drop on the group leader; however, at the point of release, the bomb mechanism on the lead aircraft was inoperative and the planes turned toward the secondary target. As they began their 180-degree turn, the second flight of planes which had failed to make the rendezvous with the leader approached the target. The first echelon joined this formation from the rear and all proceeded to the target. Due to a smoke screen thrown up by the enemy, the second echelon missed its initial point and came into the target forty-five degrees off the briefed heading. As a result, only about eight percent of the bombs fell into the target area on warehouses and railroad tracks. Most bombs fell short and to the east into a residential area. There had been no fighter opposition and little anti-aircraft fire.

While the majority of the planes proceeded to the target, one flight of three was the last to take off. They had a special mission which took them on a course at the rear of the formation to the right of the Yellow River bridge. Charles F. Thompson, a 374th pilot, tells what they did:

"Our flight of three aircraft had been briefed to fly past the bridge, then leave the formation to bomb the bridge. We flew past it and made a 135-degree turn to the left which put us on track for it. Our plane was a new Ford-built B-24L. On one side of us was [Everett L.] Mayberry and his crew; Behrn's aircraft was on the other side.

"The aircraft was trimmed for the autopilot and then the autopilot was connected to the Norden bombsight. This allowed the bombardier to control the track of the plane through the bombsight. The bombardier was Forrest E. Groves; James G. Langenegger was the pilot; I was in the right seat. Langenegger's job was to control the altitude with the elevators. My job was to control the airspeed with the throttles. When Langenegger would pull back on the yoke, I would feed in the throttles. We were perfectly coordinated. The last five minutes of the bomb run seemed like an eternity. The altimeter just hung on 14,000 feet. The airspeed indicator stayed on 155. I watched and waited for one or the other to vary. They didn't. Then I heard 'Bombs away!' We started a dive to pick up airspeed and to get away from the flak. We knew we had flown a good bomb run. When we saw the pictures the next day we knew just how good. We had flown a perfect bomb run!

"I don't know for sure but I was told that the picture of this bombing hung in the Pentagon for a number of years as an example of precision bombing.

"Since this was a new airplane, we didn't have any nose art on it yet. We got the crew together and discovered that several of the crew members had wives or girl friends named Betty; consequently, *Beeline Betty* was the name selected."

The next day, thirty-two B-24s attacked the Sinsiang Railroad Yards. This time the raid was a success with at least sixty-five percent of the bombs dropped in the first two-thirds of the yards. Again, no enemy fighters rose to the challenge; however, there was some meager but accurate anti-aircraft fire encountered at Chengsien and the Yellow River Bridge.

Another raid was dispatched against the railroad yards at Tainan with thirty-two B-24s. However, poor visibility conditions caused the leader to proceed to the railroad yards at Tsanghsien with minimal results.

Since the rail yards at Shihchiachuang had not been hit effectively, a return mission was laid on for March 16. Thirty-two Liberators reached the objective and scored hits on repair shops, warehouses, rolling stock, and railroad tracks. A violent explosion of a munitions dump or a train loaded with ammunition was observed by crews leaving the area.

The bridge over the Yellow River, which had been heavily defended by anti-aircraft fire on the March 9th mission was the target for eight B-24s on March 23. Braving intense flak and bombing from 14,000 feet, one direct hit and several near misses were scored causing a 700-foot span to drop into the water. No planes were hit but several planes had to land short of home base low on gas.

On the same morning, twenty B-24s attacked the Tainan repair shops with a large number of direct hits on locomotive repair shops which were followed by several secondary explosions. Photos taken during the raid revealed considerable destruction in a large storage depot. Flak was moderate but no planes were damaged. The mission report notes: "Fighter coverage provided by the 311th Fighter Group proved excellent."

For the second time in as many days, the bridge across the Yellow River was attacked again by nine B-24s with excellent results on March 24. Another span of the bridge was dislodged and congested road traffic was observed on roads leading to both ends of the bridge. This time the anti-aircraft fire was more effective and three planes from the 375th Squadron received small holes in various parts of the aircraft. Because of hits in a fuel line, one had to land at Hsian for repairs.

Also on March 24th, twenty-five B-24s were dispatched from the Chengtu area and attacked the Chengsien Locomotive Park with excellent results. Many secondary explosions were observed and much destruction was seen on nearby warehouses and open storage areas. Seven planes received minor damage from moderate but accurate flak.

Raids against railroad yards continued on March 27 with nine B-24s attacking the Anyang railroad repair facilities. While eight of the nine planes hit the target causing much damage, the ninth plane's bombardier could not get his bomb release into the select position because of a malfunction between the cable and pulley. He salvoed twenty bombs one mile north of the target area causing secondary explosions in a textile mill and cut the railroad line to this region. One of the secondary explosions was unusually violent accompanied by a sweeping bright red flame, indicating a possible hit on an ammunition dump. He was able to salvo the rest of his bombs on the main target.

On the same day, another flight of twenty B-24s attacked the railroad yards at Keifeng and caused widespread destruction of the yards and repair shops. Again, many secondary explosions were observed, including one particularly violent one which was believed to have been an ammunition train. No enemy flak or fighters were encountered.

On the final day of March, the rail yards at Shihchiachuang were attacked again by thirty B-24s armed with incendiary bombs as well as explosives. Two planes had to abort this mission and three others landed at Hsian and Hanchung with engine trouble. The remaining planes bombed the target successfully.

Raymond J. "Jack" Thurber, pilot of *Bee-Line Betty*, tells what happened after dropping his bombs:

"Good weather – light flak – all was great until we made our turn away from the target and then all Hell broke loose! The oil pressure on No. 2 dropped to zero and we had to feather the engine. We were flying No. 7 in the formation and it presented little problem. We stayed close to the rest of the squadron for about two hours and twenty minutes and were looking forward to getting back to A-3. This took place at 16,000 feet and all looked good. Then Murphy's Law took over! We had a runaway prop on No. 1. After a couple of frantic moments trying to correct it, we had no choice but to feather it. Two engines out on the same side – not good.

"Immediately, two lovely P-51s sidled up to us for our personal escort - great for our morale but not doing much for our being able to hold our altitude or directional control. Bill Caldwell, our co-pilot, and I each had both of our feet on the right rudder pedals and full right aileron cranked in to maintain a semblance of directional control. We lightened the plane (dumped the bomb bay tank, waist guns and nearly everything else that wasn't bolted down) yet we were still losing altitude. Our best bet (other than bailing out) was to try to get to Hangchiung.

"For the next hour and eighteen minutes there was a lot of praying going on – no panic on the part of any crew members – but I'm sure a lot of apprehension about our safety. George Liandros, our navigator, hit Hangchiung on the head and we still had 2,000 feet above the terrain. We did a large sweeping "180" and came over the fence at about 20 feet and landed on the grass runway, chopped the power on Nos. 3 and 4, and stopped perpendicular to the runway 1,500 feet from touchdown – mighty thankful and wringing wet."

Meanwhile, during the month, the 373rd at Luliang had accounted for four Jap vessels, with one sunk, one probably sunk and two damaged.

Looking back over the record of the Fourteenth Air Force, General Chennault issued an Order of the Day dated March 9, 1945:

"For the organizational year which ends 10 March, the Fourteenth

Air Force has destroyed more than 1200 enemy planes; more than 500 of them were shot down in air combat. These figures do not include more than 190 probables nor the hundred damaged in air combat, nor the probables and damaged left by our bombers and fighters on burning enemy airdromes.

"In destruction of enemy aircraft, as in the destruction of enemy installations and supply lines, our missions have been invariably outnumbered by enemy air strength. But through surprise and combat proficiency we have destroyed more than eight enemy planes in air combat for every plane of ours that has been shot down.

"Fighters and bombers of the Fourteenth Air Force since March 1944 have sunk nearly 600,000 tons of enemy shipping, with 270,000 additional tons probably sunk and nearly 450,000 tons damaged. This is a total of more than 1,300,000 tons. At least 18 enemy vessels not included in the tonnage totals were destroyed by our fighters and bombers, 14 were probably destroyed and 18 damaged.

"During the year we destroyed more than 2,600 smaller craft on which the enemy depends so greatly for supply lines on the coast and in the occupied river valleys of interior China. More than 300 of the craft in this category were probably destroyed and more than 9,000 damaged.

"Since June, units of the Fourteenth Air Force have killed more than 30,000 enemy troops and nearly 10,000 troop horses and pack horses. More than 700 enemy locomotives have been destroyed and 450 have been damaged. We have knocked out more than 100 bridges on enemy lines of communication and we have damaged nearly 150.

"As modern forces go, all this has been done by few with little, often under extremely adverse weather conditions and over the world's most unfavorable terrain. It has been made possible by incredibly more pilot and crew sorties per month than might be expected, and by indefatigable effort and devotion to duty on the part of ground personnel supporting the operations.

"Not least among the accomplishment of the Fourteenth Air Force in its second year was the protection of more than two million Chinese refugees evacuating areas of Central and South China. For the first time since the Japanese attacked China, hundreds of thousands moved under the sheltering wings of the Fourteenth Air Force, ahead of the Japanese armies, free from wanton strafing and bombing, aided by our surgeons and flight nurses.

"Fourteenth Air Force transport units and attached combat cargo squadrons have dropped thousands of tons of supplies and munitions to Chinese armies operating against the enemy, and have transported across enemy lines supplies essential to the operations of advanced bases. Repeatedly, in cooperation with the China Air Service Command and the engineers, they have completed the evacuation of our bases without materiel loss to our arms or gain to the enemy. It is notable in this connection that the enemy has thus far been unable to capitalize the bases we have evacuated under pressure of his ground forces.

"In sharp contrast, we have made untenable many of the formerly significant Japanese air bases in China, and have widely extended our zones of air supremacy and air superiority against a repeatedly surprised and always reluctant enemy. Many times outnumbered, we have beaten him to the ground. He no longer dares attack in the daylight hours, and his air strength is waning on all our fronts."

There were no enemy raids against the American bases in March, although intelligence reports indicated that the Japanese were getting ready to mount ground advances against U.S. installations at Chickiang and Hsian. The base at Hsian was occupied by the 311th Fighter Group, one of the units that escorted the 308th's bombers. If it were overrun, it would hamper the 308th's operations in the north. Laohokow, a fighter base near Hsian, was evacuated by U.S. forces that month.

The good news for the ground personnel of the 308th occurred when the much-rumored rotation plan began to take effect. After two years or more in China, sixteen enlisted men and one officer were returned home. Again, the Group historian commented on the local situation for the non-flying personnel or those resting between missions:

"With a surcease from hard work, some of the men thoroughly investigated the entertainment possibilities in the city of Chengtu. Many found their way to the famous (or infamous) Union Hotel where 'ladies of the evening' were socially encountered with the full consent of accompanying parents. The circumstances of such encounters amidst an unromantic and unsanitary environment discouraged most, and the hotel was finally put off limits to the more persevering proponents of sensuality.

"Souvenir buying continued unabated, although prices continued to rise. The rate of exchange rose to the new high of 750 CN to 1 on the black market. Embroidered silk and jewelry manufactured of local silver were the leading items purchased.

"Food at A-1 proved consistently better than that served at Kunming, although the laundry situation continued to be a problem. Clothing was returned poorly pressed with a dirty gray color, and not infrequently a buck private would wind up with a major's pajamas.

"Morale continued to be high as officers and men accustomed themselves to their new quarters. They quickly adapted themselves to the Chinese version of a shower bath – wooden buckets filled by coolies and hauled to the ceiling with ropes. Chinese ingenuity was further demonstrated in providing comforts not found in the American home, with semi-luxurious rope bed springs, soft-matted bamboo chairs, and non-flushable latrines, complete with excrement traps situated strategically hundreds of feet from the washroom."

During March, the Japanese changed their tactics insofar as using sampans for hauling cargo in the South China Sea were concerned. The 308th's planes had avoided wasting bombs on them and the enemy knew this. Some small freighters were disguised with false sails and sampan owners were paid a million yuan for one cargo trip between Hainan and Hong Kong. Rather than employ two or three large vessels which would be easily detected by the B-24's radar, they began to use large fleets of sampans. When larger vessels were used, they were hidden in the midst of large sampan fleets.

The month had its tragic side for the 308th. Two men were killed in action; one of the men killed was strangled in the turret of a 373rd Squadron plane when he was caught between the sight cradle and control handles after accidentally tripping the control switch while loading the guns.

On March 26, while returning from a 373rd mining mission in the Yangzte River area, the crew of Lt. H. L. Folsom was forced to bail out in the vicinity of Sho Gun Ho. All returned safely to Luliang in two separate groups on April 2. An entire ten-man crew of a 373rd B-24 failed to return from a shipping strike on March 30.

Mining missions had their moments of sheer terror as told in this story by Lt. Leland Miles, navigator on *Time Will Tell* of the 374th:

"Hankow was our host on the mission that gave us 202 hours and made us eligible for the Distinguished Flying Cross. With Capt. George Dawley, our operations officer, flying as co-pilot, and Lt. Warburton, a 'J' man, as bombardier, we took off in early afternoon bound for a small area of the Yangtze River ten miles south of Hankow. When we got back, Warburton exclaimed, 'Brother, that's the highest and the lowest I've ever flown in China!'

"The 'lowest' came first. We had flown through an undercast the entire 600 miles to the target area, had dropped down to 2,000 feet and flown straight up the river until we reached our bomb release point. We hit the point right on the nose, and as I turned the ship over to Warburton, I turned off the table light and pulled the curtain from the window. Under us was the broad expanse of the Yangtze, and on either bank hills loomed up out of the moonlit shadows. Our job was to get eight mines in the center of the river, each mine to be placed at a certain interval as we flew toward Hankow. Warburton had gotten every mine away within a minute, yet it is the longest minute we had ever experienced. Here we were, now flying at 700 feet up the middle of the Yangtze River, with Jap troops on either bank, three Jap airdromes two minutes ahead of us, and the biggest Jap river port in China a like number of minutes away.

"With 'bombs away,' the pilot racked [the plane] on her wing and we scurried to altitude as if the Devil himself was riding on the tail surface. That climb to altitude was a long one. It didn't end until we'd broken out of a growing overcast at 20,500 feet. None of us were dressed for high altitude; particularly was this true of Capt. Dawley, who, poor fellow, was wearing GI shoes and khakis. Oxygen supply was dwindling; the heaters had never worked before and saw no reason to start then. [T/Sgt Jack J.] Christensen [radio operator] and I got off oxygen to take the first fix and it was so cold my octant frosted up; it was a half hour before we could complete the fix. In that time Chris got so dizzy he dropped the chronometer twice and I almost collapsed, being extremely susceptible to oxygen deprivation at any altitude above 12,000 feet.

"Gradually we were able to drop down to a reasonable altitude. Dawley was swearing like a madman. 'Damn it, Miles,' he said, 'If I ever get this cold on a flight again, I'll turn in my wings!'

"We came over the field less than 10 hours from the time we departed, having flown through an overcast for 600 miles, located the target and dropped our mines 55 minutes ahead of flight plan and two hours ahead of turnback time. Capt. Dawley said he had never seen a mission that went off with such clockwork precision. He called it the most perfect mission on which he had ever flown."

During April, operations were slowed down because of the shortage of fuel. Gasoline was rationed and it became necessary for the Liberators to fly only those missions which would be of the greatest value to the overall effort. The bombing missions that were flown in North China continued to concentrate on enemy supply depots and transportation facilities as the Japanese continued their westward offensive on a broad front between the Yellow and Yangzte rivers. These missions were usually in three-ship elements. Incendiary bombing attacks were made against supply and repair centers at Yuncheng, Loyang, Linfen and Taiyuan. The 373rd at Luliang continued to score against shipping in the South China Sea and the Gulf of Tonkin. One cargo vessel was sunk, one probably sunk and two damaged.

On April 2, a 375th aircraft returning from a twenty-seven-plane mission to the Taiyuan railroad yards experienced a high rate of fuel consumption and pulled away from the formation with all of the bombs aboard. The after-action report tells the story:

"At 1516 hours, the pilot called the navigator and told him to let him know when the plane was 60 miles from Kwanghan so they could descend through the overcast on course in gradual descent. The navigator gave the pilot their position and they broke out below the overcast at 4,500 feet near Sen Tai. At 1545 hours, the No. 1 engine quit and was feathered by the pilot who also gave the order to bail out. He salvoed the bombs, pins in, which went through the partly-opened bomb bay doors, striking without exploding. The bomb bay doors were then fully opened and the empty bomb bay tank salvoed clearing the bomb bay. With one engine feathered, the pilot attempted to gain altitude after the bombs were salvoed but gained only about 400 feet in the ensuing five to eight minutes when the No. 4 engine cut out. At this time all personnel, except the pilot and co-pilot had parachutes on and were prepared to get out the bomb bay or waist camera hatch, both of which were open.

"The pilot tried to blow the bailout horn when No. 4 engine quit but it did not work. He told the co-pilot to get out and jump. At this time the men on the catwalk began to jump, followed immediately by the men waiting in the camera hatch who were watching for the bailout signal and could see through the bomb bay.

"The pilot stayed in his seat to feather the No. 4 engine and trim up the plane. This required the utmost coolness and he is to be especially commended for this action. If the plane had not been under full control at the time the crew was jumping, casualties may have been much heavier. There was very little time; the jumpers nearly collided in the rush. In one instance, Capt. Martyniuk [the observer] and Flight Officer Hardy [co-pilot] almost collided in midair. He [Hardy] started to slide off and was caught on the catwalk by his canteen and gun holster and had to wrench himself free. Lt. Petty [the pilot] followed directly behind F/O Hardy. Lt. Petty's 'chute had barely opened when his body struck the ground.

"In the waist, three men bailed out as soon as those in the bomb bay started. S/Sgt Kilcoyne [the camera operator] delayed several seconds late and his 'chute also was strung out but did not blossom when his body struck the ground..."

The ten surviving crew members landed close together and quickly assembled. They were guided to the small village of Pesuchow. Two men with fractured ankles were carried on litters by Chinese peasants. Chinese soldiers arrived and accompanied the party by trail and road to San Tai. Many relief coolies were used and when they arrived at San Tai, they were welcomed by a General Peng and an English missionary Johanna Matthison who had a missionary college there. A large dinner was prepared with the usual ceremonies. The party was lodged in a small hotel until the arrival of a detachment of the 374th Squadron with an ambulance, jeep and truck. They were taken to a nearby airfield and returned to Kwanghan by C-47.

On April 10, twenty-three Liberators dropped a total of 25,176 incendiaries on the military storage depot at Yuncheng. The area was saturated by the highly flammable bombs and many fires and secondary explosions were observed. There was no anti-aircraft fire or fighter opposition, the latter a disappointment to the escorting P-51 pilots of the 312th Fighter Group.

Three days later, the Yellow River bridge was attacked again and although no direct hits were scored, photos taken during the mission showed large numbers of railroad cars stacked up at both ends of the bridge indicating probable damage. On the same day, eighteen planes bombed an enemy storage depot at Linfen but none of the bombs fell in the assigned target area.

The city of Loyang was raided on the morning of April 14 by fourteen B-24s with incendiary clusters. Later that morning, the Yellow River bridge was the target again for nine planes bombing in flights of three, this time with excellent results. One span was buckled and another damaged. Although there was no fighter opposition, the flak was heavy on this mission and three planes were hit.

The storage depot at Linfen was hit again on April 16 with some incendiary bombs carrying delayed fuses that were set to go off up to thirty-six hours later. Numerous structures were hit and smoke columns from fires set by instantaneously-fused bombs were observed as the eighteen B-24s exited the area. On the 19th, the railroad yards at Taiyuan were struck again with excellent results.

Returning from this mission, a 375th plane experienced engine failure and the crew also bailed out when the pilot, Lt. J. K. Carroll, found he could not maintain altitude, even with full power and after dropping the bomb bay tank, extra equipment, and ammunition. Of the twelve men aboard, one suffered a broken ankle and several others received minor cuts and bruises. This group was assisted by Chinese army troops and returned to their base by wagon, mules, jeep, and airplane ten days after their bailout. This mission was the last flown by the 375th against Japanese installations.

On April 20, a 373rd plane, after making a sea sweep, lost two engines fifteen miles from Kunming. The crew bailed out; one man was killed and seven injured.

The Group historian commented on what was happening at Group headquarters in Chengtu during the spring of 1945:

> "Enlisted men generally complained bitterly and officers were not too happy when it was announced that higher headquarters had ordained a period of one hour weekly be devoted to foot drill. The fortunate rotaters walked around with a smug, self-satisfied smile as they awaited transportation on the first leg of war's most delightful journey."

The month of May saw the introduction of Azon (for "Azimuth only") bombs for use by the 308th's B-24s. These were radio-controlled bombs with movable fins that enabled a bombardier to control the bomb by adjusting the control surfaces in the tail using radio control. As Chennault says in his memoirs, the Azon bomb attack by the 308th "was one of the first true guided missile attacks of the war."

The first combat test of the Azon had been made by the 7th Bomb Group of the Tenth Air Force on December 27, 1944, and proved especially successful against railroads and bridges as skill in using it was gained by the bombardiers. It proved so successful that it was possible to reduce the number of aircraft scheduled to attack targets. It was found that best results were obtained by dropping the bombs singly from eight to ten thousand feet. General Stratemeyer reported that the 7th was exceptionally successful using the Azons, "with one mission getting four bridges with four bombs, and another getting six direct hits on two bridges with six bombs."

The Azons were also used successfully by the 425th when three aircraft were initially equipped with the system the following April. The squadron carried out attacks with them after the other three squadrons ceased tactical operations. During May, Azon missions were dispatched against the North Huto River and Yellow River bridges. On May 8, one B-24 attacked the Huto River bridge but the Azon equipment was inoperative. As a result the target was bombed visually, followed by a low-level strafing attack, then a photo reconnaissance of the railroad yards at Chihchiachuang.

A two-plane radar mission against the Yellow River bridge was ordered on May 11 from Kwanghan but only one plane reached the target for an unsuccessful attack. This plane experienced some damage from intense flak. The other plane, piloted by Lt. Ferris D. Caffey, and its nine-man crew was never heard from again. It was believed that their plane may have been downed by the intense flak that was thrown up during the runs on the bridge.

Since two important bridges at Shaho had not been attacked, another one-plane raid, with Major Harrison Marshall as pilot, was sent there with Azon bombs on May 15. One bridge on the north side of the city had one span, and possibly two, knocked down. Two runs were made against a bridge on the south side of the city with direct hits on both spans. With this encouragement and with more bombs left, the crew attacked an unbriefed bridge near Singtai and one span was knocked down.

After these successful attacks, Marshall sighted a railroad train at a standstill in the rail yards at Shaho. He decided to make a low level machine gun attack while P-51s flew cover overhead. As he descended he saw that it was loaded with enemy troops. When he roared over the yards, the B-24's nose and belly gunners blasted away. He pulled up and made two more passes but on the last one, the plane was met with intense small arms fire. Marshall turned to his co-pilot and said, "Hey, Tom, those little bastards are shooting at us!"

Those were Marshall's last words. A single bullet entered the cockpit and struck the major in the head. It proceeded through the cockpit and hit Lt. Daniel Dorchak, the bombardier, in the neck. He was not badly wounded but Marshall died instantly. The plane was flown back to the base by the co-pilot after landing at Hsian first to enable Dorchak to get medical treatment.

The Huto River bridge was attacked again on May 29 by one B-24. No spans were knocked out but near misses caused damage to rails and ties. As on all the runs against bridges during this period, there was no fighter opposition but anti-aircraft fire was experienced, sometimes intense but often inaccurate. All B-24s had fighter cover with P-51s from the 311th and 312th Fighter Groups.

While the 425th was hitting land targets during May, the 373rd was flying radar bombing missions and laying sonic and magnetic mines. Mines were laid in the Yangzte River on May 2, 13, 14, and 16. However, on the 9th, thirteen B-24s were sent from Luliang to bomb the town of Paoching. Numerous fires were started. Flak was moderate and one plane was damaged but all planes returned safely to base.

A special mission was laid on for May 15. One radar-equipped B-24 of the 373rd took off from Luliang to drop two Chinese agents and supplies by parachute into enemy territory. After the drop, the plane proceeded to Hainan Island and attacked a ship located offshore but without results.

In addition to the missing crew after the May 11 attack on the Yellow River bridge, a B-24 was lost with five men aboard on a flight from Deragaon, India, to Chengtu. For reasons unknown, the plane plunged into a river southeast of Pawngon, Burma. The bodies of two were found in the wreckage; the other three were listed as missing.

Colonel John G. Armstrong, now commander of the 308th, issued a proclamation for the group which summarized its record at the beginning of May 1945:

"Saturday May 5th marks the second anniversary of the first combat mission of the 308th Bombardment Group. Our versatility as a heavy bombardment group has been proven by day and night attacks, high, medium and low altitude bombing, mine laying and radar bombing. These sorties were against a variety of targets, most of which were heavily defended, in all kinds of weather and over poorly charted terrain. Units of this group have operated from behind enemy lines. Our men have become acclimated to enemy air raids and bombings, paucity of supplies and long periods of adverse weather conditions.

"In these two years, during which time the group has never exceeded 90 percent of its authorized strength, we have flown 4039 combat sorties totalling 34,975 hours, flown 6486 ferrying sorties totalling 21,603 hours, shot down 222 enemy planes confirmed, dropped 4090 tons of bombs, laid 433 tons of mines, expended 481,000 rounds of ammunition, hauled 9827 tons of freight and supplies, and actually sank 185 enemy vessels totalling 678,000 tons. We lost 116 aircraft and 53 crews. 164 men have been killed, 70 wounded, 312 are missing. A great many more have bailed out, but walked back safely.

"This is only part of the story. No attempt is made here to describe the devotion to duty of the officers and men of this group or the heroism of the flyers whose deeds lie behind these statistics. In paying tribute to those men who have given their lives in order that the success we have achieved could be attained, we should resolve, as we enter our third year of tactical operations to devote our energies and resources to one common goal, that of speeding in every way possible the final defeat of the enemy."

By the end of May, it was realized that the heavy bombers were no longer cost effective when compared to the new fighters in continuing an interdiction strategy. The P-51s could fly longer missions than the P-40s and packed a powerful punch against both land and sea targets with their ability to carry as much as 1,000 pounds of bombs and strafe with their six .50 caliber machine guns.

Gasoline was still in short supply in China. The question of what to do with the B-24 units was soon solved. The 308th and three of the four squadrons would retire to India and do what it had been doing for over two years: fly gasoline over the Hump from India to China. The 373rd and all of the radar-equipped B-24s would be transferred to Yontan Field on Okinawa and be absorbed into the Seventh Air Force.

When the news was official that the move would take place, the group historian noted that "gloom set in." He added:

> "Perhaps the most disappointed of all was big, keen Colonel Armstrong. He knows and loves heavy bombardment. Even his strict West Point dignity was insufficient to hold back an occasional inadvertent remark mirroring his despair...However, with typical American optimism, personnel philosophically sighed and observed, 'Well, maybe down in India we'll be able to get some decent supplies, mess and PX rations.' Although under no misapprehensions, most department heads found comfort in the thought that materiel procurement should be better in India than the heart-breaking scarcities endured in China."

The political situation in China, with General Wedemeyer in command, had improved under his leadership. However, in June, he was ordered by Generals Marshall and Arnold to reorganize the command, a move apparently intended to remove Chennault. The Tenth and Fourteenth Air Forces were to move to Chungking, with the Fourteenth's headquarters at Peishiyi, forty miles away. On July 6, 1945, eight years to the day that he first offered his services to China, Chennault requested relief from active duty. He said he would remain until Wedemeyer was fully acquainted with his new problems.

Under the reorganization, which was actually directed by General Stratemeyer, Chennault's air force was reduced to the size of a wing. Chennault had openly opposed Stratemeyer's plan for several reasons. He did not believe that a buildup of Air Force units in China could be justified if additional tonnage could not be provided. After his years of successfully managing the air war in China on his own, he did not wish to be subordinated to another commander who had been appointed by the Joint Chiefs of Staff in Washington to take over the whole air operation. Unfortunately, his "friend" in Washington, President Roosevelt, had died in April and he had no champion left in high places to whom he could unload his ideas and express his unhappiness with the reorganization. He had wanted to remain in China until victory over the Japanese was formally acknowledged but decided to retire and give ill health as his reason for leaving.

Obviously bitter, Chennault wrote in his memoirs: "Marshall and Arnold had made it quite plain that the Army held no future for me in China and that I would be barred from any significant participation in the victory. It was clearly time to go."[2]

Wedemeyer set July 31, 1945, as the date he could do without Chennault's services. Major General Charles B. Stone was appointed to take over the Fourteenth.

Chennault was not to leave China without that nation's highest decoration, the award of the Blue Sky and White Sun which was presented to him by a sad Generalissimo. General Wedemeyer presented him with a second Oak Leaf Cluster to his Distinguished Service Medal. Later, he also received similar awards from the U.S. Navy to go with earlier decorations he had received from Great Britain, France, and Poland. Before he departed the area on August 1, 1945, Chennault visited the main bases of the Fourteenth: Peishiyi, Hsian, Chengtu, Luliang, and finally Kunming.

The old warrior left China for his final flight over the Hump in a C-47. As he flew over the green rice paddies of Kunming, he mused about what he felt was "a record unsurpassed in the air annals of World War II." He had built an air force from 250 men and less than 100 planes to 20,000 men and 1,000 planes. In the three years of its operation, it had lost 500 planes from all combat causes, while destroying 2,600 enemy planes and probably destroying 1,500 more. His units had sunk and damaged 2,230,000 tons of enemy merchant shipping, 44 naval vessels, and 13,000 river boats under 100 tons; killed 66,700 enemy troops and knocked out 573 bridges.

The best testimonial of the effectiveness of the Fourteenth and its predecessors came from Lt. Gen. Takahashi, commander of Japanese forces in central China. In an interview after the war he said, "Considering all the difficulties my armies encountered in China, including guerrillas, ground armies, lack of supply, difficult terrain, non-cooperation of the Chinese, I judge the operations of the Fourteenth Air Force to have constituted between 60 percent and 75 percent of our effective opposition in China. Without the air force we could have gone anywhere we wished."

It is a sad commentary on the military politics of that era that not only was Chennault forced to leave China before the war was won, he was not invited to return for the surrender ceremonies aboard the battleship *Missouri* in September. He was formally retired in October 1945.

In a written exchange with the author in 1957 shortly before he died, Chennault had mellowed somewhat about his years in China:

"I believe that I was extremely fortunate as an air force commander.

I had the opportunity to break with tradition many times during my stay in China and get away with it insofar as some of my inflexible superiors were concerned. I believe that, as a result of my own experience, no officer of our military, especially our flying forces, should hesitate to break with tradition if, in his judgment, a departure will improve the chances of success for his unit or his side in the over-all picture. I believe that men who insist upon flexibility in all things and who retain their individualism are the ones who win battles, especially in the air. Fortunately, our nation has had enough of them when they were needed. I hope we always do."

Before he left China, the saddened and weary Chennault told Chiang Kai-shek that he would return to help restore the country, if asked. He did return a year later and organized an airline using surplus USAAF C-47 and C-46 aircraft; based in Formosa (later Taiwan), it was originally called CNRRA Air Transport but later was more familiarly known as Civil Air Transport or, simply, CAT. Chennault, fifty-seven, divorced his American wife and married Anna Chan, twenty-four, daughter of Dr. Y. W. Chan, former consul in San Francisco.

The Old Tiger returned to the States in 1958 and in July that year succumbed to lung cancer in New Orleans' Ochsner Foundation Hospital at age 67. He was laid to rest in Arlington National Cemetery with full military honors. Each year on the Saturday before Memorial Day, former members of the Fourteenth Air Force make a pilgrimage to the amphitheater near his gravesite to pay tribute to their leader. A military color guard is posted, wreaths are presented and an Air Force chaplain gives a prayer of remembrance. Mrs. Anna Chennault and others pay tribute to those of the Fourteenth who have died during the year and family members place red carnations in a ceremonial vase. Senator Ted W. Stevens (R-Alaska), who served with a B-25 squadron in the Fourteenth, usually attends. Afterwards, the group visits the gravesite about 50 yards away.

The 308th, as well as the other fighting units of the Fourteenth were sorry to see "Old Leatherface" leave China but there was nothing they could do about it, except continue to do their respective jobs against the enemy as he would have wished. Only two combat missions, both single-plane runs, were flown by the 308th in June 1945 to the Huto River north bridge, a target defended by moderate but inaccurate anti-aircraft. Both missions were with Azon bombs. On the June 2 mission, the bombs did not respond properly and the closest any came to the bridge was fifty feet.

On June 3, determined to score a hit, one plane made eleven runs over the bridge but only grazing hits were scored, to the bitter disappointment of the crew. These two missions – Nos. 566 and 567 – were the last two recorded combat missions of the 308th in China.

The 375th had already ceased combat operations and the 374th and 425th squadrons in the Chengtu area flew their last combat missions on June 3, 1945. The 374th, 375th, and the 308th headquarters began the move to Rupsi in northeast India. The 425th was assigned to Tezpur. Two weeks later, the 373rd, because of its special expertise in low altitude bombing with the B-24Js, left Kunming for Okinawa in the Pacific to join Kelly's Cobras, a Seventh Air Force Liberator Group.

Advance cadres under command of Major George Dowley left for the two bases in India between June 6 and 10 to prepare the new locations for occupancy. Many problems awaited the arrivals as they were confronted with intense, debilitating jungle heat, rain, and humidity. The Rupsi Air Base was named for a nearby village of about 100 natives which had been built by the British in 1942 for countering the Japanese in their offensive into India. With the success of the Burma campaign, the need for the base dissipated and it was abandoned. Only a few men had been retained to maintain it. It was located ten miles inland on the north bank of the Brahmaputra River. The nearest town of any size was Dhubri with about 3000 inhabitants. Tezpur was located in northeastern India not far from the Himalayas.

Most of the 308th's personnel were moved by the group's own B-24s; on the return trips to China, they flew gasoline to Chengtu; it was not considered a cost effective undertaking. The planes could not make the long haul, retain enough fuel to return to Rupsi and still carry 500 to 600 gallons for delivery.

The morale of the men was not enhanced at Rupsi and Tezpur when they began to work with the Indian natives. The historian commented:

"Used to happy, intelligent and respectable Chinese, the Americans found shiftless, black-skinned, dirty native people mostly clad only in filthy loin cloths. [Despite] the saying "to know is to love," the energetic Yankees quickly lost respect for the Indians whom they immediately came to regard as 'stupid.' It was probable, however, that the debilitating climate would sooner or later have the energies of the Americans whittled down also."

To add to their discomfort, June always marks the beginning of the rainy season in India. The men were warned about the contagious diseases that were rampant in the area, especially venereal diseases and malaria. The difficulty of getting good food with the help of natives who were unschooled in even basic sanitation, mess operation, and table service added to the misery. To assure the health of the men and prevent exposure to food poisoning, all food was taken from cans. However, for the first time, everyone had his fill of ice cold beer, Coca Cola and ice cream. In general, despite the conditions, the men believed living conditions were much better in India, with the exception of the heat which they had not experienced in China.

During June 1945, the 308th flew a total of 633 supply sorties to and from China; several hundred passengers were flown west and 130,000 gallons of high octane gas, plus an equal volume of freight, were transported to the bases at Chengtu. Again tragedy struck. A 375th B-24, with a crew of six, took off from Chengtu on June 13 for India and disappeared. Another B-24, piloted by Lt. John E. Kapsner, departed Rupsi for Daragson on a routine flight, also with a crew of six, and no contact was ever established after takeoff. It was found later in the swamps near Jorhat, India; all six men aboard had perished in the crash. Another bomber, piloted by Lt. John W. Schmierer from the 375th, was reported missing on a flight from Hsinching, China, to Rupsi on July 27. No trace was ever found.

In another incident, a B-24 was landing at Tezpur when it caught fire due to faulty brakes. In a hurried effort to evacuate the plane, a crew member ran into a spinning propeller and died of a fractured skull and severe hemorrhaging. He was buried in the Tezpur Military Cemetery.

The anonymous Group historian wrote the longest historical report found in the 308th's files to describe the situation in India in July 1945. Here are some excerpts:

"Everyone learned the tropical art of relaxing. They mastered the procedure of getting intense work done while working at a leisurely pace. The siesta, Indian style, became an institution. Along with the daily bull session circles in the evening, the inevitable Army pastime of poker took hold. In numerous barracks, games were conducted with the regularity of the hometown movie schedule.

"Mess conditions improved in geometric progression. The improvement not only in service, sanitation, but in variety and quality of food was little short of miraculous. A new-found delicacy found its way to the table: tropical fruit. Many boys were delighted with mangos, pineapples and bananas.

"The PX climbed on the ball and began procuring a case of beer each month for each man. There were great numbers of other choice tidbits such as candy and domestic accessories. However, the beer did more than anything to bring the sun from behind the cloud.

"Literally, the sun went behind the clouds after the first week of the month and didn't come back out. The monsoons which were to have started last month had come to be a laugh. Like outraged nature, the skies filled with clouds and the heavens burst quieting all who scoffed at the intensity of the word 'monsoon.'

"The weather not only brought inconvenience. It brought a humidity that threatened to strip everyone of his worldly goods. Devastating mildew attacked all clothes, especially those of leather. Breath-taking odor of wet, damp fungus filled all barracks. Clothes took on a sour smell. It became increasingly difficult to get laundry to dry.

"The rains had their bright side. It became not only possible but pleasurable to sleep at night. During the days, torrents of perspiration were dried because of the delightful drop in temperature.

"Accidents were high [during July] and ranging from collapsing nose wheels on landing to grisly crashes into the jungle. Vicious jinxes followed hard on the heels of one particular crew. It narrowly escaped death on four occasions. They had to bail out once from a ship running out of gasoline. A nose wheel collapsed. They smashed into a tree on takeoff. In a rainstorm they overshot and crashed into the end of the runway.

"During July, everyone accustomed to both American money and the Chinese yuan finally mastered the new standard of values in the Indian rupee medium in which we are now paid.

"Most persistent rumors had it that the Group would be transferred back to the States and deactivated; that they'd be sent to Calcutta to transition into A-26s; that they'd be sent back to China or the Pacific for combat; that they'd lose their identity as a bomb group and dissolve into the oblivion of an Air Transport Command base stuck away to dry up in some jungle hole permanently."

On July 1, 1945, Lt. Col. William D. Hopson, formerly deputy group commander, took command of the 308th and was destined to be its last commander during World War II.

Meanwhile, rotation of 308th personnel back to the States was nearly stopped during June, July, and August and it wasn't until August 31st that a small group received travel orders to go home under the point system.

From the bases at Rupsi and Tezpur, the three remaining squadrons of the 308th were devoted to assisting the Air Transport Command in flying gasoline over the Hump to China. More than 270,000 gallons of gas were carried in 578 sorties during July. When August began, according to the Group historian, "No one had any premonition during the entire first week of August that the month would bring anything but routine events, including more dull gasoline hauls over the Hump."

It was the news of the delivery of an atomic bomb on Hiroshima on August 6 that shaped the future for everyone involved in the CBI. But among the men of the 308th, there was disagreement that the Japanese would surrender unconditionally, especially with more than half a million armed soldiers left in occupied China. The group historian tells of the two divergent views about when the war would end:

"Major Henry Teichert and Major John Osbourne believed implicitly in the ability of the bomb to bring about an end to the war by October 1st. A vast majority of challengers thought they were out of their minds. Their arguments were not idle; they back them up with cold cash. Major Osbourne slapped down a thousand dollars on the barrel head and figuratively said, 'Put up or shut up.' Major Teichert followed right behind with five hundred dollars on the same bet. Their opponents weren't willing to shut up so they put up. Everyone settled back to watchful waiting.

"They didn't wait long. In three or four days they heard President Truman in far off America announce that the forces of Soviet Russia had been plunged into Manchuria against the empire of Dai Nippon. This enhanced the October argument. Reports of the destruction of the bomb not only continued but became more emphatic. By the tenth of the month, Rupsi Air Base was startled by the first report of surrender.

"There were celebrations at both 308th bases with much firing of
.45 pistols, rebel yells, songs, and drinking what celebratory juices were
available. After the second atomic bomb was dropped on Nagasaki on
August 9, it appeared that immediate surrender was forthcoming."

The historian of the 425th Squadron noted his observations with a different perspective:

"VJ Day [August 14, 1945] had little effect on men in the squadron,
as was the case of VE Day when the squadron was at Kwanghan. Celebrations were few and those were of a mild nature. For those men who
had been overseas since the beginning the two victories seemed to have
little to offer. Perhaps their minds were dulled to the fact that they would
get home sooner, or perhaps the end of the war came sooner than expected and they couldn't yet believe that the one thing they had been
fighting for had actually happened. There was no slackening of work
and daily routine continued as it had for more than 30 months.

"The one thing everyone looked forward to and talked about was
the day when everyone in the squadron would be home for good and
khaki exchanged for civvies. With the realization that the war seemed to
be over, the point system for return to the States and discharge was the
main topic of conversation and speculation. However, operations for the
308th continued. Gasoline still had to be hauled over the Hump and the
Group's quota remained throughout the month of August. The 374th
was cited for flying the greatest total gasoline loads into China with the
smallest number of aircraft. At this time, most of the squadron gunners
and bombardiers, no longer needed, were leaving for the States. The
others remained and made twenty-eight crossings of the Hump hauling
gas and bombs."

Several 308th crews flew over the Hump to Hsian and dropped leaflets
to Allied prisoners of war confined in camps at Keijo, Peiping and Weishien
in China, Korea and Mukden in Manchuria. They assisted in the repatria-
tion of many survivors who had been captured on Wake Island, Bataan, and
Corregidor. Some Fourteenth Air Force fighter pilots who had been captured were also flown out.

On August 24, 1945, three of the four surviving Doolittle Tokyo Raiders

- Sgt. Jacob DeShazer, Lt. Robert L. Hite and Lt. Chase J. Nielsen – who had been captured after their historic raid on Japan of April 18, 1942, were flown from Peking (now Beijing) to Shanghai by a 374th plane for transport to the States. George Barr, the fourth survivor of the eight Tokyo Raiders captured, was too sick to travel and was evacuated later. On August 29, a 374th plane evacuated two American generals from General Jonathan Wainright's staff who were captured on Corrigidor and eight Royal Netherlands East India Army generals from a prison at Mukden, Manchuria.

The 308th crews returned to Rupsi and Tezpur with sad stories of the physical state of the former prisoners and the arrogance of the Japanese. Scores of Japanese pistols, swords, and other war souvenirs were "liberated" from the Japanese and returned home with the victors as mementoes of their service in the CBI.

During the month, the Group tried to continue a normal routine. A new officers' club opened and parties were held frequently there and in the enlisted clubs. Hopson was promoted to full Colonel and the 308th was awarded its second Presidential Unit Citation for its work in China.

Naturally, rumors were a daily fare. Some said that the entire Group would be returned to the States and deactivated. Others believed they would be deactivated first and then sent home as individuals. The detachment that had remained in Kunming was removed and many officers and men received orders to proceed to the States individually.

The slowdown in flying activity gave the personnel much free time to travel to see the sights in India: Calcutta, with its bazaars featuring ivory and exquisite handiwork, the Great Western Hotel, Firpo's, and the Kanarney Estates were the main attractions. New Delhi was another favorite destination. Many, realizing they would probably never return to India, visited the world-famous Taj Mahal. As the Group history states, "By August, these places were luring rank and file personnel into the crowded and filthy streets of 'Calicut.' Tales of 'white' women, good Stateside whiskey and all that goes with them were bandied over the beer bottles in the clubs at Rupsi."

Others, who had no interest in sightseeing, took advantage of the opportunity to hunt wild animals in the jungle. At least two leopards were killed and several members of the 308th stalked the famous Bengal tiger but without results. Meanwhile, the monsoon rains vented their fury and the bases were not spared. The nearby Brahmaputra rose and raged over the countryside, covering villages and paddies. The mosquitoes increased but the malarial control unit was able to effect some measure of control. No new cases of malaria were reported.

The "vacation" for the 308th had to end. Most of the crews and many ground personnel received orders to return to the States. The last flights across the Hump were made in mid-September. Capt. Charles W. Swanson, 374th intelligence officer, made this last entry in the squadron record:

> "18 Sept 45 - The gas haul is finished. Here I come, Shangri-La. The wogs can have Rupsi; we will fly our Hump-weary planes home."

Lt. Leland Miles, 373rd navigator, recalled his feelings as he was flying west as a passenger in a C-46:

> "I stuck my head up in the celestial dome just behind the pilot and looked westward where the sun was sneaking one last peep over mighty 14,000-foot Tali Mountain. It was a pretty sight. Considering the direction in which I was traveling, it was more than pretty. It was downright beautiful."

On September 15, 1945, General Wedemeyer radioed a message to Colonel Hopson: "On the occasion of the third anniversary of the 308th Bomb Group, I wish to extend heart-felt congratulations. The record of achievement in the China Theater is a great credit to the officers and men who have loyally, selflessly and effectively contributed to victory. You can feel justifiably proud as you reflect upon the years of excellent service which you have rendered. Sincere good wishes to each and every one of you, continued success and happiness."

Karl Hartung, a member of the 375th's communications section, had joined the squadron in mid-October 1942 and was still with the squadron at war's end. He remembers that Colonel Hopson had "fixed it" so the squadrons could fly their own planes home.

"Not one of us believed he could work it out," he said, "and we knew that it took some doing, but he was successful in getting permission. In addition to the air crews, each plane was scheduled to carry along ground personnel with those who had been overseas the longest (75 points or more) getting first priority. That included me and I've been grateful to Colonel Hopson ever since.

"Someone had the foresight to list us as 'gunners.' That made us crew members, and we couldn't be bumped on the way home by men with more points or brass trying to pull rank. I was on the first plane to leave India for home. That was on the morning of October 15, 1945, a date I'll never forget."

As many of the air crews flew their own B-24s back to the States, the general route was via Karachi, Abadan, Cairo, Tripoli, Marakesh, Dakar, Belem, Georgetown, British Guiana, and Borinquen Field, Puerto Rico. The final landing for most was at Morrison Field, West Palm Beach, Florida.

Although the Group's squadrons had been withdrawn from combat in China in June 1945, it was not until December 7, 1945, that the last contingent of the Group left India for the United States aboard the *S.S. General Black*. They landed at New York and were transported to Camp Kilmer, New Jersey for disposition on January 5, 1946. The Group and its four squadrons were officially inactivated the following day.

In one of the last official acts of the 308th's war saga, Major General Charles B. Stone, commander of the Fourteenth Air Force on VJ Day, issued General Order No. 114 to commend the Group which summarized the latter part of its service in China:

"Between 24 May 1944 and 28 April 1945, this group preyed relentlessly on the Japanese sea shipping lanes between the Japanese homeland and her conquests throughout southern Asia and adjacent insular territories.

"During most of this period, this Group was the only organization among all the Allied Forces in a position to conduct interdiction operations against this vital supply line.

"Operating from bases in China, the Group swept the East and South China Seas, the Straits of Formosa and the Gulf of Tonkin through all kinds of weather, sinking and damaging nearly three quarters of a million tons of vital Japanese shipping. They sank 107 merchant vessels and sank 12 enemy naval vessels, including three cruisers and seven destroyers. They probably sank 29 vessels and damaged 48 for a total of 427,252 tons of shipping sunk, 102,765 tons probably sunk and 187,045 tons damaged.

"Pressed by the constant need for economy of operations from air-supplied China, the Group forsook the usual style of bombing to attain accuracy and minimum expenditure of bombs. Heroically and deliberately, the combat crews developed and employed low-altitude tactics that brought their slow, heavy bombers down to within 400 feet of their targets during attacks. This exposed their aircraft to murderous fire from the armed merchantmen and naval vessels they attacked.

"On a number of occasions, the crews carried out attacks at 400 feet over entire convoys of eight to twelve armed merchantmen and naval ships. Throughout the cited period, the Group was forced to fly much of its own gasoline and bombs over the 'Hump' (Himalaya Mountains) into China, and in the same period, was forced to evacuate from three bases before the advance of enemy ground forces. For several months the Group launched its sea-search missions from a base behind enemy lines in East China.

"The phenomenal achievements of the 308th Bombardment Group (H) in its interdiction of these vital enemy shipping lanes are the result of extraordinary heroism, gallantry, determination and esprit-de-corps demonstrated by the members of this organization. Their attainments are consonant with the finest traditions of the American military service."

Perhaps the greatest praise for the 308th came from General Chennault himself in his memoirs:

"They took the heaviest combat losses of any group in China and often broke my heart by burning thousands of gallons of gas only to dump their bombs in rice paddy mud far from the target. However, their bombing of Vinh railroad shops in Indo-China, the Kowloon and Kai Tak docks at Hong Kong, and the shipping off Saigon were superb jobs unmatched anywhere. When the Army Air Forces Headquarters in Washington tallied the bombing accuracy of every bomb group in combat, I was astonished to find that the 308th led them all."[3]

The 308th had lost many men during its tenure in the CBI. Most of those who were buried in the American cemeteries in China or in remote villages by Chinese peasants were returned to the United States after the war. But the burial sites of some were not known until long after the war. That was the case of the crew of the *Red Hot Riding Hood*, piloted by Wayne Schlentz, that exploded during a mission of the 374th Squadron on October

9, 1944. Pieces of the plane and bodies of the ten-man crew were located five years later scattered along the banks of the Yangtze River about 200 miles southwest of Wuchang. In addition to Schlentz, the other crew members found were James W. Brown; Harold R. Dawson; William S. Clarke, Ira S. Ingle, George A. Leschner and Thadeus Nocek.

Local Chinese peasants had gathered the remains of the crew and buried them so nothing would fall into the hands of the Japanese. Unfortunately, their bodies were damaged so that individual identifications could not be made with certainty. Long after the war, the American Graves Registration Service found the graves and brought the remains back to the United States. A group burial was conducted with full military honors at Jefferson Barracks National Cemetery, Missouri on September 29, 1949.

Old sorrows were revived again on December 7, 1973, the 32nd anniversary of the Japanese attack on Pearl Harbor, when five members of the 425th Bomb Squadron were buried together at Arlington National Cemetery. The five men, all in their twenties, were reported missing on August 7, 1945 while returning to India from a gas-hauling mission to China. Their remains were found in early 1973 in dense jungle high in the mountains near Imphal, India. The five were Flight Officer Richard H. Franken, pilot; Lt. James W. Cantrell, co-pilot; Flight Officer Francis P. Yuskaitis, navigator; S/Sgt. Harvey E. Brockmiller, radio operator; and Sgt. William J. Cannady, flight engineer.

Because of the condition of the remains, it was decided to bury them together. In addition to thirty-six surviving relatives, two former members of the 425th also paid their last respects at the gravesite. They were Leo Dufrechou, who had been a co-pilot on that crew previously, and John G. Bolton, an armorer.

There is a monument on the Imphal Trail to Burma near where the crash occurred. It was erected by the Burma Star Medal Association of Great Britain to honor British soldiers who had died fighting for the cause in the CBI. Its words also seem appropriate for all the members of the 308th who made the supreme sacrifice:

When You Go Home Tomorrow
Tell Them Of Us And Say
For Your Tomorrow
We Gave Our Today

Chapter 8

THREE POWS
TELL THEIR STORIES

I t is not known exactly how many of the members of the 308th Bomb Group who bailed out or crashlanded fell into the hands of the Japanese and became prisoners-of-war. Some of those who bailed out were killed or seriously wounded by enemy fighters as they parachuted to earth. Reliable sources behind the lines or in Japanese-held territory reported that some were killed by revengeful Japanese soldiers after landing safely. Some may have died of disease, torture, or starvation while in captivity and their deaths were never reported after the war. Others may have evaded capture only to die in the jungle from disease, injuries or attacks by animals.

An inquiry to the American Ex-Prisoners-of-War organization in Arlington, Texas, revealed that there are only six former 308th personnel who were listed as members of that organization. They were Paul W. Abernathy, Hildebran, North Carolina; Don Z. Davis, Mt. Zion, Illinois; Jay Hawe, Jacksonville, Florida; Glenn A. McConnell, Annapolis, Maryland; William H. Thomas, Cummings, Kansas; and Earl S. Vann, Murfreesboro, North Carolina. It was learned that Don Davis died in 1987. However, as will be seen, there were many more 308th POWs, including nine of the ten members of William Thomas's crew, who survived captivity and eventually returned to the States.

The author interviewed Col. Glenn A. McConnell in his Annapolis home in May 1994. Here is his story:

Glenn A. McConnell, a resident of Hollywood, California, enlisted in the Army Air Corps in 1941 and completed the aircraft armament course. He applied for aviation cadet training, was accepted and completed flying training with Class 43D. He was commissioned a Second Lieutenant at Douglas, Arizona, in April, 1943.

McConnell wanted to fly the B-26 Marauder but was assigned to B-24s instead. He completed the training phases and arrived in China in September 1943 as a co-pilot aboard a B-24D assigned to the 373rd Bomb Squadron.

After flying a variety of search, bombing, and Hump missions as co-pilot out of Yankai and Kweilin, he moved to the left seat in January 1944. At that time, the group had two radar-equipped B-24Ds without belly turrets. The requirement for trained personnel to operate the radar meant the aircraft flew with eleven-man crews on sea searches from the forward base at Kweilin.

The usual tactic was for two aircraft to take off on parallel tracks, although neither crew would normally see the other, and arrive over their assigned ocean patrol areas. After leaving the land areas, they would fly at about 200 feet.

On March 19, 1944, McConnell and his crew flew a particularly successful mission from Kweilin. At the end of the mission they were to land at Suichwan and prepare to go on another mission.

They crossed the shoreline and descended to begin their search. As they droned along under a low overcast, the radar operator saw what he thought was the other B-24 circling ahead. It wasn't. It was a Kawanishi 97, a large Japanese four-engine flying boat (code name: Mavis). McConnell started in pursuit as his gunners began blasting away when it came into their sights. The gunners on the flying boat returned the fire. As the Liberator edged closer, the Kawanishi's No. 3 engine began to smoke and the pilot pulled up into the clouds. Although he caught sight of it through the clouds a few times, McConnell gave up after a few minutes and returned to his search track at low altitude.

About forty-five minutes later, McConnell looked ahead and saw an enemy flying boat heading straight toward him! Both planes took immediate evasive action. Sam Auslander, the co-pilot, was flying the B-24. He reacted immediately by turning on a switch on his wheel which was hooked up to two .50 caliber guns in the nose. McConnell, watching the enemy plane turn away, saw Auslander's shots hit the tail surface. The top turret gunner and the right waist gunner began shooting as the B-24 passed underneath.

At this moment, a single bullet blasted through the center section of the windshield, went past McConnell's throat, hit his armor plate and shattered into shrapnel. McConnell was hit in the arm with flying glass. One of the crew members behind the flight deck was also hit by bits of the bullet and glass. The flight engineer, standing between the two pilots, suddenly disappeared. The impact of the blast had driven him backwards to the rear of the aircraft. When McConnell turned around to see what happened to him, he was making his way forward with his head bleeding; fortunately, he was not seriously wounded.

The damage to the aircraft included the destruction of both radio compasses and the electric compass. Another bullet cut a hydraulic line and knocked out most of the electrical system, while two more hits caused a bad oil leak in the No. 3 engine. As the crew watched the other plane overhead, its wing started to burn between the Nos. 3 and 4 engines. McConnell took over the controls and turned the plane away quickly in case the flying boat blew up. Crew members saw a large piece of wing fall off and watched the plane dive into the water. The last thing they saw was the tail and rear fuselage sticking out of the waves. One of the crew members had a camera and was able to take several photos to document their "kill."

While McConnell headed for Kweilin instead of Suichwan, two crew members entered the bomb bays which were flooded with hydraulic fluid, cranked open the bomb bay doors and salvoed the bombs. When they arrived over the field, the nose wheel refused to go down. Expended machine gun casings from the nose guns had jammed the gear mechanism but the engineer and bombardier were able to break them loose by using the barrel of one of the machine guns as a fulcrum to break the jam.

Meanwhile, they had no hydraulic pressure because a bullet had cut through an emergency hydraulic line in the bomb bay. The gear was cranked down but there was no fluid left for braking after the landing. McConnell was able to land and eventually stop before coming to the end of the runway. McConnell and two other crew members were taken to the dispensary and treated for their wounds. All three received the Purple Heart. The crew later received a letter of commendation from General Chennault for their unusual aerial victory.

The aircraft was repaired at Kweilin but, after flying a trip to Kunming and then Yankai, a mechanic discovered a hole in the No. 3 engine nacelle. Sitting on top of the engine's supercharger was an unexploded 20mm shell. If it had exploded at any time, the supercharger, rotating at an extremely high speed, would have caused much damage as it shattered.

The mission of April 18, 1944, was to be the last for *Sweepy Time Gal,* the name chosen for McConnell's aircraft. On that date, two "Sniffers" were dispatched from Kweilin on a sea sweep, flying separate parallel courses. The other plane completed its mission and returned to Kweilin without sighting any targets or dropping any bombs. Glenn McConnell piloted the other plane; its eleven-man crew consisted of McConnell, pilot; Lt. Samuel Auslander, co-pilot; Lt. Robert Carney, navigator; Lt. R. F. Moessner, bombardier; T/Sgt Peter S. Maholick, flight engineer; T/Sgt Robert Berman, radio operator; S/Sgt Barton W. Owens, assistant flight engineer; S/Sgt T. Spadafora, assistant radio operator; S/Sgt C. W. Holley, armorer; S/Sgt J. Oroyecz, tail gunner and S/Sgt. Erwin H. Posner, radar operator. The crew was supplemented by Lt. John V. Mroz, a non-rated radar specialist who wanted to go along to see how the equipment operated in combat. The weather was marginal and McConnell exited the land area at St. John's Island for a sea sweep at 200 feet.

About an hour out over the South China sea, Posner called over the interphone, "I've got a target!" It was about twenty miles ahead and got larger as they approached. The blip on the radar scope turned out to be a Japanese destroyer with a smaller steamer trailing in its wake.

McConnell lined up at an angle to the two and made two bomb runs with 500 lb. bombs while the destroyer blazed away with its anti-aircraft guns. The turret gunners who could see the targets fired rounds with their .50 calibers. The bombs missed on both runs and McConnell was admittedly "mad as hell," as was Sam Auslander. Auslander was so eager to get the freighter that he opened the window and pumped away with his .45 automatic pistol when they flew by.

As they pulled up and away, McConnell decided to return to base. In the subsequent flight back, he believes the top turret guns firing right over the nose agitated the repeater compass excessively and induced a 20- or 30-degree error. Instead of crossing onto the mainland at St. John's Island, they ended up near Hong Kong at 200 feet. By the time McConnell realized they were far from their assumed position, the plane picked up ground fire. Simultaneously, three Japanese fighters – probably Army Oscars – appeared suddenly and made a pass. The lead fighter fired a burst; the other two didn't.

McConnell thought they had missed at first but that one burst had taken out the B-24's Nos. 3 and 4 engines and they couldn't be feathered. Both engines began to burn as McConnell struggled to keep the aircraft in level flight at 200 feet; the right wing began to burn and break off. With both engines on the right side and the right wing deteriorating and thus creating excessive drag while the left wing provided lift, the plane began to drag on the wave tops. The last time McConnell saw the air speed indicator, it read 95 miles per hour. The right wing – what was left of it – caught on the waves and the plane cartwheeled and smashed into the water with the nose down. The front of the aircraft disintegrated. McConnell and the co-pilot catapulted out through where the windshield had been and McConnell found himself about twenty feet underwater. As he rose to the surface in the darkness, he saw an island nearby. An excellent swimmer, he decided to shuck his life jacket and swim to shore. He believes he saw Sam Auslander surface a time or two and possibly two or three other crew members but is not sure who they were.

Meanwhile, the three enemy fighters returned and started strafing. They missed hitting McConnell on the first pass and made as many as ten more passes shooting at the wreckage and anyone getting out of the plane. McConnell dove under the water each time and could see the machine gun bullets hitting the water, flattening out and coming down toward the bottom.

In a few minutes, McConnell was picked up by a Japanese patrol boat, along with Tony Spadafora, the radio operator/gunner, who had been badly injured. The boat crew came toward McConnell shooting as the fighters pulled away but they either missed or deliberately fired over his head to be sure he would not resist. When they hauled him aboard, he was blindfolded and had his hands tied behind him. He believes Spadafora was also taken aboard at the same time but didn't see or hear him.

Both men were taken to a Hong Kong confinement facility called the St. John's Ambulance Yard where the camp commander, who spoke excellent English, later showed McConnell a photo from the Hong Kong paper of the wreckage of the *Sweepy Time Gal* which had been picked up and placed on a barge. McConnell believes that the bodies of three other crew members may have been picked up at this time. Of the twelve men on board, only these three, plus Spadafora and McConnell, were ever accounted for. Spodafora suffered a compound fracture of the right knee, an injury that was never properly treated during his subsequent captivity.

Back at Kweilin, when McConnell's aircraft did not return, a report on the 308th's Mission No. 93 was submitted to Group headquarters by the squadron intelligence officer:

"No direct information from American sources has been received from this crew, but Chinese ground reports from Hong Kong indicate with reasonable certainty that the plane was shot down near Lyemun Pass, or Channel, at Hong Kong. Chinese reported that two airmen got out of the plane when it hit the water, inflated a rubber raft, and were later captured and brought into Hong Kong. One other crew member was reported to have parachuted, and was killed by gun fire during the descent. No information is available concerning the fate of the remaining crew members. A part of the plane also was taken into Hong Kong and put on display there. The two captured crew members were reportedly taken into the Causeway Bay Military Prison. No information has been received which throws any light on the identity of the captured men."

While there were some elements of the report that were accurate, it is not exactly what happened. No raft was inflated and no one could have possibly parachuted out of the crippled B-24.

For the next few days, McConnell was interrogated by Japanese Navy personnel and tortured because he would give only his name, rank and serial number. He was whipped repeatedly on his thighs between his knees and buttocks with a heavy ship's hawser. "You can handle this all right in the mornings," McConnell told the author, "but in the afternoon, the blood vessels swell, your senses get aggravated and the nerve endings are so sensitive that it is unbelievably painful. You find that you urinate without control. When this kind of beating is repeated for several days, you lose all thought of resisting and want to tell them anything that will make them stop."

McConnell says they had been told in briefings by unit intelligence officers that when the enemy tortures got to the point they couldn't stand it and name, rank, and serial number were not enough to call off the beatings, they could tell their interrogators anything they wanted. Consequently, McConnell gave them all kinds of fictitious but plausible information and told confusing stories that he hoped would befuddle his inquisitors.

The interrogation by what appeared to be naval personnel included questions about the flying units in China, his training, how many aircraft were in the theater and back in the States. If he gave an answer that they believed to be false, he was beaten repeatedly. Sometimes he was beaten for no reason. Towering over his captors, a few of the guards, always shorter than he was, seemed to take delight in inflicting pain on the tall American.

The camp commander, who never identified himself, took over some of the questioning but seemed more interested in what was going on in the United States. His questions were on a higher level concerning the overall American economic situation. Was it business as usual? Was the American industry putting out consumer goods as well as military products? What about commercial transportation? How did people get around? What was the general public attitude toward Japan and the war? McConnell could only answer vaguely and he does not know today what intelligence value the enemy could garner from the answers to this kind of questioning.

After several days, the physical abuse ceased. He had been handcuffed the entire time he was in custody but was able to slip the handcuffs off to soothe his wrists at night and relax his arms and shoulders when the guards were not looking. Twelve days after the crash, McConnell was readied for transfer but since the handcuffs belonged to the jail, they had to be removed. However, in trying to unlock them, the guards broke the key off in the lock and were at a loss as to how to get back their handcuffs. When they seemed unable to solve the situation, McConnell slipped them off and handed them to his captors who were greatly embarrassed. "That didn't go over good at all because they had lost face," McConnell says. "However, they didn't knock me around over this but did tie me up tightly from then on with rope."

After twelve days in Hong Kong, McConnell was put in a cage on a Japanese destroyer for a three-day trip to Formosa, "hoping every minute we weren't going to be attacked by a B-24," he said. "I knew the Japanese would not have cared about what happened to me if the ship were attacked and was going down."

There were no other prisoners aboard and the cage was so small he couldn't stretch out. He spent the time cramped up in a sitting position until the ship docked in a Formosa port. He spent one day in a jail there blindfolded and tied and was then placed on a bomber. The plane landed at one of the Japanese islands where he was placed in a cell at what he believes was a college campus or military academy. After one night there, he was led aboard a passenger train with a Japanese Navy warrant officer as escort. He continued to be blindfolded and a sort of lampshade was placed over his head. He had had no shoes since he was captured and was wearing shorts. Strangely, he had been given Sgt. Berman's leather A-2 jacket; he has no idea where it came from unless they had recovered Berman's body.

McConnell does not recall how long he traveled on the train but it may have been two days with the warrant officer as his escort. He made no effort to escape because he felt that his chances of surviving would be short-lived as a Caucasian in an Oriental country, especially barefooted and dressed as he was. At intervals along the route, he was led blindfolded onto the station platforms and taken for a walk. He heard Japanese civilians ooh, aah and whisper as he walked by but none made any moves against him nor were they held back from attacking him if they had wanted to.

McConnell was taken to a secret Navy interrogation camp at Ofuna, a suburb of Yokohama and former Japanese film colony, on May 1, 1944. When he arrived, it held about forty Army, Navy, and Marine and Allied officer and enlisted personnel who were captured at various locations. One of the prisoners was Major Gregory "Pappy" Boyington, famous Marine ace and commander of the famous Black Sheep Squadron, who had been shot down on a mission to Rabaul. He had been seriously wounded with the most serious injuries being a shattered ankle and a large hole in his inner thigh.

In his autobiography, Boyington explained that Ofuna was not like ordinary prisoner-of-war camps: "The idea was to try to make you miserable enough so that they could pry military information out of you. This went on for a year to eighteen months for each prisoner. Not every prisoner went through Ofuna, but people they thought had some special value to them were sent there. There were submarine survivors, pilots, and technicians of various kinds, besides anyone with any rank they were able to get hold of."[1]

Boyington added, "We were all warned that we were special captives of the Japanese, and that we were not prisoners of war, and that we would not be entitled to the privileges of prisoners of war. We were to be held strictly off the books. In other words, the Japanese did not notify our government through the Swiss that we were alive. To our people back home or anyone else we remained missing in action or dead."[2]

Although he had not traveled with McConnell, Tony Spadafora of the *Sweepy*'s crew was also transferred to Ofuna; his injuries were unattended and giving him great pain. Newly arrived prisoners were usually placed in solitary confinement for the first few days, then placed in wards with the others. The reason was probably so that the new arrivals could not tell the others what was going on in the war zones. As Boyington explained: "They wanted to keep us depressed and uninformed for control. The mix of prisoners from each of the services also seemed to be deliberate, probably so a variety of intelligence information could be extracted from us."[3]

During the summer of 1944, the prisoners thought they could tell how the war was going by the conduct of the guards. "They would get surly and highly emotional," McConnell said. "We could sense they were very touchy and the result would be a bashing. A guard would look around and when he saw someone he didn't like or he felt had been disrespectful, he would grab that individual and beat him with great relish in front of the others."

McConnell was beaten severely with a baseball bat on one occasion for about ten minutes by a particularly mean guard, along with several others. After a thrashing, the protocol was that the prisoners had to bow toward their assailant, about face, and return to the ranks. Weakened by the sparse diet, McConnell bowed, turned and fell over in a faint as he tried to rejoin his position in ranks. It had been reported to the inmates that anyone who fainted would be hauled away and beaten to death. McConnell's prison mates promptly yanked him to his feet and he was not punished further.

One memory that remains uppermost in McConnell's mind about his imprisonment at Ofuna was the food. There was soup, flavored with bean paste that had the color and consistency of peanut butter, and a brown grain, probably some kind of barley, served three times a day. There were a few greens included which were probably carrot tops, plus potato peelings; an occasional fishhead or two would be found but very little other kinds of identifiable meat. McConnell, normally weighing 190 lbs when he was captured, was reduced to about 135 in a short time.

"We were always hungry," he says, "and food was always the main topic of conversation. Sex was never mentioned and we rarely even talked about flying. Instead, the guys would talk about recipes, writing cookbooks, running a restaurant, working in a grocery store or anything connected with food when they got back home. All I wanted to do when I got back home was drive a bakery truck. If you could get a job working in the kitchen with the Japs, that was the best you could hope for because you could then steal some food when they weren't looking."

When Fall came, keeping warm also became uppermost in the POWs' battle for survival. They were issued some used Japanese jumpers and a medium weight cotton jacket and pants. McConnell eventually got a pair of shoes but was never issued any socks. One of the highlights of his days at Ofuna was finding a filthy handkerchief dropped by someone with a major sinus problem. He said it was like finding gold because after months of using his sleeve, he now had his own handkerchief.

Prisoners were kept in separate cells and slept on the floor with two cotton blankets. They were too short for McConnell and he always had a part of him uncovered. During the cold weather when the sun was shining, they would stand outside against their prison barracks facing the west in two or three lines. The ones nearest the wall were warmed by the heat of the sun reflecting against the building. After a few minutes, the back line would come to the front and the second line would move against the wall; the front line would become the second line. This ritual would be repeated as long as the sun shined on the wall.

McConnell was moved in January 1945 to Omouri (also spelled Amori) on the outskirts of Tokyo to make room for new prisoners, many of whom had been crew members in B-29 Superforts. He stayed there about six weeks and was moved to Shumida Gowa, a working camp, with other officers. The other inmates there included about 150 American Army, Navy, and Merchant Marine enlisted men, plus a few foreign nationals.

In both camps, McConnell vividly remembers seeing and hearing the B-29s flying over toward their targets, mostly at night. Although the prisoners were glad to know they were attacking the enemy nearby, there was the ever-present fear that they would be bombed because from the air the prison camp looked like any other enemy cantonment area.

The treatment of prisoners at Shimada Gowa was better and the officers were treated as officers which meant they were placed in charge of work details unloading sacks of grain or coal from barges at the nearby port. McConnell felt that he was blessed when he was made mess officer and never was sent on a work detail. He later received the Bronze Star for supervising the food service personnel and seeing that meals were prepared as sanitarily and as efficiently as possible despite blackouts, air raids, food and fuel shortages.

At no time during his captivity did McConnell ever see another member of the 308th other than Spadofora. He attributes this to the belief that many of the B-24 crew members whose planes were shot down were unable to get out of the planes once the pilots lost control due to the centrifugal force imposed on the plane which they were unable to overcome. He also feels that some may not have wanted to jump into occupied territory because of the reputation the Japanese had for summarily executing prisoners, especially those who had bombed their installations.

As the number of B-29s increased overhead, so did the number that were shot down. The prisoners watched as one would be hit by flak or incapacitated by a defending Zero. "It was heart-rending to see one get hit and go into a death spiral," McConnell says. "We would watch to see if anyone got out and agonized when they didn't. We heard later that of those who were captured many were tortured and killed by the Kempei Tai, the notorious Japanese police."

When the devastating B-29 fire raids against Tokyo began, the Shumida Gowa camp was spared because it was located in the railroad yards and there was nothing to burn there. Block after block of the city was leveled and the inhabitants fled by the thousands into the suburbs.

In the summer of 1945, a number of six-foot poles, sharpened at one end, were brought into the camp and placed in the guard house. The prisoners were told that they were to be used by the prisoners against civilians that might revolt and storm the prison and try to kill all foreigners for causing the loss of their homes and livelihood.

McConnell and his camp mates knew the war was over on August 15, 1945, a half hour after the emperor finished his surrender speech at noon. They had known when huge bombs had been dropped on August 6 and 9 which had caused great damage and many casualties, but they didn't know they were atomic bombs. There was great apprehension among the prisoners concerning their fate. Would they be summarily executed? Would they be tortured, locked up, starved and abandoned? Or would the gates be opened and they be allowed to fend for themselves?

Although the guards were less vigilant, there was nothing the POWs could do but wait to see what was going to happen. Japanese Red Cross officials arrived and advised them to put the initials "PW" on the roofs of the camp buildings. A day or two after the surrender, a couple of U.S. Navy fighters flew overhead, saw the letters, circled and flew low over the camp at slow speed with flaps down.

"As we cheered, others followed and began dropping notes, candy bars, cigarettes, scarves, gloves, whatever they had to let us know it wouldn't be long until our ordeal was over," McConnell said. "A B-29 came over slowly and dropped a cargo pallet full of boxes. As soon as it hit the slipstream, the boxes went their separate ways and came down on us at about 125 miles per hour. They were filled with clothes, medicines, food, shoes and all kinds of goodies we had not seen for many months.

"It was such a good feeling to see those guys," McConnell says. "It's a sight I'll never forget and it still brings tears to my eyes to think about it. We had not been forgotten."

The first Americans that McConnell saw were Navy personnel who came ashore in landing craft on August 30. The now-former POWs were taken to a Navy hospital ship offshore, checked over by medical personnel and then transported to Atsugi Airdrome where they were surprised to see a captured B-17, two or three P-40s and several Japanese experimental aircraft parked on the ramp. Some C-54s arrived with American airborne troops and as they debarked, the newly-freed men got happily aboard and flown to Okinawa. They were then flown to the Philippines and returned to the States by a Navy troop transport in mid-September 1945.

Despite the beatings he received, McConnell is not bitter about his 499 days as a POW. When he was given the choice of a discharge from the service or remaining in uniform, he opted to stay in and retired in 1971 as a colonel. Today he resides in Annapolis, Md.

• • •

Another 308th prisoner-of-war survivor was William H. Thomas of Cummings, Kansas, who graduated from the AAF Armament School at Lowry Field in March 1943. After completing gunnery school, he was assigned to the 374th Bomb Squadron and arrived in Pandergar, India, in mid-November. This was the period when the 308th and 7th Bomb Group in India combined forces briefly for missions against the Japanese in Burma. Thomas, then nineteen, was the tail gunner on his crew. The rest of the crew consisted of Lt. Newton J. Kellam, pilot; Lt. Fred J. Schwall, co-pilot; Lt. John D. Marcello, navigator; Lt. George E. Harman, bombardier; S/Sgt. Perry Marshall, flight engineer and top turret gunner; S/Sgt. Thomas E. Seneff, radio operator; Sgt. Charles W. Perry, assistant engineer; Sgt. Norman E. Albinson, ball turret gunner; and Sgt. Don Z. Davis, nose turret gunner.

Ten days after their arrival on its second mission, Kellam's crew was assigned to a bombing raid on Rangoon. When they left the target, the No. 2 engine had to be shut down and they fell behind the formation as it pulled away. Later, the No. 4 engine died but the prop could not be feathered. Not sure of their position, the crew decided they would stay with the plane until their fuel was exhausted and then bail out. When the fuel was nearly exhausted, the pilot ordered five of the crew into the bomb bay with the understanding that when the engines quit, they were to bail out. Thomas tells what happened next:

"Someone from the flight deck opened the door and shouted that we were under attack by Japanese fighters. This meant removing my chest parachute and returning to the tail turret because I couldn't fit into the turret with it on. After entering the turret, one fighter came from the two o'clock position. The waist gunner on the right side fired, the top turret gunner and I fired as the fighter flashed by the tail and down. We didn't know why he never made another pass. Maybe he was also out of fuel.

"I got back in the bomb bay and was ready to jump again. The flight engineer opened the door and said that the pilot's 'chute had burst open when someone picked it up to hand to him. With a quick vote, we decided to ride the plane down with him.

"About two hours later there were three of us in the rear of the plane. We were lying down with our feet forward and up against a step near the waist guns. I don't know where the rest of the crew were but they were spread somewhere around the flight deck.

"As we got lower we could hear the bottom of the plane hitting the tall elephant grass. I thought it was an easy landing but my mind must have gone blank for a few moments. The plane had stopped and had sunk through the grass into mud and water. When my mind cleared, I was lying across the ball turret. The first thing I thought of was fire. I jumped through the waist window and fell into waist-deep water. The two other men were close behind. As we cleared the plane by about 30 feet, the top hatch came open and the other crewmen climbed out. They were covered with mud from head to foot because the bomb doors, which had been closed, were ripped open and the mud and water had been scooped up and thrown forward into the flight deck. No one was injured except Seneff who had a cut on his leg.

"After waiting to make sure the plane wasn't going to catch on fire, we returned to get out our emergency rations from our parachute packs, first aid kits and other survival materials, including an American flag with Burmese and Chinese lettering which promised to pay a large sum of money for help to American flyers."

Carswell's Medal of Honor was presented to his widow and son at ceremonies held at Goodfellow Air Force base, Texas in 1946. The rear of the medal is always engraved with the recipient's name, branch of service, place and date of the action for which the award was granted. (Photo courtesy of Peter M. Bennethum)

The monument erected to honor Carswell was placed at his gravesite on Carswell Air Force Base, Fort Worth, Texas. When the base was deactivated in 1993, his body was moved to a cemetery in the city. (Photo courtesy Peter M. Bennethum)

A Curtiss C-46 of the Air Transport Command takes off from the Chabua airfield at Assam, India with a load of freight destined for China. (USAF photo)

A sight no pilot likes to see. The propeller of the No. 4 engine is feathered as Capt. Howard H. Morgan starts over the Hump toward China. (Photo courtesy Howard H. Morgan)

Jinx Falkenburg, Hollywood actress, signs a leg cast for an injured pilot of the 374th Bomb Squadron. Visits by attractive movie starlets were morale boosters for American servicemen in all theaters during World War II. (USAF photo)

The 14th AF Band was directed by Lt. Addie Bailey (right). Bailey was a band leader in a New York City nightspot before joining the Air Force. S/Sgt Robert G.Cobb, third from right in rear row, was the only 308th member in the band. (USAF photo)

Life for men of the 308th was not always comfortable. Here is a scene in the officers' barracks at Agra, India. (Photo courtesy Howard H. Morgan)

Dances were held as often as possible at the major 308th bases. This scene at Chengkung was at a dance in the officers' club sponsored by the 375th Squadron. The 14th Air Force Band plays in the background. (Photo courtesy Howard H. Morgan)

Billie's Cafe in downtown Kunming was a favorite destination for off-duty meals and libations. (Photo courtesy Buford C. Carpenter)

Capt. Lunt treks from the 12-hole latrine at Chengkung. The visits were made very uncomfortable in sub-freezing weather. Lt. Col. Harvard W. Powell, C.O. of the 374th, solved the problem by cutting a hole in a bath towel, heating the towel, placing it under his arm pit inside his shirt for the dash outside, then positioning it on the seat. When word spread of its success, this became standard practice. (Photo courtesy Howard H. Morgan)

Sgt. Robert G. Cobb, left, played first trumpet in a 14-piece 14th Air Force orchestra at Kunming. An armament crew chief with the 425th, he was transferred to the band after four combat missions and credit for one enemy plane shot down. (Photo courtesy Robert G. Cobb)

The trials of a long, difficult life are reflected in this man's face in Kunming. (Photo courtesy Clarence L. MacDonald)

Ox-drawn carts used by farmers were a common sight in wartime China. (Photo courtesy Charles F. Thompson)

Two generations of Chinese are seen here at the entrance to their house in Kunming. (Photo courtesy Milton H. Werner)

Street scene in Kunming. Rickshas were the popular method of intra-city transportation. (Photo courtesy Charles F. Thompson)

Comedian Monte Blue and movie actor Melvyn Douglas pause before departing for another base to entertain the 14th Air Force troops. (Photo courtesy Hubert A. Krawczyk)

Monte Blue exits after his act amusing the crowd at a base in China. The United Services Organization (USO) sponsored morale-building trips by celebrities wherever American troops were stationed. (Photo courtesy Hubert A. Krawczyk)

Capt. Howard H. Morgan poses outside the austere but solidly-built 375th officers' barracks at Chengkung. Most barracks had been hastily built by Chinese coolies at the air bases occupied by 14th Air Force units. (Photo courtesy Howard H. Morgan)

The enlisted men's club at Chengkung. (Photo courtesy Clarence L. MacDonald)

The Ding Hao Follies were held in a hangar at Kunming. The "girls" are (l to r) Bob Cobb, Dick DeSonir, Larry Easter, Harry Kleiber and Harry Shipman. The woman on the right is unidentified. (Photo courtesy Bob Cobb)

Paulette Goddard was another movie star who visited 14th Air Force units in China. Here she has just signed "short snorter" bills for a group of admirers. (Photo courtesy Hubert A. Krawczyk)

Bob Cobb and Harry Kleiber sing Addie Bailey's parody of "Oh, How I Hate to Get Up in the Morning." (Photo courtesy Bob Cobb)

Chinese soldiers stroll down Kunming streets under typical Oriental archways. (Photo courtesy Clarence L. MacDonald)

An early model of the Consolidated B-24 awaits its crew at a mid-western air base in the States. Over 18,000 Liberators with many variations were built and served in all theaters of war. (USAF photo)

A late model B-24 showing belly, nose and tail turrets flies over Fort Worth, Texas on a test flight. (Consolidated Vultee photo)

Mrs. Thelma Thompson, wife of Charles F. Thompson of the 374th Squadron, painted a portrait of "Ubangi Bag III" that flew more than 50 missions. It had been preceded by Ubangi Bag and Ubangi Bag II. (Photo of painting courtesy Charles F. Thompson)

Several B-24As were modified to carry passengers and used to fly Roosevelt cabinet members on diplomatic missions. The Army Air Force Ferry Command insignia can be seen near the tail. (Photo courtesy W. J. Binder)

When the 308th started to fly low-level, night sea sweep missions, the bottoms of the aircraft were painted black. (Photo courtesy Jeff Ethell)

The U.S. Navy procured a number of single-tailed B-24 models for sea patrols and designated them PB4Ys. Note gunner's blister on the side of the fuselage. (Photo courtesy Jeff Ethell)

A B-24D undergoes a thorough maintenance check at a Consolidated factory base before being turned over to a ferry crew. (General Dynamics photo)

The C-87 Liberator Express was a B-24D modified to carry passengers, freight or fuel. Note windows in bomb bay area. (Photo courtesy General Dynamics)

Instrument panel of a Consolidated C-109. The C-109s were B-24s converted into aerial tankers. They were used in the European and China-Burma-India theaters. (Photo courtesy Jeff Ethell)

This unnamed B-24J flies over the Hump from China to Chabua, India. Each 308th crew had to make several flights over the Hump to supply the group with bombs and ammunition before combat missions could be flown. (USAF photo)

Thomas and the rest of the crew hacked their way out of the swampy areas. Completely tired when night came, they lay down and slept soundly. At daylight, Fred Schwall, the co-pilot, woke everyone up because he heard shouting in a foreign language. It was a Japanese patrol who began firing their rifles. The crew returned the fire with their .45s as they fled into the tall grass. George Harman, while still in the open, was hit in the back; the bullet barely missed his spinal column. After a number of shots were exchanged, Newton Kellam, the pilot, shouted to his crew that they were badly outnumbered and had to surrender. He told them to thrown down their weapons and give up. Thomas continues:

"We were surrounded by about fifteen Japanese soldiers who didn't understand English but we were made to understand that if we tried to escape we would be shot. They allowed us to examine Harman and we put sulfa powder from our parachute packs into his wound, bandaged it and gave him a shot of morphine.

"We were searched and relieved of all of our watches and gold rings. The Japanese wanted to know where the plane was so we led them back to it. Two soldiers were left with Lt. Harman but I didn't think we would ever see him again because of the stories we had heard about the Japanese.

"We weren't worried about the Japanese finding anything of military value on the plane because the front of it with the bomb sight inside, was crumpled underneath the plane in the mud. There were no guns left because we had dumped them overboard before we crashlanded. After they climbed into the plane, the only thing that seemed to interest them was the drift meter which was about three feet long with an eye piece in one end. They thought it was a bomb sight and we had to carry it back to where Lt. Harman was being guarded.

"The Japanese made us understand that we had to move out. Lts. Kellam and Schwall tried to tell them that Harman could not walk and they made motions that they would shoot him. I'm not sure whether they meant it but one of them cut some bamboo poles about ten feet long and two for cross members and tied them into a crude stretcher. I think a blanket from the plane was used to cover it.

"With four of us carrying the stretcher and one carrying the drift meter, which weighed about 50 or 60 pounds, we started to their camp.

As we walked and took turns on the stretcher we were able to talk to each other. Lt. Kellam told us we had better have a story other than being on a bombing raid to Rangoon. We decided that we would tell them we had been on our way from the States to Calcutta and had gotten lost in a storm and somehow wound up in northeast Burma. We also agreed on a different route than we had actually taken. This probably doesn't sound important but it seemed very important to us at the time. How nine people could keep a story straight, made up almost on the spur of the moment through numerous interrogations, is still a wonder to me.

"We all thought we were tired from carrying Lt. Harman that first day but we didn't yet know what tired was. And it was very cold at night, although it was warm during the day.

"When we arrived at their camp, we were interrogated by an English-speaking Japanese, one at a time. It was not an intense questioning and they didn't take a lot of time at it.

"About an hour before dark we were grouped together, sitting around the bombardier who was nearly out of it from pain. The English-speaking Jap came to us with the announcement that we would be killed because it was so far from a POW camp. I suppose this didn't come as a great surprise to any of us so we lit a last cigarette or two that some of us had, and passed them from one to another and talked. I can't remember all that was said but it was a frank and intimate conversation between nine young men from 18 to 21 years of age.

"At about dark, we were tied together and were walked down into a wide, deep gully; a couple of soldiers carried the bombardier down with us. I think all of us were pretty much resigned to the fact that we were going to die.

"A group of soldiers were marched into the gully and turned to face us. An officer walked to one side of his men, drew his sword and shouted some commands. I can remember I turned to Don Davis and said, 'Jesus, Kid, I sure wish they would shoot us. I hate to think of that damned cold steel.' I wasn't making a joke. I had already tried to make peace with my God. I think most people, whether religious or not, will try to talk to the Lord at times like this. Scared? Yes, but I was so sure of death that I suppose I was numb.

"With one command, the squad worked the bolts on their rifles and put a round into the chambers. Another command and they raised their rifles to their shoulders. One more command and it would be all over.

"From the top of the embankment, someone shouted something down to the officer in charge. He gave the squad a command and they lowered their rifles to their sides. After much conversation between the two officers, the squad marched away and I heard Lt. Schwall say, 'Probably going for a sunrise serenade.' It was no joke, just what we all thought.

"Since I was on the end and Don Davis was next in line, we were untied and taken by a guard to their cooking fire where we were given a wooden bucket of cooked rice. We carried it back to the others and we ate it from the bucket by the handsful.

"At this time, a Japanese soldier gathered wood and built a fire at each end of the line of tied-together prisoners. I don't think it was meant to warm us but so we would be easier to guard. Even though all of us were sure we would be killed in the morning, we laid down on the rocky ground and slept most of the night."

After daybreak, Thomas and Davis fetched another bucket of rice and the outlook of the crew improved. They reasoned that if they were going to be executed, why would they be fed? Shortly afterward, the English-speaking interrogator told them they would be taken to Mandalay. After about four days of difficult walking they were met by a Japanese general who spoke excellent English. He had been educated in California and had attended the same college as Harman, the bombardier. He told the prisoners that they would be transported to Rangoon and placed in a camp with other Americans and have good American food. They continued walking for three more days carrying Harman and the drift meter.

"We became so tired during this time that we would fall asleep as soon as the Japanese gave us a rest," Thomas continued. "The walking wasn't so bad but carrying Harman was really rough. It became so hard that we could not carry him more than 10 minutes before trading off. Every so often, the guards, who were changed daily, would carry the stretcher for a few yards to show us how easy it was. At times I became so tired that I thought about killing one of the soldiers with the drift meter. Trading my life for a Japanese life sounded reasonable to me. The only trouble with that was that they would have probably killed the whole crew.

"The bombardier was out of his head most of the time. When he groaned aloud and made any kind of noise he was given a shot of morphine. He never recognized, in any way, the effort the crew put out for him."

The prisoners were taken to Mandalay and then transported by bullock carts and a truck to a Rangoon prison which was to be their home for the next year and a half. Until that time they had never undergone any physical beatings or torture. The jungle troops were tough but Thomas thought they seemed to realize the Americans were soldiers the same as they were and were only to be taken to prison.

The group was divided with three enlisted men and two officers together in separate cells. At this time, about 18 days after their capture, Harman was able to get on his feet with help and move about.

"After separating us, we were visited by a Japanese guard and received the first of many beatings," Thomas said. "The guard who did the beating was short and walked with a limp. He unlocked the cell door and shouted something like 'Kiskae!' This, we were to learn, meant 'Attention!' After showing us what 'Kiskae' meant, he gave us a pretty good working over. This beating was a regular thing for new arrivals at the camp and was nearly always done by 'Limpy' or another guard we called 'Tarzan.'

"I think the first beating was a sort of softening up process and also because the Japanese Army used this form of corporal punishment for their enlisted men. But I must say, it's very hard to stand at attention and let a little five-foot bastard knock you around.

"After this we were left alone for the rest of the night. We were able to converse with some of the other POWs that night and found out some of the rules that were to be followed. Any time a guard was in the building, we were to stand facing the door at attention. If the guard came by the cell, we were to call each of them 'Master.' We found out that most of them couldn't understand English so 'Master' usually came out 'Bastard.' If you happened to meet with one that understood English, you would be in for a beating.

"We learned about more of the rules from the other prisoners which they had learned from others or the hard way. It really didn't seem to make any difference. If the Japs thought a beating was due, they didn't need a broken rule to do it.

"In each cell was a metal ammunition box which was used as a latrine (benjo). Each day one man from each cell was allowed to take it out and empty it. This was under guard, of course, during which we occasionally suffered a few hits. But some of the guards would allow you to stay outside for a few minutes to get fresh air and sunshine.

"There isn't much that two or three men can do in a cell that is 12x12 feet, with half of it taken up by a raised wooden platform about a foot high. This platform was for sleeping. You could sit or stand on the platform but if they caught anyone lying down, they wouldn't just work one man over but everyone in the cell, and maybe the next cell, too, if they hadn't worn themselves out.

"There were several two-story prison buildings in the compound and each was surrounded by a wall 10 or 12 feet high. Each cell had one barred window without any covering. From the window of our cell we could look over the wall and see the upper floor of the next building. News of the outside, or war news from new prisoners, was passed from one building to the next by hand signals. Words were spelled out by making the letters by hand and arm movements.

"We were fed twice a day but there didn't seem to be a regular feeding time, just when it pleased the guards. Morning chow was boiled rice and a thin tasteless gruel. The evening meal was usually rice and some kind of soup. There were always bugs and mouse droppings in the rice; at first we tried picking them out but after a while we ate the food without noticing the extras.

"Life in this form of solitary confinement was a dreary time. Exercising took up a great deal of time because the three of us in our cell decided that in order to weather this confinement we needed to be in as good a shape as possible."

Thomas and the rest of his crew spent forty-five days in their two-and three-man cells, then were moved to another building with about forty other Americans and more than a hundred British officers and enlisted men. This compound had four large cells on each floor of the two-story structure. There were four windows in one side of each cell that went from floor level to about seven feet high. There were steel bars in the windows but no covering. The rains during monsoon season poured in and the prisoners felt like they were wet and damp for months.

"One thing I remember about those damp months," Thomas recalled, "was that you couldn't lay what clothes you had out on an ant hill so the ants could eat the lice. The ants would clean out the lice but the warm sun would help hatch a new bunch of them when you put the clothes on.

"The floors inside were home to all kinds of bugs – any kind that live in filth and dirt. The mosquitoes also had free access through the open, barred windows. Not many birds flew in but only a few were ever lucky enough to get out. Rats were numerous and we killed them when we could but I don't know of anyone eating a rat.

"Each morning we were awakened just after dawn by the shouting of the guards from outside the compound. This meant we had to form two lines outside the building for 'tenko' or prisoner count. The officers were in the first group in two lines. The American enlisted men and other people in the second cell upstairs were in the second group in two lines. On command, the front row would count off from right to left in Japanese. It didn't pay to screw up the tenko because that would lead to hits and beatings by the guards.

"Some of the guards carried boards or short poles instead of their rifles. These were easier to hit with and hurt a hell of a lot more. If something was really wrong, they would have the first row of prisoners step forward and turn to face the back row of prisoners. Then we were to take turns hitting each other. It was just as well to make the punches mean something or the guards would show us how and then we would start over.

"Shortly after morning tenko, it was time for breakfast. This was a pan of rice with a small amount of bran porridge or gruel that tasted bad, plus a can or cup of water which had been boiled. After morning rice, the work parties were formed for walking or being transported by truck to a warehouse, the docks or to dig defense entrenchments. We unloaded boats, built blast walls around searchlight batteries and anti-aircraft guns, cleaned up areas after air raids, built a huge air raid shelter and dug wells.

"One of the unusual projects was making candles. This was done by those too sick to go outside on work parties. They had a building set up as a factory. The POWs would cut and wrap wax paper into tubes about two inches in diameter and six inches long. We were told that the candles were used to heat a Jap soldier's food ration in the field.

"A daily list of work parties to be formed and the officer in charge of each made up a list of those who were to go on them. There were always one or two officers on each work party but they did not work. The rest of the officers stayed in the camp; some of them worked in a garden that the Japanese allowed them to have. The rest of us worked seven days a week. The only days the work parties didn't go out was Christmas Day 1944 and the Emperor's birthday. The only bad thing about the Emperor's birthday was that the guards were mostly drunk and seemed to be in a hitting mood. Many bruises were handed out that day.

"One of the guards I remember especially was called 'Speed-o.' This was the only word of English that he knew. He was in charge of the garden project. We could never move fast enough to suit him and he was a good hitter. He usually carried a wet, twisted towel that he hit with. He could also slap with both hands while flipping the towel from hand to hand.

"Most of the slappings and beatings hurt but if you saw a Jap carrying a sliver of bamboo, watch out! That thing stung more than anything they used. The bamboo, being limber, had a lot of hurt in it.

"The work on most parties was very hard but I made up my mind early that being outside of the camp and away from the filth was more healthful. Normally at noon we took a break of about 30 minutes. Afterward, it was back to work but there would be a ten-minute break for a hot drink in the afternoon; then we would work until about an hour and a half before dark, have the evening meal and then a tenko. After the tenko, we could usually mingle with the other POWs in our compound. The Japanese didn't put a curfew on because there were people up and moving throughout the night. With dysentery so prevalent, there was always somebody going to the benjo.

"Normally, after the evening meal, since we had no lights, we just talked. This was the loneliest time and the talk between close friends would always turn to our loved ones. This was, I think, because when the moon rose I would think about this as being the same moon that would shine on my home in just about 12 hours. I don't know why but the moon always seemed so large that you could almost touch it.

"Another topic of conversation was food. Every type of food that anyone had ever eaten or heard of was talked about.

"In addition to diarrhea, for which we had no medicine, beri-beri, caused by a lack of vitamin B-1, was a disease some had. It would bother only the feet at first and then became worse as it moved up the body. No one lived long when the swelling reached the stomach. In about November 1944, cholera broke out briefly in the camp. No Americans were stricken but about 20 British and a large number of Indians died in about six or seven days after contracting the disease. Those who died were cremated instead of being buried.

"The Japanese were very nervous about cholera because it was a quick death. They gave all of us shots which was the only time I knew of them to do much medically for the POWs. I didn't worry about the disease because we had received our cholera shots just shortly over a year before.

"Any kind of a scratch or cut would usually turn into what we called 'jungle sores.' The infection seemed to keep spreading and the sores would become larger and larger. I saw sores on some men that had eaten into the bone. Death usually followed in cases like that.

"Ringworm was another skin disease that almost everyone had. I had ringworm and scabies over most of my body from my waist down. One thing we did get to help alleviate skin diseases was what we called "blue stone" (probably blue vitriol or copper sulfate) which was crushed into a fine powder and mixed with water to varying degrees of strength for applying to the affected areas. No matter how weak the solution was, it always burned like fury when applied to sore and itching areas.

"In August 1944, Norman "Red" Albinson, our ball turret gunner, decided he could no longer eat the food. After eight months of hard work and poor diet, we were all very thin and not in very good physical shape. When he stopped eating, there was only one way to go. He became thinner and weaker and died. He was the only one of our crew to die in prison camp, although all of us were ill at one time or another.

"At about this time, the food that we were furnished became somewhat better and there was more of it. The officers combined their cooking with the enlisted men's cookhouse. We, the enlisted men, were told that we were being paid for our work but the pay all went to pay for the rice we received. The officers were paid even though they didn't work and were able to buy things from the outside. Eggs, sugar, salt and cigars were the most common items. One prisoner made a cigarette rolling machine with parts and pieces picked up by work parties. He rolled smokes for some of the officers for a small percentage, maybe a cigarette for every twenty he rolled.

"Needless to say, the officers ate better than we did. I think that when they combined the cookhouses, they thought, as did the Japanese, that it would look better when freedom came if we were eating the same prison food. I am not saying this was right or wrong; I'm just telling it like it was.

"Going to bed meant getting onto your spot on the wooden floor. You worked all day wearing a 'fondushay' or loin cloth. You put your clothes on at night to keep the mosquitoes off. The lucky people who had a blanket of some sort or even a burlap sack, would cover up with it. You needed something to cover your feet and head. Those with shoes would put them on at night. The only trouble with wearing your clothes at night was that the body heat made the lice start moving around. Also, the bed bugs came out from between the boards and gave you trouble.

"There were two or three pairs of scissors in the compound for hair and beard cutting. The barber who owned the scissors normally charged a cigarette for a hair or beard cut. He also had a kitchen knife about four inches long which had been broken off. He sharpened it by honing it on a concrete window sill. It was sharp enough to scrape a beard but a lot easier just to clip the beard off. Some people let their beards grow but I think they found out that the heat, filth and bugs made a beard unacceptable. The only good thing about hair and beards was that they helped keep the mosquitoes away from bare skin.

"The only time we were bothered at night by the guards was for surprise searches of the compound. All of us became quite adept at stealing from the Japanese. When working at some of the warehouses, we sometimes were able to break open a box and steal whatever we thought we could carry back to the compound.

"At one time some of the men stole some short-sleeved white shirts of the type worn by Japanese officers. When nothing happened for awhile, the fellows thought that the Japanese hadn't missed them. After a few days, however, a large number of guards came into the compound late at night and found most of the shirts. The thieves were badly beaten.

"This didn't stop the pilfering, though. Something that we could eat on the spot or cigarettes which could be smoked at the time was best if we weren't caught. One time we stole a meat grinder and smuggled it into camp. We had no meat to grind but at least we had a grinder. Stealing became a sort of contest between us and the guards.

"We carried our food to work in wooden buckets slung on bamboo poles about three or four inches in diameter. The poles were hollow and made a very good place to carry contraband back to camp. They were split and held together with twine so we would untie it, hide whatever we had inside and retie the twine. As far as I know, the Japanese never caught on to this. At one warehouse, I remember we found a case of toothbrushes and we smuggled about 100 of them into the compound. They were not very good because the bristles fell out very soon. But it didn't make any difference to us whether we needed what we stole. It was a challenge to see if we could get away with it.

"Air raids were a thing of fear and beauty. To see from 60 to 100 B-24s and B-29s in formation and watch them jettison their bombs from a high altitude was really fascinating. But to be bombing the railroad yards or the dock areas, both of which were only a half mile away, was scary as hell. It was hard to imagine that in these planes were people like us. Only they could go back to a clean, safe place with good food and drink and at least have written contact with loved ones.

"On March 1, 1945, things started changing. Carts filled with wood came into camp and were unloaded by Indian personnel. Much rice in 100-lb sacks was unloaded and stored.

"We knew things were happening but we didn't know what. The Japanese guards were more nervous and hit and slapped with little provocation. The air raids picked up, also: Americans in the daytime, the British at night. During this time we heard that the British were in Prome, only about 150 miles north of Rangoon. I'm sure the rumors and news bothered the guards as much as they buoyed our spirits so we could face another day. The only news the Japanese passed to us was when President Roosevelt died on April 12, 1945. This news really saddened us.

"We didn't know how the war in Burma was going but we could tell there were big changes. There were more strange guards, more food and many more air raids, not only by the heavies but P-47s, P-38s and British planes I didn't recognize. It was a beautiful sight to see a group of P-38s peel off from a formation at 15 or 20 thousand feet and dive to bomb Mingladon Airport about 10 miles to the north.

"We felt sure the location of the camp was known to the British and Americans so, barring an accidental string of bombs, we wouldn't be hit. However, we found out later that Lord Mountbatten had issued a Top Secret order dated February 16, 1944, that if a target near a prison camp was considered vital, the risk of hitting the camp had to be taken. Just as well we didn't know about this.

"The routine was the same every day. Tenko, morning rice, work party, evening rice, tenko, bed. The only thing that broke the monotony were the rumors and the war news that we got from the Burmese on the work parties. This was normally a whispered 'Not long now' or 'British in Mandalay.' We found out when an invasion of northern Burma was underway by the British 14th Army. The question on everyone's mind was what the Japanese would do when the British arrived. We wondered if the Japanese planned to defend the camp when the British came. Surely they would not just turn the prisoners over to the British after the treatment we had received. We hoped that the invasion would be from the air by paratroopers.

"After September 1944, when the amount of food was increased and became better, the guards sometimes brought a hog or, on one occasion, a water buffalo into camp for butchering. One of the officers was a butcher. He cut the meat into small cubes and boiled them in the soup for evening meals. With no refrigeration, the meat couldn't be kept very long but one hog didn't go very far when divided among four cell blocks.

"Another treat was the dried fish that the Japanese brought into camp occasionally. Another special food was the eggs which we were able to steal or get from the Burmese while on a work party. We smuggled them back to camp and ate them raw over the rice. The Burmese made a confection which looked like peanut brittle which they smuggled to us. We called it jagari. If you were caught with it, you got slapped around.

"When we moved into the large compound, we each had a square metal rice dish and a soup cup. These were made by Lt. Jack Horner who had been in the camp longer than any other American. He made them out of corrugated metal roofing. A spoon was all the utensils that we ever used or needed. Lt. Horner made ours from a small piece of metal that he beat from a bar of steel.

"When we finished eating, we could go to the end of the corridor and wash our rice pan in a bucket of water. Probably 150 pans were washed in one bucket of water. The water became very thick.

"My sleeping and eating space was next to Sgt. John Hubbard who never washed his pan. After eating he would set his pan outside the barred window. The sparrows would peck at the small pieces of rice that were caught in the corners where the metal was folded over. Maybe he did the right thing because I don't remember that he was ever sick the whole time we were in camp.

"The morning of April 26th was not like any other morning. Tenko and then morning rice with pork. Also we had more hot water to drink than anyone could remember. Normally, one cup of hot, boiled water or tea as it was called, was all we received at one meal. Then we spent all day in the compound without any work parties being sent out.

"Sometime during the next morning, the fit people were paraded in their respective compounds and marched out of camp. There were a number of new guards accompanying us. Supplies were piled on large, two-wheeled carts and eight or ten POWs would push and pull them. The first afternoon and night turned out to be a tough march which may have been 25 miles. Most of the prisoners were barefoot and wore their loin cloths because that's what we were accustomed to wearing. Going without shoes for all the time we were in camp had toughened the soles of my feet to almost leather. Later, when we are able to get shoes that fit, they were hard to wear.

"There were no breaks in the march the first night. The guards were talking about 'toxan michi' (much food in the morning). At first light we were marched from the road into the woods to be hidden from aircraft during the day. The Japanese were more nervous than ever, although they did not do as much hitting of the prisoners. As it turned out, the 'toxan michi' was the rice and pork we had brought with us.

"The daylight hours of the 28th were spent resting. By this time, the sky belonged to the Allied air forces. No Japanese planes were to be seen. There were Allied fighter aircraft in sight throughout the day and also a formation of B-24s probably heading to Rangoon or south of the city where the seaborne invasion was to be made.

"The second night of the march was another long, hard walk of 25 miles. By this time the wheeled carts had been abandoned because we were off the macadam road to Pegu and sometimes we walked the railroad tracks. The prisoners carried what supplies remained and also all the Japanese belongings except their rifles and clubs. A rice ball made from the last of the cooked rice was all the food for that night. As usual, we had an overpowering thirst. We were afraid to drink any water that wasn't boiled.

"We had a close call on the morning of the 29th. The Japanese kept the march going until after daylight, probably because the British Army was coming fast from the north and they wanted to go as far as possible before stopping. We didn't want to be spotted on the road any more than the Japanese because I'm sure that just about anything caught moving was a target for the fighters.

"We found this to be all too true the next day. While we were hidden in the woods, the ranking officers, a Colonel Gilbert, an American, and General Hobson, a Britisher, circulated the word that if the column got far enough north to turn east around the bay, we would try to overpower the guards. We knew that some people would be killed but the chance of surviving was better than marching around the bay, then south to Moulmein, and be put on a ship to Japan for more captivity; no one wanted more of that. At this time, we were just south of Pegu.

"On April 29th we were on the move again. We had become used to a short food supply. But we were now drinking any water we came upon. Ditches, creeks, rivers or anywhere else. We passed through Pegu shortly after dark and saw very few people. The town had been bombed very badly. The guards were very nervous this night and so were we. We didn't make much distance that night because of the planes overhead. It takes some time to get 350 people moving again after diving into ditches or off the railroad tracks whenever a plane came over. It takes especially long when these people don't want to make good time.

"At morning light we were herded into a woods adjacent to the railroad tracks. It was a small junction north of Pegu. We could hear the sound of artillery in the distance. The Japanese captain called a meeting of the ranking officer prisoners and told them that they were releasing the prisoners and that if we stayed in the woods where we were we would be overtaken by the British Army.

"Can you imagine the happiness of the POWs upon seeing the Japanese leave? We were free of them at last. Now we needed to get to the British to our north. We could hear them plainly now – the larger guns and the tracked vehicles.

"Sometime later in the day, the commanding officers decided that we needed to be seen from the air. They had some pieces of cloth that they put on the ground next to a small haystack which was set afire. A small spotter plane over, made two or three passes, wagged his wings and flew away. We expected to be contacted by the British soldiers at any time.

"Shortly afterward, a flight of British fighters made a pass at the woods and, to our surprise, dropped their bombs. The woods, about four or five acres in size, was good camouflage but there were not enough large trees for cover from the machine gun and cannon fire that followed as they made three or four more passes.

"After the first pass, many of the prisoners, including me, left the woods and made a run for some one-man holes – probably fox holes made by the Japanese – near the railroad tracks. After the planes left, we returned to the woods to find that there was only one fatality. It was Brigadier General Hobson. He had been shouting to his men to take cover and didn't find cover for himself.

"After the bombing and strafing, most of us, if not all, left the woods and railroad tracks. I suppose we were like terrified animals. The group I was with wandered into the jungle without any destination or plan in mind. This fear that I think most of us had was worse than the fear we had when we were captured. At that time, we were sure we were going to be killed but now we were so near to freedom and yet it seemed so far. The happiness of the first few hours of freedom was wiped out quickly.

"After wandering around for a while, we were approached by a Burmese lad who could speak a little English. He made us understand that if we would go with him to his village we would be fed by his people and that the British soldiers would meet us there.

"After the previous three days without food we were very hungry so we followed him to his village. When we arrived, the Burmese killed some chickens and put them in water to boil, along with some rice. It wasn't long before we had a very good meal. It was the first chicken I had eaten in a year and a half. The meal was followed by cheroots (cigars) which they passed out to us. It was almost too much to have a whole cigar to smoke at one time. Most of the fellows smoked some of the cigar, then put it out and saved the rest for later.

"There was no sign of the British soldiers and we wondered if this could be a trick and our hosts were really working for the Japanese. While we were trying to make up our minds, another Burmese walked into the village and told us he had been sent to guide us to his village where the British would meet us. We were suspicious but decided to take a chance and go with him.

"It was now early in the morning – probably about 2 a.m. When we arrived at the second village, everyone was asleep and there were no British. We were then told that we were to sleep there the rest of the night and the British would meet us in the morning.

"By this time, we were certain that this was a Burmese plot to return us to the Japanese. At this time, some of the POWs who had become separated from us from the day before came out of a building and told us they thought the Burmese were sincere and were truly trying to help us. We were put into a house on stilts with the floor about eight feet off the ground. It was about 30x30 feet and must have been a village meeting house. When we got inside, we found quite a few other POWs so there were about 40 of us in this one big room. We were all so tired we were quickly asleep.

"I knew nothing until I heard the sounds of chickens and pigs underneath the building. Then I heard a commotion outside and saw an armed soldier, about the size of a Japanese, coming down the street very warily. He had on dark green fatigues and a green wide-brimmed hat with one side pinned up to the crown. He had a rifle and a large scabbard at his side. He could be nothing but a Gurkha, one of the finest type of soldier in the British Army.

"He was very watchful as he made his way into the village center. He was a point man for a platoon of Gurkhas and two British sergeants. He gave a hand signal and a group of soldiers came into view. Our ordeal was over.

"There were handshakes all around and we were told that there were trucks close by that would take us into the British camp. We were loaded into them and as we headed toward the camp, a Japanese soldier was flushed out of the brush and started to run. One of the Gurkhas jumped off a truck and ran after him. The Japanese dropped his gun instead of trying to shoot his attacker. That was a mistake. The Gurkha killed him with the long, curved knife that they all carried."

The American POWs were treated royally when they arrived at the British camp. They were issued mess equipment and began to eat and drink real tea spiked with a little rum immediately. They received British fatigues and shoes if they wanted them but few did. They took a bath in a creek nearby with soap they hadn't had for many months. They bedded down with new blankets and enjoyed the freedom they had all longed for so long. They were besieged by reporters and photographers who had been waiting to interview any POWs that came their way.

Thomas and the other prisoners were flown to Akyab where they were met by three American Red Cross ladies with coffee and doughnuts at the airport. They were also met again by reporters and photographers but were on their way within two hours to Calcutta where they were all hospitalized and given physical and dental checkups. Those with skin or other problems were treated immediately.

"After being there three or four days," Thomas said, "we were visited by General Stratemeyer who welcomed us back. He later sent us two cases of bourbon. Some of us later visited the British POWs across town in the British hospital. It didn't appear that they were as well treated as we were. While there we heard what happened to those who had stayed in the Rangoon prison.

"The Japanese left the prison on April 29 but left a note saying that maybe sometime in the future they would meet again on another battlefield but until that time wished them luck. These were not the original guards that we had in the camp. As soon as they left, the prisoners took some whitewash and painted in large letters JAPS GONE on one side of the roof and on the other side BRITISH HERE. This didn't seem to do much good because a British Mosquito bomber dropped bombs on the outer wall of the camp. After this episode, someone then climbed up and painted the words EXTRACT DIGIT which meant 'get the finger out' which was a British colloquial expression that their pilots would understand to mean to cut out the bombing."

The POWs stayed in the camp with the outer doors locked from the inside, more to keep out the Burmese from the food supply, rather than the

Japanese who might have returned. Before leaving, the Japanese had stockpiled much food and wood and the water had been turned on in the compounds. The prisoners left in the camp had some frustrating days after Thomas and his fellow inmates had left the camp on April 27th. They couldn't get the attention of anyone who could tell them the Japs had gone. However, on May 3rd, supplies were airdropped into the camp from a B-24 and British troops arrived two days later to let them out of the compound.

Thomas returned to the States in late May 1945. He was assigned to a base at Salina, Kansas, after taking a recuperation leave and was discharged on November 1, 1945. All of his crewmates except Sgt. Albrinson, the ball turret gunner who died in prison, survived their ordeal and returned safely to the States.

• • •

Earl S. Vann, a flight engineer assigned to the 373rd Squadron, was aboard *Pistol Packin' Mama*, a name the crew had selected but had not yet painted on their B-24. Their target on September 15, 1943, was the airfield at Haiphong, French Indo-China. In addition to Vann, the crew consisted of Lt. Earl Johnson, pilot; Lt. Tom Chambers, co-pilot; Lt. Jack Quarrant, navigator; Lt. Joseph Manella, Bombardier; S/Sgt. Abe Trachenberg, assistant engineer and top turret gunner; S/Sgt. Herschel Nelson, radio operator and waist gunner; S/Sgt William L. Lambert, assistant radio operator and waist gunner; S/Sgt. Frank Robbins, armorer, bottom turret gunner; and S/Sgt Paul Cybowski, tail turret gunner.

Vann tells his story in a cryptic style:

"Five planes without fighter escort made a bomb run on the airfield in CAVU weather. The lead plane broke radio silence and requested all planes hold bombs, cross over field, make 180-degree turn for second bomb run. While making this unnecessary maneuver 65 Japanese Navy fighters located us and began making strafing runs on us. We were in Vee formation. They would go out in front of formation, do a chandelle, come back and rake us from stem to stern on both sides of formation. They were a little late firing and missed the lead bomber. It got back into cloud layer and ran for home, leaving the rest with engines out and dead crew to do the best we could.

241

"In these attacks we lost pilot Johnson, radio operators Nelson and Lambert, gunners Robins and Cyboski. Navigator Quarrant and bombardier Manella bailed out. Our plane had two engines out and one with partial power. We were losing altitude over wooded area. Co-pilot and I decided it was time to leave as we were down to 1,000 feet. He gave the alarm and Trachenberg and I jumped at about 700 feet. By this time the plane was over a river and pilot and co-pilot decided to stay with the plane and ditched it in the river. All on board died. Learned later that a Vietnamese Catholic priest gave them a decent Christian burial.

"Momentum carried Trachenberg and me over the river. We landed in waist-deep water near an island where two natives were fishing. We could not communicate and insisted on them taking us in the direction of China on their sampan. When about 30 yards offshore we saw six Japanese soldiers step out of the bushes with rifles. I had a .45 pistol and decided it would be best to surrender. Out of sight was an entire squad of Japs. We were searched, disarmed and loaded on a truck and taken to Hanoi. There we were imprisoned in a make-do jail in the cellar of an official-looking building. We were stripped of all clothes except our undershorts, made to sit cross-legged, wog fashion, on a rice straw mat. When it became dark we were made to lie down and at first light we were made to sit up. We were taken to latrine once each day and fed a ball of gooey rice with vegetables along with a cup of tea two times a day.

"Most days the guards would take us one at a time upstairs to a conference room for interrogation. By now the other three survivors from my crew had been put in the cell with Trachenberg and me. The officers at the interrogation usually spoke English and would talk about baseball, boxing's Joe Louis and other sports figures. Most had been educated in the U.S. When the interrogations began it was done through an interpreter. They would ask lots of simple, inconsequential questions and occasionally ask where we came from, about our planes, etc. When anything of a military nature was asked, I would reply, 'On my honor as a soldier I cannot answer that.' They would smile and change the subject. I was never slapped or hazed in any way. I later learned that other crew members were slapped around a bit when they responded that they did not know. They were told they did know and they were lying. They were slapped around a bit.

"After two weeks or more we were put on a train loaded with Japanese troops going south. We ended up in Saigon and were put in a large cell with about a half dozen native men and women. There were no toilet facilities except a big stone large-mouthed jug in which you could relieve yourself. The accommodations were rice straw mats and food was more of the same gooey rice with little vegetables made into a ball the size of a large orange and a cup of tea twice a day.

"Once each day the guards would require one of us to carry the jug used for a toilet out to an open sewer, dump it and wash it out with our hands, with no soap to wash our hands. There was no interrogation while here.

"Just prior to leaving Hanoi, we were taken outside for a news conference of some kind. Pictures were made of the group and the Japanese supplied all the information.

"After about three weeks in Saigon we were put on board a ship loaded with Japanese soldiers. We were handcuffed to our bunks which were bolted to the bulkhead. In front of the door was an armed guard.

"About the third day out there was an alarm. The Klaxton horns went off. The guards dropped their rifles, picked up life preservers and headed out on deck. We were left handcuffed to the bunks. After about five minutes, they came sheepishly back, put up the life preservers, picked up their rifles and resumed pacing in front of the doors.

"Each evening while at sea, the troops would go on deck and do exercises. After they were dismissed, they would parade by our doors to take a look at us. We had not shaved or bathed since the time of capture. One Japanese spoke a little English, looked at our hairy chests and bearded faces and said, 'You monkey man. Me no monkey man.'

"I noticed the life preservers and other items on board were stamped 'Ile de France.' From that I assumed it was a French ship that had been captured by the Japanese.

"The Japanese said we were headed to Nippon. However, we could tell by the sun we were sailing south and we ended up in Singapore. When we arrived we were put in a barbed wire, heavily-guarded compound with the British Gurkha troops. Leftenant Bob Skeen, British Gurkha officer, told us the Gurkhas have no word for surrender and the Japanese did not trust them. He also told about the Gurkha troops operating behind the lines in the jungle. They were given a bonus for every pair of enemy ears they brought in. All Gurkhas carry a heavy knife called a krokery. A young man must be able to cut the head off a bullock in order to prove his manhood and be accepted in the army.

"After about 30 or 40 days with the Gurkhas, we were released into the camp at Changi Gaol with the British, Aussies, Dutch, Javanese and Americans. The Japanese said the reason we were put with the Gurkhas was because American bombers had bombed Tokyo and the emperor's palace. We were made to do penance for sinning against the emperor. [This referred to Doolittle's famous raid on Japan but the palace was not bombed.]

"The Americans in Singapore at Changi were survivors of the *USS Houston* sunk in the Macassa Straits, the Texas 131st Field Artillery, and a few merchant seamen. There were five airmen from our plane and five from another 373rd plane on the same mission. There was one airman who had been captured in the Philippines.

"In the early days, the Japanese made prisoners stand parade and roll call each afternoon. One day a chicken from a native company came over in front of the American detachment as we were counting off. As soon as the parade was dismissed we formed a circle around the chicken and that evening about 50 of us had chicken and rice.

"Another time there was an old British major who had a bull dog. He was starving himself in order to keep the dog. The British commander ordered him to get rid of the dog. Some of the Americans bought the dog, took him to a cell on the top floor of the Changi Gaol, sealed the cracks with blankets to keep the odor of cooking meat from getting out, dressed and cooked the dog. Dog tastes something like pork.

"I was put up with the British warrant officers. One had a pet cat. One day Petty Officer Kelly came over with a bucket of water with a burlap bag over the bucket. My job was to lure the warrant officer away so Kelly could steal the cat by catching him with the bag and hold him under water until he drowned. That night we ate cat. It tasted like rabbit.

"There were about 150,000 men of all ranks in the Changi prison camp. About 60 or 70 American enlisted and about 30 or 40 officers. We lost one American during the two years I was there. He died of cancer.

"There were two secret radios in the camp. One that I knew about was operated by the Royal Air Force prisoners. When any news of importance was picked up, Wing Commander Howell got it and reported it to Sgt. Carpenter, an American with the 131st Field Artillery. In the camp, it was never called 'news.' It was called 'drift.' Sgts. Carpenter, Gordon, Ficklin, Stewart and others operated a black market. Most of it consisted of watches bought from the British officers and sold to Chinese and Malays while on working parties. I recall one Mido automatic stainless steel wrist watch that sold for 40,000 Japanese invasion dollars. We bought it for about 400 dollars. While the British camp police were running down Sgts. Carpenter and Stewart, I was sitting in the warrant officers' hut with the 400 dollars around my waist. When the camp police caught them they were clean. This is the same Sgt. Carpenter that James Clavel wrote about and called him 'King Rat.' Clavel, the author of *King Rat* and *Shogun*, was a prisoner at Changi.

"Many of the prisoners were ill with malaria, beri beri, tropical ulcers and dysentery. All water had to be boiled before drinking so we drank hot tea. If you got water in your ears while taking a shower, fungus would start growing in your ears and you would have a hell of an earache which would require about a week in the hospital hut.

"The guards at Changi were mostly Koreans pressed into service by the Japanese. The sergeant of the guard was Japanese. Those escorting work parties were usually Japanese. Trachenberg and I were on a work detail digging up coconut palms so they could lengthen a runway. The British were working very hard and had moved ahead of us. We had malingered and were standing in the hole with the stump. The Japanese sergeant came over, pushed his rifle against the stump and it fell over. He saw our rank insignia was different and asked if we were British. We replied: 'Americans.' He said Americans were like Nipponese 'bonoru ich' meaning number one. Then he told us an American 'negi-go-kou skoke' (B-29 airplane) and 'Nippon skoke go bomb-boom-boom. Nippon skoke go down crash.' Then the sergeant took us to where the British were working, saluted us and went on supervising the work party. Whenever he found the British malingering he would rave and threaten them. He seemed to admire us for not working hard for the enemy.

"Our plane was shot down Sept. 15, 1943. We Americans were liberated about September 1, 1945. Shortly after Japan surrendered, a U.S. C-54 landed at Singapore, picked up all the sick, took them to base hospital in Calcutta. It came back the following day and picked up the rest of us. All who were fit about a week later were flown directly from

Calcutta to Walter Reed Hospital in D.C.

"Japanese did not recognize Red Cross. We did not receive Red Cross packages as POWs of the Germans did. The POW doctors and hospital did not have drugs for treating malaria, dysentery, cholera, etc. All POWs suffered from malnutrition and beri-beri and were in worse shape than prisoners of the Germans.

"We were allowed to send one post card about a year after we were captured. Parents never received this. Near end of the war, parents received radiogram from War Department."

Vann was discharged as a master sergeant in January, 1946, and carried on with the family cotton gin business in Murfreesboro, North Carolina. He earned his pilot license in 1971 and built his own aircraft. He says, "I had no hard feelings towards the enemy when I was a prisoner and have none today."

Chapter 9

THE CARSWELL STORY

The former Air Force base at Fort Worth, Texas, now a Joint Navy and Air Force Reserve base, is named after Major Horace Seaver Carswell, Jr., a member of the 374th Squadron of the 308th. Naming an Air Force base after one of its former members is a rare honor reserved for heroes and outstanding airmen after they have gone.

Born on July 18, 1916, in Fort Worth, Carswell graduated from North Side High School in 1934 and had been a quarterback on the football squad. His school annual noted, "Horace Carswell was injured most of the season, but played about as much as the other backs. He was just finding himself when the season ended. Sorry we have to lose him by graduation."

Carswell had a reputation for playing hard but couldn't make the freshman college football squad at Texas A&M, College Station, Texas, which he attended listing agriculture as a major during the fall semester of 1934. He enrolled at Texas Christian University, Fort Worth, in the fall of 1935 and played on the varsity baseball team for three years and the football team for two.

He graduated with a Bachelor of Science degree in Physical Education on August 25, 1939. After graduation, he worked for an insurance firm briefly and entered pilot training as a Flying Cadet in the Army Air Corps in March 1940.

Carswell was awarded the Medal of Honor posthumously in 1946, America's highest award for conduct above and beyond the call of duty. Since he was the only member of any U.S. unit assigned to the Fourteenth Air Force and its predecessor units in China to win this medal, his story deserves a chapter in the 308th's history.

Horace S. Carswell, a compact, tough, determined individual, was said to have been nicknamed "Stump" because of his physique and that running into him was like running into a tree stump. To one of his former superiors, he was considered "a rugged individualist." He graduated from flying school and was commissioned a second lieutenant in early 1941 and was assigned to Goodfellow Field, San Angelo, Texas, as a basic flying instructor flying Vultee BT-13s. Major (later Major General) Harry Crutcher, then director of training at Goodfellow, remembers Carswell as "very clean-cut, every inch a soldier, very confident" and "always interested in his students' progress and looking for improved teaching techniques." He met and married Virginia Ede there and they had one son, Robert Ede Carswell.

John B. "Jack" Carey remembers Carswell as a flying school classmate. "We did everything in alphabetical order in those days," Carey said, "so Carey and Carswell ate together, bunked together and marched together. He was a very determined individual and had a love for the military and military protocol. He knew the rules and he played by the rules. This might have been interpreted by some of our non-volunteer airmen to mean something other than what it was.

"He was neat and punctual and although he was of a quiet nature, he had a sense of humor. He was compassionate and reservedly friendly. He once remarked that "little old ladies and dogs like me.""

"He was a fierce competitor as evidenced by his playing as a lineman (guard) on the TCU football team when he weighed at somewhere only around 150 pounds. I liked him."

After leaving the Gulf Coast Training Command as an instructor, Carswell was an instructor and operations officer with three Stateside B-24 operational training units before going overseas. He joined the 308th in China in April 1944, first on the group headquarters staff and later as operations officer for the 374th Squadron at Chengkung. Because of his previous experience as a B-24 instructor, he flew with different crews to check their proficiency and observe their reactions and those of any other aircraft in the formation.

On the afternoon of July 22, 1944, Carswell's plane joined with twenty-four others to bomb Changsha for the fourth successive time in ten days. It was a daylight mission and the weather turned sour en route. However, seventeen planes were able to drop more than thirty-five tons of incendiary bombs on the target "with excellent results," according to the group history. However, on the return flight, Carswell's aircraft became lost and arrived in the Kunming area after the weather had closed in and was unable to land.

When the gas reached a critical point, Carswell ordered the crew to bail out and he followed. The plane crashed in the vicinity of Tsuyung; none of the ten crew members were badly injured. They were assisted in their trek back to base by Chinese guerrillas and arrived at Chengkung eight days later. Carswell arrived just in time to stop the message to his wife that reported him missing.

At this time, the four squadrons of the 308th had several B-24Js assigned to each. These were radar-equipped for low altitude bombing and were to be used primarily for interdiction of the sea lanes extending from French Indo-China to Formosa. After three months of combat flying, Carswell was sent to command the detachment of B-24Js at the advanced base at Liuchow. The base was located about 400 miles southeast of Kunming directly in the path of advancing Japanese ground forces.

With all of his B-24 experience as an instructor, Carswell knew his airplane's capabilities and limitations probably better than most other pilots. Lt. Charles F. Thompson, then a co-pilot who had not been through the B-24 transition school in the States, believes he may have flown more missions with Carswell than any other pilot in China.

"I remember the time we were on a bombing mission on a north China target and he suspected the formation was loose," Thompson recalled:

"We were leading the formation and he said, 'Fly the airplane,' He got out of his seat and went back to the rear so he could see the entire formation. Upon returning to the flight deck, he ordered the radio operator to notify all other radio operators to tell the bombardiers to hold their bombs. He then got on another radio frequency and talked to the pilots directly. By this time we were already committed to overfly the target and encountered some flak. The major told the pilots we were going to slowly descend to 1,000 feet and start a slow turn to the right, make a 360, and come back over the target. The bombing run was a success. That was Carswell.

"Another time after a particularly successful mission, he said, 'I'm going to show you a fighter plane landing with a B-24.' We came in on the approach to the runway with engines churning and the airspeed indicator showing about 200 mph. He had told me to do exactly as he said when controlling the wing and cowl flaps, and landing gear.

"We came screaming over the runway at just a few feet, then he pulled her up and went into a steep turn to the left. At this point, he started shouting instructions to me. Just at the last moment, he called for gear down. I lowered it and I believe we touched down just as the wheels came fully into position. The man could fly!"

October 15, 1944, was a date that Carswell's squadron mates well remember. Late that afternoon, with Capt. Donald N. "Smilin' Jack" Armstrong in the pilot's seat and Carswell riding as co-pilot, they took off from the advanced base at Liuchow for a night sea sweep over the South China Sea looking for targets of opportunity. About 150 miles east of Hong Kong, a group of six vessels was sighted. At this point Carswell took over the controls. Diving to 400 feet in the direction the ships were steaming, the B-24 encountered concentrated fire from the heavily armed ships. Lining up for a stern-to-bow run, one direct hit and two near misses were scored on a destroyer which brought it to a halt. A second run was made and more bombs were dropped on the ship which was by now signalling frantically to the other ships for help.

Meanwhile, Sgt. Kenneth A. Barber, radio operator, had transmitted Carswell's message that they had sighted a destroyer and five 'unknowns.'

"I thought at the time that probably the destroyer was escorting merchant ships," Carswell said in an interview after the mission that was reported in *C.B.I. Roundup*. "I soon found out what we were up against."

Others aboard reported a nearby cruiser. Carswell decided to make a third run, this time aiming for the new target.

"We were right on her," Carswell said. "I told [Nolan S.] Klepinger to let her have the last six bombs. He was pretty cool. Why spend six when three can do the trick, he told me. Seeing the results he got, I had no kick coming.

"There was a big explosion and we were right over it. We could see stuff exploding in front and behind us. It was aimed stuff. It was like an ammunition dump going off in every direction. At the same time, the plane tilted nose down."

Armstrong said, "I thought we had our tails blown off. We pulled back as hard as we could. The plane leveled out and started climbing. Then tailgunner (Sgt. Reginald R.) Leonard called out through the intercom, 'that cruiser's blown up all over the sky!'"

With tracers angling up at the lumbering B-24, Carswell decided to make a third run on the destroyer to finish it off. Just as he was about to line up on the stricken target, however, he sighted a larger ship, the largest enemy ship the crew had ever seen - possibly a navy cruiser. Again Carswell made his run from stern to bow while the bombardier, Lt. Klepinger, toggled off three more bombs. As the plane streaked over the vessel amid heavy defensive fire from it and the other ships, there was a blinding flash below followed by a tremendous explosion. As Carswell swung around to look, the ship folded up in the middle and began to sink. Within a few minutes, as the B-24 left the area to loiter about thirty miles away, the radar confirmed that there were now only five ships left.

With three bombs left in the bomb rack, it was decided that a fourth run would be made on the slower of the ships now streaking for port. No direct hits were scored but there were two near misses. With fuel running low, the crew headed for Liuchow. The mission had lasted twelve hours, fifteen minutes. Later that day, the U.S. Navy confirmed that two enemy warships had been sunk.

Everyone sweated out the journey home because it was not known if the B-24 had suffered any damage. "The navigator (Lt. Alfred T. Withian) did a beautiful job getting us back," Carswell said. "If we had gotten lost, we would have been cooked. When we landed, we had about an hour's gas left."

On the trip home, the crew broke out some K rations and chatted over the intercom about their experience. It was still dark when they landed. Later that day they examined the plane and found not even a scratch. A censored news report stated:

> "A single sea-sweeping B-24 blew up a heavy cruiser and sank a destroyer in a 55-minute low-level attack on a six-ship Japanese naval formation moving towards Formosa.
>
> "The bomber probably put a crimp in the Japanese naval reinforcement of that island stronghold which has recently taken a blasting American attack. At any rate, the sinking ranks as one of the most notable one-plane achievements of any air force - all the more notable at a time when the 14th is fighting to retain a narrowed foothold in southeast China."

For this mission, Carswell earned the Distinguished Flying Cross for "the exceptional courage, gallantry, cool judgment and skill demonstrated by Major Carswell in attacking such a large task force with his lone plane in the face of almost certain destruction."

Lt. Carlos J. Ricketson, the usual co-pilot on the crew of this aircraft, had gone along as a spare pilot. He had no particular duties during the flight and acted as an observer. He told the story about the flight from his special viewpoint:

"About an hour out Major Carswell and Capt. Armstrong changed seats. For a while, I helped Al (Lt. Alfred T.) Withian, our navigator, with visual check points after it grew dark. I went back to the waist of the plane and shot the breeze with the gunners. 'Sleepy' (S/Sgt Leonard), our tail turret gunner and armorer, kept running back to his guns every two minutes or so checking to see if there was a Nip sneaking up on us. The boys began kidding him about his 2-minute trips and he just laughed it off. 'You know, Lieutenant,' he said, 'maybe only one time in a thousand there'll be something back there, with it growing dark and with us out in the middle of nowhere, but if that thousandth time ever occurs, I intend to be there.'

"We crossed over the coast and started our letdown to sweep altitude. The majority of the mission was without event and for a while I busied myself with looking for a few targets. About 10 p.m. I decided that I'd catch a few winks so I propped myself against the pedestal between the two pilots and slept. About 1 a.m., the major tapped me on the shoulder and said we had picked up some targets and that I should get ready. Al and I tried to identify the targets. Everybody was at their stations and eager to hit 'em. Al said, 'Rick, I'll bet you a buck that those ships are all naval.' I hoped that they were and then again I hoped that they weren't because even one naval vessel can throw up a hell of a lot of flak and here were six of the bastards. We flew around downwind of them so we could look them over and plan our attack without them hearing us and thereby not alerting them. It's a damn good idea to try to surprise them, especially if they're warships. While doing this we let down to our very low attack altitude of 400 feet. As soon as the specific target was picked out and Klep had opened the bomb bay doors, I got set in my position in the bomb bay. I picked this spot to observe from as it is the best position on the plane to do so. Al and I decided that when we were two miles from the target, he would signal me with his flashlight as the bomb bay does not have an interphone system. I wanted to know when we were fairly close so that I could get set to make my observations. On these runs in the black of night, one hardly knows what to expect in the way of gunfire from the decks of these ships and my heart was beating like a trip hammer.

"Al flashed and then a moment later I heard the click of bombs going away. As we passed over the vessel, I saw it was a destroyer. The first bomb hit aft of amidships on the starboard side and right alongside the vessel. The second bomb hit directly amidships and the third forward of amidships and right alongside the vessel on the port side.

"In the flash of the bombs, I saw the superstructure silhouetted and was able to identify it as a destroyer of the Terisuki class, one of the Emperor's newest and most modern of his destroyers. We must have really surprised them as not a shot was fired at us. As soon as Klep closed the doors, I rushed up on the flight deck shouting, 'Boy, oh boy, old Klep really laid them in there!' and informed the major and Don what I had observed, which I thought was plenty. We knew he was crippled, if not sinking. Sleepy came over the interphone saying that he was stopped.

"We swung around for the second run and I hoped like hell that it was for the kill. I got set again in the bomb bay; Al gave me the signal and a few seconds later bombs went away. Those few seconds seemed like an eternity to me. I knew that this wouldn't be a free one and that we would catch hell. I was getting mighty apprehensive. It's really amazing how long just a couple of seconds can drag out. As soon as the bombs had gone, it started. The tracers seemed to be coming from everywhere. The destroyer we were bombing wasn't firing. They either weren't able to or else we had gotten them clean out of the fighting mood. That sure didn't mean that the others weren't hot for us. Most of the stuff seemed to be coming from a cruiser that was nearby and it wasn't light machine gun fire, either. Machine gun tracer fire is red. This stuff was white and green and not as rapid. It was probably 20 or 40 mm stuff and maybe some heavier. How we came through it without getting knocked out of the sky, I'll never be able to understand.

"This run was made practically across the beam. About the time the bombs exploded, the doors were coming closed, so my observations weren't as good as they should have been, but the first bomb seemed to hit on or near the bow and exploded with a white flash. The two other bombs fell over. I rushed up to the 'office' and informed the boys as to what I had seen but by that time they were getting a blow-by-blow description from Sleepy in his turret. From the cockpit of a B-24, it is practically impossible to see what you hit. Everyone felt sure that it was sinking this time but the decision was made to make sure and as we swung around for another pass, we could see the destroyer frantically signalling and shooting flares, evidently for aid from the other vessels in the force.

"As I got set again, I wondered how in the hell he was still floating after the pounding we had given him. This time I started praying, praying that we wouldn't get hit and spread all over the water and I knew that if we ever did get hit by that flak with its intensity that there would be no two ways about it, we would be. By this time, I guess I was too excited to be really scared. Al signaled again and I was saying to myself, 'Come on, Klep, you can do it. Lay those eggs down the middle.' I couldn't be up there at my job, but I was giving him all the moral support I could.

"Bombs away and did they start filling the sky with tracers!

"Oh, man! I had my feet dangling over the catwalk but I sure pulled them up in a hurry and, brother, I started making as little a target out of myself as possible. Looking down I got one of the biggest surprises of my life. I had expected to see the destroyer again but what I saw made me almost fall out of the bomb bay. There directly under us was what looked to me to be the biggest damned ship in anybody's navy. It wasn't, however, and thank God. It was a cruiser. From bow to stern it was lit up from the gun flashes. I couldn't start to count the number of gun positions firing at us. The first bomb hit just a little aft of amidships and on deck. The second practically amidships and the third on the port side forward of amidships and right alongside.

"All this time they kept up their terrific barrage and the tracers kept inching into us and just when it seemed that they were finally going to get right on us, I saw a sight that I have never seen before and hope never to see again, not even in the movies. As the bombs exploded, there was a blinding white flash and then a terrific explosion wherein the whole center section of the vessel blew up and the ends of the ship folded up like an accordion. The heat of it was amazing and for a moment I actually thought that my face had been burned.

"In the explosion, I could see chunks of the ship flying through the air and I thought at the time, 'Good Lord, Klep must have put one down the stack or in a magazine.' It must have been in a magazine because I remember seeing what looked like tracers in with the explosion. When the ship blew up, the plane gave a terrific lurch nosedown and seemed to bob around like a cork on the ocean and I was hanging on for dear life.

"I thought the plane was out of control but in a moment it got straightened out and started to climb. Later, Don told me that he and the major, not being able to see what was going on, thought that from the way the plane lurched that we had been hit and had blown up ourselves and that it took all the strength they had to pull up and keep us from plunging into the sea.

"When the [bomb bay] doors closed, I rushed up to the flight deck and started pounding Al on the back and yelling, 'Al, Klep blew that bastard clean to hell!' I have never been so excited in my life. I believe that if we hadn't hit him, he sure as hell would have gotten us because those tracers kept coming closer all the time.

"I wanted to find out exactly what kind of cruiser it was while the picture of it was still so clear in my mind. I went down into the nose to take a look at Klep's identification manual and was able to identify it as a cruiser of the three-stack *Kuma Natori* class. Klep was grinning from ear to ear and I wanted to congratulate him but he said, 'Get the hell out of here, we have more work to do.'

"I had wondered if we were going in again as we still had three bombs left. I didn't think we would get chewed out for bringing three bombs back, considering what we had done, and considering the odds we were up against, but we were really out for blood now and to hell with the flak.

"I wondered about the gas at the time because I knew we must be getting low as we had been out an awfully long time but there was no time to check it now. This time the run was made across the beam of a destroyer but the bombs fell short of the stern and I didn't see enough of the vessel to be able to identify it.

"I believe we sweated out that last run more than any other. We were all eager to get the hell out of there and start home. I guess the Japs were pretty mad at us because they were really spraying the sky but without much accuracy. 'Lucky' (T/Sgt Lusk, our engineer), came forward and checked the gas. He found we had just enough to get back provided we went straight home and going home meant coming uncomfortably close to a couple of major airfields that the Japs had near Canton, but we had no alternative. We wanted to find out what had happened to our destroyer but that was an impossibility due to our gasoline situation. As it stood, we would only count it as a 'probable' because we couldn't be sure that it actually did sink. As it turned out later, we got confirmation of it actually sinking.

"Coming back, we opened up some K rations (cheese and dog biscuits) and celebrated. That is, everyone except Al who was 'just too damn busy to eat.' He did a beautiful job of navigation and brought us back, splitting the field. If he had made just one little mistake, we would have wound up walking back. When we landed, we had about 30 minutes of gas left.

"It gives a man a pretty damn warm, satisfying feeling to be able to fly and fight with the determined, aggressive and courageous team that I have the honor and privilege of doing."

Three days after this mission, Carswell scheduled himself for another sea sweep with another crew but en route to the target area, the plane had complete radio and radar failure. When it was determined that no in-flight repairs could be made, he reluctantly turned back to Liuchow with the full bomb load. Ordinarily, the bombs would have been salvoed and the gas burned off to lighten the load but in China where bombs and gas were always in short supply, Carswell decided to land with the bombs aboard after about an hour's flight. He made a soft landing which impressed the crew and those who learned later what he had done.

At this time, several of the B-24s were grounded for the installation of extra bomb bay fuel tanks which would give them a 3,500-gallon capacity, up from the 2,750 gallons normally carried. Able to stay aloft for nearly sixteen hours, the purpose was to use them as unarmed reconnaissance aircraft to locate enemy forces moving toward the Philippines at the time General MacArthur's forces had landed on Leyte Island to begin the liberation which he had promised many months before.

The first 308th long-range reconnaissance mission, without a bomb load, was flown on October 21, 1944. It was made almost in sight of Lingayen Gulf and down the coast of Luzon toward Manila and Bataan. Three days later, Capt. Armstrong and his crew flew along the French-Indo China coast to check out suspected enemy convoy routes. After a long period of no sightings, they were returning to Liuchow in deteriorating weather when they spotted three different convoys totalling about twenty-five ships. With no bombs to drop, all they could do was radio what they had seen to Liuchow.

When Armstrong arrived at Liuchow, the weather had gone below minimums and he had to land at Chengkung. The crew recorded fourteen hours, five minutes of flight time in their log books.

On October 26, eleven days after his previous successful mission, Carswell and the crew he chose to fly with that day took off on their epic night mission. They were briefed by Edward G. Menaker, the Group's radar expert, and their objective was to locate and attack a convoy whose approximate location had been reported earlier. The co-pilot was Lt. James H. Rinker, a former flying sergeant. Three other officers in the crew were Lts. James L. O'Neal, the regular co-pilot; Walter W. Hillier, bombardier; and Charles A. Ulery, navigator. The enlisted men on the crew were Sgts. Charles A. Maddox, Jr., engineer-gunner; Kaemper W. Steinman, armorer-gunner; Ernest P. Watras, radio operator; Norman Nunes, gunner; Carlton M. Schnepf, gunner; and Adam Hudek, radar specialist.

Carswell lifted the Liberator off from Chengkung at about 5:15 p.m. It was dark when they crossed the coast and headed down the South China Sea in bright moonlight to locate a large convoy consisting of eight naval and merchant vessels that were reported southwest of Hong Kong. At about 8:15, the radar operator spotted twelve vessels, instead of the previously reported eight – two destroyers and ten other vessels, which were probably gunboats and cargo ships.

Carswell, well aware of the importance of lining up on a target so that the plane would receive a minimum of defense fire from the convoy, planned the run carefully. He aimed the plane at one of the destroyers. When the run was completed, Carswell reported to his crew on the interphone that they had damaged the ship. No defensive fire was seen.

Following is the official intelligence report of this mission which was filed after crew interrogations on November 12, 1944:

"Two LAB runs were made on vessels in the convoy. The first was made on a destroyer from 600 feet altitude at 90 degrees to the bow, across the starboard beam. 6 x 500 RDX bombs were dropped, one of which was a 20-foot near miss short of midships, undoubtedly damaging the vessel. No gun fire was received on this first run and since it was made from a direct angle of approach, the attack was believed to have been a surprise to the enemy.

"On leaving the immediate area and circling for 35 minutes, a second run was made on a 350-foot freighter or tanker from the same altitude as the first run, 600 feet, quartering the port stern. The run was directed at 45 degrees to the bow. Three bombs were dropped, the first landing in water 70 feet short and from two explosive blasts observed, the other two are reported as direct hits. Further observation was impossible but the vessel is claimed as probably sunk. The fact that heavy concentrated gun and pom-pom shells were bursting all around the aircraft at its altitude and tracers from anti-aircraft were well-directed, is evidence that the plane was tracked and the gunners set for altitude and range. Fire was held until the plane was directly above the convoy and with a bright clear moon, it must have stood out clearly at that altitude.

"The plane dropped to just above the water's deck with No. 1 and No. 3 engine shot out, No. 2 engine hit and sputtering, the hydraulic system out, hole in No. 2 gas tank and numerous other holes throughout the plane. The pilot had great difficulty in righting the plane and regaining altitude. The three remaining bombs were jettisoned in the water and the crew began throwing everything removable overboard. Lt. Ulery explains that in getting up to 4,000 feet, the highest altitude attained before reaching the coast at Hainan Island, the pilots would put the plane into a climb until it almost stalled out, then point the nose down in order to pick up speed to go into a climb again. At no time could more than 125 to 130 mph be maintained and with two engines feathered and another damaged, it was with great difficulty the plane was held on course.

"Twenty minutes after heading on return course away from the attack, Lt. O'Neal, the regular co-pilot of the crew, noticed that Lt. Rinker had a severe wound in his right hand from shrapnel. The front of his clothing was covered with blood and he was almost in a faint when Lt. O'Neal grabbed him and lifted him from the co-pilot's seat. Although in this condition, he had remained at the controls with Major Carswell, without mentioning his wound. Lt. O'Neal took the co-pilot's seat and Lt. Rinker was administered first aid by the navigator and bombardier. A tourniquet was tied around his arm between the elbow and shoulder, sulfanilamide applied to the wound which was then bandaged and a tube of morphine was injected into the arm. His condition seemed improved after a short time and he talked with other crew members. The fact that he was weakened by loss of blood, however, was very evident.

"When the plane flew over the coastline which was approximately one hour before it crashed, it was flying at 3,500 feet altitude with great difficulty. Members of the crew interrogated state that they had expected to bail out on reaching this point but believed the reason for not doing so was because the parachute of Lt. Hillier, the bombardier, had been hit by bomb fragments and he refused to jump in it. Rather than jump he was determined to remain with the plane.

"An hour later, No. 2 engine sputtering, the plane was losing altitude and it was impossible to hold it on course. No. 2 engine cut out and the order was given to bail out. Realizing their predicament, all crew members were on the catwalk waiting for the order except the two pilots, Major Carswell and Lt. O'Neal and Lt. Hillier who still refused to jump. Lt. Hillier had been persuaded to go to the catwalk also but when seen by the last man to leave the plane, he was standing behind the pilot and co-pilot in the cockpit. The other eight men jumped at 2315 hours from an estimated altitude of 2,000 feet. The plane was out of control with its pilots trying to dodge mountain peaks, which extended almost to their altitude. Its crash was observed by the explosion on impact against a mountainside ten miles farther west.

"Beside Major Carswell, Lt. O'Neal, and Lt. Hillier, who were killed in the crash, the bodies of Lt. Rinker and Sgt. Steinman were found the following day. Lt. Rinker, in his weakened condition and right hand rendered almost useless from the wound, apparently was unable to pull his ripcord. The body of Sgt. Steinman, with his parachute open, was found on the top of the mountain, where he landed, but no doubt before his 'chute had opened fully. Of the remaining six men who jumped, none were injured but all report having landed on mountainsides and struck the earth only a few seconds after the impact of the 'chute's opening."

The official report does not explain all that happened that night. While Carswell and his crew may have wanted to rejoice in the score after their attacks, they knew immediately that the plane had been hit and damaged badly. One shell had burst in the bomb bay and shell fragments had ricocheted around inside. Lt. Rinker was hit by a piece of shrapnel that entered the back of his right hand and exited through his palm, causing him to begin bleeding. Another shell blasted the front of the plane and Lt. Hillier's chest parachute, lying on an ammunition box, was punctured by bits of shrapnel. Holes in the hydraulic lines caused the fluid to spill all over Sgt. Schnepf's parachute.

A quick assessment of the damage showed that the No. 1 and No. 3 engines were inoperative and No. 2 was damaged but still turning with reduced power. One gasoline tank was punctured, the hydraulic system was not functioning and there were gaping holes throughout the fuselage. The bomb bay doors would not close completely; the aircraft would have flooded and sunk quickly if the plane were ditched.

While Carswell was fighting to control the aircraft and Rinker was trying to help despite his badly-injured right hand, it lunged downward toward the sea. With Rinker bleeding and going into shock, Carswell managed to level the plane off at about 150 feet above the water. He headed toward the shore and tried to inch the disabled plane upward. He knew he had to reach better than 4,000 feet to get over the mountains toward possible landing fields.

Meanwhile, O'Neal came up to the cockpit to assist Carswell at the controls. The crew began to throw everything possible overboard. Tool boxes, ammo cans, flak vests and machine guns were thrown out. The remaining bombs were quickly salvoed.

Rinker, blood-splattered and weak, was lifted out of his seat and laid on the flight deck floor. Ulery, Hillier, and Maddox gave him first aid, put a tourniquet on his arm and gave him a morphine shot from the ship's first aid kit.

As they limped toward shore, Carswell reportedly instructed Watras to radio Liuchow that they had two engines out and they would try to reach an alternate airport. [Watras denies this because of the prohibition about transmitting in a combat area.] There was an overcast and Carswell plowed into it still trying to get to 4,000 feet.

Although no one spoke about it, they all knew they would have to bail out if that No. 2 engine, which was not delivering full power, were to quit. Those in the rear stayed near the open bomb bay doors on the catwalk just in case.

As the B-24 labored westward, the No. 2 engine coughed and slowed down nearly to a stop. The loss of power sent the big bomber down a thousand feet but Carswell and O'Neal, now in the co-pilot's seat, somehow managed to get the engine going again and nursed the plane ever so slowly back to 4,000 feet. This same sequence happened four more times. By this time, they were about eighty miles inland but Carswell and O'Neal could see they were below the level of hills on both sides of them. Carswell gave the order to bail out.

Charles F. Thompson, a pilot assigned to the 374th who had flown many times as co-pilot with Carswell, commented years later: "In my opinion there were not more than a handful of pilots in the entire Air Force who could have kept a B-24 from crashing into the water after losing an engine at 150-foot altitude. It was hard enough to maintain altitude with one engine out. Major Carswell was able not only to maintain altitude but gain more and get the aircraft back over land for other crew members to bail out. I heard one of the surviving crew members tell how he did it. He would feed in the throttles to the maximum point of the engines, all the time working the flaps up and down to gain lift, to gain airspeed, to level out and repeat the procedure time and time again, sometimes gaining as little as 20 feet at a time. The procedure must have been exhausting."

Rinker dropped out of the bomb bay first but his parachute failed to open. Ulery, Maddox, Watras, Hudek, Nunes, and Steinman followed but Steinman's 'chute also failed. The others made hard but safe landings in the mountains below.

This left Carswell, O'Neal, Hillier, and Schnepf in the plane. Hillier, with his punctured 'chute, stood between the seats. There were no spare parachutes on board. Schnepf decided to wait briefly before leaping out. However, desperation overcame reluctance and he jumped. When he pulled the D-ring to release the 'chute from the pack, nothing happened. He pulled frantically at the pack and managed to rip the silk out in time for it to blossom. He landed hard a few seconds later.

Ernest Watras recalled his jump:

"I recall looking back toward the pilots' area as I stood on the near end of the catwalk to, sort of, wish them well as I asked God to help them to land safely somewhere nearby so that we could get together and rejoice in reunion. My brain was numb with sadness at this point, not fear. I gave myself to God – maybe He could help. I looked straight at Lt. Hillier, my friend, who was in serious distress, then I dove out of the aircraft. I flipped over onto my back, looking straight up at the bottom of the aircraft. Suddenly, the aircraft pulled away from me. I distinctly remember watching the grand B-24 for those few milli-seconds. It was not on fire, it was not shattered, it flew along smoothly.

"Suddenly, the plane disappeared as if God plucked it right out of the sky like I asked Him to do. At the same time, as if watching a fast-forward tape on my VCR, I saw a huge fire reflection penetrate the overcast sky. During this split-second time interval, I pulled my 'chute cord. Instantly, I felt the tug of the canopy opening and at the same time I felt the branches of an evergreen tree tangle with my feet, then I fell across this tree, shaving off all the branches on one side with the small of my back, and lying there with parachute canopy neatly covering me, still showing the folds like it was never used. Needless to say, I have a painful back problem to this day."

As Schnepf lay dazed after his jump, he also saw a huge fireball light up the sky to the west. It was their B-24 slamming into a mountain only a few feet from the top.

No one will ever know what happened in the cockpit or what any of them was thinking during the ensuing few minutes after the last man bailed out. It is unthinkable that Carswell and O'Neal would jump and leave Hillier to die. Both were fighting to control the crippled plane and attempt to get more lift out of it. When he realized it couldn't clear the mountains, Carswell's only alternative was to try to crash-land in an open space in the dark. He had no time to find one.

The next day, Maddox, Hudek, Watras, and Ulery met and were assisted by a Chinese who was a member of the British Air Aid Group (BAAG) who told them that Nunes had been found alive. [The BAAG was a secret unit organized in southeastern China to rescue Allied airmen and escort them to safety.] Later, they heard that Schnepf had been picked up and was in safe hands. He joined them soon after, as did Nunes. They also learned that three bodies had been found in the aircraft wreckage and two others along the bailout path. They were told by the first Chinese they encountered who could read the "Pointee-Talkee" that the Japs were only seven miles to the northwest and that numerous puppet troops were in the vicinity. It was evident that the natives were afraid to give them aid because of the possibility of being caught by the Japanese. The intelligence report picks up the story:

"Monday, October 30: A message was received from Liuchow requesting the names of men killed and those walking back which delayed the start for an hour. After this information was given, the six crew members, the Chinese sergeant from the BAAG with 20 soldiers as guides and the magistrate and Mr. Liu departed from the Catholic mission at Tungchen. Sedan chairs were supplied for the party with bearers and the soldiers acting as scouts, traveling ahead and bringing up the rear. They arrived at the mission that afternoon at 1530 hours. They were met by Father John J. Tierney, a native of Ireland who ran the mission, and Father James Fitzgerald and Father Edward Mueth, both from the U.S. who had been driven out of their respective missions by the Japs.

"The bodies of Lt. Rinker and Sgt. Steinman had arrived in sealed caskets shortly before the party and placed in the small chapel. After receiving food at the mission, all attended the ceremony in the chapel where Catholic rites were given the two bodies. The caskets were taken to a spot on a hillside 1/4 mile back and to the left of the chapel, where graves had already been dug. A short closing ceremony was given by Father Tierney and the bodies were lowered into the graves at 1700 hours. One volley was fired by the six members of Lt. Rinker's crew and a volley was also fired by the Chinese soldiers. The night was spent at the mission.

"Tuesday - 31 October: As the party was preparing to leave at 0730 hours, three sealed caskets bearing the remains of Major Carswell, Lt. O'Neal and Lt. Hillier were brought in. The men were not permitted to remain for the burial as their guides were quite concerned about their safety and advised moving on. Father Tierney assured them he would take care of everything including records and name plaques on the graves. The party left for Sunyi, arriving at 1600 hours. The men spent the night in a schoolhouse where Nunes was treated for fever (temperature 103) by a Chinese doctor.

"Wednesday - 1 November: Nunes's temperature was normal and the men left with the BAAG sergeant and his soldiers (20 in number). Traveled seven hours in rain and over rough terrain arriving in a schoolhouse in the mountains where they were met by a Chinese colonel who insisted the men put on coolie clothing which he had arranged for them. They learned the Japs were pushing south toward their direction. The colonel mapped their route for the following day.

"Thursday - 2 November: Travel started before daylight and after 12 hours walking in the rain through mud and mountainous terrain they arrived at a small village where they spent the night in a native hut.

"Friday - 3 November: After 11 hours of walking in rain they reached Watlam. They were taken to headquarters of the village mandarin who told them that they would not be able to get through to Liuchow as the Japs had that route blocked and their only possible escape would be to Nanning, which would take them 10 days to reach. Leaving the mandarin's headquarters, they were taken to a Catholic mission in the town run by a priest, Father Macdonald, whose home is in Boston. Here they were joined by a P-51 pilot, Lt. Charles E. Porter, who had been shot down northwest of Macao while flying escort on a 308th Bomb Group mission to Kowloon docks, Hong Kong, 16 October 1944. He had been all this while walking out with another BAAG since. The night was spent with Father MacDonald at his mission.

"Saturday - 4 November: The six men of Lt. Rinker's crew, Lt. Porter, the two BAAG guides and their men started for Hingyeh following a main road which led to the town. They had been informed that this journey would be dangerous but they might get through. The road had been blown up by the Chinese and native evacuees encountered were numerous heading with their belongings toward Watlam. After covering half the distance to Hingyeh, they were met by a runner carrying the message that the Japs were entering the town of Hingyeh and advising them to change their course immediately. The party abandoned the road, cutting across rough mountains to Singhwang which they reached after dark having travelled fourteen hours in steady rain. The mandarin of the village, which was practically evacuated, advised against their remaining overnight as the Japs were driving in that direction. The men were so fatigued from travel, going further without rest was impossible. They remained overnight."

It took nine days for the survivors to walk, ride in sedan chairs and on sampans to get to Nanning. After several days there, they were transported to Kunming and arrived at Chengkung, the home base of the 374th, on November 9.

Reviewing this mission more than fifty years later, at least two of the survivors believe the second bombing run should not have been made on the convoy. Ernest P. Watras, the radio operator, says, "I recall that after our withdrawal from the area of the first bomb run and circling about 20 miles away (our usual procedure, to size up the situation and to plan a second run, abandon the target, or whatever else is appropriate), took longer than on previous missions. The officers did not consult with the enlisted men:

"While we were circling, the radar operator, Adam Hudek, reported that the convoy was continually rearranging itself, indicating that the convoy commander was well aware of our presence and location. I recall the more-than-usual discussion by Major Carswell, the navigator, and the radar operator. I did not hear any comments from our own pilot, Lt. Rinker. Co-pilot O'Neal was attentive but quiet, and Hillier the bombardier, was at his station below deck.

"During this time being used to formulate a plan, the convoy was maneuvering and placing its gunboats and destroyers in 'Purple Heart' Corner – the area an enemy would anticipate we would strike; i.e., the lone target straggling behind and away from the main target as bait for us. We took the bait.

"Adam Hudek watched the enemy movement very closely with greater than normal excitement, reporting that this convoy was very large and evidently of great importance because of its continuing rearranging action. I became quite scared at this point and wished we didn't have Major Carswell aboard because by this time we would have recognized that we had met our match and started for home base. There was more than sufficient information to give the major a warning that he was playing with a determined and capable enemy.

"The final decision to make a second run was announced to the planners only, and the rest of us knew we were on the way to doom by what we could see out of our windows. The wake these ships were stirring up proved that they were well-trained in evasive action and determined to protect themselves.

"As we approached the target ship, our original planned target had sneaked out and was replaced by a heavier sea craft. That target and other nearby naval vessels fired on us just as we released our ordnance. What a beautiful target we made at about 600 feet on a moonlit night!"

Watras has no doubts that the second run on the target was a tragic mistake in judgment, "since we had ample information about the enemy to know it would be a suicide run." He says that during the long walk back to their base, the others agreed with him. Ulery says that in his opinion, "the procedures employed in the last mission should not have been used."

For his service in China, Carswell had been awarded the Distinguished Flying Cross, the Air Medal, and the Purple Heart. For the October 26, 1944, mission, he was posthumously awarded the Medal of Honor in 1946. It is not known who made the recommendation and there is some feeling among the survivors that others on board such as Lts. Rinker and O'Neal should also have received it for helping to keep the aircraft flying. However, it has long been Air Force policy that such awards for heroism have been given in similar cases only to the senior person on board, not others who were present during the event. A case in point is General James H. "Jimmy" Doolittle who received the Medal of Honor for leading the famous raid on Tokyo in April 1942. He felt he did not deserve it and, as he told the author, "I accepted it on behalf of all the men who took the same risk that I did."

The Carswell citation for the Medal of Honor, signed by President Harry S. Truman, which accompanied the award concluded: "With consummate gallantry and intrepidity, Major Carswell gave his life in a supreme effort to save all members of his crew. His sacrifice, far beyond that required of him, was in keeping with the traditional bravery of America's war heroes."

The Medal of Honor was presented to Carswell's son Robert at Goodfellow Field, San Angelo, Texas in 1946. A huge, six-engine Consolidated B-36 from the air base at Fort Worth droned overhead in tribute during the ceremony.

In the spring of 1940, when the nation was beginning to gear up for a possible war and to support the President's call for lend-lease equipment, the Fort Worth Chamber of Commerce and other civic organizations had contacted various aircraft manufacturing companies to tout the advantages of locating their new factories in that area. One of the first to respond was Consolidated Vultee Aircraft Corporation, headquartered in San Diego, which was interested in an inland site. Six months later, the War Department authorized the company to build a plant for manufacturing B-24 heavy bombers on the outskirts of the city.

From a bomber assembly plant with a modest dirt runway, the area grew into a huge combination of an assembly plant and crew training base. The field was named Tarrant Field and construction began on June 28, 1942; the base was officially activated on August 21, 1942. In May 1943, the name was changed to Fort Worth Army Air Field. More than 3,000 B-24s were manufactured there during the war.

After the war, in January 1948, the base had three names during that month. On New Year's Day, it was Ft. Worth Army Air Field but the next day the name was changed to Fort Worth Air Force Base because the Air Force had become a separate service the previous September. On January 13th, it was renamed Griffiss Air Force Base after Lt. Col. Townsend E. Griffiss who had been killed in an aircraft accident on February 15, 1942. Griffiss was the first U.S. airman to lose his life in Europe during World War II in line of duty.

As has been customary over the years, most Air Force bases are named after deceased Air Force heroes who had lived in the local area. Citizens of Fort Worth believed that one of their own who had won the nation's highest medal for valor should have the base named after him. On February 27, 1948, the base that had turned out so many B-24s, possibly including the one that Carswell and his crew had flown, was officially dedicated as Carswell Air Force Base to honor the 308th's and the China theater's only Medal of Honor winner. Griffiss was later honored by having the Air Force base at Rome, New York, named for him.

At the dedication ceremony, attended by many state and federal dignitaries, a letter from General Hoyt S. Vandenberg, vice chief of staff of the Air Force, was read which said it was "most fitting that the Carswell Air Force Base should be known by the name of one of the great heroes of World War II. It is equally appropriate that the installation should be named for a Texan and a life-long resident of your city. Major Carswell was a hero many times over."

After the war, Carswell's body had been recovered from the grave in China, returned to the United States and laid to rest at Shannon's Rose Hill Memorial Park in east Fort Worth. However, when his son heard in 1984 that the family grave plot was overgrown with weeds, shabby and unkempt, he was upset and made his unhappiness known. Personnel on the base and citizens of Fort Worth, led by Earle North Parker and John B. Long, raised $166,000 and had his father's body disinterred and transferred to a new gravesite on the base called Carswell Memorial Park. The park and a large granite memorial tombstone were dedicated on October 17, 1986. A B-24 from the Confederate Air Force, escorted by fighters, flew over the crowd.

Robert Carswell gave a short talk and a memorial wreath was laid at the burial site. In a final tribute, there was a "missing man" flyover by a flight of McDonnell-Douglas F-4 Phantom jet fighters.

The event marked the first and only time in the history of the U.S. Air Force that the person for whom a base was named was actually buried on that base.

In early 1993, the Department of Defense announced that the base would be closed as an Air Force operating base on October 1, 1993, and designated as a Joint Navy and Air Force Reserve installation. It was rumored that the base would drop the Carswell name. Representative Pete Geren (D-Ft. Worth) and a number of Fort Worth citizens felt strongly that the name should be retained. The Navy decided to retain the Carswell name and the official designation is now Naval Air Station Fort Worth-Joint Reserve Base, Carswell Field.

Many were concerned that the base might eventually be fully closed and the Carswell gravesite would go untended once again. Carswell's body was removed in March 1993 and a final reinterment ceremony was held at Oakwood Cemetery, the city's oldest burial ground. Carswell rests there today beside his mother and father who had been moved to the Oakwood site from Shannon's Rose Hill Cemetery.

There is a saying at Texas A&M University that "once an Aggie, always an Aggie." Since Horace Carswell had attended the university, even though for only one semester, he was considered a member of the Class of '38. On February 27, 1993, Carswell and six other former Aggies who had won America's highest award for valor were honored with an unveiling of their portraits and a dedication of a Medal of Honor memorial at the Sam Houston Sanders Corps of Cadets Center. A large portrait of Carswell is also displayed in the city's library.

Chapter 10

FLYING THE HUMP

I n March 1942, the Japanese cut off the Burma Road, the only over land path from India to China and all overland supply had ceased. As one of the initial objectives when Japan launched its march of conquest between December 1941 and May 1942, they had overrun all of the Malay Peninsula and almost all of Burma. British, Burmese and Indian forces, aided by Royal Air Force and the AVG, did their best to resist. Chinese forces under American General Joseph Stilwell arrived to defend the Burma Road but were forced to retire from North Burma into India.

When the monsoon rains came in June 1942, the Japanese held all of Burma except for fringes of mountain, jungle, and swamp on the north and west. It was during these early days that the Tenth Air Force was formed in New Delhi, India, and among its first activities was cooperation with the Allies in the evacuation of Burma.

The Allies came back with a response to the severance of the Burma Road that was unprecedented in scope and magnitude. They began to muster planes and pilots to fly over the world's highest mountain range – the Himalayas, known better as the Hump – to supply Chinese and American troops and, only if space permitted, Chennault's struggling air units. However, the 308th was destined to do most of its own hauling of gasoline, bombs and ammunition.

Though the distance is relatively short, the Hump is considered the most dangerous ever assigned to air transport. The reason is apparent from this description contained in the official Air Force history:

"The distance from Dinjan to Kunming is some 500 miles. The Brahmaputra valley floor lies 90 feet above sea level, the mountain wall where the principal American valley base rises quickly to 10,000 feet and higher.

"Flying eastward out of the valley, the pilot first topped the Patkai Range, then passed over the upper Chindwin River valley, bounded on the east by a 14,000-foot ridge, the Kumon Mountains. He then crossed a series of 14,000-16,000-foot ridges separated by the valleys of the West Irradwaddy, East Irrawaddy, Salween and Mekong Rivers. The main 'Hump' which gave its name to the whole awesome mountainous mass and to the air route which crossed it, was the Santsung Range, often 15,000 feet high, between the Salween and Meklong Rivers."

Pilots had to struggle to get their heavily-laden planes to safe altitudes; there was always extreme turbulence, thunderstorms and icing. On the ground there was the heat and humidity and a monsoon season that, during a six-month period, poured 200 inches of rain on the bases in India and Burma. When the sun was out, shade temperatures of from 100 to 130 degrees Fahrenheit rendered all metal exposed to the sun so hot that it could cause second degree burns if touched by the human hand.

The route over the Hump between India and China was dangerous. By the end of the war, more than 450 planes had gone down along what was called the "Aluminum Trail." There were few radio aids and no emergency fields. It was not until late in the war that a small search-and-rescue operation was formed to try to locate and extract survivors from the most inaccessible areas in the world.

It is difficult for anyone who has not flown in India and China to visualize what it was like for the Hump crews during those chaotic days of World War II. E. Franden James, gave his impression in *Plane Talk,* a 1944 Consolidated Vultee Aircraft Corporation publication:

"If you lay out your right hand on the table, palm upward, with fingers closed and thumb outstretched, you have a rough map of India. The thumb will be Assam, the narrow eastern province that reaches out and touches China. Most of Assam is low and flat, and the great Brahmaputra River that drains through it spreads out like the lower Mississippi.

"But suddenly rising at the tip of the thumb are the great Himalaya mountains, where the lowest peaks are higher than the tallest of our Rockies. There are the great walls that must be leaped to pass between

India and China. This is the Hump that all flying men from the Far East theaters speak of with awe. Over this we are flying supplies to our bases in China.

"From Assam in India to Kunming is China is only 250 miles. But the route is over mountains that rear themselves three miles high in the air; and if a plane, having climbed far enough to clear these, gets off course however slightly to the west, it may crash into the sides of still greater peaks that line the three-mile-high 'pass.'

"The air valleys between the desolate white peaks are filled with eternally swirling mists and roaring winds. A plane falling here could probably never be found, whatever the signals its slowly freezing crewmen managed to send by radio. Planes that have survived have picked up, on their radios, the voices of American crews hopelessly lost in blizzards at 20,000 feet, facing certain destiny by singing just before they crashed.

"Crews flying the Hump usually wear a small flag sewn on the back of their blouses, either American or Chinese. If they crash in potentially friendly territory, the flag helps identify them; they also carry identification cards in four languages. Beneath the flag is a silk map of Burma and China, which they may want in time of emergency.

"It is no secret that many planes flying the Hump have been lost without trace. Pilots have reported down-drafts that threw a plane 2,000 feet and almost wrenched off its wings. The 250-mile flight may take one hour, or several hours, or forever – depending on the winds and a pilot's luck. There is often no visibility; practically all the course must be flown by instruments. Fliers may leave India in noonday heat of 125 degrees, sweltering in the lowlands where 200 inches of rain fall a year; they must swiftly climb to sub-freezing heights of as much as five miles to clear the jagged wall. A good part of the route is subject to Jap attack, and Jap patrol planes operate dangerously close to some of its segments."

From the time of its arrival in China throughout the month of April 1943, the aircraft of all four squadrons of the 308th were used principally to ferry supplies, spare parts, gasoline, oil, bombs, and ammunition over the Hump for use when the group was ready to start offensive operations. On each trip, the planes also brought over various members of the ground echelon who had arrived in Chabua after making the trip across India. By May

1st, the group had accumulated about 100,000 gallons of gasoline and about 200,000 pounds of 500- and 1,000-pound bombs.

The 308th B-24 plane with the most Hump flights must be the *Doodlebug*. On its nose near the cockpit, it carried eleven stenciled bomb figures symbolizing that many combat missions, ten Japanese flags representing enemy aircraft shot down by its crew members, and 120 snow-capped mountain peaks to record the number of its Hump flights.

Chabua, a base in Assam that flying personnel of the 308th would see many times as the western terminus of their turn-around flights, was anything but comfortable. Edwin Ballenger, a crew chief with the 375th remembers:

> "We slept in tents and the sand storms were awfully dirty and made a mess of our personal clothing and equipment. It would be two years before I would again see my skin white. In China and India, it was always reddish-brown. That was also the color of the water.
>
> "The food was poor and greasy in Chabua. We had to wash our mess kits in cold water which made the next meal even less appealing. At night you went to bed early to get under the netting away from the mosquitoes. The early days of Chabua were famous for dysentery and malaria."

Ballenger recalls his first trip across the Hump:

> "My Rand-McNally World Atlas was not too helpful for our first flight over the Hump. All my map said was 'unexplored territory.' Fortunately, the weather was clear and calm. The flight was uneventful but we did see why it was so awesome. Some of the mountain tops we cleared were 26,000 feet."

Lt. John T. "Red" Cochran, a 373rd pilot of *Big Sleep*, remembers the takeoffs from Chabua:

> "Stand on the brakes at the end of a steel mat runway and hope we could get it up enough to clear the trees about 3,000 feet in front of us. Made eight or nine successful trips and eight or nine near misses on the trees."

Lt. John M. White, a pilot in the 425th Bomb Squadron, also remembers the loaded takeoffs from India and one particular flight over the Hump:

> "I carried a piano up in the bomb bay, 35 cases of liquor and 140 cases of beer. After six long, dry months in Kunming, we discovered a warehouse in Calcutta with beer and booze consigned to us. Nearly didn't get off the runway at Barrackpore (north of Calcutta) with this load but knowing all those dry fellows in Kunming were waiting for this precious cargo, we tried a lot harder.
>
> "There were high winds over the Hump, both vertical and horizontal. We would leave China empty and take three to four hours to get to India, then make it back loaded in less than two hours on heavy wind days. I was anxious to get back to a party at the base once and made it back in just over 1 1/2 hours, flying around the peaks on the southern route.
>
> "Sometimes there were thunderheads which we couldn't see; we would fly into one of these and drop 2,000 feet per minute, then hit an updraft which would carry us up at 2,000 feet per minute. We finally learned to ride with these, for over-compensation [on the controls] would put too much strain on the ship."

Lt. Jack Keene, pilot of *The Pelican*, recalled one trip from China to Chabua:

> "We went to 26,000 feet and right into solid overcast weather. The ship started icing and soon our radio compass went out. We knew we were some place over the field, and we fooled around for a half hour trying to find a hole in the clouds. Then we gradually descended, thinking we were in a valley. At 13,000 feet a peak appeared directly in front of us. We missed that one by a few feet."

After an hour and a half trying to find a hole and feeling hopelessly lost, Keene finally picked up a signal from Chabua that he could home in on.

> "By that time, we had just ten minutes gas supply left and we were ready to hit the silk. However, we swung around at about 600 feet and tried coming in on the final approach, but we lost the field and had to

climb back again to 2000. The next time, and how I still don't know, we landed safely."

Don McCormick of the 373rd was stationed at Chabua and tells about Lt. Colonel James C. Averill, executive officer of the 308th, who allowed the ground crew to load his plane to the hilt with bombs, gasoline, cigarettes, food, mail, and tools. He recalls the takeoff:

"We weren't sure the tires would hold, but Colonel Averill paid us no mind. We watched him taxi to the far end of the runway, rev up the engines while standing on the brakes, then gently they started to move; really, they seemed to crawl. It was like he took forever, but at about two-thirds down the runway the plane lifted - inches - and they had no more than five feet of altitude when they passed us at the end of the runway. They left a cloud of chopped jungle grass behind.

"We could see them gain altitude while circling upward. I don't think they had 2,000 feet when they finally straightened out and headed for China. Many of us figured that we had seen another victim on the Aluminum Trail.

"But they made it to Kunming! The China ground crew called to tell us that there was grass jammed into the bomb bay racks."

Later, at a 1989 reunion in Portland, Oregon, McCormick talked with Averill about that takeoff:

"When I mentioned the particular overloaded flight, Col Averill remembered more about it than I did. He, too, was concerned with the load he was carrying and was aware when he reached the end of the runway that he was barely airborne.

"He said that from Chabua to Kunming he handled that plane as if it were a baby. He limited himself to a five degree bank and kept an extra sharp watch on altitude and airspeed. In any case, they made it to China and the crew offloading the plane couldn't believe the load. They reported a gross weight of over 70,000 pounds, and the plane was supposed to fly with no more than a max gross of 63,000 pounds."

Edward G. Menaker, a radar expert on the 308th Group staff, was a passenger on the first radar-equipped B-24 to fly the Hump and he also had an overload story. Bill Cashmore was the pilot of *Monsoon Maiden*:

"Our planes were the first to operate in China using radar with the Hopson LAB Project. The only way we could get anything for the Project in China was to carry it along on the combat aircraft. We were instructed to be able to operate for three months with only what we carried with us. As Project Radar Officer, I settled, after consultation with our technicians, on two maintenance men per plane and all the necessary supplies and equipment for that period.

"Each plane thus carried, in addition to its normal crew of 10 (including the radar operator) and their belongings, two passengers with their belongings and a substantial supply of tools and equipment.

"The day before takeoff from Langley Army Air Field in Virginia, we finished loading the plane and lashing all the cargo in place. The load limit was 64,000 pounds gross. Presumably, we would be the heaviest 24 ever to take off from Langley. At the end of the loading, some cargo was removed to get the weight down to the limit.

"After nightfall, the real work began. Everyone going had extra stuff he wanted to take. The crew had gotten the word that China would be at the end of the line, with minimal amenities. The extra stuff was loaded on by crew members and passengers jamming it into every bit of space they could find. It comprised not only personal effects, but items of equipment for entertainment and relaxation. I stayed away, not wanting, as the senior officer, to know what was happening.

"How high the gross went above 64,000 pounds, no one will ever know. We had a sizeable audience for the takeoff because everyone knew, even if they were ignorant of the after-dark additions, that we would be the first to try a takeoff at the new high official gross weight.

"Takeoff went fine, as did all our takeoffs.

"The before-dawn takeoff from Natal, Brazil, for the flight to Ascension Island was memorable. It was hot and we were carrying all the fuel possible. We barely got airborne when we ran out of runway. My passenger spot was on the floor behind the co-pilot so I could watch the instrument panel and the pilots' activities, and listen to their conversation. Unable to gain altitude, Bill Cashmore, the pilot, said rather than turn back, we would fly at our altitude of less than 100 feet above the sea until we had used up enough fuel to be able to climb. It took a good hour in the dark. It was not a relaxing start.

"Ironically, we had the opposite trouble at Khartoum. It was probably hotter there that afternoon than I've ever experienced before or since. The rising thermals above the runway were such that we didn't settle to touch down after flaring out from final. More and more runway started appearing behind us. When we finally touched down with our hearts in our mouths, we were barely able to stop as we came to the end of the runway.

"I can't claim any specific record for *Monsoon Maiden*, since no one will ever know how much above the 64,000 we were. But all took pride in the achievement."

Eugene F. Messerly, a 375th gunner on the *Ramp Rooster*, recalls that the base operations at Chabua was, at one time, located in a huge tree. He made many trips there to load bombs and reminisces in mixed tenses:

"Upon leaving Chengkung, we headed north close to Yannanyi, then continued past Fort Hertz. On this day the Hump weather was closing in around 32,000 feet and Navigator Guzik said the outside air temperature was minus 82 degrees Fahrenheit. Oh, well, it would be about 110 degrees in the Assam Valley in about two hours. Good old India is always hot but should get down to a cool 90 degrees when the fuel truck pulls in and the driver and I start loading 3,500 gallons of gas.

"Well, this was a red letter day as we flew higher than Mt. Everest, although we are east of it by 500 miles at Chabua. I sure hope the armament man gets around to our plane before early morning as when he is short on time, he'll dump his bomb load and it will be up to me to slide them in under the bomb bay and hang them on racks, one end at a time. This time they are only 500 pounders and only ten of them.

"In a few minutes it will be time to roll onto the runway, roar out over Chabua Valley towards the Ledo Hospital. I always looked to see if any nurses were watching or waving to us. I never once saw a nurse out on the lawn as was done in those World War I movies. No matter as our pilots were busy making the *Ramp Rooster* fly like a Buck Rogers rocket ship and I was making my eyes act like radar.

"Once we crossed the Himalayas in three and a half hours instead

276

of five – what a tail wind. About now I began to wonder where we would use our new supplies. Would we revisit Hanoi, Haiphong, Vinh, Hainan Island, Hong Kong, Victoria, Kowloon, Formosa, Bataan, or would we go to India to bomb Rangoon, Akyab or the Mallaca Straits?"

Paul Tenello, a gunner with the 375th Squadron, noting the weather was bad, made two entries in his diary about flying the Hump:

"We're running out of gas and bombs. I'd rather go on a mission than fly the Hump in this stuff. It's scary. If you bail out, it's a long way back.

"Radio man sick. He hates the Hump worse than I do, He usually throws up darn near every time we are airborne but won't stay down. The only way home is flying."

Sgt. Emerald B. McNeer, a radio operator on the *Rum Runner*, kept a log of his trips which he felt might help others who followed him. He recorded his feelings about the flights over the world's roughest mountains:

"The Hump is fine – peaks reach 20,000 feet, and there isn't enough level land to spread a handkerchief. (Rumor has it that birds even walk across it.) Besides all this, it's dangerous 'cause I read so in the *C.B.I. Roundup* that it was and anybody knows if it says so in the newspapers, it's bound to be true. But we gotta sustain Hap's point that B-two-fours can be self-sustaining.

"Crew Ten flew the Hump until all about went Hump Happy. In time, a supply of gas and bombs was accumulated. Food and ground personnel were flown over, too. Payloads pushing 60,000 pounds were flown over before it was officially announced by Group that it couldn't be done. After two trips without the proper code for weather, we found that was impossible also.

"Part of the trip is over Jap-held territory but we flew skeleton crews – pilot, co-pilot, navigator, radio operator and engineer; latter two manning top turret and tail turret respectively."

On August 25, 1944, Major James E. Maher, the 308th's Executive Officer issued Operations Memorandum 55-7 under the title "Longer Life in China." In the introduction, he noted:

"It is a well-accepted fact that navigation in this theater is the toughest in the world. Terrain, abnormal winds, eccentric and freakish weather, ice, lack of radio facilities and operational data all contribute to the ever-increasing number of lost aircraft and bailouts.

"Although unavoidable conditions would naturally keep this figure high, still the contribution we make to the Jap war effort by losing aircraft is appalling. Nearly all accidents are caused through negligence and ignorance."

Since weather and navigation were the two worst enemies of flying the Hump and the mountainous areas of China, Maher gave five pages of advice to pilots. It is not known if Maher was a pilot; however, he noted that it was prepared by Capt. Frank W. Russell in collaboration with other flying and staff officers. Capt. Russell compiled 500 hours of combat flying in China. He never had a turn back on a combat mission, but he stated, "I can't say I was never lost." Here are some excerpts:

"When icing conditions are known to exist, never go on instruments if it can be avoided. Pick out light spots or holes to go through. When ice becomes excessive, do not hesitate to make a 180-degree turn. Get in the clear, seek a new altitude and try at a new place.

"It is very awkward to ice up and spin in before making a decision.

"It is just damn negligence and a help to the Japs when a pilot leaves a plane and jumps when he still has four engines running.

"It has been proven time and again that a B-24 can stay in the air over 14 hours with 2750 gallons of gas. There is no excuse for the pilot to jump before the plane actually runs out of fuel. It takes real courage and shows the will to win when a plane is brought back when lost or fuel is low.

"Pride, ego and ability are quickly brought to light in formation flying. Always fly better than the next person and your chances of going home are greatly enhanced."

Leo M. Miller, a pilot with the 375th Squadron, recalls a flight over the Hump to Dum Dum Airport near Calcutta. He had been ordered there to pick up a load of flak suits which were to be used by crew members on combat missions. The heavy suits were loaded into the rear of the aircraft and they were getting ready to leave for China when someone asked Miller if he would take an upright piano to be used in one of the enlisted men's day rooms. Since there were no bombs in the bomb bay on this flight and the plane's weight would not be over limits, he gave the OK provided the piano could be strapped in the bomb bay safely.

The piano was loaded and Miller took off. En route to China, the plane ran into severe icing conditions and when Miller could no longer hold his altitude, he knew he had to dump some weight. He didn't want to dump the flak suits so he ordered the flight engineer to open the bomb bay doors, cut the straps and let the piano go.

"We knew there were Japanese troops down below," he said in a video-taped interview, "we could imagine what they were thinking if a piano came down on them and piano keys were scattered all over. I was never asked about it when I got to Chengkung because it wasn't for our squadron and I don't think anyone knew the piano was coming over."

Miller tells a tragic story which was related to the Hump trips. B-24s were sent to Chabua for routine engine changes and the crews had to wait until the work was done before flying back to China. The wait was boring for the flight crews and much time was spent in playing cards, gambling, and otherwise passing the time until the planes were ready. After an engine change, a short test flight was required before departing for China. It was a chance for the ground maintenance personnel to ride in a B-24 so a few were usually invited as a reward for their efforts.

A pilot, whose name shall not be used, asked Miller if he wanted to go along for a test hop. The ground crew had set a record for speed in changing an engine and several wanted to go along. Miller agreed to fly as co-pilot. Five ground crewmen and the flight engineer got aboard, one in the nose and four in the rear where they had a view out the side windows.

The pilot took off and after testing the new engine, he decided to fly over the Bramahputra River at a low altitude "to give these guys a thrill." He lowered the plane to nearly wavetop level and aimed at the many small fishing boats making their way along the wide river. He would climb up and over the boats and down again and head for another boat. After doing this about twenty times and there were no more boats in view, the pilot went down even lower.

"I couldn't believe we were that low," Miller recalled:

"So I called to him and I said, 'You're getting awfully low!' At that moment, the plane began to shudder and shake and I knew we were dragging on the water. The instrument panel began to shake and we couldn't read the instruments. The two of us grabbed the wheel and began to yank the nose up. All I could think of was that a wingtip might grab the water and we would go cartwheel and tear everything all to pieces. We barely got it off the water and were doing only about 150 when we had been going about 220 when we hit. The instruments seemed to be normal so I looked back toward the rear of the plane. The whole bottom of the plane was gone and I could see straight through to the rear turret. The catwalk, bomb racks and bomb bays were gone. And the four men were gone.

"Meanwhile, the engineer who had been standing behind us was holding on for dear life and everything was shaking. The whole flight deck was torn loose. The man in the nose was screaming 'Get me out of here!' but refused to come out of the nose. The pilot wanted to have everyone bail out but when the man in the nose refused, he decided to land the plane on the pierced steel-planked runway.

"The pilot made a normal landing pattern but we had lost our hydraulic pressure and had no flaps or brakes and we were leaking fuel. The gear came down all right but it meant we would have a hard time stopping. Our radio was out and we couldn't tell the tower what our problem was. Fortunately, there was no other traffic. My concern was that when we hit that metal runway, the sparks would ignite the fuel and we would be blown up.

"[The pilot] made a normal approach and a smooth landing. As the plane slowed down it drifted off to the right where I could see some construction work going on. We headed toward a very high pile of gravel, hit it, came down the other side and hit another pile. We went over that and went toward two gullies. When we hit that, the nose wheel broke off and the plane broke in half.

"The man in the nose was still there and still screaming. I thought he must be dying. The pilot, flight engineer and I got out as fast as we could and as I left the cockpit I was drenched with gasoline. The pilot got a fire ax and tried to chop the man out of the nose but he couldn't do it. A rescue crew finally got him out and, amazingly, he wasn't hurt too badly."

The result of such a senseless act by the pilot was the loss of four men, injury to another, and the loss of an airplane. After the ensuing investigation, the pilot was arrested and later dismissed from the Army which meant he had lost his rights to any credit for his service.

But Miller's experience on that trip to Chabua was not over. When he returned to China, he was assigned to fly co-pilot with Capt. John Z. McBrayer. The plane was loaded with 1,000-pound bombs. When they rolled down the runway, the tire on the right landing gear blew out. They were past the middle of the runway and rather than abort the takeoff and attempt to stop before reaching the end, McBrayer continued the takeoff and they proceeded to Chengkung for a landing on the gravel runway there.

"We could see the tire was all torn to shreds," Miller said. "We agreed that when we touched down, I would handle the throttles for the engines on the right side to counteract the drag when the right wheel hit the ground. We got it down and, surprisingly, very little damage was done. The plane was repaired overnight and was ready to go the following day."

Many flights over the Hump carried a few passengers provided the planes were not over the weight limit. Capt. Jones C. Laughlin, a medical officer, may have wished he didn't hitch a ride on a B-24 tanker on November 12, 1944. About three hours from Chabua for Suichwan and climbing above a solid overcast, the No. 1 engine developed a runaway propeller. Efforts to feather the prop were unsuccessful. Shortly afterward, Zeroes were sighted below crossing underneath at 90 degrees.

Laughlin was riding in the tail looking out the tail window where the guns emplacements had been removed. Fifteen minutes after the runaway prop, Laughlin thought something happened to the No. 2 engine. The left wing went down, the nose dipped, and he felt like the plane was about to go into a spin. As he was the only passenger on the plane within easy reach of an exit, he thought the others would have great difficulty getting out. He jumped out of the tail window and his parachute opened immediately. Meanwhile, the pilot got the plane under control before it went into the overcast and landed it safely at Suichwan.

Laughlin landed safely in a tree on the bank of a stream near Liling which was occupied by about 3,000 Japanese troops. The Chinese in the area were extremely hostile to the Japanese occupation forces which caused the Japanese to surround the city with a barricade of barbed wire. They only emerged for foraging expeditions. The Chinese guerrillas frequently engaged them in running fights in which the Japanese were said to come out second best.

Laughlin's luck held. He was picked up by Chinese farmers on landing and turned over to the guerrillas who had been looking for him. The report of Laughlin's experience was noted in an intelligence report:

> "The significance of this is that American airmen who are forced to land in this area will be assured of safe conduct to the guerrilla head-quarters, and stand an excellent chance of evading the Japanese unless they land directly in the town, or in the midst of the Japanese patrols. It was learned on one occasion, General Yuang Sha How, the guerrilla chief and also commanding officer of the Chinese Second Army, sent a detachment of men into Jap-held territory to bring out an American pilot who had been hidden and cared for in the Changsha area for a period of three months. Several of the Chinese and Japanese were killed in the fight that followed and the pilot was rescued."

The general organized a party which consisted of a Lt. Mo who was his adjutant, four Chinese soldiers, two Japanese prisoners and four coolies. Although uninjured, the prisoners and coolies were to carry Laughlin in a sedan chair which Laughlin later said he used only 25% of the time. For the next fourteen days, he was led from village to village with overnight stays in small hotels or Chinese houses, and in one night, a school. When the hills were too steep for the chair, the party hiked. At one time, a horse was provided for him and a donkey for Lt. Mo. The final leg was made by a charcoal burning boat that took him to Suichwan. There are no records that quote exactly what Laughlin told the intelligence interrogator when he returned or what the crew of the B-24 said when he finally arrived at their base.

Chapter 11

MEMORIES
OF CHINA

E
ach survivor of the tour in China returned home with his own memories of what life was like on the ground and in the air. Following are excerpts from many who answered Howard Morgan's questionnaire, responded to the author's letters, or had their stories printed in the *Jing Bao Journal*.

Robert E. Cook, engineer and top turret gunner, 374th Squadron remembers:

> "An item of pride for the 308th was having the top gunner in all the air forces during World War II. He was T/Sgt Arthur J. Benko of Bisbee, Arizona. A full-blooded Indian, he was Arizona skeet and rifle champion in 1939-40. He was a top turret gunner on the *Goon*.
>
> "Art belted his own ammunition, removing all tracers. He did this for two reasons: (1) He didn't want the enemy to know he was being shot at; (2) tracer fire gave a false trajectory by losing weight as it burns in flight.
>
> "There was some skepticism at group headquarters as Benko's score mounted so they sent an intelligence officer on one mission. Art sent seven Japs down that day and made a believer out of the officer.
>
> "Art's record stood at 16 confirmed victories. Then homeward bound from a Hong Kong mission with one engine out and one faltering, the pilot, Sam Skousen, hit the bail-out button so that maybe the plane could clear a mountain range. Benko and Lt. Sanders landed on the Jap side of the river and were captured. Later, a Catholic missionary sent the Air Force photographs of their crucifixion."

Jack Averitt, radio operator and aerial gunner, 425th Squadron, tells of some of the things about China that stick in his memory:

"Complaints from navigators about inaccurate charts.

"Rats coming up through the floor of our hostel in Kunming, sometimes interrupting poker games.

"The eerie feeling of pulling guard duty inside a B-24 revetment at Kunming – and hoping those weren't the nights that the Japs decided to bomb the field.

"Learning the hard way to use the relief tubes during flights instead of opening the bomb bay doors. (The wind blew the urine back in the plane).

"The Chinese house boys who were agents for the black market (and maybe the Japs as well).

"Going hunting for geese with a Colt .45 near Kwanghan – and missing every bird I shot at...and being chewed out in Chinese for trespassing in their air space.

"Wings of our B-24 bobbing up and down over the Hump, flapping like a bird.

"The acrid odor of flak that floated through our open waist windows on my second mission.

"I also remember being told what to do in the event our IFF malfunctioned – Get on the voice mike and broadcast these words: 'My cockerel isn't crowing.'

"I thought it was about the silliest thing I ever heard of until I was told about the B-24 that inadvertently was shot down by one of our Black Widows (P-61s) because its 'cockerel' wasn't crowing."

"Not shooting at a Zero that zoomed underneath our formation because a P-40 was in pursuit and I was afraid I might hit the P-40."

One of the lasting impressions of most of the 308th's personnel stationed in China was the pungent smell of yucch, a name not found in any English dictionary. One day when David L."Tex" Hill and Johnny Alison of the 23rd Fighter Group were driving along, Alison tried to rid his nose of the sickly odor.

"You know what it is, don't you?" Tex asked.

"Yeah," Johnny replied. "But what do they put in it to make it smell so bad?"

Capt. Jim Kinder, a flight surgeon assigned to the 1st Bomb group, later stationed at Kweilin, thought the nose-boggling essence was a chemical problem which he could solve and forever rid all of China of the yucch smell, especially the sixteen-hole latrines which everyone had to use daily or more often as needed. The standard treatment was to throw lime into the latrines but it didn't work. He thought he had a better idea. He wrote his aunt at home in Gerardeau, Missouri, and asked her to send him four packages of foil-wrapped Fleischmann's yeast every week. He mixed the yeast in warm water, added some Chinese sugar, including bugs and twigs, put the mixture into eight bottles and let it ferment near the stove in the dispensary.

After several days, the bubbling of the fermentation process slowed down and "Doc" Kinder poured the concoction into each latrine hole. He did this for a week. Kinder recalled:

"It took time to work. In fact, it was several weeks before there was a decided change. Then men would approach the latrine, sniff and sniff again. A big grin would result when they realized that the yucch had become unstunk. Some of the Tigers actually maintained that the latrines now had the aroma of Aramis After-Shave Lotion."

Perhaps Kinder thought his achievement was worth a medal. The October-November 1990 *Jing Bao Journal* reported: "Doc waited for official recognition for his scientific achievement. He cleaned and pressed his Class A uniform which he expected to wear while General Chennault pinned on colonel's eagles on his shoulders and the Distinguished Service Medal on his breast. It never happened. He then languished year after year awaiting word from the Nobel Committee. Nothing."

However, he rated a story in the *Journal* and he has now earned mention in the history of the 308th.

Sgt. Melvin E. Johnson, an intelligence specialist in the 373rd Squadron, tells what he remembered about his stint in China:

"The commander of the base guard battalion at Yangkai was a Colonel Stewart. He was an Australian, and the story was that he had been a truck driver on the Burma Road. Somehow, he had accumulated sufficient money to buy a commission in the Chinese Nationalist Army. I remember him, a tall and imposing presence, and in full Chinese regalia, coming from the S-2 situation room to show us some of the latest advances of the Japanese ground forces. His method of obtaining supplies for his troops was unique. He simply drove a half-track with a contingent of troops to the nearest Chinese supply depot and threatened to blow it up if they didn't give him what he needed.

"I believe the brunt of the ground troop hardship was borne by the aircraft mechanics and armorers. Maintaining engines and loading 500 and 1,000 lb. bombs in all kinds of weather was hardly child's play.

"When I got home in the fall of 1945, I was perusing my discharge certificate and discovered that I had been awarded the Bronze Star Medal by the Fourteenth Air Force. I thought about this for a while and couldn't come up with any compelling reason for it. I finally decided it was simply for endurance."

Lt. John M. White, the pilot of *Chug-A-Lug* in the 425th Squadron:

"Early in March of '43 we flew into Kunming to begin ops. After several trips over the Hump we had enough supplies for our first mission, which was to bomb Canton. We had already lost a ship at Salina (Kansas), another at Georgetown (British Guiana), and a third on our initial flight over the Hump.

"I was on the second mission over Hankow – and we were badly shot up. We lost Louis Kne, who was filling in as tail gunner.

"I also laid the mines off the Hoogley River, south of Rangoon. These mine-laying missions were sort of enjoyable, going in at 200-400 feet in complete darkness.

"I was also on the missions over Rangoon when we lost so heavily. We had just picked up a new ship, *Chug-A-Lug, Jr.* in Agra, having bailed out over eastern China and walking back to Kunming.

"We met our new C.O. in Calcutta and he told us not to go back to China but to meet at Pandaveswar for a combined mission. Some of the group was at Panagar, a small town just east of Pandaveswar.

"Two ships which crashed that first morning had watered gas and had been sabotaged. We took off over the burning wreckage at the end of the runway, bombs going off, a scary maneuver.

"During the months of July and August 1943, when the ATC received the Presidential Unit Citation for flying supplies over the Hump, our B-24s carried more tonnage over the Hump than the ATC."

George Plantz, an engineer-gunner on *Shootin' Star* of the 374th Squadron, recalls what it was like to get ready for a mission:

"A day on the job, mission is on. A little bubble of excitement prances around in your stomach. A familiar little friend, your companion all day. The bubble would vanish during takeoff to be replaced by boredom, anxiety, fright and sometimes stark terror.

"Waiting until the aircraft had been loaded with bombs, the crews briefed and bundled in fleece and leather, and transported through the rain and mud to the revetment and now, 'Let's get it over with.' Sometimes the mission was scrubbed and some men said it was the same feeling you got when you made love badly and you wished you hadn't made love at all.

"The engines have been run up and as the vibrations are drumming through the members and stringers the *Shootin' Star* waddles out on slender oleo legs, belly heavy with high explosive and incendiary bombs. Airplanes are fascinating things – metal-clad monsters with beautiful parts, propellers, wings, canopies and functional [gun] turrets. The audacity of the whole business never seemed to diminish the fascination, the little man-made worlds rattling bravely into the air, kept aloft by a precarious balancing of forces, a waggling of surfaces to direct a stream of air, blind faith in flimsy structures.

"The crew crammed in a Jeep, bulky in flying gear, jammed on all sides with parachutes and flight bags, makes its way to the flight line.

"The *Shootin' Star* awaits her crew, her one hundred and ten feet of wing spanning the hard-packed earth in the embanked revetment. She was painted the dreary camouflage green and brown and her nose bristled with the teeth of a tiger, or was it a shark. Her lines were clean and her size neatly proportioned, a regal lady. She dwarfed the men who had come to take her out. She seemed vast and immovable and as you stood beside her you wondered how anything this huge could actually get off the ground. The walk-around was a never-ending ritual, gazing intently at the wings, rudders, ailerons, elevators and tires. The rule was, take a good, hard, long look at the airplane before you get in it, making sure everything is stuck on where it's supposed to be stuck on. The *Star* was showing signs of wear and tear. The leading edges were almost completely stripped of paint, the soft metal edges of her cowling were dented and bent; oil had dyed her upper wing surfaces in streaks to the trailing edges. Middle age was creeping up on the *Shootin' Star* but she seemed to us to carry her age with dignity. She was the oldest lady in the squadron.

"The B-24 provided minimum space for those who rode in her; she had no wasted inches but cramped or not, depending somewhat on the physical size of the crew, she was functional. Five of the crew members were within touching distance, in an emergency such proximity might make all the difference.

"'Pilot to crew. Testing intercom. Navigator?'

"'Navigator O.K.'

"'Bombardier?'

"'Intercom O.K., Skipper.' And so on through all the turrets and gun positions. Everyone's intercom was working. The ground crew moved back and away from the swirling dust and debris. They had done their stuff and now it was in the hands of the air crew.

"The throttles engaged full power. The *Star* shivered, not able to at this point to convert all the power to motion. She rolled slowly at first, gathering speed, propellers slicing the air, hurling it around and thrusting it back, dragging the thousands of clumsy pounds along, forcing the air to swarm over her wings and tail. Then with speed came strength as she lumbered down the runway. The airspeed indicator registering 80, 85, 90. Now she wants to go, a workhorse chomping at the bit. A firm pull back on the wheel, runway dropping away. Wheels up and locked, flaps up.

"The crew relaxes. Once again the *Shootin'Star* had successfully dragged herself off the ground without a hitch. Takeoffs were the nastiest part of flying. Now airborne, in the pilots' seats, Ken and Mac sweat from the sheer physical labor of hurling the big bomber around the sky. The target was in Herb's sight, the gunners poised for probable attack, it was bombs away and LeRoy gave a heading for home.

"'Pilot to crew. Letting down now.' Throttles back a few notches, column gently forward, nose inching down, the *Star* begins her return to earth. Then wheels down and locked. Tower: 'Cleared to land.'

"'Pilot to crew. Stand by for landing.' Flaps 20, speed 140, the mud-

NOSE ART GALLERY

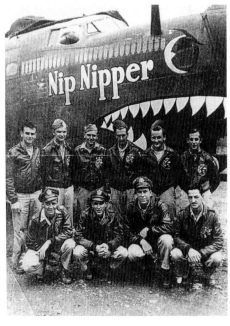

and straw-thatched village at the runway's end seemed to rush up. Fifty feet, full flaps. At the beginning of the runway, she was no more than 25 feet in the air and ready for a long braking roll to a halt. Then, nothing moving, controls motionless, the old girl was at rest, another landing. The crew had to have confidence in its skipper; it was vital. Thanks are not enough.

"The crew relaxed. Once again another mission was accounted for, a measurement which would culminate into an end of tour and going home.

"A real fine bunch, this crew, the very best. Soon they would all be going their separate ways returning to the everyday working world. It took time for ten airmen to become a crew. Too many didn't get time enough. They would probably never see one another again. They would talk about reunions and hopefully make a few as the years pass so quickly.

"The bodies age, changes occur, values are adjusted, but in all of this change the memory with all of the drama of one of our lives' greatest experiences will forever hold a niche in the hearts of those who came and saw and remembered."

Letters to his family by Lt. Lyndell T. Highley, a navigator assigned to the 375th Squadron, revealed some interesting sidelights:

"October 17, 1943 - There's a funny incident that happened near here which shows the relationship between the Chinese and American soldiers. When we first got here, there was a small boy dressed in the usual Chinese rags, tending a flock of goats nearby. He was dirty, foul-smelling and his hair was down to his ankles. Some of the fellows decided to adopt him. His folks were dead and the best information we could get was that they were killed coming out of Burma.

"The fellows dressed him up, gave him a bath, a pair of shoes, some clothing, a haircut, fed him and made him a Private-First Class. He was a bright kid about six years old and followed these boys around. Every word they would speak, he would try to imitate them. The first words he picked up were 'piss poor' so that became his name. Gradually, he picked up the American vocabulary and he could really tell someone off with his cuss words.

"The climax happened the other day. He wandered off into town and was picked up by a Chinese Red Cross girl. She took him to the Red Cross headquarters where there were some American girls, some American officers and some enlisted men. They tried to find out where he belonged. He stood it for a while but finally got mad. He expressed a few American words to the Chinese girl that made the American girls turn and run. The Chinese girl could also talk American and maybe you think she wasn't embarrassed. Finally, he got back here where he can say what he pleases."

In a letter, dated August 20, 1943, Highley wrote:

"Now that we've been over here for over six months we are getting pretty well acquainted. There's a college located close by and there are some nice Chinese girls there. Some of the fellows have met some very nice Chinese girls. They are funny as hell. You ask them a question and all they can say is 'Yes' but there's many a time a fellow has got his face slapped as they really didn't mean yes. I guess we are also hard to figure out."

Highley wrote another letter on September 7, 1943 and commented further about meeting Chinese girls:

"We are planning a big party here about the 14th of the month to celebrate the formation of our squadron. We will be one year old. The Special Services officer, through the help of the Red Cross, is trying to round up enough Chinese girls to have a dance. That isn't too hard to do but most of them can't speak English and I'm not very good at Chinese or sign language. I do know a couple of the most essential words but they wouldn't carry on a very sociable conversation. A hotel in town will let us use their ballroom for the dance. The hotel is located about 30 miles away and transportation is good over here.

"In town they have a club for the enlisted men of our organization. It is a very unique affair. The government (Chinese) hires a bunch of girls to go to the club. For $100 Chinese ($2.00 U.S.) you can get a girl for an hour. That is, to dance with, to drink with, etc. The girls can't leave the dance hall but according to all reports it gets pretty rugged on the dance floor. It's strictly a clean affair supervised by the American authorities. I think it's pretty nice and am jealous as hell because the officers aren't treated as well. The officers are supposed to mingle with the higher Chinese girls and let me tell you that there are some nice looking girls and they speak perfect English. How would you like to have a Chinese daughter-in-law?"

Ming Chen Hsu, now one of the five commissioners of the Federal Maritime Commission, then eighteen years old, was living in Kunming, when she was invited by the Red Cross to attend a dance at a hangar on the base. The Fourteenth Air Force had just been formally established and the affair was to mark its beginning. Educated in an American school in Shanghai before the Japanese invaded the area, she had fled with her family to Kunming because her father was a high official in Chiang's government working with the lend-lease program. He was captured and imprisoned by the Japanese in the Philippines when the war began. Her knowledge of English was helpful to the Red Cross women in setting up dances and parties on the base for the enlisted men:

"They often came to me for advice about whom they should invite, what kind of food they should serve and where the events should be held. The officers had to organize their own dances without the help of the Red Cross. I was invited to both.

"I recall a dance planned by the officers of the 375th at the American consulate in the fall of 1943. I was contacted by three officers in Kunming who asked me to help in organizing a big dance. They said they wanted to invite Chinese girls but didn't know how to go about it.

"The wife of the president of the university had organized an informal group of Chinese girls attending the university who spoke English. They were anxious to practice English but had to get their parents' permission to attend dances. The parents did not discourage this because the dances were heavily chaperoned and there was no reason for parents to be concerned.

"When I say 'heavily chaperoned,' I mean that we had to go to these dances together. We would be picked up by a truck that stopped at each of our houses. We would be brought to every dance and we could not leave on our own with a date. We had to leave together and were returned directly to our homes.

"Sometimes this posed a problem. There were several dances when we weren't having a good time and wanted to leave but we had to stay there until every dance was over. There was no way that we could leave separately. Even if we wanted to have a date with someone, there was no transportation available.

"It was at the dance of the 375th that I first met Colonel Beebe. He was very handsome and the fellows in the squadron really respected him.

"I met General Chennault on several occasions at the headquarters in Kunming. He was a magnificent figure. When you saw him, you couldn't help but be in awe of him. My impression of him was that he was going to win the war for us. He projected confidence and made you feel wonderful. After having fled from the Japanese for several years, I was sure that General Chennault was going to take care of everything. High Chinese officials to the man-in-the-street, and the men of the 308th thought the world of him. It was unusual that anyone could be held with such respect and affection. They trusted him and would do anything for him. They all thought it was an honor to serve under General Chennault.

"I met Generalissimo and Madame Chiang Kai-shek when I was a young teenager. He was also a commanding person who did a lot to unite China during those war years."

Paul Tenello of the 375th wrote in his diary during a raid on his base at Kunming by the Japanese on May 15, 1943:

"The report and news from Tokyo Rose [shows] they do know the 308th has joined the Flying Tigers. She named the four squadrons and mentioned Colonel Beebe by name. Wow!

"The three ball alert is up and just about everyone who can get away is scattered on the hillsides. I've got my rifle and canteen. The enemy plane formations can be heard long before you can see them. They are flying a tight formation. Looks as though a good 40 or 50 planes are up there. You can see the glint of sunlight on the fighters as they move back and forth. Those are Zeros unpainted. Our P-40s are painted Army drab.

"Saw two planes crash, don't know which. Our 24s have flown north away from the base with makeshift crews. Our 40s have been up some time before the enemy showed.

"A flight flying west to east has dropped bombs. I think the air base and Kunming have been hit. You can see large puffs raise from the ground as the bombs explode. Wish I had the field glasses we keep in the plane. Looks as though the bombs made a beeline from the end of the field right into the city. Sure hope not. There's just one pall of black smoke I see. Could be a plane on the line.

"Our field wasn't even touched. When the pole came down, we moved towards camp. Our bombers have all returned and landed. Wonder how much gas we burned this time. The fighters usually re-load, gas up and follow the enemy back as far as possible. Good."

Allan A. Crockett, C.O. of the 373rd Squadron, recalls soon after his arrival in China, he was assigned a North American BT-14 basic trainer which had a 650 h.p. engine installed in place of the usual 450 h.p. version.

"I believe these were loaned to us by the Chinese to provide the CO of the 373rd a means of getting to group headquarters without having to make the awful one-day each way road trip or using valuable gas in a B-24. The 373rd was at Yangkai, only about 60 air miles from Kunming. I tried driving once. It nearly killed me. Never again. I would put my squadron bombardier and navigator in the back seat of the BT-14, one on a seat pack chute, the other with a chest pack, and fly over the 7200-foot pass to group briefings.

"The 373rd later moved to Luliang, even farther from Kunming, and for some reason my BT-14 was returned to the Chinese and replaced with a Stearman [bi-winged trainer], soon named *Crockett's Rocket* and appropriately painted. I loved the airplane, having flown it in primary, but it was too slow, and couldn't handle two in the back seat. Later I was given a P-40."

Elmer E. "Bud" Haynes, a pilot with the 375th Squadron, remembers:

"I was one of the crews in the LAB B-24 project that left Langley Field in the spring and summer of 1944 and arrived in China with Bill Hopson who became C.O. of the 308th. I personally flew almost all of my missions either hitting Japanese shipping in the South China Sea or flying recons during the winter of 1944-45 to spot convoys and naval vessels for the Navy as well as our own strikers. In fact, I flew around Hainan Island so many times, I picked up the nickname of 'Hainan Harry Haynes.'

"Once we scared the living hell out of a bunch of ATC boys when we crashed and slid up the runway towards the ATC Coffee Shop the morning of October 27, 1944. Another incident in Chengkung was the evening a lone Jap fighter came in and dropped some bombs down the runway. My navigator, McClure, and I had just crossed that runway in a jeep headed for the hostel area of the 3rd Mapping Squadron boys. Never a dull moment!

"As I was in the radar-equipped B-24s, I didn't fly many daylight missions over land targets, but the ones in which we were involved, I sure appreciated the cover the fighter boys gave us."

Edward Menaker, also a LAB crewmember, summarizes their problems:

"The list of obstacles we faced was formidable: single-plane missions at maximum range from base; minimal aids to navigation, and scant information on weather; complete dependence on newly-developed and still unreliable electronic equipment; minimal logistical support, particularly for the electronic equipment; operation from bases which were under attack by land and air; and an initially skeptical command and general staff structures."

Scrounging was a way of life for the 308th in China. Always short of supplies, parts and tools, the 308th demonstrated the Americans' inherent ability to improvise thousands of times during the days when everything had to be ferried over the Hump in the group's own B-24s. Tony Santoro of the 375th Squadron was one of those who proved that necessity was truly the mother of invention. He made a scooter for his many forays up and down the flight line. It had rubber wheels from a portable generator, an engine from a refueling pump, one wheel brake and a built-in governor. He also built a washing machine from meshing gears of undetermined origin, a heavy-duty 3/8" drill, some rods, sheet metal, angle irons, and a barrel.

Karl "Moose" Hartung, 375th Squadron, also had a claim to fame as a scrounger:

"I was squadron bootlegger in January, 1944. Bottles were hard to come by. I had two musette bags. I took the straps off of both of them and fastened the hooks together. Then I folded a piece of cardboard over the hooks and wrapped them with masking tape. With the bags full of bottles I hung the bags on my shoulders and headed for the village by the lake.

"I walked the taxi strips around the north end of A.T.C. hill, then walked the rice paddy dikes the rest of the way. I would get the bottles filled with jing bao juice and head back. It was about a mile each way.

"What I was doing was no secret. It was all out in the open. I remember one day walking down the taxi strip with my bottles when Lt. Wurtsberger pulled alongside in his bomb truck and said, 'Where you headed, Moose?'

"I'm going to Oo-Lam-Poo to get a load of booze," I replied.

"He said, 'Hop in. I'll give you a ride part of the way.'

"No, the lieutenant was not one of my customers."

Donald H. Engert, a mechanic in the 374th remembers:

"In between raids we drank a lot of Jing Bao juice. It was made up of one quart of Red Star gin, one large can of grapefruit juice, lemon powder from our C rations, Chinese brown sugar (which had small sticks or straw left out), mixed in a one gallon thermos jug from a crashed B-24."

Orval Mattice, an aircraft and auto mechanic with the 374th, made notes of some of the memorable events during his tour in China and reminisced on tape for this history. "You may remember me," he said, "if you flew out of Kweilin or Luichow. I was the one with mustache and goatee who met all the 308th planes and gave the crews a Jeep ride to headquarters, then supervised servicing of the planes."

Mattice was particularly proud of a ring crafted for him by the grateful people of Liuchow. Some excerpts from his notes and tapes:

"Got orders to appropriate (steal) anything that we could use in China and small enough to get into our planes...Stole tools and motorcycles for the guys...Also received orders to get a whole polo ground full of equipment loaded and over to China...Dr. removing 20mm shell from a tail gunner's shoulder that hadn't quite penetrated below skin level...The first time I fired the twin 50s in combat I nearly shot down one of our own planes...How the Chinese guerrillas were able to bring back an American who had landed on White Cloud Air Base at Canton after bailing out...A rumored secret flight by the *Escalator* over Japan to get aerial photos...Plane that buzzed river too low and had the belly ripped off...Thirteen beautiful Eurasian ladies shot by firing squad...When evacuating Liuchow, radar had priority over GIs...The Chinese custom of shooting off firecrackers to drive away evil spirits, celebrate a wedding, or dedicate a new house...Having to be ready to stop a truck or Jeep abruptly because of the Chinese natives' belief that it would kill off evil spirits that might be following close behind them...finding a mummified corpse in a revetment...loading special meteorological equipment aboard B-24s that would be parachuted into remote areas and report weather information..."

Mattice recalls an incident when a Chinese boy, while playing with a GI's .45 automatic, accidentally shot himself through the hand. He was taken to a doctor at the Kweilin base infirmary but the doctor said he couldn't give him an anesthetic. Mattice used a CO_2 fire extinguisher to freeze the hand so the doctor could operate.

Len Gelhaus, co-pilot of *Monsoon Maiden,* of the 425th Squadron, told a story which is related by Bob Cowan:

"On November 14, 1944, the *Maiden* took off from Kunming to Suichwan to transport gasoline, RDX bombs and .50 caliber ammo to this beleaguered advance base. The five-man crew consisted of Bob Revard, pilot; Len Gelhaus, co-pilot; T. Lopez, navigator; John Turner, engineer; and Ray Daniels, radio operator.

"ETA at Suichwan was about 2100 hours. But when they arrived, the base was under attack by Japanese bombers and they were redirected to Kanchow, a nearby fighter strip of the 14th.

"When they dragged Kanchow, they found the strip was very short for a bomber with a full load of bombs, etc. They were able to land the *Maiden* but had to pop the parachutes of Turner and Daniels out the waist windows, anchored to the machine gun mounts, to get more braking power on the short strip. A hairy caper!

"The P-51 squadron there had been out of gas, bombs and ammunition for over a week. The next day they flew 15 sorties with the load the *Maiden* and crew brought.

"On the trip back, they got lost. Although Revard and Gelhaus had a good idea where they were, the navigator, thinking they were near home, suggested they drop down and take a look but they immediately started to pick up flak. They had flown over the ex-14th's base at Hengyang, now held by the Japs. Needless to say, they got the hell out of there before the Japs sent up some Zeros.

"Sometime later, Daniels reported he was having difficulty with the radio and could not raise Kunming. Turner went back to the command deck to check out the radio equipment and found that the *Maiden* had been hit by flak at Hengyang which had wiped out the radio and gas lines. By this time, it was night, very dark, and they were at 17,000 feet altitude.

"A short time later, they could smell the gas and were concerned that a spark of any kind could blow them up. The bomb bay doors were opened for ventilation. Later, by the amount of air traffic, they figured they were near Kunming but there was a heavy undercast. A decision had to be made. Without a radio, any kind of an instrument letdown was impossible.

"They did not know that Luliang and Yunnanyi were clear and open, and with the gas leak, did not know how much gas was left. They turned on the gas crossfeed and the decision was made to bail out. Daniels was the first to jump, Turner next, but Lopez was hesitant, so Gelhaus went out, with Lopez following him. Revard put the *Maiden* on automatic pilot and followed them out. As he was about to jump, one of the engines stopped, apparently out of gas. The *Maiden* went into a spiral and the centrifugal force kept him on the catwalk. He finally shoved himself out, ending up at the outer edge of the spiral. But the *Maiden* kept coming at him, one time even spilling his 'chute. He saw the *Maiden* finally hit the ground.

"Turner and Daniels, having used their parachutes at Kanchow for braking power, almost decided not to take new ones when they left there. Revard insisted they do so, which was the saving of their lives later. All five made it back to Kunming after a few days of roaming around in China."

The July 1944 issue of the *CBI Roundup*, published in New Delhi, India, tells about a piano player who helped keep morale up for members of the Fourteenth Air Force:

"Lt. Addison "Addie" Bailey has been pounding the ivories for well over a year in this theater of CBI-land with two rather curious results: First, he is probably the best known American soldier in China; and second, despite the number and diversity of his following, Addie Bailey's triumphs in China have received far more publicity in the United States than in this neck of the woods.

"The explanation for this second happenstance is anchored on Addie's 12 years as Pianoissimo at Leon and Eddie's on 52nd Street [in New York City] as Eddie Davis's accompanist.

"When Eddie arrived in China on March 1943, he was tagged to play the piano on the 10th of that month at the gathering celebrating the activation of the Fourteenth Air Force. The Japs, never sufficiently appreciative of Cole Porter, rudely selected that particular evening for a raid and managed to contrive a 15-minute blackout at the party. Addie calmly filled this interval with a little Porter, musical tidbits from Rodgers and Hart and some straight Bailey.

"He was congratulated on his calmness for a neophyte when the lights went on, but quipped, 'Well, it would take more noise than a bombing to unnerve any guy who's worked in a New York night club.'"

Addison Bailey, in his own diary entry for March 25, 1944, wrote a sample verse for "Leap Year Blues," a song he wrote for men named Cobb and Kleber, to celebrate the lack of a social life for Americans in China. It was sung at a concert in the hangar at Kunming on April 4, 1944:

"We do the next best thing. It's not what you think.
"We just stay at home and have taken to drink.
"We're shy with the girls and we're scared of air raids.
"We're G.I. editions of two damned old maids."

Major (later Brigadier General) Harvard W. Powell, C.O. of the 374th in 1944-45, recalls a contribution he made to a better life at Chengkung. It involved the fact that, at 6,500 feet above sea level, the six-hole latrine located about forty yards from the officers' barracks, was always cold. It made it difficult to tend to one's daily call of nature.

"I decided that there had to be a way to warm the seat so I took a towel, cut a hole in the middle, and held it near a small heater until it was very warm. I then put the towel under my arm inside my shirt, rushed to the latrine and placed it on the seat. Never had any problems after that.

"By the time I left China, almost everyone in the 374th was using the same technique to answer nature's call. I learned later that the enlisted men, after hearing of my solution to this problem, called me "Hot-Ass Harv.""

Jack Clifford, navigator, one of the few crew members on *The Frendlin* (The Friendly Gremlin) who bailed out twice during their China tours, as reported in the July 29, 1944 *Chicago Daily News*:

"We had just strafed a convoy from a height of only 200 feet in the South China Sea when we got the fireworks. A big hole was torn in the side of our *Frendlin* and there were holes in our wings. We barely made the coast when two of our engines gave out.

"One of our crew was badly shot up and we all jumped. I got out at 6,000 feet and fell on top of a mountain. It was dark and the only thing to do was sleep out in the open. The rain woke me and I got up. I took off my clothes, wrung them out as much as I could and put them on again. Then I covered myself in my parachute.

"Our crew was scattered over 10 miles but we were together in a few days. The three weeks we were reported lost we really were on our way to our base 300 air miles away but twice that far over primitive trails. All the people we met were very kind to us. They fed us, gave us what clothes they could and finally got us back to our base.

"I'll never forget the dinner the Chinese gave us in one village. It was in 14 courses and between each one Chinese girls would come over and wipe our faces with perfumed towels. The Chinese are so happy to see American soldiers that they shoot off firecrackers wholesale whenever a group of men comes through a village. Whole strings of them are thrown right into the trucks we ride."

From a history of the 308th after the move to Chengtu in 1945:

"The men continued to get along splendidly with the local Chinese, taking cognizance of their many quaint customs. One of these, the little game of taking the pig to market, is truly indicative of the low value placed on human effort. The porker averages from 250 to 300 pounds. It is not desired that he lose any of this avoirdupois en route to the slaughterhouse. An undersized human beast of burden is hired for a pittance and he trundles the squealing pig in a wheelbarrow many miles over the dust-choked, rutty highways. Two methods are employed to keep the huge pig docile as he proceeds to market on his back, lashed to the wheelbarrow. Either his eyes are gouged out previously or his eyelids are sewed shut."

James Gibson, co-pilot on *Homesick Susie*, composed a tribute to his plane after he and his crew had to bail out of it on November 15, 1943:

The States were falling behind us
The darkness lay heavy as lead
The sea rolled below us in her age-old fuss
And we wondered what lay ahead

"Homesick Susie" purred into the night
Then there's a break in the engines' roar
A weakness in Susie's might
But onward and onward we soar

Over mountain and valley and ocean
Susie never letting us down
Her flight a comforting motion
Taking us half the world around

Over desert and veldt and prairie
Our confidence mounting fast
Aloft, past the eagle's aerie
Our destination at last

Susie carried us into battle
To bomb the Nipponese foe
Amid all the action
She suffered a mortal blow

She faltered but her heart wouldn't fail
Tho' crippled, she homeward flew
Limping over mountains and vale
She collapsed with the field in view

Susie's flying days are now over
But her mem'ry will ever remain
In the hearts of the men who flew her
And wish they could fly her again

Don McCormick, 373rd Bomb Squadron:

"The 308th had a permanent detachment in Chabua, generally 100 to 125 of us from the four squadrons. Our main function was to keep the 308th supplied in China with the weapons of war.

"Among us were about 30 aircraft mechanics whose job it was to change high-time engines. It was easier to fly the plane to India from China for an engine change rather than haul the engine to China.

"A plane would arrive during late afternoon and engine change would begin immediately; when complete, the engine would be ground-run for about an hour, and then be flight-tested for an hour. By the second morning, they would be loaded and ready to fly home to China."

Roy Brown, a P-40 pilot with the 16th Fighter Squadron, tells about an escort mission he flew with the 308th's B-24s:

"In 1943 I led a flight of four P-40s escorting a squadron of B-24s to bomb Gia Lam Field at Hanoi. The bombers had taken heavy losses at Hanoi going in without fighter cover and they were grumpy people. In briefing they surlily demanded peace and tranquility on this trip. They gave, as argument, that (1) they had their butts shot off on two recent missions down there; (2) the Japs had placed some 15-18,000 Allied

POWs on Gia Lam to discourage bombing attacks and bombardiers insisted on not being disturbed by Zeros on bombing runs so they could hit the hangar lines instead of the POW camp; and (3) they were fed up with unfriendly Nips and preferred not to get their butts shot off any more. All that made sense and we agreed to take the Zero heat off them. Or try to, anyway.

"We were not in good shape, as our 16th Fighter Squadron had been moved to Chengkung to regroup after heavy action at Hengyang and worn-out P-40s were pulled out of service for much-needed maintenance and overhaul. But we scraped up a flight of four serviceable ships for the mission and off we went.

"About 150 miles out, my second element leader wingman came alongside to signal that he was siphoning fuel overboard through the vents, a fretful thing. It usually stopped without excessive fuel loss. This time it didn't and I thumbed him back to base. Keeping radio silence, I fumed to myself this bad luck. I felt a sense of foreboding.

"After finally resigning myself to making do with only three P-40s, I stared in dismay when my element leader hove alongside holding his nose and pointing back, and I'll be everlastingly damned if *he* wasn't spraying a plume of fuel out behind, too! I nearly had a hissy fit at the thought of losing two of my four-ship flight. Four fighters were too few if the Zeros did their usual swarming act, and two just couldn't cut the mustard.

"I sat in frustrated fury, wishing with great feeling that I was back in West Texas sitting under a mesquite bush and far away from all this crap. But that didn't help, so I resignedly waved him away and we continued, though I stayed wide of the B-24s. I suspected they were having a fit seeing their escort dwindle away. Those guys weren't interested in just a little bit of tranquility, they wanted the whole thing. No way could only two hard-pressed P-40s provide that.

"About 50 miles out of Hanoi, my wingman swung in tight from his wide ranging position and I shrugged and held up my hands to say, 'It's all ours, chum; don't sweat it,' when I saw he wasn't paying any attention. He was jabbing his finger toward his engine and moving his hand across his throat in a cutting motion. I saw smoke puffs coming out of his stacks, then I saw his engine was backfiring and cutting out. I dropped back with him and prayed he could get that damned engine running right. So when he finally gave thumbs down with weary head-shaking finality, I waved him away, hoping he could make it home.

"Then I sat in disgust, pondering with a sense of awe how I could get into such a foul mess. I knew the B-24 guys would think it was a foul mess, too. How in God's name could you lose three out of four airplanes before ever reaching the target?

"It had to be gremlins. And complaining to the Engineering Officer would accomplish nothing. Because I was the EO and I knew our maintenance was damned good.

"It had to be the whims of unreliable gods in that vicinity. Only Unfriendly Presences could make it happen to three out of four in one flight. What were They holding in store for me? Were They also going to snafu my plane, or were They going to let me go in lonesome as a coyote and get the living hell shot out of me? I received no sign from Them and considered turning back, too. Then I found I didn't have the guts. One shivering soul in his rackety P-40 couldn't provide the B-24 guys with their prized peace and tranquility, but I supposed it was better than nothing, so I swung in close to the bomber formation, knowing they were wondering what in hell was going on with their escort.

"Sure enough, as I flew alongside in lonely splendor, they waggled their wings ponderously in urgent question, and as we neared Hanoi and radio silence was no longer necessary, I heard profane voices asking me where the hell those other P-40s were, and incredulous curses when I cringingly told them I was all there was left. I got the feeling they weren't as concerned about going all alone as they were about going in with just me.

"Anyway, there was no more time to discuss it, as the city spread out below with fleecy clouds around, and Gia Lam in the clear. The River Rouge lived up to its name, with its red muddy water separating Gia Lam from the rest of the city.

"I saw no Zeros and was immensely pleased. Then I heard, 'Bandits 12 o'clock low coming up!' and I commended my butt to God and went diving down to deal with these no good bastards. I didn't see a thing. Then I heard, 'The sonsabitches are in that cloud at 9 o'clock!' So I sailed back over the formation with trigger finger quivering to try to keep the faith. I saw nothing. Now the bombers were at their IP, beginning their bomb run and they went in tight and steady as if they owned the place, paying no attention as far as I could see to the heavy flak puffs that smoked around them. Then bomb bay doors opened and strings of bombs trailed down with explosions blooming along hangar lines and ramps and runways. None fell in the POW encampment off to the side that I could see. All the time there were calls over the radio reporting bandits here or there, but I never saw any. Nary a one. I wasn't unhappy about that, though; I was keyed up and mad enough to wish I could take a pop at something. But I knew I'd been conned out of boots, first by the evil devils and then by the B-24 devils. I figured the Zero pilots were probably sitting around in slit trenches cursing, unable to get their engines started. You just never could tell about the gremlins.

"I left the bombers about halfway to Chengkung and made my own way home, beginning to get a tight pucker about fuel. I dropped it onto the long bomber runway at dusk with relief and taxied in to see the whole squadron waiting to hear about the mission.

"I set the brakes hard, pulled the mixture control back to idle cutoff. When the engine sputtered and died, I pushed the throttle to full open: the standard shutdown procedure. I stripped off a glove in the silence and snapped my safety belt and parachute buckles open - and the engine caught with a full-throated roar! Surging against the locked brakes at full power, apparently from a cupful of gasoline still in the carburetor, the P-40 went onto its nose, the whirling prop dug in and the engine ground into silence again!

"I hung out half over the windshield trying to keep from being catapulted into the prop and dazedly wondered what in hell had happened. Everyone had run or fallen flat and now they came back to help me down. I felt murderous. Like a murderous jackass.

"Several new pilots stood eyeing me, then my bent-up prop. I had lectured them severely about proper taxiing and parking to avoid nosing over, ruining engines and props. No one said anything except my long-suffering crew chief. He climbed up off the ground and stood cursing steadily as he looked at the airplane.

"Finally, the CO came over and said, 'You okay?' I mumbled that I was, and was silent for a little while. Then he growled with some wonder, 'Well, I'll be triple goddamned if this doesn't beat anything I ever saw. That makes four out of four. A whole flight goes sour on a mission and you still have the tape on your guns. Not a shot fired. Well, at any rate, you got there and back in one piece. But you couldn't leave it at that, could you?'"I knew very well what it was all about. It was clear that those goddamned unholy gods and devils had hung with me to the end. It was clear as hell to me, and I hope it now is to everyone else. I started to bring this to the CO's attention, then I hesitated, then I decided not to. It ought to have been clear as glass to him without explanation. Besides, it just didn't seem like the best time for it."

And speaking of gremlins, Art McIlhone, a bombsight specialist with the 425th, told the *Jing Bao Journal* that he believes in one type of gremlin. He calls it the Feather Gremlin and it followed *The Impatient Virgin* everywhere it flew. Without warning, the propeller of one engine would feather. After it happened twice over a target, the props, prop controls, and wiring were checked after the mission and all four engines were pronounced fit for duty. Unfortunately, the plane's Feather Gremlin was not replaced. McIlhone tells what happened when the plane had been cleared for flight after the second feathering incident:

"Some idiot had devised a way to carry forty 100-pound bombs on a B-24, even though there were only twenty bomb stations. *The Impatient Virgin* was freak-loaded with the 40 bombs and a test flight was authorized. The test crew consisted of pilot, co-pilot, engineer and me. Why me? How the hell would I know? I guess I was the least-needed elsewhere.

"Anyway, the plan was to climb to 10,000 feet and then run through all engine settings and prop speeds while watching for abnormal behavior. We didn't have to wait long because just before the wheels left the ground an engine feathered. I'll swear until the day I die that at that instant I saw a gremlin sitting on the prop, laughing away. Nobody believes me when I tell them about it, so I don't mention it anymore – but it happened!

"Well, we all know that a B-24 does not take off very well on three engines with a full load of gas and two tons of bombs from the altitude at Kunming. We just skimmed over the village at the end of the runway, clearing the roofs by inches. We made for the lake where there were a dozen or so fishing boats placidly being worked. We capsized them all!

"We got far enough out to salvo our bombs and then turned for a straight-in landing. We were so low that we made a track in the up-to-then calm lake.

"O.K., we made it and the gang tore the engine apart. You know damn well what they found: Nothing!

"We were sure that *The Impatient Virgin* was jinxed from here to hell but you can't red-line a plane because of an unseen gremlin. So we loaded with twelve 500-pounders and left for a mission.

"Half hour out, guess what happened. You're right. An engine feathered. How did you know?

"By unanimous vote the crew bailed out and walked back. All were O.K. except the bombardier, who broke a leg.

"Of course, *The Impatient Virgin* crashed and burned and there were tears of joy in the eyes of every crew member when they saw the flames.

"And so I say that, yes, there are gremlins and only foot-slogging feather merchants would doubt it."

Evans Kranidas, radio operator/gunner with the 425th on *Malicious*, remembers one of his four-plane missions against White Cloud Airdrome near Canton:

"White Cloud was a major Japanese airfield and, supposedly, had the only concrete runway in China. We'd been briefed that if the lead aircraft had problems, the rest should keep going. Sure enough, the lead turned back. I heard him on the radio but didn't say anything to my pilot.

"We broke out of heavy clouds near the target and discovered we were completely alone. We were a cocky bunch and went on in. On the first pass, the bombardier wasn't lined up and said we'd have to go around again.

"We were a little ticked off with him but things were going pretty well, so we made another run. On the second pass, we could actually see aircraft warming up and taxiing.

"The bombardier made the most of his reprieve and laid the bombs right across the runway and into the revetments. Nothing came up after us, and we were lucky.

"It was tradition after a mission for aircrew members to be given a shot of whiskey 'for medicinal purposes' to settle you down. This time they just handed us the bottle and told us to have at it.

"And that's what made this mission notable."

Eugene F. Messerly, a gunner on the *Ramp Rooster*, a 375th aircraft that flew near the Philippines on a sea sweep:

"Once we surprised about 20 ships west of Bataan in the northern Philippines and I believe our foray caused MacArthur's command to warn General Chennault to stay away from there as I'm sure we and a wingman caused the ultimate sinking of six sizable ships.

"I pray to God that we never skip-bombed any disguised ships that we believed were armed freighters because the Japanese loaded some with American POWs. The above-described convoy did fire several rounds of AA or a new signalling gun which suddenly quit. I was suddenly aware that the airplane couldn't swim and I might not float very long.

"I remember that our crew was interviewed by Colonel Beebe at Wendover Air Base. He commanded the 308th during its baptism of enemy fire over Hainan Island in the South China Sea. When we hit that airfield with its numerous runways and taxi strips, I believe we surely destroyed over half the airplanes the Japanese had based there. I was happy that we didn't stick around to make a head count, but if it had been required, not one man would have skipped the fun."

From the history of the 308th after the Group settled down in India after the stint in China:

"When shots became due at the dispensary, many of the boys had forgotten the shock of health and sanitary conditions in India. They dragged in haltingly in twos and threes to the shadow of the needle. Just about that time, the Doc received a call from a perturbed young fellow.

"This young fellow thought maybe he was falling apart and figured it behooved him to take a powder to the Doc. When Major Laughlin turned the man over and had a look, he said, 'Humpfh,' then proceeded to extract a fourteen-inch parasitic worm from the hapless boy's intestines.

"The Doc immediately was besieged by worried-looking individuals who wanted to know just how likely they were to be housing some worms. With diabolic complacency, the Doc nonchalantly purred, 'Don't worry. Lots of us have 'em. But they won't worry you until they crawl out of your nose.'"

It had been said by some that at one time or another, the 308th was planning a bombing mission to Nagasaki, Japan. Many thought this was only a tall tale and there is no record of such a mission being considered in official files. Although the mission was apparently disapproved in Washington, Jack Carey, former C.O. of the 373rd, confirmed in the *Jing Bao Journal* that it almost took place:

> "It's true. There was such a mission planned and it was to stage from Kweilin and Suichwan. Twelve B-24s were to go in at 9,000 feet. The group and squadron staffs were secretly briefed by Group CO Bill Fisher with the threat of eternal damnation if a word leaked out. Since we were aware that some of our hostel people would sell their mothers [to go on the mission], a leak about the mission could lead to 12 planes going and none returning."

Samuel W. Cooksey, a supply sergeant in the 373rd who transferred to the 374th when the former was sent to Okinawa, recalls his return home:

> "I remember that I left Calcutta on September 26, 1945 and at midnight October 16-17 passed through Gibraltar. The 17th was my birthday. We landed in New York on October 24 early in the morning. Went by train from the ship to Camp Kilmer overnight and then left the next night by train down the coast. There were seven passenger cars on the train and they were lined up as to where they were going so that when a train hit a certain stop, that car was cut off. When the train got to Camp Gordon, Augusta, Georgia (my stop), there were two passenger cars cut off, leaving one passenger car with the engine to go on down to Orlando, Florida. I was discharged five days after arriving back in the States."

Tony Lavelle of the 375th wrote in his diary after a year in China:

> "Our diet doesn't vary. No food from the States. All we have is pro-

vided by the Chinese. It could be much worse. What coffee we have is brewed like tea which isn't the way to make coffee. The salt we joke about is really priceless. You should see the prices on the black market. We are allowed one pack of cigarettes and one bag of Bull [Durham] per week. One bar of soap and one tube of toothpaste per month. There's no beer, Coke, no soft drinks period. Glad to eat at the mess in Chabua. I brought some goodies back the last time over the Hump. Beans, peaches and pineapple juice. Tried for a ham. No.

"Oo-Lam-Poo [the Chinese liquor store] must be doing a land rush business. The white mule or wine we buy is something. Be awful if it runs out; small chance of that. Haven't raised the price, either. Cigarettes are $24.00 a carton. Mine are worth more than that to me. Some of our boys are smoking English cigs from Chabua. Six dollars a carton. Funny thing, I've not had a hangover on the Jing Bao Juice yet. I want to tell you, don't try getting up. The thing to do is fall over on your back and lie still."

Howard H. Morgan, a 375th pilot on the *Battlin' Bitch*, retained letters he had written from China to his father. Here are some excerpts:

March 25, 1943. "The climate here is plenty cold at present. This is due mainly to our altitude of 6000 ft. Quarters are much nicer than expected and the food tastes good. However, I did get a case of dysentery our first day here. Very little drinking water and all of it has to be boiled good. Some of the boys can't stand to take a shower; it's hard to blame them when the water is brown and almost freezing.

"You'd be surprised to see the dirt and filth that most of these people live in. The other afternoon I was taking a short cut across a hill to my plane and walked right into a human bone pile. The worst of it was, it wasn't all bone. Practically whole bodies were left up there to be eaten by large dogs that resemble the chow. These dogs are vicious and it's best to stay away. Believe me, you very seldom see me without my .45 cal. pistol.

"Weather hasn't been too good recently so have had lots of spare time to play poker. Managed to scrape up a few corny mystery stories to read but that is about all. Reading material is very limited in these parts."

April 11, 1943. "It's Sunday afternoon again but not like on the farm.

The monsoons have started so everything is very gloomy and damp. They have monsoons in China every year and they last about two months. This bad weather slows down our progress about fifty percent. My room is dark and sad-looking. My windows are made of dark wax paper with a cheese cloth screen. We have no lights during the day, so with cloudy weather, I can hardly see to write.

May 9, 1943. "Well, Dad, here I am back in India. Just finished knocking hell out of the Japs but as usual am over here for an engine change. Had quite an experience on our last mission. Hope you've watched the papers about this date. We lost an engine about two hours out, but continued into combat with only three. We were very lucky – accomplished our purpose and returned safely to friendly territory. Had a forced landing because of gas shortage but eventually got home the following day. We flew ten and a half hours on three engines. When we arrived here [India] we were dead tired. We'll probably be here for a week, so I'm going to a larger town for a little rest and recreation. I told you I haven't seen a white woman in three months. It will be nice to hear some music and get a good drink again.

May 20, 1943. "Just got back from a short time in New Delhi, India. The city is the best we've seen since the U.S. but it's as hot as can be. Always over 100 degrees.

"We got to New Delhi about one week ago and, of course, asked for the best hotel in town. At dinner that evening, we found ourselves eating with a bunch of majors, colonels and generals. This place was only for high ranking officers and there were plenty of them. So happened we eased into the only vacant room. It really belonged to a colonel on temporary duty elsewhere. We were treated very nice, had good meals and comforts of a modern hotel.

"The transportation is very poor and the tonga, drawn by a horse, is used extensively. There are three or four good theaters in town which we patronized almost every evening. The girl situation is very bad. I saw some very nice looking British girls but they seem to have a funny outlook on the American fellow. You always have to be very properly introduced to get to first base. Who the devil did I know to give me an introduction? Anyway, all the British women and American nurses were booked up way in advance and most were going steady. It was possible to get some good liquor, and some poor. All good scotch is rationed and can only be had during certain hours.

August 16, 1943. "One good thing is, we have a picture show three times a week now. Usually it rains during the pictures and we have to leave (outdoor camera). The mosquitoes are so thick that we have to smear our faces with repellant and wear mosquito bars over our heads. We can't complain because it is swell entertainment.

October 23, 1943. "I am at the rest camp now. My crew had orders to come up here for a week for a rest. The trouble is, there's absolutely nothing to do besides swim and row, and the boats are few and very awful. We have no light up here so that eliminates reading and writing at night. We do play Monopoly, Parchesi and dominoes by candlelight. Great fun.

"A week ago I flew over the Hump to India. There is a camp of American nurses about 60 miles away from our Indian air base, and all they take care of are Chinese refugees. No Americans. A few of us drove for two hours over a God-awful road to see them. We had a swell time dancing to a phonograph and drinking, but my gal proceeded to get me good and tight. The evening was really a pleasure but I certainly paid for it on the return trip home.

November 2, 1943. "The other night our squadron officers had a dance in town - the first we've had over here. The place was small but 25 girls were asked to attend. Four American Red Cross girls and 21 Chinese girls. The competition was plenty tough but a little luck netted me, I thought, the nicest of the lot. She is half Chinese and half Scotch and talks perfect English.

December 10, 1943. "After we finished our work in India, we had a day or so to spend in Calcutta. Of course, the day I was there, the Japs bombed it. I've been in bombings before but never felt so helpless as I did in the famous Firpo's restaurant in the center of the city. Just as the bombs were dropping, an ack-ack gun next door went off. I'd have sworn that that noise was bombs dropping in train right down the street and that each one was getting closer. You should have seen me drop my ice cream and turn both left and right trying to decide which way to go. After thinking a moment, I just walked over to the window and looked up for the planes. Only a minute or two had passed when the band struck up with a new tune. Those things are easier to take when you have a slit trench nearby."

311

Fred B. Barton, a writer for *Plane Talk*, a publication of the Consolidated Vultee Aircraft Corporation, made a trip to China and reported what he found in the September 1944 issue. Here are some excerpts:

"In China you live in a barracks built by the Chinese. The floors are wood and are swept with hearth-brooms and then mopped. The walls are of mud-brick. The roof is tile, and under China's severe rains the roofs have been known to leak. You have occasional hot water for your shave and shower. A modest Chic Sale is a few muddy rods away.

"The food is Chinese-cooked and is supervised by GI mess sergeants and watched over by our Army veterinarians. It is neither very bad nor very good: generally it is merely monotonous. You don't get much to eat between meals. An occasional candy bar at your PX, flown over the Hump from India and carried by boat or plane all the way from the States. A mid-morning cup of coffee you can get sometimes: price about a dime U.S., or $20 Chinese.

"A $50 sack of peanuts – that sum is worth about a quarter in U.S. currency – is to be had. But the peanuts are pretty small. Chinese peanut brittle, however, is not too bad.

"Anything from home is a treat. Catsup, jelly, jam, canned baked beans – anything. The butter is Army stuff, guaranteed spoil-proof and melt-proof. Unfortunately, it tastes a lot like axle-grease. Most of all you miss milk. This powdered stuff is chalky and tasteless, and the taste of the queer native water, which is boiled 45 minutes and then chlorinated, comes through it and you don't like it. Every American overseas is homesick for Mother's cooking. But most of all he is homesick for a glass of clean, creamy milk.

"Manpower is scarce overseas and so native labor is brought in to do all manner of military jobs. It is a neighborly gesture, too, to employ Chinese coolies. There are millions of them. You see them everywhere. They carve away a hummock and move the dirt in flat baskets supported from a shoulder-bar, a spoonful at a time – but within a matter of days a new area is level and rained and graded. They carry gravel with their shoulder-bars, and whenever an ambitious GI challenges the effectiveness of their work he is surprised to find he probably can't even lift the load, let alone carry it. They bring the charcoal that is China's fuel; they carry farm produce long miles to market; four of them can carry a heavy log coffin, or an automobile engine, or any load you can mention.

"Yellow-skinned, slant-eyed, bare-legged and foreign they undoubtedly are. You don't speak their language. Yet you don't need to regard them as strangers. They are quick to smile; not the insincere and mechanical smile of the Japs, but a warm smile from the heart. They find Americans understandable, sure of their own minds, and democratic. A universal language has sprung up; 'Ding-how,' very good, hello. Ding-how gets you through the day. Now and then, for variety, you say No to something. For that you need 'Boo-how': bad. That gets you by.

"When you go shopping you may or may not buy all manner of souvenirs...Prices are high. When you and a shopkeeper bargain and you can't understand his price, he sometimes writes out a figure for you. Also, he counts out the price – several hundred CN it will be. A bottle of your favorite American fountain pen ink will cost you anywhere from $1,000 to $2,500 Chinese – and you either pay him or do without.

"You can sell almost anything, and at incredible profit. A used pair of trousers is worth about $20 American. You can sell a carton of American cigarettes for $10 gold. But don't do it! The Army has strict laws against selling items you buy at your PX. And there is a stiff fine and further penalties if you get caught.

"China is a country of 450 million people: a country of 21 separate provinces, and many mountains, and a variety of dialects. In some areas there are bands of outlaws who support themselves by a sort of polite brigandage. If you have to bail out, it makes a lot of difference whether you light in occupied or unoccupied China.

"Any American flyer or soldier who has fought alongside the Chinese in Burma or along the Salween will tell you what admirable soldiers the Chinese are. They form the majority of General Stilwell's army. In the war they don't look like much - underfed, ill-equipped, bothered with skin diseases and such - but given GI clothing and guns and training and food, they develop quickly. They have the fighting spirit."

While the flying was always full of unexpected moments of terror, a flight wasn't over until an aircraft was parked safely on the ramp and the engines shut down. Kenneth E. Henson, a 374th pilot, tells about a typical problem all pilots experienced at one time or another:

"I had a fuel hauling trip to the forward P-51 base at Suichwan. After landing, I was directed to a certain taxiway. I thought I was taking the right one but I was wrong. As soon as I rolled off the runway, my main gear sunk into the ground. Only the tops of my main gear tires were above the ground and the bottom of the bomb bay seemed to be resting on the ground.

"I was supposed to fly back to Chengkung that night but instead, we spent the night listening to a thousand Chinese coolies chanting and pulling. When daylight arrived the next morning, the airplane was back on solid ground, fueled up and ready to go."

Jack L. Pierson, a bombardier with the 375th, reminisces:

"Somehow we managed to get hold of two 12-gauge shotguns. One was a nice double-barrel and the other a pump model. We had plenty of shells so between raids we hunted. The country was alive with mourning doves and with many small lakes full of ducks and geese near us, it was a hunter's dream. Every village had a school and when we were hunting nearby, the teacher would dismiss class so the kids could see Americans. They were wonderful children; some of the boys would retrieve our birds for the empty shells. We would also give them a few CN. Some days we shot over a hundred doves or perhaps twenty or thirty ducks or geese. Our kitchen would cook them for us and we would all feast. On one hunt, a boy went into [the water] to retrieve a duck and sank out of sight in a deep spot. We got him out but it was too late. It broke our hearts. We never did much hunting after that."

Leland Miles, navigator on the eleven-member crew of *Time Will Tell*, recalls what he did on the first Sunday morning after landing in China in October 1944 with the 374th:

"Capt. Browne's stories of how so many crews had been lost, bailed out, and walked back via the Chinese underground, had prompted me to action. I cut up the cumbersome pack which had been issued to me at Langley and made a small pack, say 9"x14"x2" which I sewed on to my parachute harness. Small and light as the kit was, I got all of the following into it, after a lot of tugging, pushing and swearing: a compass, first aid kit, fork, two handkerchiefs, a pair of socks, a flare, 50 small game cartridges for my .45, two bars of Baby Ruth, one field ration (chocolate), one wash cloth, wash towel, soap, toothbrush, mosquito head netting, insect repellant, and, last but not least, a pack of playing cards."

Miles also remembered an unusual sight while he was returning in a Jeep to his base near Kunming with two of his squadron mates:

"We turned a corner and beheld a strange sight. A procession of some two hundred Chinese – from old wrinkled men to toddling infants – winding their way slowly into a village square. At the head of the procession were three men carrying what can best be described as totem poles. They were 20-foot columns of crepe paper with all sorts of weird designs and objects dangling from the main structure, which probably was bamboo. Behind this startling advance guard came the Chinese version of the local band – thirty or so men and women beating like mad on instruments that looked like a cross between a Spanish castanet and a toy drum like an American kid might get for Christmas. I turned to the captain and said, 'Some wedding, huh.'

"'Wedding hell,' he said. 'That's a funeral.'

"I laughed in disbelief until the next section of the parade passed by our now creeping Jeep. It was a large raft-like affair carried on protruding poles by about 20 men. Atop the raft, shiny, polished and black, was a casket. If I expected to see any grief on anyone's face, I was to be sadly disillusioned. As the pall bearers passed, they laughed and yelled 'Ding Hao!' at us. The kids who made up the tail end of the procession were having a big time gorging themselves with food and scrambling to climb on the Jeep. I asked the captain why everybody was so happy. He said the Chinese were always happy at a funeral because the deceased was then on his way to a happier life with his ancestors."

Hal Fenton, a mechanic with the 425th, submitted these recollections to the *Jing Bao Journal*:

"At Kunming, we had a super rec hall called "Loafers Lounge." It was comfortable, had lots of reading material, and was a good place to spend idle time. However, a strong memory in my mind is of the "Syndicate," a group of enterprising gentlemen who set up a Las Vegas-style felt-covered gambling table every month after pay day. It stayed open for two or three days, long enough to reach a secret, pre-arranged profit. We were paid in American money then, and I have it on good authority that a few G.I. millionaires were born.

"As an airplane mechanic with the 425th, I very often would pre-flight one or all of the four engines on the B-24. It was also part of my job to taxi the planes around, sometimes to change revetments. As a kid who grew up in New York City, I never had a driver's license and was driving those B-24s around before I ever drove a car!"

Howard H. Morgan, remembers one of his mine-laying missions in November 1943:

"My crew was one of seven that were to lay mines in Hong Kong harbor near the Kowloon docks. I believe the 374th was to bomb the docks from altitude after the 375th departed the harbor. Timing was important. The weather was no factor and the moon was bright and shiny over the target area. One aircraft in our squadron aborted and the six remaining flew loose formation to the staging area about 50 miles southwest of the target at about 12,000 feet. We had been given extensive briefings for this mission and each aircraft had a U.S. Naval officer who supposedly had lots of knowledge about the kind of ordnance we were using. The mines were not the usual small type but were about 10 to 12 feet in length and the maximum girth that would fit into the bomb bay. The naval officer was to arm the mine just prior to the drop.

"It was midnight when we deployed. We broke at one minute intervals, all navigation and formation lights out. We retarded the throttles to reduce the glow of the four engine exhausts and slowed our speed to 120 mph as we entered the target area.

"I believe I was third to break. The six aircraft had a similar pattern of dropping the mines on a string throughout the run. The moon was so bright that one could see the surrounding hills and the gateways between them.

"Our navigator, Lyndell Highley, was to signal the bombardier, Al Monitto, when we reached the release point. I was certain we were on target. What stuck in my mind was that I was looking up at the lighted portholes of the large ships as we passed by them. We maintained 50 feet over the water throughout the run and then climbed up and away. The mission was a huge success. We nailed the enemy by compete surprise. We didn't see any blackout of lights on shore or experience enemy fire. We were glad that the Navy liked our performance."

Returning from a bombing mission could be just as nerve wracking as any bombing mission. Jack Keene explains:

"One night in December 1943, we bombed Formosa and had to navigate back to Kweilin with an undercast the whole way. It wasn't until we were within 20 or 30 minutes of Kweilin before the ADF started coming in. This afforded us one pass over the station followed by an immediate compass letdown. If you've seen pictures of Kweilin with its countless volcanic-appearing (actually eroded limestone) spears shooting into the sky, you had to place a lot of trust in that single letdown aid. Capt. Jack Edney, who was my copilot on that mission, can attest to how hairy it was."

Henry G. "Hank" Brady, former CO of the 375th, wrote this poem in tribute to the 308th and the 341st Bomb Groups with which he served during two tours in China:

We sank many ships in the South China Sea,
And near the river at Saigon,
And we bombed some boats that we saw afloat,
In the harbor at Haiphong.

We hit the airfield at White Cloud,
By the city of Canton,
While we laid our mines, at the darkest times,
In the channel to Hong Kong.

We know the hills at Kweilin,
And the airstrip at Lingling,
And we shared a glass with a Chinese lass,
In a cafe at Kunming.

Then on at night to Formosa,
From a field that couldn't last,
It's a hell of a trip, when you can't find the strip,
And you're just about out of gas.

We stuck our nose in a hornet's nest,
The Zero base at Hankow,
So we paid the price, which wasn't nice,
And we still remember it now.

Once we flew out to Suichwan,
With a plan to bomb Nagasaki,
But the brass intervened, too risky it seemed,
In fact, some thought we were wacky.

For R&R we sometimes flew,
To Agra and the New Delhi,
The Taj Mahal enthralled us all,
But not the "Delhi-Belly."

The Mekong, Salween and Irrawaddi,
We knew like the palm of our hand,
And the stormy Hump of the Himalayas,
We tried to understand.

When we bombed some bridges in Burma,
The Zeros swarmed all around us like bees,
And we saved our hides and little besides,
In a crash landing at Yunnanyi.

Finally came the time to rotate,
For the missions we had tallied,
When the plane headed back, we followed its track,
From a base in the Assam Valley.

For the memories never leave us,
Of the friends we left behind,

Some we couldn't save, some in a shallow grave,
Lost long before their time.

To all who returned triumphant,
Who served and came back alive,
We drink to your pluck, and of course your luck,
And we're all very glad you survived.

Chapter 12

'THE MOST-PRODUCED BOMBER OF WORLD WAR II'

One man's vision and leadership deserves the credit for giving birth to the Consolidated B-24 Liberator, one of the two heavy bombers used during World War before the Boeing B-29 Superfortresses saw action. That man is Reuben H. Fleet, co-founder and president of Consolidated Aircraft Corporation. He had won his wings at the Signal Corps Aviation School in 1917 and had been in charge of the Army Air Service's pioneering of the air mail in 1918. After helping to design and test several military aircraft at McCook Field, Ohio, he resigned his commission in 1922 and was hired by Gallaudet Airplane Corporation. However, the company was in poor shape financially and Fleet left to form Consolidated Aircraft Corporation in 1923 with Colonel V. E. Clark as partner. Two other men who deserve prominent mention for giving birth to the Liberator are David R. Davis and Isaac "Mac" Laddon. Davis was a young engineer who had innovative ideas about wing design. Laddon was Fleet's chief engineer and Davis's boss.

One of the first projects after Consolidated was formed was the purchase of the TW-3 trainer design from the Dayton-Wright Co. It was completed in 1924. They designed another in 1924 called the "Trusty" which was accepted by the Army and designated the PT-1 (for Primary Trainer, first model). Fifty aircraft were produced and Consolidated became a leader in building trainer aircraft, not only for the U.S. Army and Navy, but for several foreign nations as well.

The success of the company led to a move to San Diego, California where Consolidated began to build flying boats. One of the most famous of these was the PBY Catalina which performed prominent service as a patrol bomber and air-sea rescue aircraft during World War II and several years after.

Chapter 12: 'The Most-Produced Bomber of World War II'

It was during 1938, when it seemed probable that the United States would be involved in the war in Europe, that the young engineer named Davis was hired. Davis had many aircraft design concepts of his own which he was anxious to see adopted. He thought a wing might be designed that would be shaped something like a drop of water. "Mac" Laddon, thought it might have possibilities and approved wing tunnel tests at California Institute of Technology. The "Davis airfoil" was the result and was notable for its exceptionally high aspect ratio – the ratio between wing chord and wing span.

The Davis wing proved so efficient that Fleet, Laddon, and Davis immediately incorporated it into a flying boat design. The result was the Consolidated Model M-31, a high-wing, twin-engine design with twin rudders. It was equipped with retractable Fowler flaps which improved its takeoff and landing performance. The first flight took place on May 5, 1939. It was quickly shown that it outclassed the Catalina in speed and could carry a greater load for a longer distance.

Meanwhile, the Army Air Corps had issued a specification in 1935 for a four-engine bomber which would have a 300 mph top speed, service ceiling of 35,000 feet, a range of 3,000 miles and carry a bomb load of 8,000 lbs. Fleet had his growing staff design such a bomber using the Davis wing and designated it Consolidated Model M-32 to meet those specifications. Rather than the conventional tail wheel, the Model 32 would have a tricycle landing gear using a steerable nose wheel. The main gear would retract into the wings. There would be four Pratt & Whitney engines each developing 1200 horsepower.

It seemed like a very bulky design, compared with the four-engine B-17 then being built by Boeing Aircraft Co. However, Model 32 was accepted on March 30, 1939, and the Army Air Corps designated it XB-24. Shortly thereafter, with war seemingly even more imminent, a worried Congress approved the production of more combat aircraft and an order for seven YB-24s (Y for service test) was confirmed for Consolidated. The total cost for the eight aircraft, including the XB-24, was to be $2.7 million, a small sum compared with today's production costs.

The XB-24 had its rollout from the factory at Lindbergh Field, San Diego on December 26, 1939, nine months after the contract had been issued. Consolidated's Chief Test Pilot William R. "Bill" Wheatley made the first flight on December 29, 1939.

After the war in Europe began in September 1939, and before the first production article for the Army Air Corps was produced, France placed an order for sixty aircraft and took options on 120 more under the designation of LB-30 MF (Land bomber, Consolidated No. 30, Mission Francais). When France was overrun in August 1940, the war had progressed too far for the French to have received even one of them.

The British Government Purchasing Commission took over the French contract and ordered 120 LB-30As. When Air Ministry personnel learned that Consolidated referred to the plane as the *Liberator*, they inquired about the source of the name. Reuben Fleet replied, "We chose the name 'Liberator' because this airplane can carry destruction to the heart of the Hun, and thus help you and us to liberate those nations temporarily finding themselves under Hitler's yoke."

The Consolidated design had a number of innovations. In addition to the Davis shoulder-mounted wing, tricycle gear and twin rudders, it featured roll-up bomb bay doors which prevented buffeting and drag when they were opened for bombing. The wings were actually fuel cells employing a concept known as a "wet wing" which saved weight. The bomb bay for the 8,000 lbs. of bombs was divided into front and rear compartments where the bombs could be stowed vertically. The fuselage keel beam of the plane formed a walkway through the bomb bay between front and rear.

The XB-24, after weeks of testing and a number of modifications, was formally accepted by the Army Air Corps on August 13, 1940. In addition to changes in the interior and exterior of the plane, the engine nacelles were redesigned and the engines were fitted with improved superchargers for high altitude flight. Self-sealing fuel cells were installed and the empennage was redesigned for better stability. These improvements caused the XB-24 to be redesignated the XB-24B.

One of the most authoritative books on the B-24 tells of the arrangements made with Consolidated so that the British could receive their aircraft as soon as possible:

"While tests were being flown with the XB-24B prototype, work had continued on the seven YB-24 service test aircraft. The changes that were called for by the Army Air Corps on the XB-24B were incorporated into the first YB-24 before it was rolled out. When the British government took over the French contracts, Consolidated sought, and was granted, permission to divert the first six Army Air Corps YB-24 service test aircraft and twenty B-24A production aircraft to the British order as LB-30As (YB-24) and LB-30Bs (B-24A). The British LB-30Bs would be the first Consolidated Liberators to see war service when they were assigned to RAF Coastal Command under the designation Liberator I. The seventh and final YB-24, now designated simply the B-24, rolled out in January 1941 and was delivered to the Army Air Corps in May."[1]

The first of six LB-30As, built to British specifications, first flew in January 1941. All six were used as unarmed transports flying Lend-Lease supplies across the Atlantic from Montreal to Prestwick, Scotland. Two aircraft crashes cost forty-four lives; the remaining four original Liberators eventually became civil transports flying British Overseas Airways Corporation (BOAC) routes.

The twenty Liberator Is were assigned to the Royal Air Force Coastal Command and flew 2,300-mile patrol missions in search of German submarines and naval vessels. The Liberator IIs were redesigned to new British specifications. About three feet were added to the nose and British four-gun turrets were added to positions in the upper mid-fuselage and the tail.

There were to have been 139 Liberator IIs delivered to the British but only eighty-eight had arrived by the time of Pearl Harbor. The remainder were taken over by the Army Air Corps. Three of them joined two B-17s in the first bombing missions by this model of the B-24 manned by American crews in a raid against Kendari in the Celebes on January 16, 1942.

Most of the rest of these former Liberator IIs were sent to Hawaii, Alaska, and Panama and used as patrol aircraft. Others were lightened for training gunners or converted to transports.

The successful testing, production and employment of these early B-24s proved that this huge plane with its bulky fuselage was going to be lively competition for the Boeing B-17 Flying Fortress. Both planes would be built in large numbers but the Liberator was destined to become the most-produced airplane of World War II with 18,432 of them manufactured. To accomplish this task, a Liberator Production Pool program was established in early 1941 in which three other companies participated with Consolidated. Factories were built and operated by Ford Motor Co. at Willow Run, Michigan; Douglas Aircraft Co. at Tulsa, Oklahoma; North American Aviation at Dallas; and the Consolidated factories at San Diego and Fort Worth, Texas.

The U.S. Army Air Corps accepted the first of nine B-24As in June 1941 and assigned them to the Air Corps Ferrying Command. They were flown between the States and Prestwick, Scotland, with passengers and mail. The bomb bays were sealed and benches were installed for passengers. Two unmounted .50 caliber machine guns were carried "just in case."

A number of significant long range flights were made with these B-24As. In September 1941, two of them flew the Harriman mission to Moscow and one then continued around the world. The other returned via Africa and South America. Two other aircraft were scheduled to fly reconnaissance missions over islands in the South Pacific before war was declared but only one had arrived in Hawaii by December 7, 1941. It was destroyed on the ground at Hickam Field during the attack. The other B-24A flew many flights for the Air Transport Command until it was scrapped after logging over 10,000 hours.

The B-24C was really the first of the production run to satisfy the need for an increased number of four-engine bombers, although only nine were built under this designation. The changes and recommendations for improvements as the result of experience by the British were incorporated in the C models. Machine gun turrets were installed in new locations. Engine refinements caused engine nacelles to be redesigned. Although none of these aircraft ever saw combat, the training and test flights revealed areas where improvements should be made.

It was the B-24D model that began a long production run and would eventually be assigned to the 308th. The first of these was delivered to the Army Air Corps in early February 1942. Although many modifications would be made as the numbers grew, the original D models featured retractable belly turrets, an upper fuselage turret and a tail turret, all fitted with .50 caliber machine guns. A single machine gun in the nose was later augmented with additional guns which were mounted in ball sockets on each side of the plexiglass nose.

As production increased at the five manufacturing locations, new armament was installed such as five-inch forward-firing rockets and waist guns. Since the B-17s and B-24s could not be assured of fighter protection on long-range missions, two heavily-armed and armored prototype bombers were derived that would accompany formations of bombers for protection. One was the YB-40, an off-shoot of a B-17F, and the XB-41, a gunship converted from a B-24D.

There was only one XB-41 built and it was tested at Eglin Field, Florida in early 1943. The number of defensive machine guns was increased from ten to fourteen. One of two top turrets was capable of being raised to increase its field of fire and lowered to decrease drag. With all of this additional weight, however, it was slower and could not maintain formation position with bomb-laden B-24s; therefore, the idea was abandoned. The lone XB-41 was later redesignated a TB-24 and was used by the Air Training Command to train B-24 student mechanics and armament specialists.

There were B-24E and B-24G models built which were similar to the main production run of B-24Ds. The B-24Es were turned out by the Ford Motor Co. at Willow Run; the B-24Gs by North American Co. at Dallas. There were only minor differences in armament and turrets that caused these designations to be made.

Another of the B-24D modifications was a cargo version that was designated the C-87. The first one was rebuilt from a crashed B-24D to meet an Army Air Forces specification for a heavy transport aircraft. All aircraft armament was removed and a solid hinged nose for easy loading replaced the plexiglass nose; the tail gun position was faired off. A floor was installed in the bomb bay for cargo; plexiglass windows were installed along the fuselage under and aft of the wing. A large cargo door was installed on the left side of the aft fuselage.

Three C-87As were modified to carry VIPs. One of them was christened the *Guess Where II* and was the first plane built especially for the president of the United States. It provided a long-range capability that would mean fewer stops for fuel and reduce security considerations and provide a special loading ramp for President Roosevelt, crippled by polio. Although it provided unusual internal comforts, the President never used it.

Many pilots did not like the C-87. Ernest Gann, famous pilot-writer who flew them during World War II with the Air Transport Command, said, "They were an evil companion, nothing like the relatively efficient B-24 except in appearance. The C-87s would not carry enough ice to chill a highball."

There were 286 C-87s built; six were modified with sleeping accommodations; five were redesignated AT-22s and used for advanced gunnery training. The U.S. Navy ordered thirty-four cargo models which were designated RY-1 and RY-2.

The next model was the B-24H which was developed because of the experience gained in combat when enemy fighters discovered that the B-24 was vulnerable if attacked head-on. There had been some measure of success with hydraulic-powered nose turrets in some late B-24D models so the B-24H was developed with electrically-powered turrets that required many changes in the B-24D airframe because of the added weight in the nose. However, the H model was considered successful and over 3,100 were manufactured.

It was the B-24J model that would eventually be assigned to the 308th during its tour in China to supplement and replace the D models. The first of the Js was delivered to the AAF in August 1943. Most noticeable difference between the D and J models was the A-6 nose turret which made it the longest of the B-24 variants. In addition, the J had an improved automatic pilot, bomb sight, and fuel transfer system.

According to B-24 historian Larry Davis, each of the factories under the Liberator Production Pool program were building the B-24Js with different parts which were not always interchangeable. He notes: "Ford/Willow Run Liberators varied slightly from North American-built machines, which also differed from Convair/San Diego machines. Even the two Convair factories produced slightly different aircraft. This lack of standardization created a logistical nightmare for parts and repair depots around the world, who had to maintain parts for all of the variants, as well as parts for the various block changes within the variant."[2]

There were other B-24 models after the J was in production. Lighter-weight gun mounts at the various gun positions were installed and other changes were made, all designed to reduce the total weight of the aircraft by about 1,000 pounds. These were designated B-24Ls and over 1,650 were produced.

The B-24M followed which was the last production model of the B-24. Its major features were an improved windshield and tail gun improvements. More than 2,500 of this model were produced, some too late to be flown to the various theaters.

There were other variants in the saga of the B-24. Photo reconnaissance models, called the F-7, were produced. These were modified B-24Js which had all armament removed and eleven stations for cameras installed. About 185 of these were produced.

Still another variant was the C-109 tanker. About 215 of these were modified B-24 airframes with fuel tanks installed which carried 2,400 gallons of fuel. These were principally used in the CBI to ferry fuel over the Hump for the B-29 units in China.

The U.S. Navy saw the wisdom of increasing its long-range patrol and reconnaissance capability shortly after war began and ordered the Navy version of the Liberator called the PB4Y-1 to supplement its force of smaller patrol planes which could carry only small bomb loads. The Navy Liberators were mostly standardized B-24Ds, although a few J, L, and M models were also procured but with various kinds of armament to satisfy special Navy requirements. About 975 of these were manufactured. In 1942, Consolidated designers had decided that the Liberator would be more stable if it had a single vertical stabilizer instead of two. Consequently, a B-24D was modified and labeled the B-24K. It was more stable and in April 1944, a new designation was pinned on the Liberator – the XB-24N. One was built for test purposes and seven YB-24Ns were produced before production was halted in May 1945. These single-tail models had radar-directed guns installed. A thermal de-icing system for wings and empennage also provided cabin heat.

Since many of the PB4Y-1 Navy Liberators were to be used at low levels for patrol work, the Navy asked for the single-tail variant because they proved their stability in turbulence on low-level missions. This model would not need supercharged engines and would have non-supercharged engines installed in order to lighten the weight. It was also requested that a flight engineer's station be added such as the Navy flying boats had. The result was the PB4Y-2 Privateer, a single-tailed Liberator, with various kinds of gun turrets for low-level strafing and protection. About 740 of these were produced. The Navy retained many of these after the war; several were used as target drones and transports. A number were sold to the Nationalist Chinese Air Force, France, and Honduras. Some were used during the Korean War for patrol and flare work.

The last of the Privateers was kept in Navy service until 1962, while several were flown by the Coast Guard until the mid-1960s. A few saw later service as water bombers by civilian forest fire fighting units.

The saga of the B-24s was not over when the PB4Ys were placed in production. Larry Davis explains why:

"In November 1939, Army Air Corps Chief of Staff, General Henry H. Arnold, asked the War Department for permission to initiate development of a four-engine heavy bomber that would surpass the capabilities of both the B-24 Liberator and the B-17 Flying Fortress. The new bomber would be developed with high speed and long range as primary considerations, rather than carrying a massive bomb load. The Army Air Corps specification was circulated to the leading manufacturers on 29 January 1940, calling for an aircraft that would carry a 2000-pound load at a range of 5,000 miles at speeds up to 400 miles per hour."

The result was the B-32A Dominator which used much of the B-24 technology but was a larger aircraft. The prototype first flew on September 8, 1942. It crashed on one of the first test flights because of design flaws which resulted in many production delays. After tail redesign, based somewhat on the Boeing B-17 and B-29 single tail configuration, the B-32 showed promise at first and orders were issued for 1,200 aircraft; however, only 115 were built. Several B-32 Dominators flew combat missions with the 312th Bomb Group of the Fifth Air Force against the Japanese in the summer of 1945. None were saved when the war was over.

The Liberator contract was completed in June 1945 and some aircraft were flown directly from the factories to the aircraft "bone yards" in Arizona and other storage facilities for melting down into scrap which later became post-war household products such as cooking utensils. A few were saved for use by civilian firms as forest fire-fighting water bombers and cargo planes; others were put on static display at various Air Force bases.

The record of the B-24 is closed now. At this writing, there is believed to be only one still flying. A dozen or so others are on static display in aviation museums around the world.

The Liberator never received any beauty prizes but it served a mighty purpose. Designed as a high altitude bomber, it was found that it could perform low-level strafing like a fighter and was capable of destroying enemy fighters that made the fatal mistake of attacking. It was also used as a pilot and gunnery trainer, photo reconnaissance platform, cargo and passenger hauler, a radio-controlled drone bomber, and long-range patrol bomber. Between 1939 and 1970, the Liberator had been flown by the air forces of thirteen nations and was flown in all the World War II theaters of war. Before the B-29 came into service, a B-24 made the longest combat mission on record: twenty-four hours. The B-24 was a rugged workhorse and deserves a permanent niche in the Aircraft Hall of Fame.

Appendix

CHRONICLE OF THE 308TH BOMBARDMENT GROUP (H) IN WORLD WAR II

308th Bombardment Group

Constituted as 308th Bombardment Group (Heavy) on January 28, 1942. Activated on April 15, 1942. Trained and equipped with Consolidated B-24 Liberators. Moved to China in March 1943, with the air echelon flying its planes by way of Africa, and the ground echelon traveling by ship across the Pacific.

Assigned to Fourteenth Air Force. Made many trips over the Hump to India to obtain gasoline, oil, bombs, spare parts, ammunition, and other items needed to prepare for and sustain its combat operations.

The 308th Group supported Chinese ground forces; attacked airfields, coalyards, docks, oil refineries, and fuel dumps in French Indo-China; mined rivers and ports; bombed shops and docks at Rangoon; attacked Japanese shipping in the East China Sea, Formosa Strait, South China Sea and Gulf of Tonkin.

The group moved to India in June 1945 and ferried gasoline and supplies over the Hump. Sailed for the United States in December 1945. Inactivated January 6, 1946.

The 308th received a Distinguished Unit Citation for an unescorted bombing attack, conducted through anti-aircraft fire and fighter defenses, against docks and warehouses at Hankow on August 21, 1945. Received second Distinguished Unit Citation for interdiction of Japanese shipping during 1944-1945.

373rd Bombardment Squadron

Lineage: Constituted as 373rd Bombardment Squadron (Heavy) on January 28, 1942. Activated on April 15, 1942. Inactivated January 7, 1946.

Operations: Combat in China-Burma-India theater, May 4, 1943, to June 3, 1945; combat in Western Pacific, July 21, 1945, to August 14, 1945.

Campaigns: India-Burma; Air Offensive, Japan; China Defensive; New Guinea; Western Pacific; China Offensive; Air Combat, Asiatic-Pacific Theater.

Decorations: Distinguished Unit Citation: East and South China Seas, Straits of Formosa and Gulf of Tonkin.

374th Bombardment Squadron

Lineage: Constituted as 374th Bombardment Squadron (Heavy) on January 28, 1942. Activated on April 15, 1942. Inactivated on January 6, 1946.

Operations: Combat in China-Burma-India Theater and Western Pacific, May 4, 1943, to May 11, 1945.

Decorations: Distinguished Unit Citations: China, August 21, 1943; East and South China Seas, Straits of Formosa, and Gulf of Tonkin, May 24, 1944, to April 28, 1945.

375th Bombardment Squadron

Lineage: Constituted as 375th Bombardment Squadron (Heavy) on January 28, 1942. Activated on April 15, 1942. Inactivated January 6, 1946.

Operations: Combat in CBI and Western Pacific, May 4, 1943, to April 19, 1945.

Decorations: Distinguished Unit Citations: China, August 21, 1945; East and South China Seas, Straits of Formosa and Gulf of Tonkin, May 24, 1944, to April 19, 1945.

425th Bombardment Squadron

Lineage: Constituted as 36th Reconnaissance Squadron (Heavy) on January 28, 1942. Activated April 15, 1942. Redesignated 425th Bombardment Squadron (Heavy) on April 22, 1942. Inactivated January 6, 1946.

Operations: Combat in CBI and Western Pacific, May 4, 1943, to June 3, 1945.

Decorations: Distinguished Unit Citation: East and South China Seas, Straits of Formosa and Gulf of Tonkin, May 24, 1944. to April 28, 1945.

Chapter Notes

Chapter 1: Prelude to War for the 308th

1. Emile Gavreau, *The Wild Blue Yonder*, New York: E. P. Dutton Co., 1944. P. 171.

2. Report by Naval Attaché in Chungking Re: Operations U.S. Forces, CBI, as cited in Memorandum by Major General Thomas T. Handy to General George C. Marshall, December 12, 1942.

3. Henry H. Arnold, *Global Mission*. New York: Harper & Brothers, 1949. P. 398.

4. Letter from President Roosevelt in Casablanca to Chiang Kai-shek, January 25, 1943.

5. Arnold, op. cit. P. 418.

6. Ibid. P. 420.

7. W. F. Craven and J. L. Cate, editors, *The Army Air Force in World War II*. Chiacgo: University of Chicago Press, 1950. P. 418.

8. Arnold, op. cit. P. 429.

9. Claire L. Chennault, *Way of a Fighter*. New York: G. P. Putnam's Sons. P. 213.

10. Ibid. P. 214.

11. Ibid. P. 216.

12. Claire L. Chennault, as told to Col. C. V. Glines, "Individualism: That Controversial Leadership Trait," *Air Force Magazine*, November 1967.

13. James MacGregor Burns, *Roosevelt: The Soldier of Freedom*. New York: Harcourt Brace Jovanovitch, Inc. P. 376.

14. Chennault, *Way of a Fighter*, op. cit. P. 217.

15. Craven and Cate, op. cit. P. 442.

16. Chennault, op. cit. P. 226.

17. Ibid.
18. Craven and Cate, op. cit. P. 445.

Chapter 2: The 308th Comes to Life

1. Arnold, op. cit. Pp. 193-194.
2. Letter, General H. H. Arnold to Colonel Eugene H. Beebe, July 13, 1942.
3. Interview of General Beebe with Dr. Murray Green, Long Beach, Calif., August 12, 1970.
4. Chennault, op. cit. Pp. 232-233.
5. Ibid. P. 219.

Chapter 3: Baptism of Fire

1. Interview, Office of Air Force History, Washington, D.C. April 22-28, 1979.

Chapter 4: Neutralization of Haiphong

1. Chennault, op. cit. P. 249.
2. Chennault, "Individualism: That Controversial Leadership Trait," op. cit.
3. Craven and Cate, op. cit. Pp. 453-454.
4. Ibid. Pp. 480-481.

Chapter 5: January to June 1944

1. Chennault, op. cit. P. 270.
2. Ibid. P. 253. Between June 18, 1943, and January 9, 1945, Chennault wrote twelve letters to the President.
3. John S. Chilstrom, "A Test for Joint Ops: USAAF Bombing Doctrine and the Aerial Minelaying Mission." *Air Power History*, Spring 1993. P. 37.
4. Edward G. Menaker, "Making Technology Work in World War II." *IEEE AES Systems Magazine*, June 1993. P. 18-19.
5. Ibid. P. 19.
6. Arnold, op. cit. P. 505.

7. Chennault, op. cit. P. 256.

8. Craven and Cate, op. cit. P. 545.

Chapter 6: July to December 1944

1. Chennault, op. cit. Pp. 265-266.

2. Ibid. P. 266.

Chapter 7: The Year of Victory

1. From *Briefing*, an unidentified newsletter, Winter, 1983.

2. Chennault, op. cit. P. 351.

3. Ibid. P. 257.

Chapter 8: Three POWs Tell Their Stories

1. Boyington, "Pappy", *Baa Baa Black Sheep*. New York: G.P. Putnam Sons, 1958. Pp. 272-273.

2. Ibid. P. 275.

3. Ibid.

Chapter 12: "The Most Produced Bomber of World War II"

1. Davis, Larry, *The B-24 Liberator In Action*. Carrollton, Texas: Squadron/Signal Publications. 1987. P. 6.

2. Ibid. P.34.

Bibliography

Arnold, Henry H. *Global Mission.* New York: Harper & Brothers, 1949.

Chennault, Claire L. *Way of a Fighter.* New York: G.P. Putnam's Sons, 1949.

Craven, W.F., and Cate, J.L. *The Army Air Forces in World War II. Vol. 1. Plans and Early Operations, January 1939 to August 1942.* [U.S. Office of Air Force History] Chicago: University of Chicago Press, 1948.

Davis, Larry. *The B-24 Liberator in Action.* Carrollton, Texas: Squadron/Signal Publications. 1987.

Feuer, A. B. *General Chennault's Secret Weapon: The B-24 in China.* Westport, Connecticut: Praeger Publishers, 1992.

Glines, Carroll V. *The Compact History of the U.S. Air Force.* New York: Hawthorn Books, 1963. New and revised, 1973.

Hotz, Robert B. *With General Chennault: The Story of the Flying Tigers.* New York: Coward-McCann, 1943.

Maurer Maurer. *World War II Combat Squadrons of the United States Air Force.* Woodbury, NY: Smithmark Publishers, 1992.

Air Force Combat Units of World War II. New York: Franklin Watts, 1963.

McClure, Glenn E. *Fire and Fall Back.* San Antonio, Texas: Barnes Press, 1975.

Romanus, Charles F. and Sunderland, Riley. *Stilwell's Mission to China.* Washington, D.C. Office of the Chief of Military History, Department of the Army, 1953.

Schultz, Duane. *The Maverick War: Chennault and the Flying Tigers.* New York: St. Martin's Press, 1987.

Scott, Robert L., Jr. *Flying Tiger: Chennault of China.* Garden City, N.Y., Doubleday, 1959.

Spector, Ronald H. *Eagle Against the Sun.* New York: Random House, 1985.

Spencer, Otha C. *Flying the Hump.* College Station, Texas: Texas A&M University Press, 1992.

Stilwell, Joseph W. *The Stilwell Papers.* Edited by T.H. White. New York: William Sloane, 1948.

Toland, John. *The Rising Sun: The Decline and Fall of the Japanese Empire, 1936-1945.* New York: Random House, 1970.

Tuchman, Barbara W. *Stilwell and the American Experience in China, 1911-45.* New York: Macmillan, 1971.

White, Theodore H. *In Search of History.* New York: Harper & Row, 1978.

Index

Unfortunately, many of the names in this Index are not complete. The official reports and other sources cited in the text did not always refer to the first names and middle initials of crew members.